# JOHN CONSTANTINE HELLBLAZER
# ALL HIS ENGINES

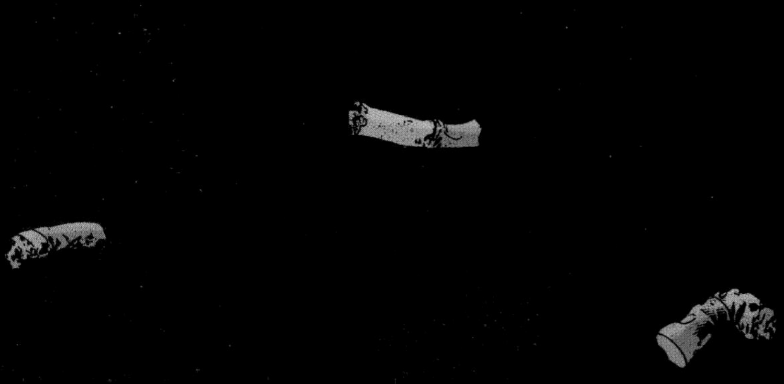

WRITER
# MIKE CAREY

ARTIST
# LEONARDO MANCO

COLORIST & SEPARATOR
## LEE LOUGHRIDGE
## & ZYLONOL STUDIO

LETTERER
## JARED K. FLETCHER

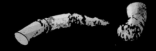

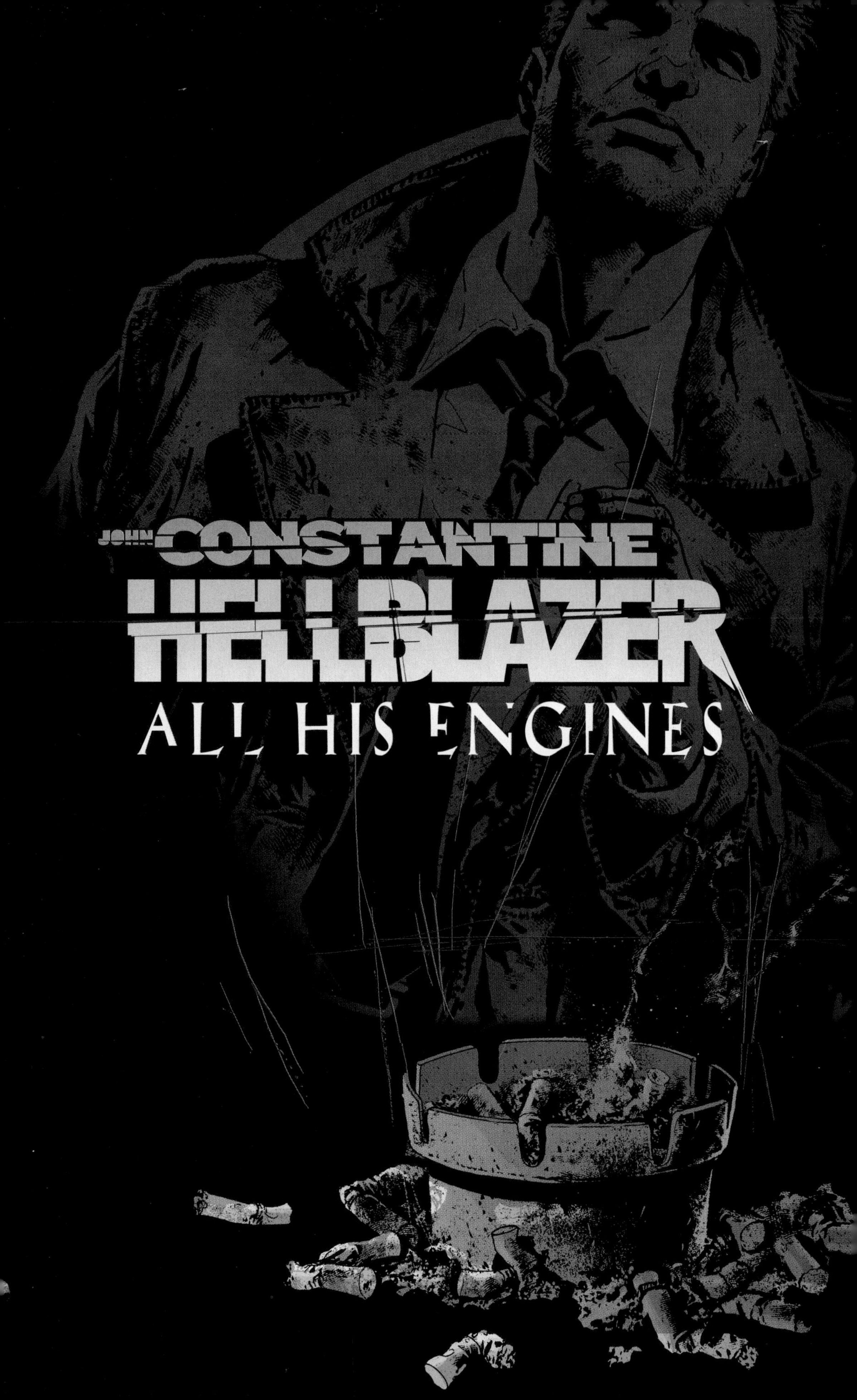
JOHN CONSTANTINE
HELLBLAZER
ALL HIS ENGINES

**Karen Berger**
VP-EXECUTIVE EDITOR

**Will Dennis**
EDITOR

**Casey Seijas**
ASSISTANT EDITOR

**Amie Brockway-Metcalf**
ART DIRECTOR

**Paul Levitz**
PRESIDENT & PUBLISHER

**Georg Brewer**
VP-DESIGN & RETAIL PRODUCT DEVELOPMENT

**Richard Bruning**
SENIOR VP-CREATIVE DIRECTOR

**Patrick Caldon**
SENIOR VP-FINANCE & OPERATIONS

**Chris Caramalis**
VP-FINANCE

**Terri Cunningham**
VP-MANAGING EDITOR

**Dan DiDio**
VP-EDITORIAL

**Alison Gill**
VP-MANUFACTURING

**Rich Johnson**
VP-BOOK TRADE SALES

**Hank Kanalz**
VP-GENERAL MANAGER, WILDSTORM

**Lillian Laserson**
SENIOR VP & GENERAL COUNSEL

**Jim Lee**
EDITORIAL DIRECTOR-WILDSTORM

**David McKillips**
VP-ADVERTISING & CUSTOM PUBLISHING

**John Nee**
VP-BUSINESS DEVELOPMENT

**Gregory Noveck**
SENIOR VP-CREATIVE AFFAIRS

**Cheryl Rubin**
SENIOR VP-BRAND MANAGEMENT

**Bob Wayne**
VP-SALES & MARKETING

JOHN CONSTANTINE HELLBLAZER:
ALL HIS ENGINES.
Published by DC Comics. Cover and
compilation copyright © 2005 DC
Comics. All rights reserved. VERTIGO
and all characters featured in this issue,
the distinctive likenesses thereof, and
all related elements are trademarks of
DC Comics. All Rights Reserved. The
stories, characters and incidents featured
in this publication are entirely fictional.

DC Comics
1700 Broadway
New York, NY 10019

A Warner Bros. Entertainment Company

Printed in Canada
Second Printing

ISBN – 1-4012-0317-5
ISBN 13 – 978-1-4012-0317-7

Cover art by LEONARDO MANCO
Cover color by LEE LOUGHRIDGE
Logo design by NESSIM HIGSON

NOR Nor aught availed him now
TO HAVE To have built in Heaven high TOWERS
NOR Nor did he 'scape CAPE
BY By all his ENGINES
BUT But was headlong SENT
WITH With his industrious CREW
TO To build in Hell HELL

—ML Milton "Paradise LOST"

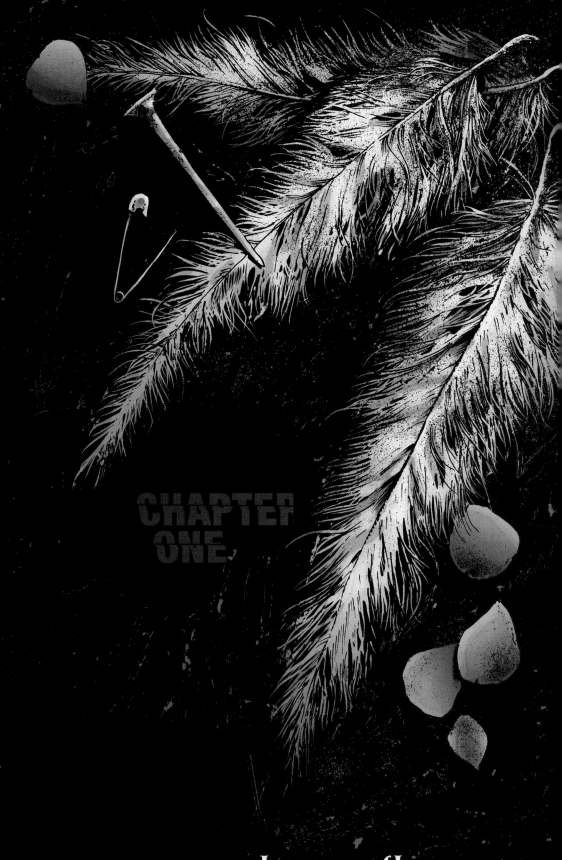

proserpine gathering flowers

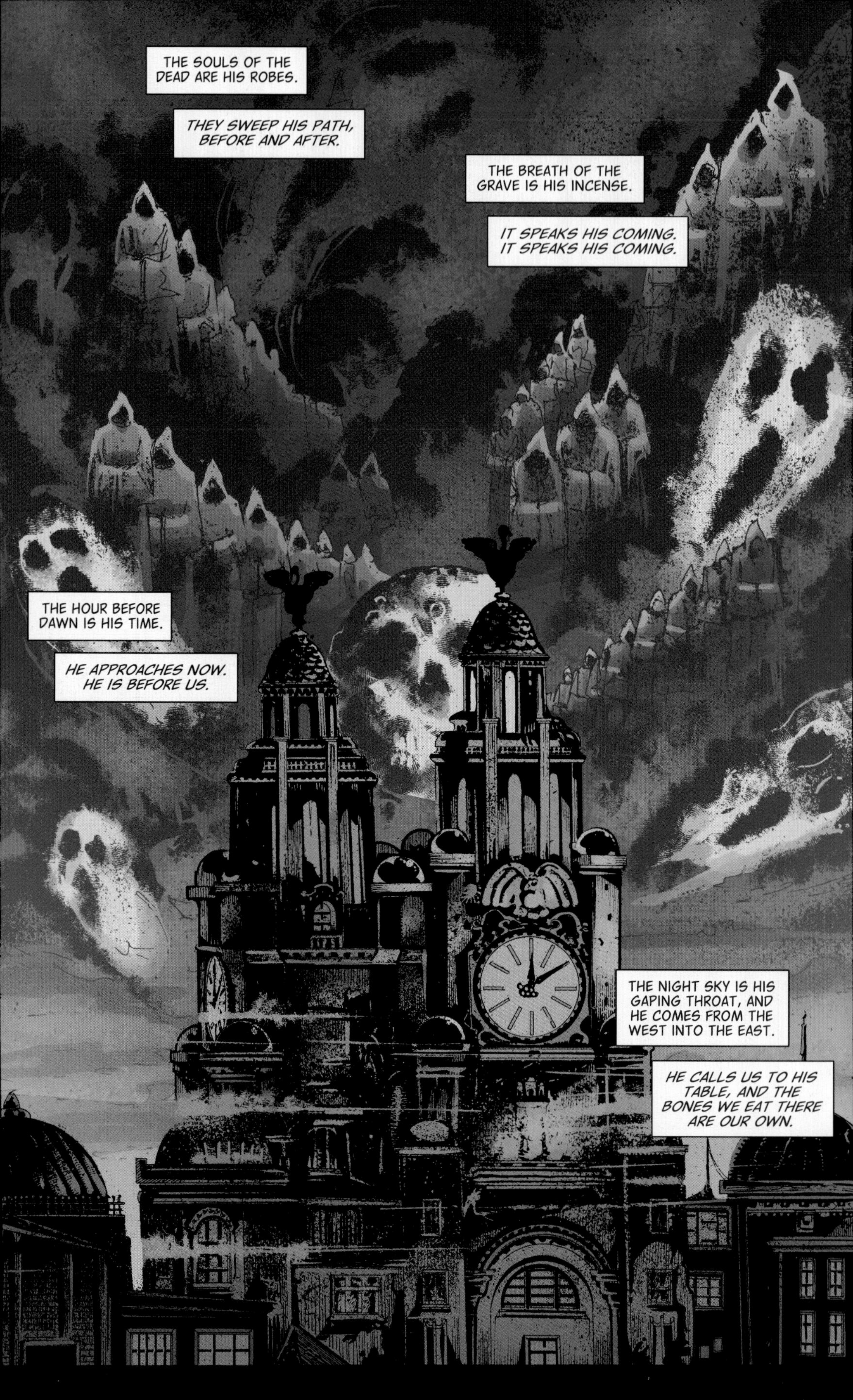
THE SOULS OF THE DEAD ARE HIS ROBES.
THEY SWEEP HIS PATH, BEFORE AND AFTER.
THE BREATH OF THE GRAVE IS HIS INCENSE.
IT SPEAKS HIS COMING. IT SPEAKS HIS COMING.
THE HOUR BEFORE DAWN IS HIS TIME.
HE APPROACHES NOW. HE IS BEFORE US.
THE NIGHT SKY IS HIS GAPING THROAT, AND HE COMES FROM THE WEST INTO THE EAST.
HE CALLS US TO HIS TABLE, AND THE BONES WE EAT THERE ARE OUR OWN.

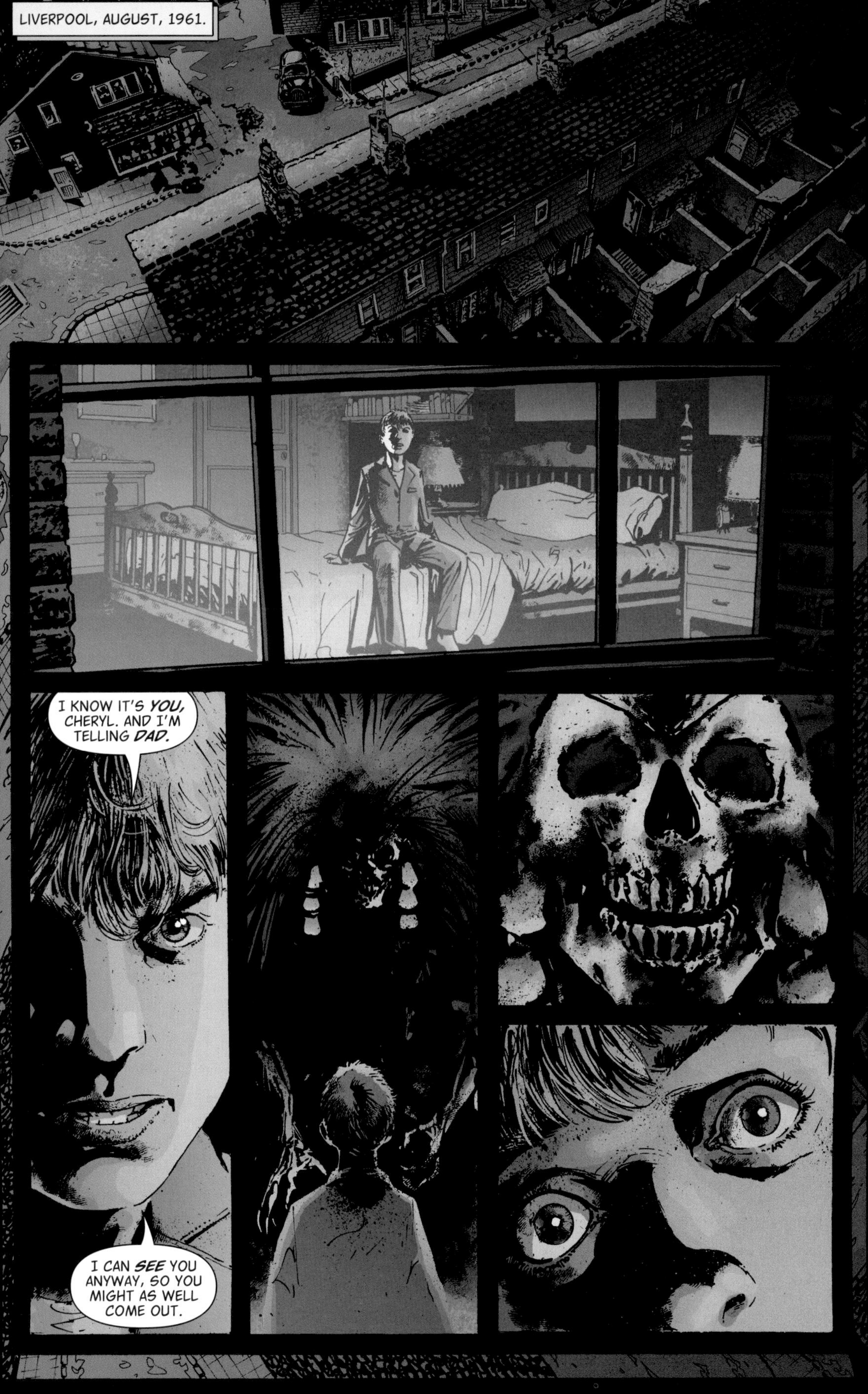
LIVERPOOL, AUGUST, 1961.
I KNOW IT'S YOU, CHERYL. AND I'M TELLING DAD.
I CAN SEE YOU ANYWAY, SO YOU MIGHT AS WELL COME OUT.

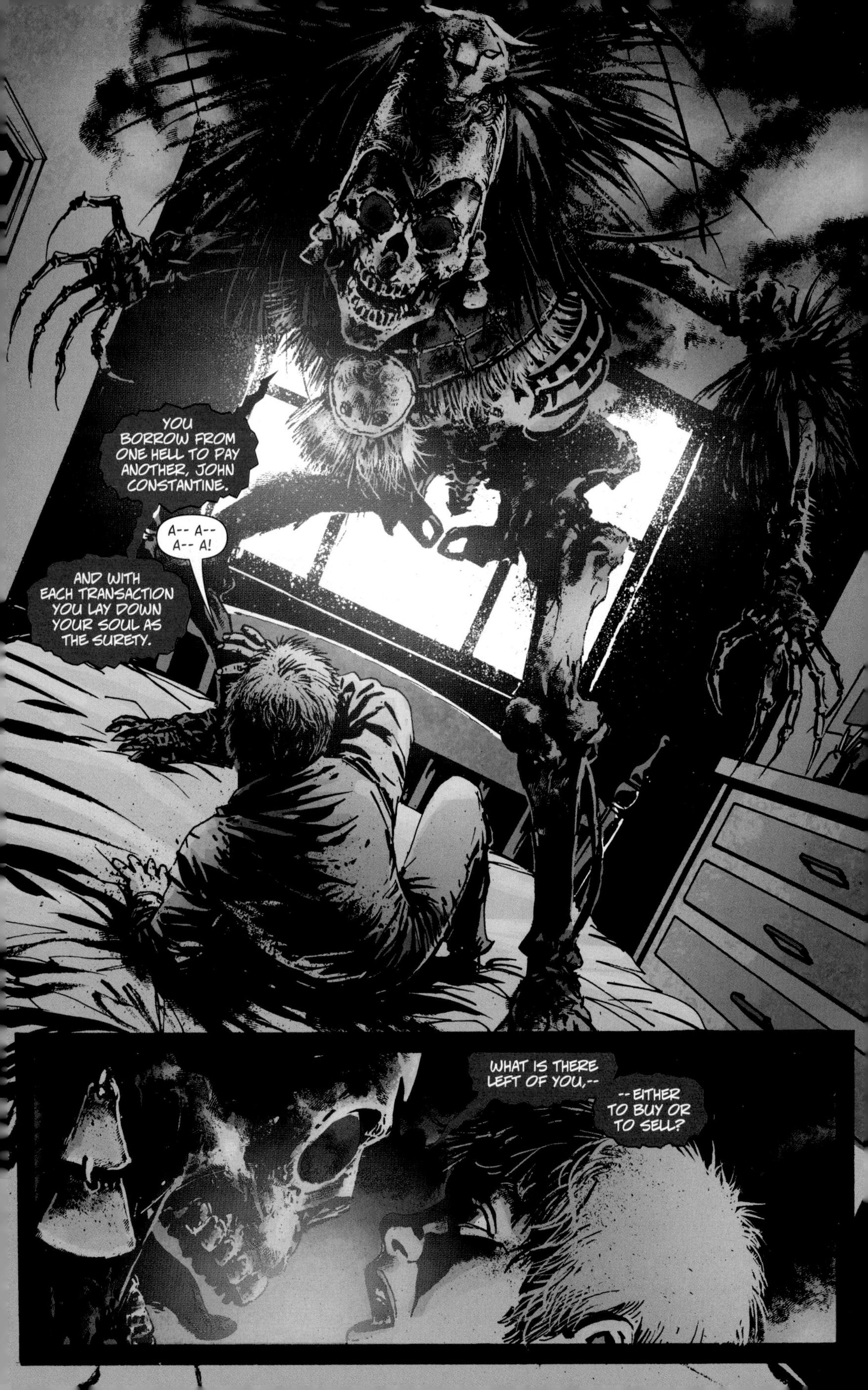
YOU BORROW FROM ONE HELL TO PAY ANOTHER, JOHN CONSTANTINE.
A-- A-- A-- A!
AND WITH EACH TRANSACTION YOU LAY DOWN YOUR SOUL AS THE SURETY.
WHAT IS THERE LEFT OF YOU,--
--EITHER TO BUY OR TO SELL?

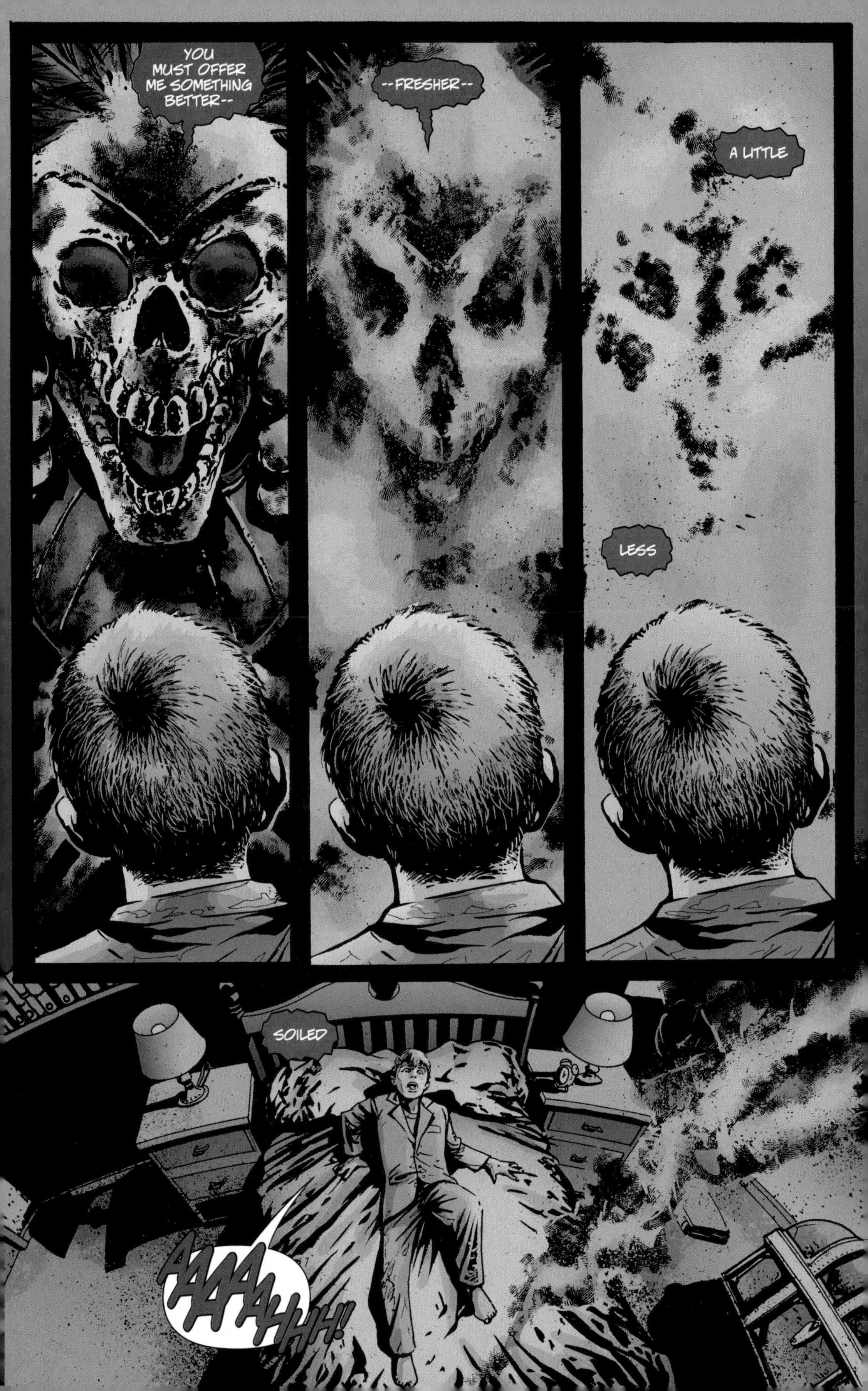
YOU MUST OFFER ME SOMETHING BETTER--
--FRESHER--
A LITTLE
LESS
SOILED
AAAAAHHH!

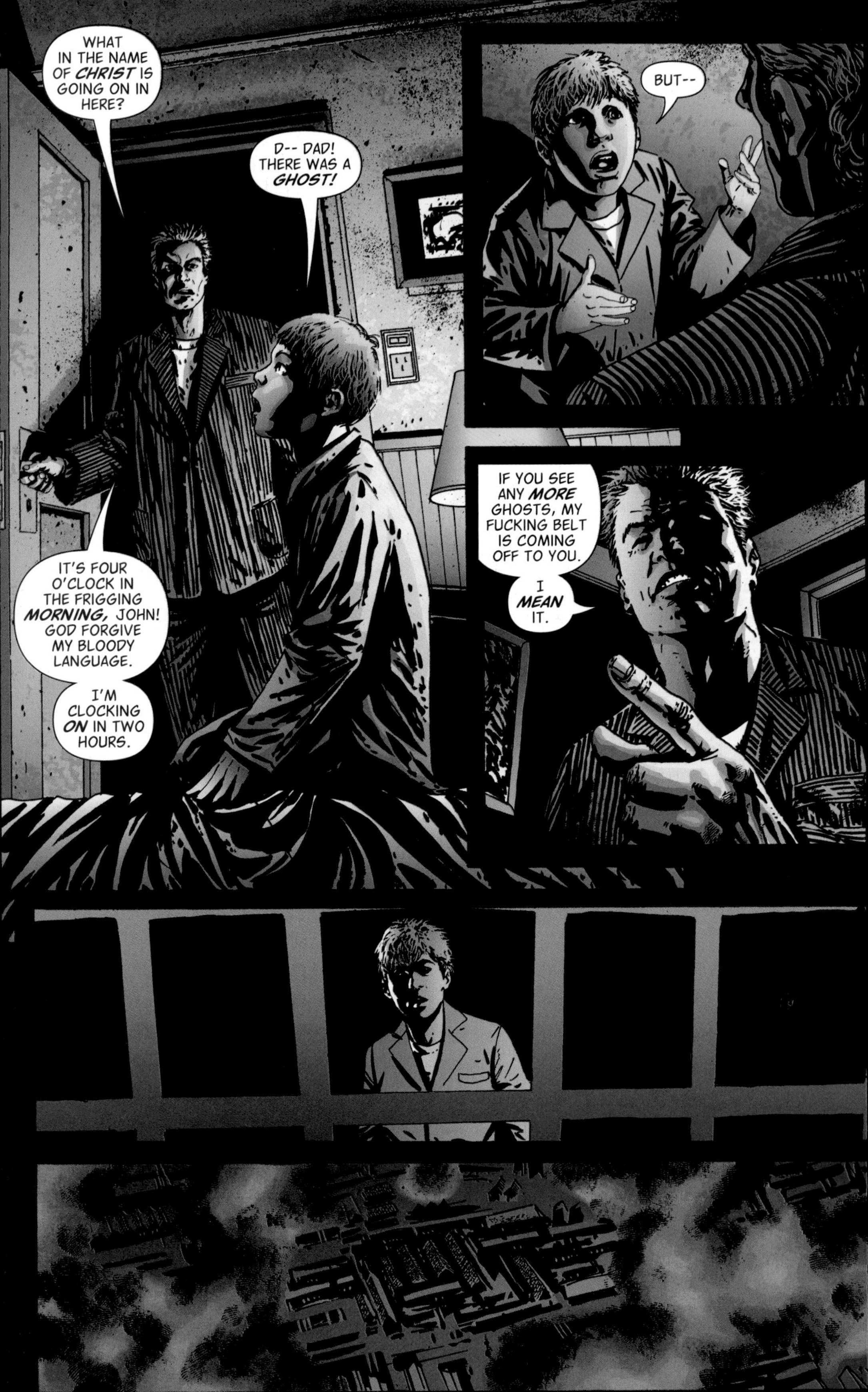
WHAT IN THE NAME OF CHRIST IS GOING ON IN HERE?
D-- DAD! THERE WAS A GHOST!
IT'S FOUR O'CLOCK IN THE FRIGGING MORNING, JOHN! GOD FORGIVE MY BLOODY LANGUAGE.
I'M CLOCKING ON IN TWO HOURS.
BUT--
IF YOU SEE ANY MORE GHOSTS, MY FUCKING BELT IS COMING OFF TO YOU.
I MEAN IT.

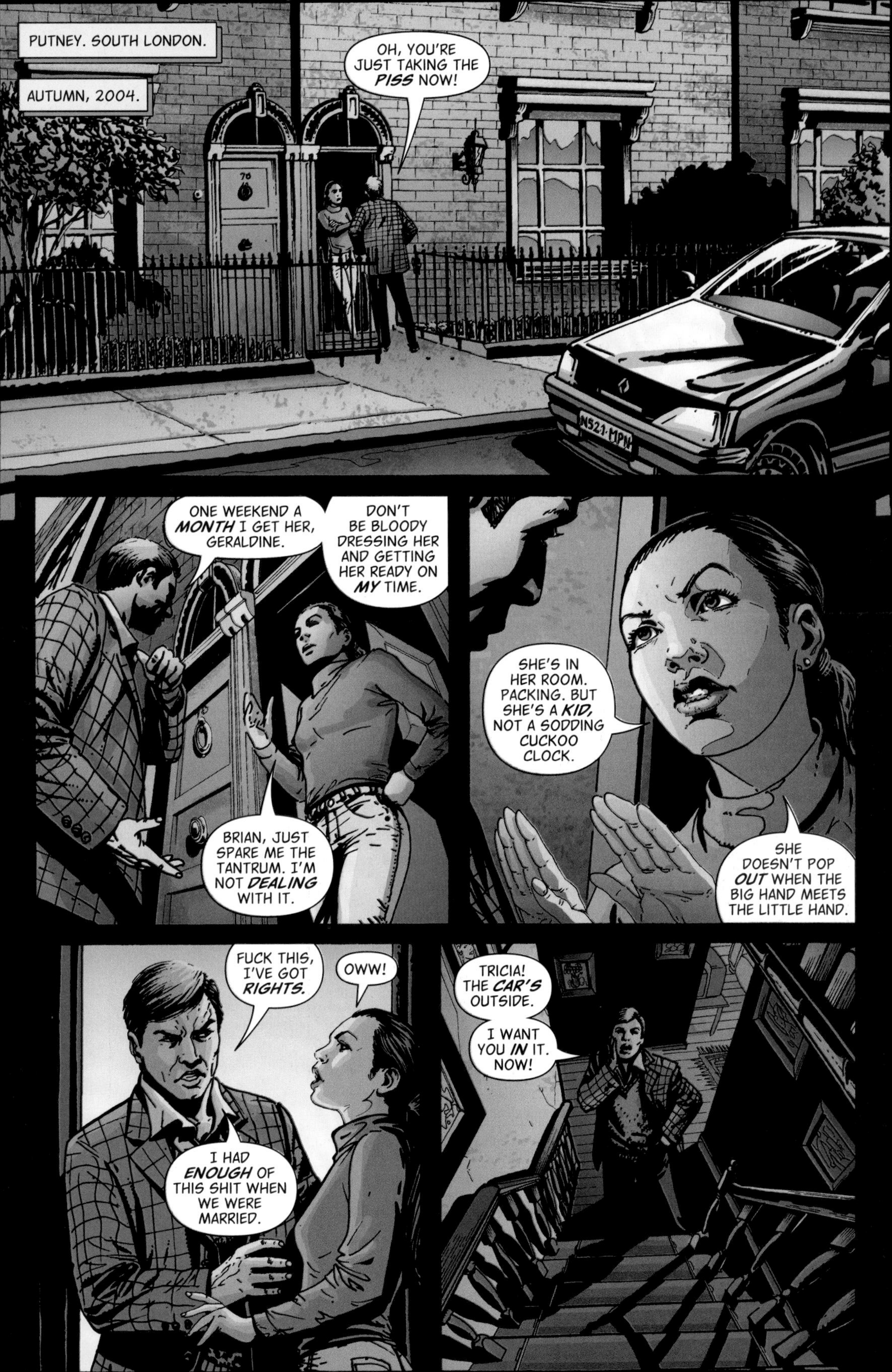
PUTNEY. SOUTH LONDON.
AUTUMN, 2004.
OH, YOU'RE JUST TAKING THE *PISS* NOW!
N521 MPN
ONE WEEKEND A *MONTH* I GET HER, GERALDINE.
DON'T BE BLOODY DRESSING HER AND GETTING HER READY ON *MY* TIME.
BRIAN, JUST SPARE ME THE TANTRUM. I'M NOT *DEALING* WITH IT.
SHE'S IN HER ROOM. PACKING. BUT SHE'S A *KID,* NOT A SODDING CUCKOO CLOCK.
SHE DOESN'T POP *OUT* WHEN THE BIG HAND MEETS THE LITTLE HAND.
FUCK THIS, I'VE GOT *RIGHTS.*
OWW!
I HAD *ENOUGH* OF THIS SHIT WHEN WE WERE MARRIED.
TRICIA! THE *CAR'S* OUTSIDE.
I WANT YOU *IN* IT. NOW!

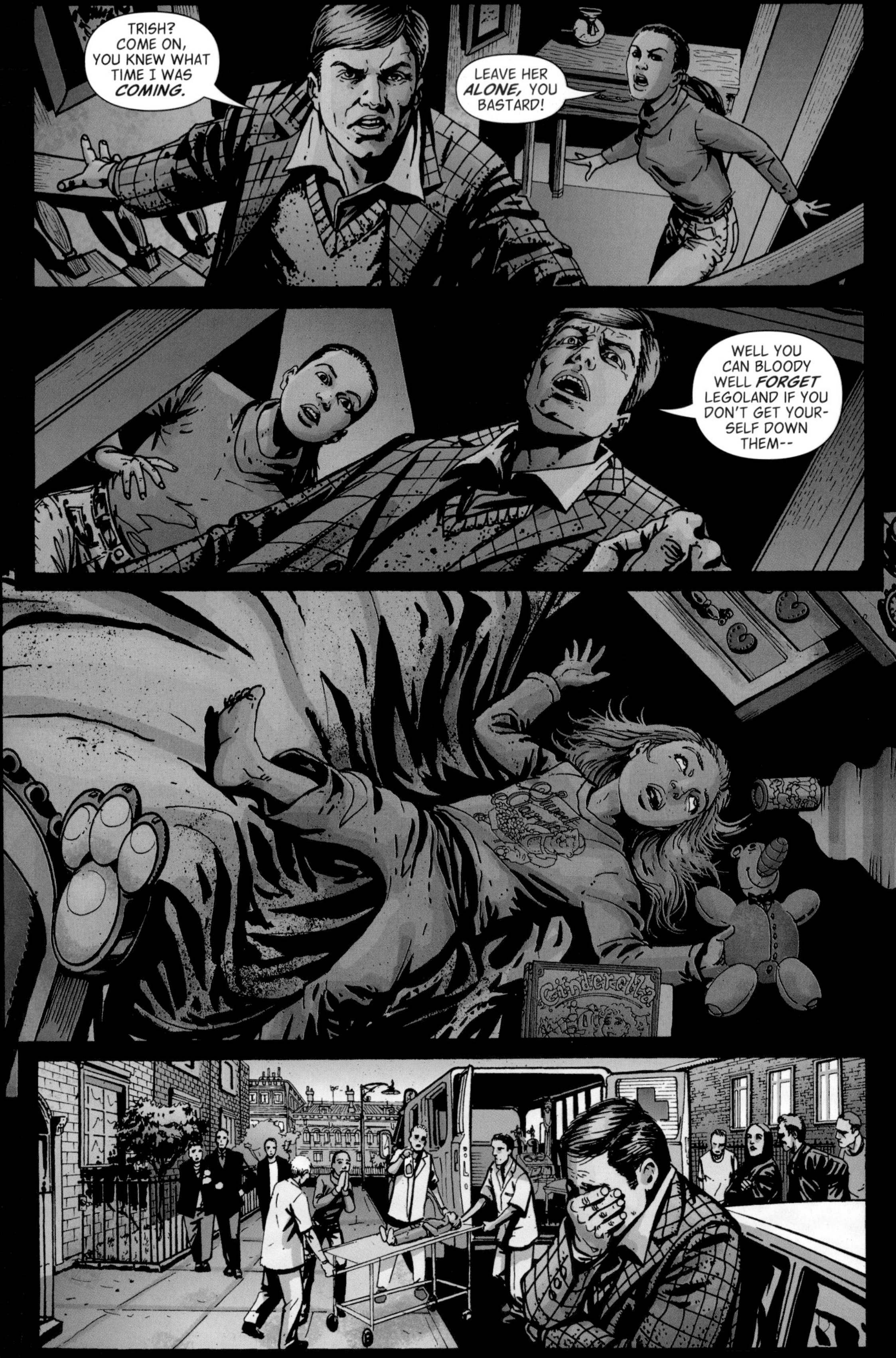
TRISH? COME ON, YOU KNEW WHAT TIME I WAS COMING.
LEAVE HER ALONE, YOU BASTARD!
WELL YOU CAN BLOODY WELL FORGET LEGOLAND IF YOU DON'T GET YOUR-SELF DOWN THEM--
Cinderella

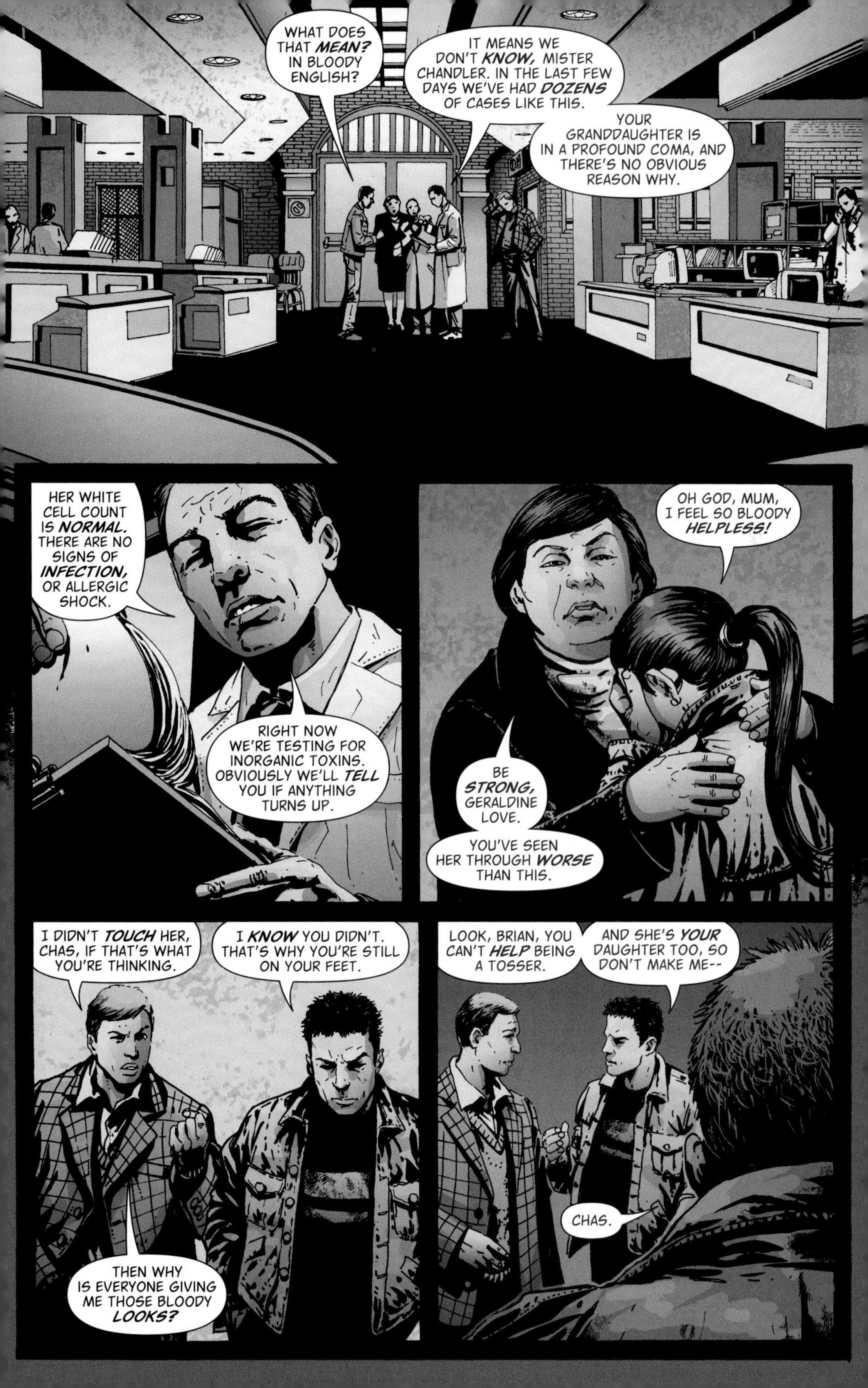
WHAT DOES THAT *MEAN?* IN BLOODY ENGLISH?
IT MEANS WE DON'T *KNOW,* MISTER CHANDLER. IN THE LAST FEW DAYS WE'VE HAD *DOZENS* OF CASES LIKE THIS.
YOUR GRANDDAUGHTER IS IN A PROFOUND COMA, AND THERE'S NO OBVIOUS REASON WHY.
HER WHITE CELL COUNT IS *NORMAL.* THERE ARE NO SIGNS OF *INFECTION,* OR ALLERGIC SHOCK.
RIGHT NOW WE'RE TESTING FOR INORGANIC TOXINS. OBVIOUSLY WE'LL *TELL* YOU IF ANYTHING TURNS UP.
OH GOD, MUM, I FEEL SO BLOODY *HELPLESS!*
BE *STRONG,* GERALDINE LOVE.
YOU'VE SEEN HER THROUGH *WORSE* THAN THIS.
I DIDN'T *TOUCH* HER, CHAS, IF THAT'S WHAT YOU'RE THINKING.
I *KNOW* YOU DIDN'T. THAT'S WHY YOU'RE STILL ON YOUR FEET.
THEN WHY IS EVERYONE GIVING ME THOSE BLOODY *LOOKS?*
LOOK, BRIAN, YOU CAN'T *HELP* BEING A TOSSER.
AND SHE'S *YOUR* DAUGHTER TOO, SO DON'T MAKE ME--
CHAS.

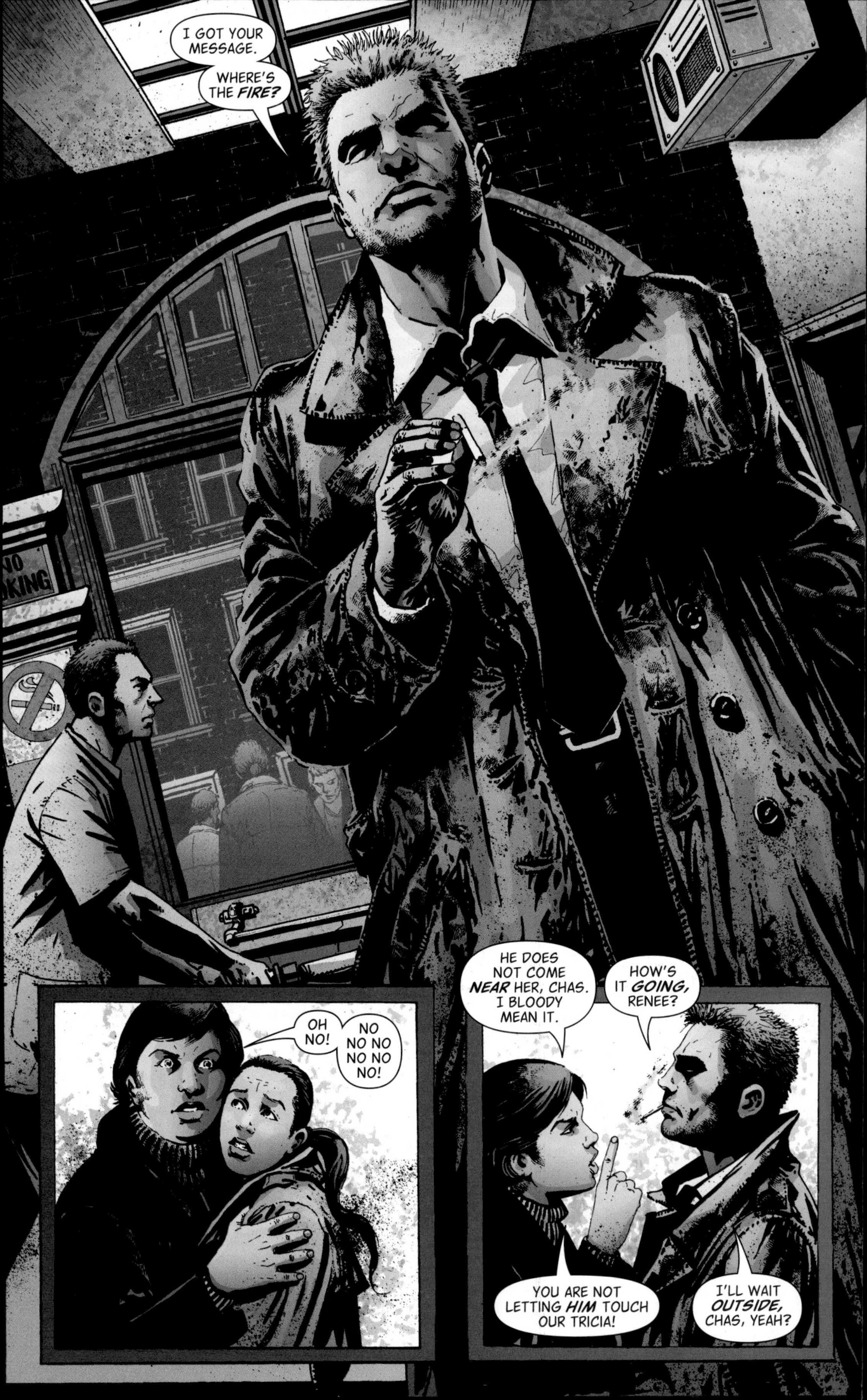

I GOT YOUR MESSAGE.
WHERE'S THE *FIRE?*
OH NO!
NO NO NO NO NO NO!
HE DOES NOT COME *NEAR* HER, CHAS. I BLOODY MEAN IT.
HOW'S IT *GOING,* RENEE?
YOU ARE NOT LETTING *HIM* TOUCH OUR TRICIA!
I'LL WAIT *OUTSIDE,* CHAS, YEAH?

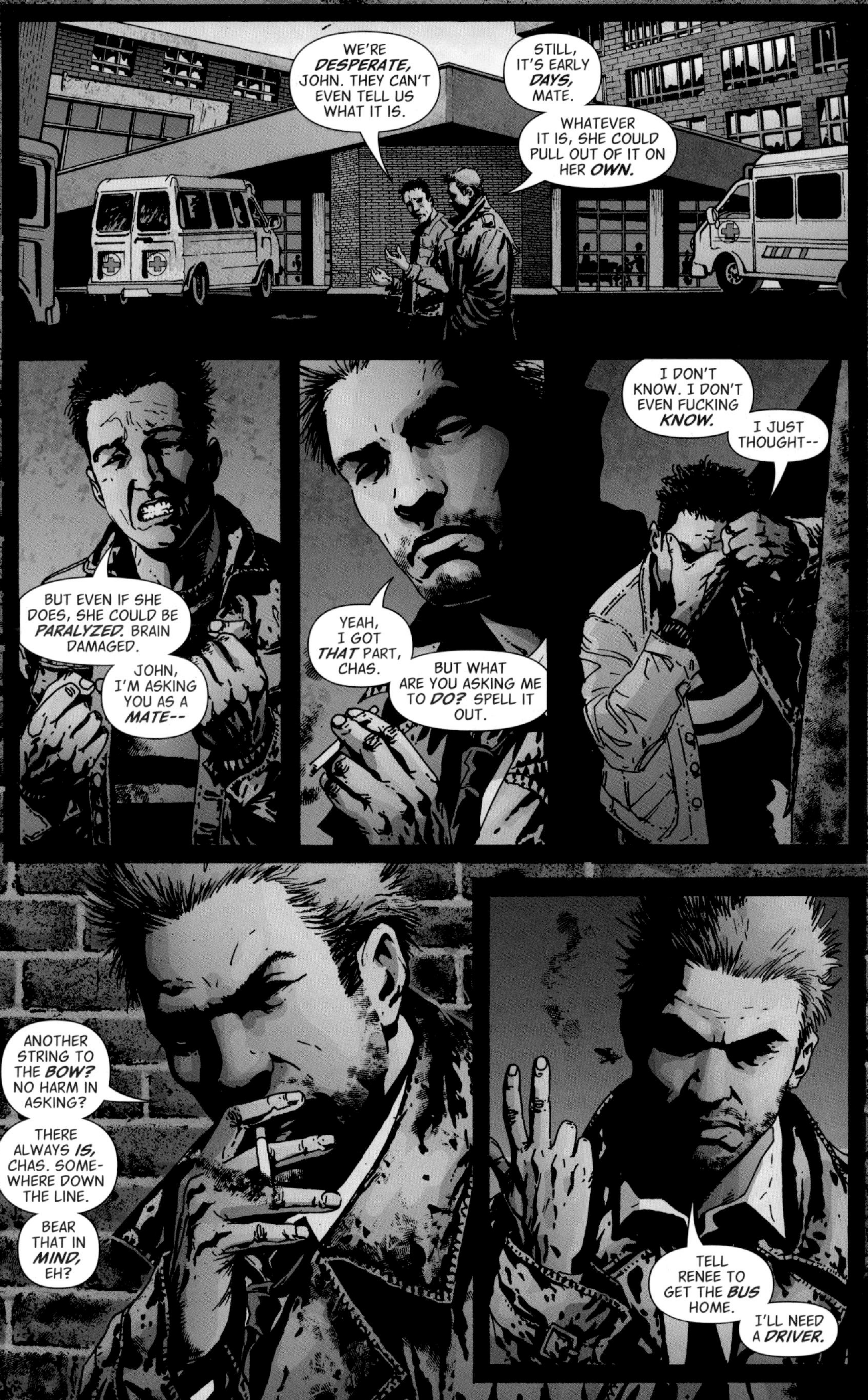
WE'RE *DESPERATE,* JOHN. THEY CAN'T EVEN TELL US WHAT IT IS.
STILL, IT'S EARLY *DAYS,* MATE.
WHATEVER IT IS, SHE COULD PULL OUT OF IT ON HER *OWN.*
BUT EVEN IF SHE DOES, SHE COULD BE *PARALYZED.* BRAIN DAMAGED.
JOHN, I'M ASKING YOU AS A *MATE--*
YEAH, I GOT *THAT* PART, CHAS.
BUT WHAT ARE YOU ASKING ME TO *DO?* SPELL IT OUT.
I DON'T KNOW. I DON'T EVEN FUCKING *KNOW.*
I JUST THOUGHT--
ANOTHER STRING TO THE *BOW?* NO HARM IN ASKING?
THERE ALWAYS *IS,* CHAS. SOME-WHERE DOWN THE LINE.
BEAR THAT IN *MIND,* EH?
TELL RENEE TO GET THE *BUS* HOME.
I'LL NEED A *DRIVER.*

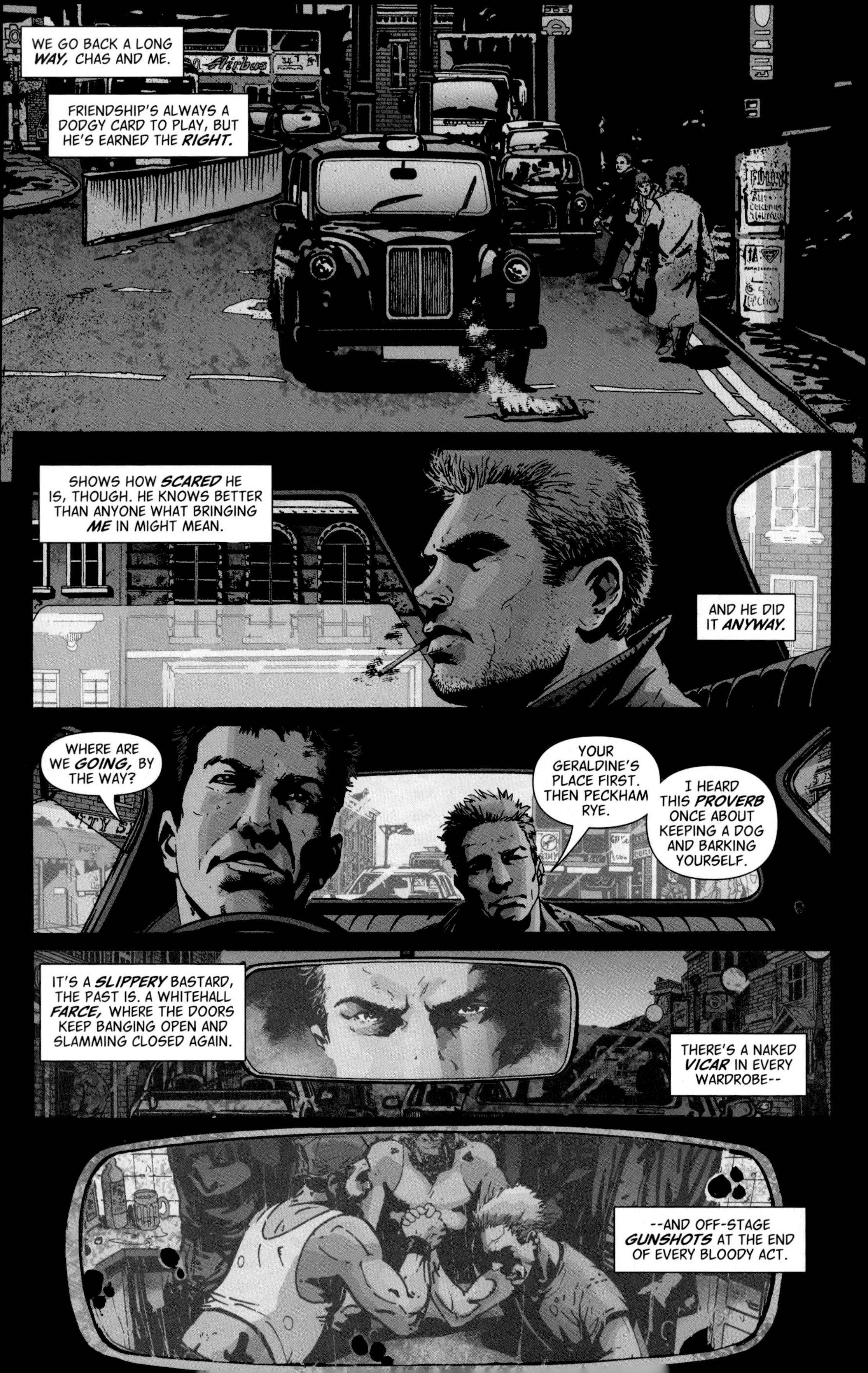

WE GO BACK A LONG *WAY,* CHAS AND ME.
FRIENDSHIP'S ALWAYS A DODGY CARD TO PLAY, BUT HE'S EARNED THE *RIGHT.*
SHOWS HOW *SCARED* HE IS, THOUGH. HE KNOWS BETTER THAN ANYONE WHAT BRINGING *ME* IN MIGHT MEAN.
AND HE DID IT *ANYWAY.*
WHERE ARE WE *GOING,* BY THE WAY?
YOUR GERALDINE'S PLACE FIRST. THEN PECKHAM RYE.
I HEARD THIS *PROVERB* ONCE ABOUT KEEPING A DOG AND BARKING YOURSELF.
IT'S A *SLIPPERY* BASTARD, THE PAST IS. A WHITEHALL *FARCE,* WHERE THE DOORS KEEP BANGING OPEN AND SLAMMING CLOSED AGAIN.
THERE'S A NAKED *VICAR* IN EVERY WARDROBE--
--AND OFF-STAGE *GUNSHOTS* AT THE END OF EVERY BLOODY ACT.

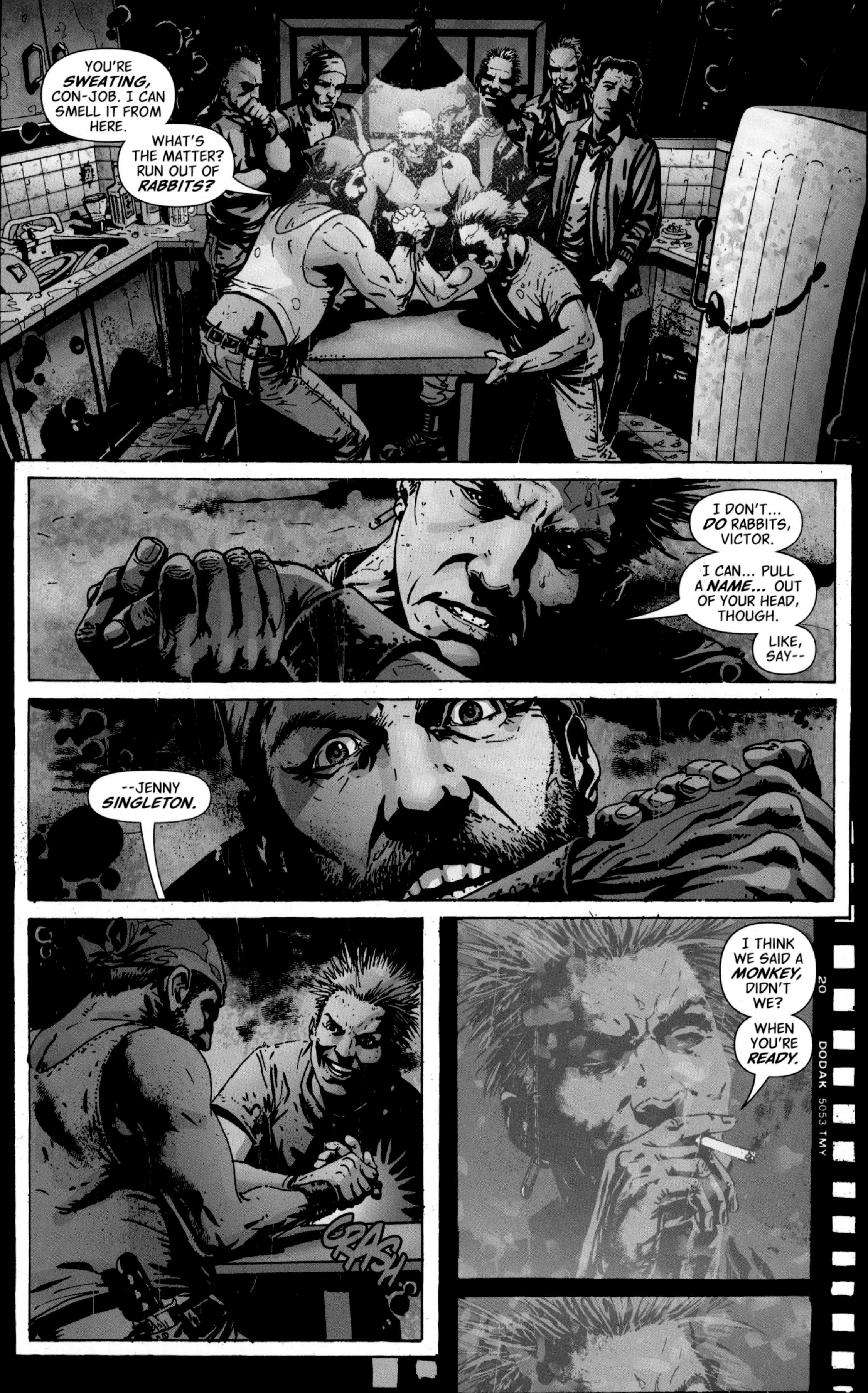

YOU'RE SWEATING, CON-JOB. I CAN SMELL IT FROM HERE.
WHAT'S THE MATTER? RUN OUT OF RABBITS?
I DON'T... DO RABBITS, VICTOR.
I CAN... PULL A NAME... OUT OF YOUR HEAD, THOUGH.
LIKE, SAY--
--JENNY SINGLETON.
CRASH
I THINK WE SAID A MONKEY, DIDN'T WE?
WHEN YOU'RE READY.
20
DODAK 5053 TMY

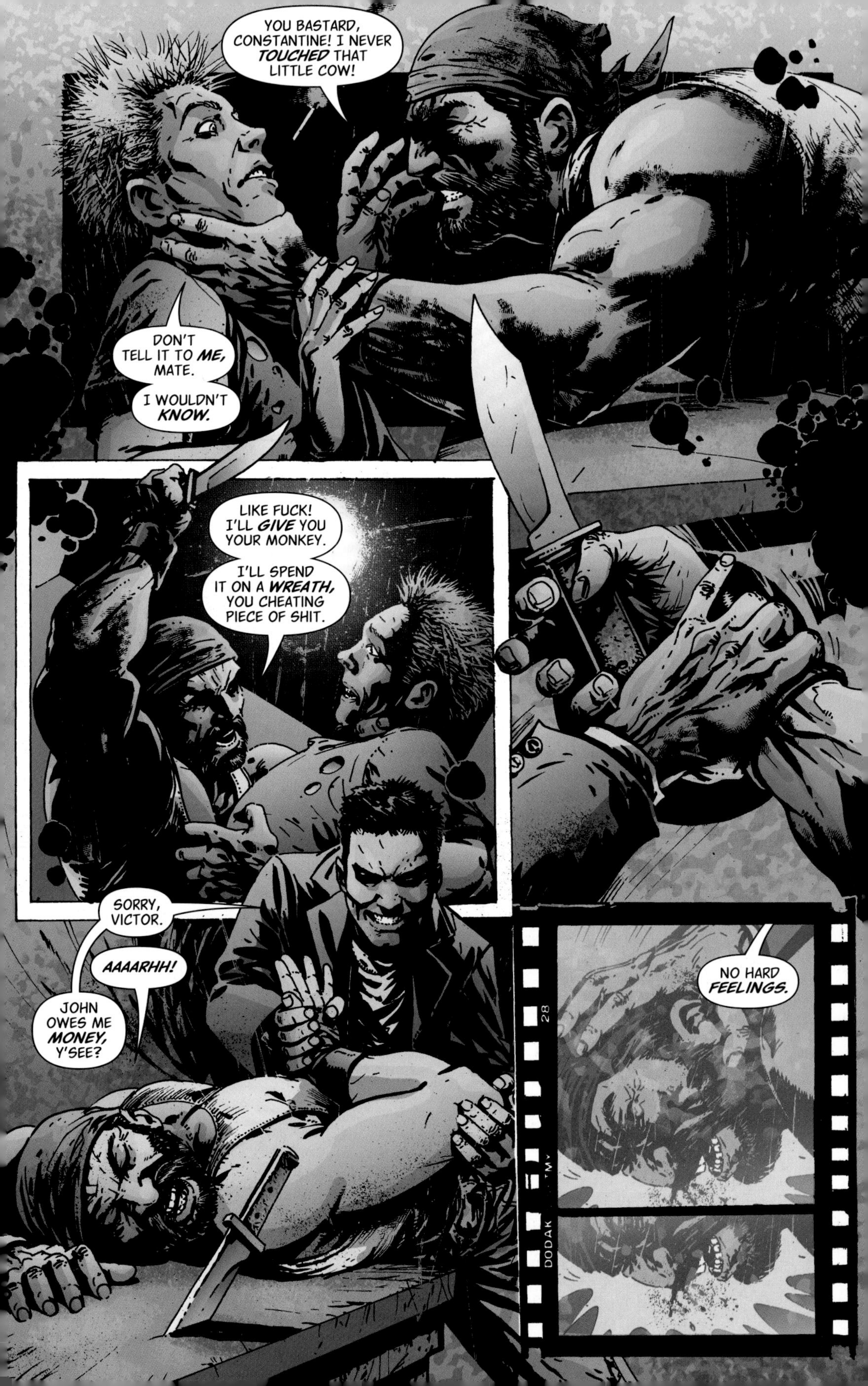

YOU BASTARD, CONSTANTINE! I NEVER TOUCHED THAT LITTLE COW!
DON'T TELL IT TO ME, MATE.
I WOULDN'T KNOW.
LIKE FUCK! I'LL GIVE YOU YOUR MONKEY.
I'LL SPEND IT ON A WREATH, YOU CHEATING PIECE OF SHIT.
SORRY, VICTOR.
AAAARHH!
JOHN OWES ME MONEY, Y'SEE?
NO HARD FEELINGS.

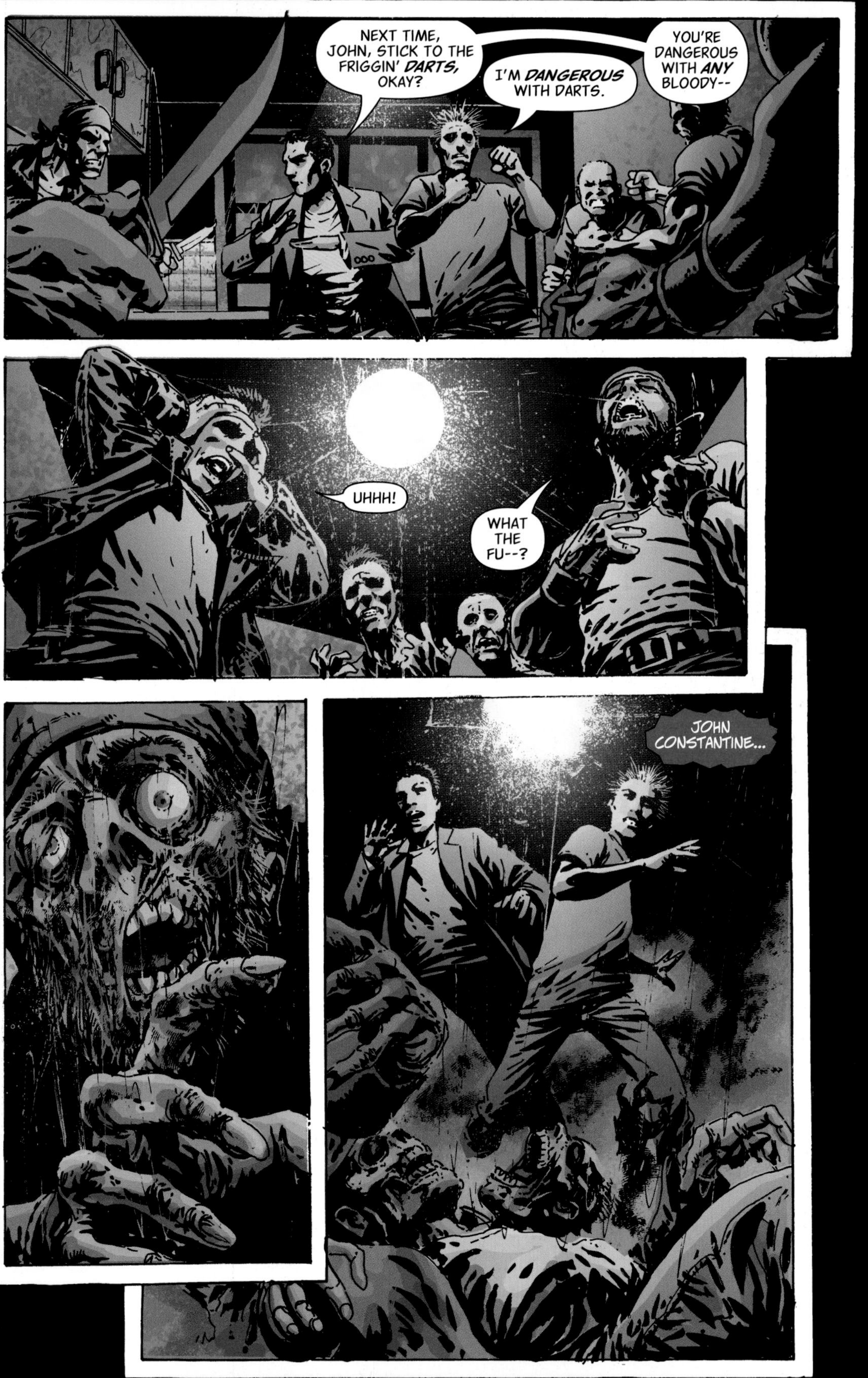
NEXT TIME, JOHN, STICK TO THE FRIGGIN' *DARTS,* OKAY?
I'M *DANGEROUS* WITH DARTS.
YOU'RE DANGEROUS WITH *ANY* BLOODY--
UHHH!
WHAT THE FU--?
JOHN CONSTANTINE...

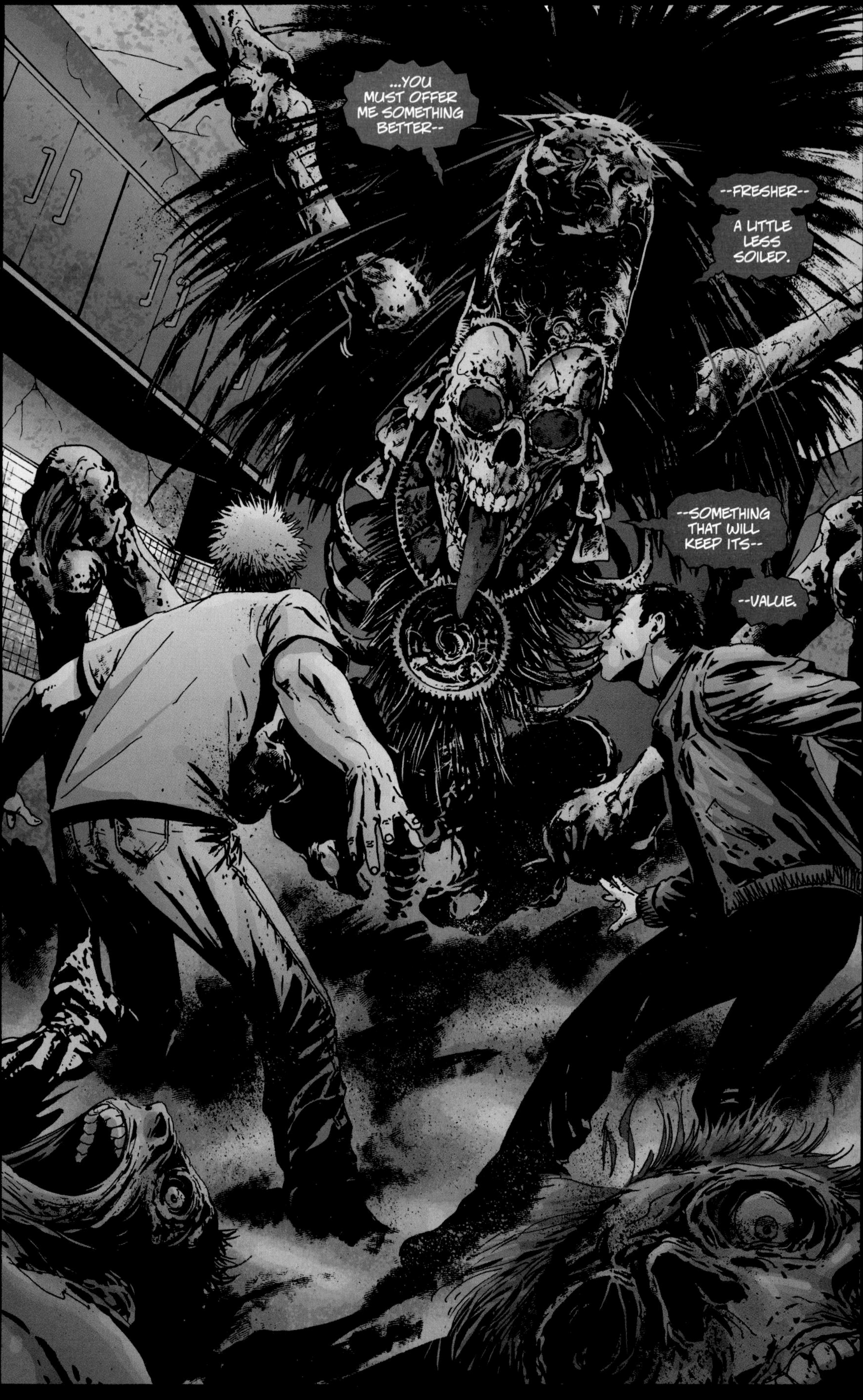
...YOU MUST OFFER ME SOMETHING BETTER--
--FRESHER--
A LITTLE LESS SOILED.
--SOMETHING THAT WILL KEEP ITS--
--VALUE.

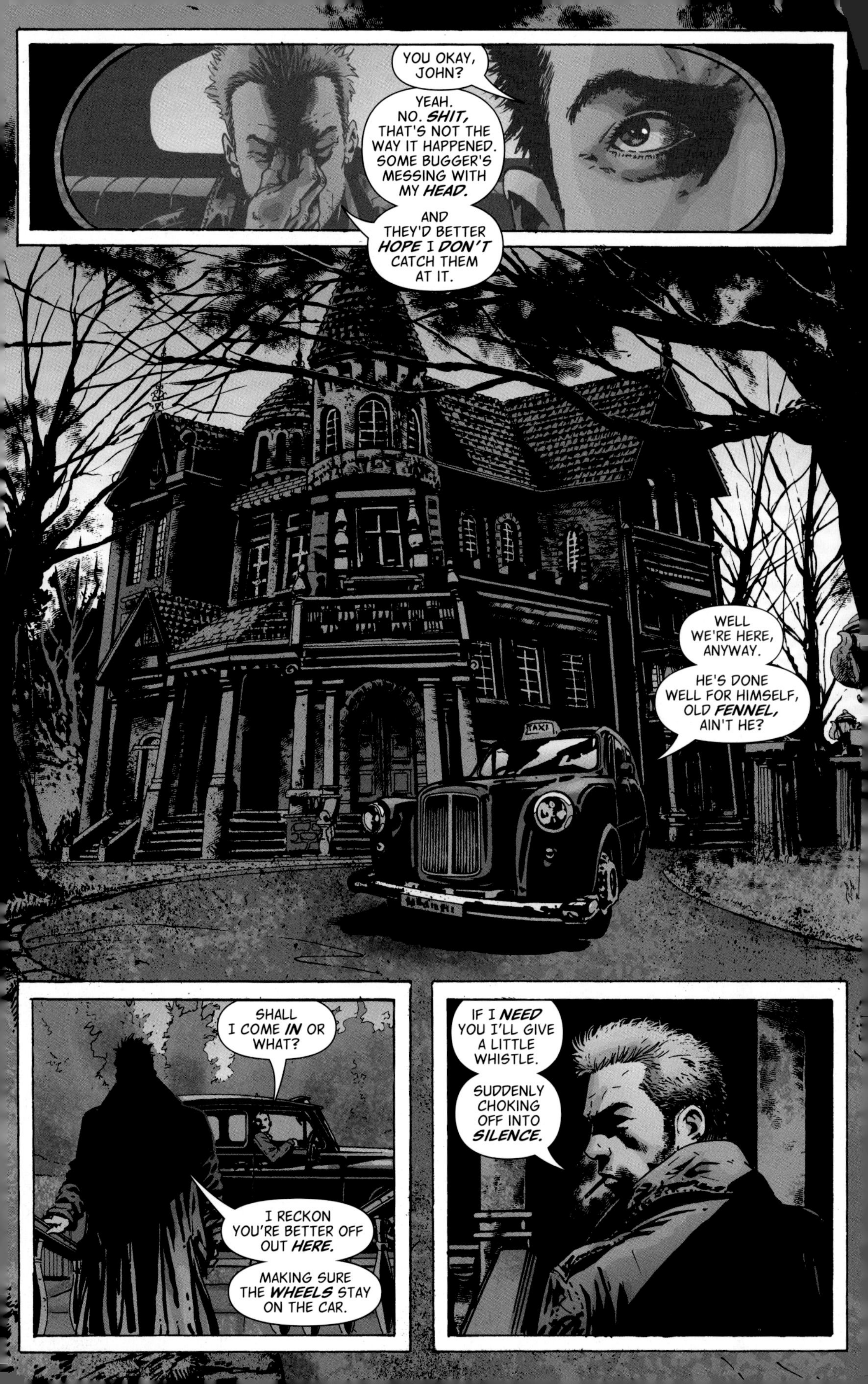
YOU OKAY, JOHN?
YEAH. NO. SHIT, THAT'S NOT THE WAY IT HAPPENED. SOME BUGGER'S MESSING WITH MY HEAD.
AND THEY'D BETTER HOPE I DON'T CATCH THEM AT IT.
WELL WE'RE HERE, ANYWAY.
HE'S DONE WELL FOR HIMSELF, OLD FENNEL, AIN'T HE?
TAXI
SHALL I COME IN OR WHAT?
I RECKON YOU'RE BETTER OFF OUT HERE.
MAKING SURE THE WHEELS STAY ON THE CAR.
IF I NEED YOU I'LL GIVE A LITTLE WHISTLE.
SUDDENLY CHOKING OFF INTO SILENCE.

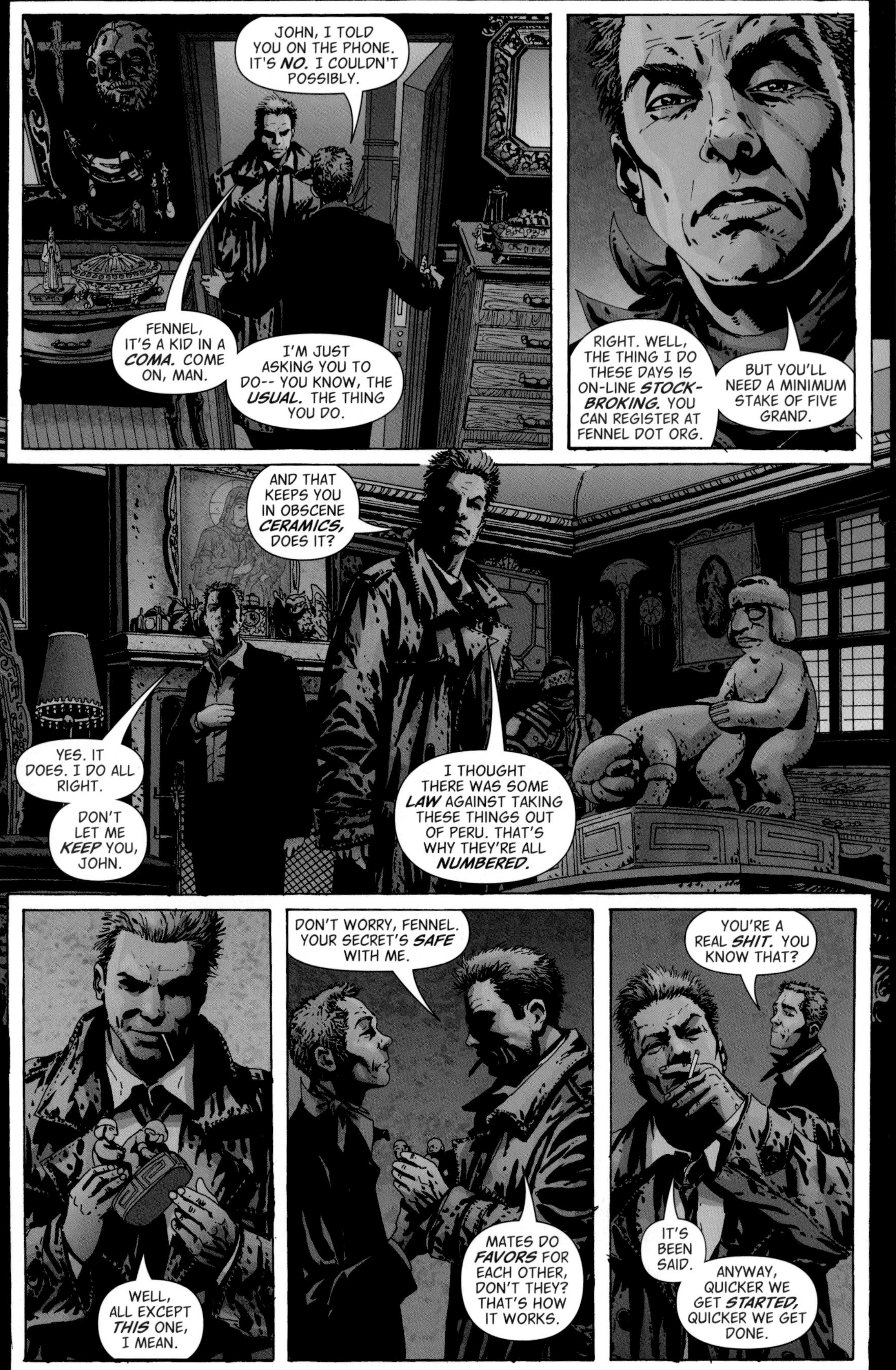
JOHN, I TOLD YOU ON THE PHONE. IT'S NO. I COULDN'T POSSIBLY.
FENNEL, IT'S A KID IN A COMA. COME ON, MAN.
I'M JUST ASKING YOU TO DO-- YOU KNOW, THE USUAL. THE THING YOU DO.
RIGHT. WELL, THE THING I DO THESE DAYS IS ON-LINE STOCK-BROKING. YOU CAN REGISTER AT FENNEL DOT ORG.
BUT YOU'LL NEED A MINIMUM STAKE OF FIVE GRAND.
AND THAT KEEPS YOU IN OBSCENE CERAMICS, DOES IT?
YES. IT DOES. I DO ALL RIGHT.
DON'T LET ME KEEP YOU, JOHN.
I THOUGHT THERE WAS SOME LAW AGAINST TAKING THESE THINGS OUT OF PERU. THAT'S WHY THEY'RE ALL NUMBERED.
WELL, ALL EXCEPT THIS ONE, I MEAN.
DON'T WORRY, FENNEL. YOUR SECRET'S SAFE WITH ME.
MATES DO FAVORS FOR EACH OTHER, DON'T THEY? THAT'S HOW IT WORKS.
YOU'RE A REAL SHIT. YOU KNOW THAT?
IT'S BEEN SAID.
ANYWAY, QUICKER WE GET STARTED, QUICKER WE GET DONE.

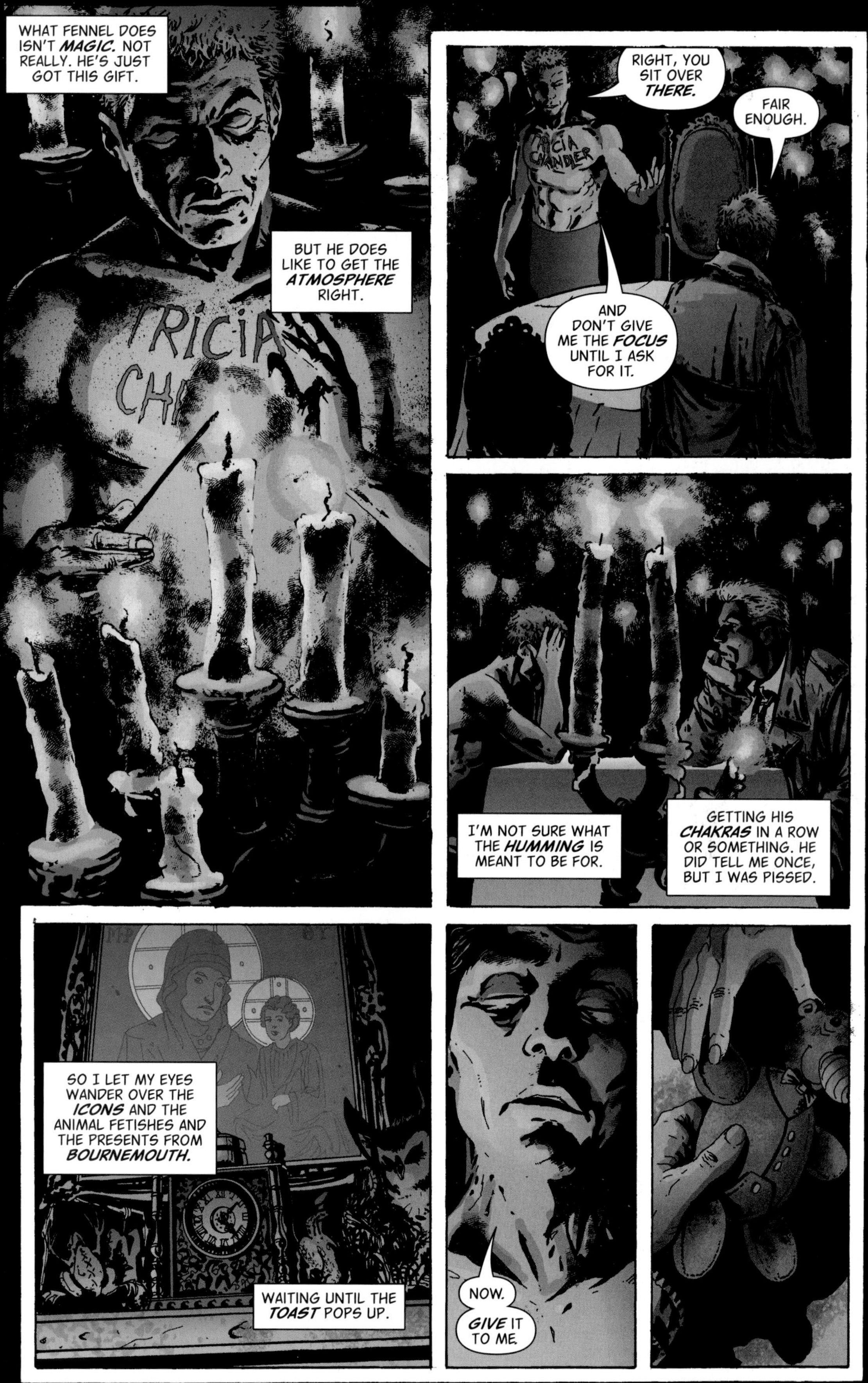
WHAT FENNEL DOES ISN'T MAGIC. NOT REALLY. HE'S JUST GOT THIS GIFT.
BUT HE DOES LIKE TO GET THE ATMOSPHERE RIGHT.
TRICIA CH
RIGHT, YOU SIT OVER THERE.
FAIR ENOUGH.
TRICIA CHANDLER
AND DON'T GIVE ME THE FOCUS UNTIL I ASK FOR IT.
I'M NOT SURE WHAT THE HUMMING IS MEANT TO BE FOR.
GETTING HIS CHAKRAS IN A ROW OR SOMETHING. HE DID TELL ME ONCE, BUT I WAS PISSED.
SO I LET MY EYES WANDER OVER THE ICONS AND THE ANIMAL FETISHES AND THE PRESENTS FROM BOURNEMOUTH.
WAITING UNTIL THE TOAST POPS UP.
NOW.
GIVE IT TO ME.

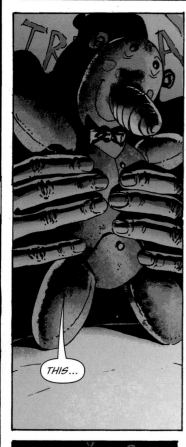

THIS...

...THIS ISN'T MY BED. IS IT?

TRISH?

THIS ISN'T MY ROOM.

YOU'RE IN HOSPITAL, LOVE. THAT'S A HOSPITAL BED.

BUT I'M ALL CHAINED UP. AND NOBODY'S COME.

YOUR MUM AND DAD ARE RIGHT THERE, LOVE. JUST OPEN YOUR EYES.

NOBODY'S COME EXCEPT THE NASTY MAN.

WHAT NASTY MAN? TRISH?

WHO'S THERE WITH YOU, LOVE? CAN YOU SEE A--?

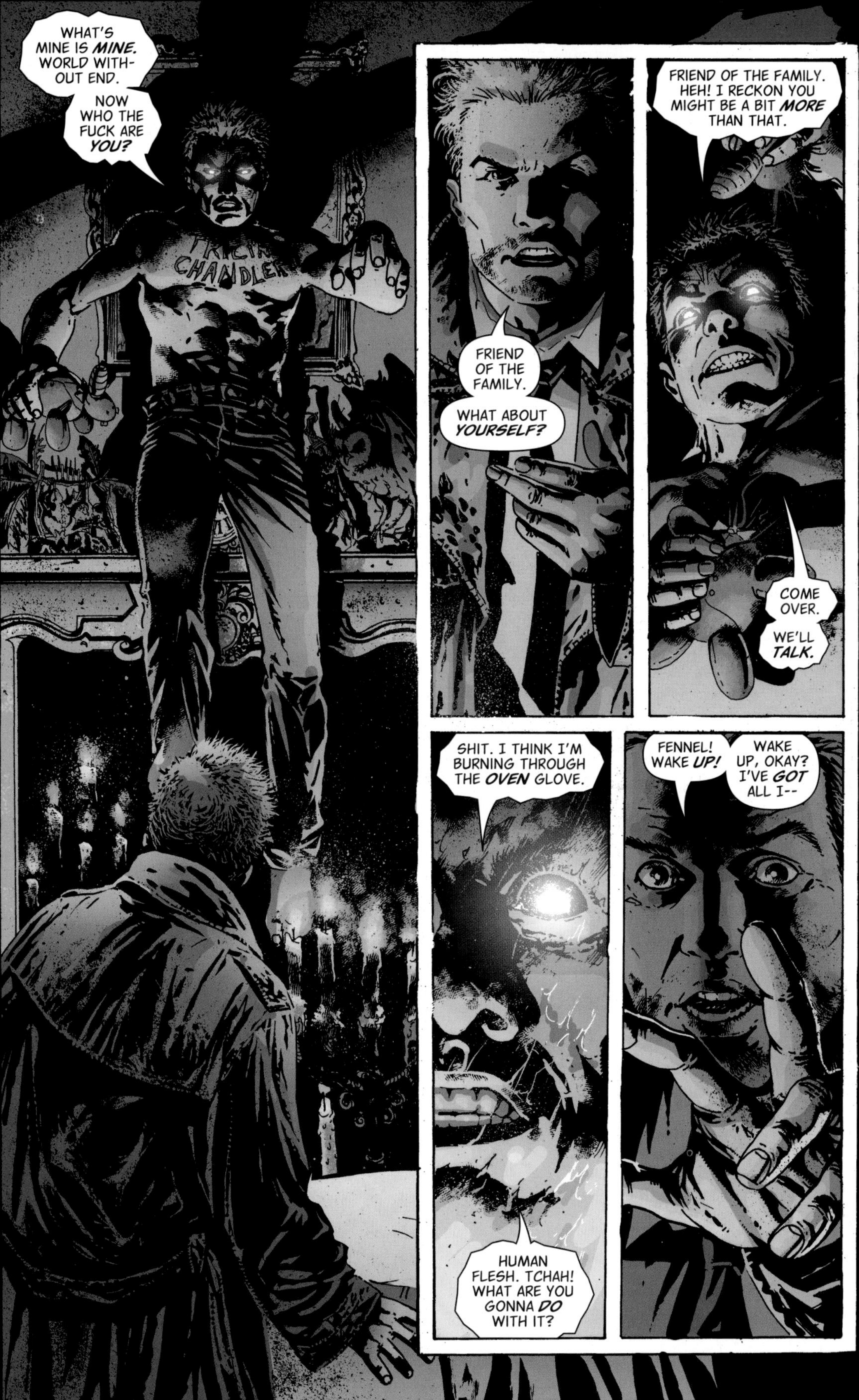
WHAT'S MINE IS *MINE.* WORLD WITH-OUT END.
NOW WHO THE FUCK ARE *YOU?*
FRIEND OF THE FAMILY.
WHAT ABOUT *YOURSELF?*
FRIEND OF THE FAMILY. HEH! I RECKON YOU MIGHT BE A BIT *MORE* THAN THAT.
COME OVER.
WE'LL *TALK.*
SHIT. I THINK I'M BURNING THROUGH THE *OVEN* GLOVE.
HUMAN FLESH. TCHAH! WHAT ARE YOU GONNA *DO* WITH IT?
FENNEL! WAKE *UP!*
WAKE UP, OKAY? I'VE *GOT* ALL I--

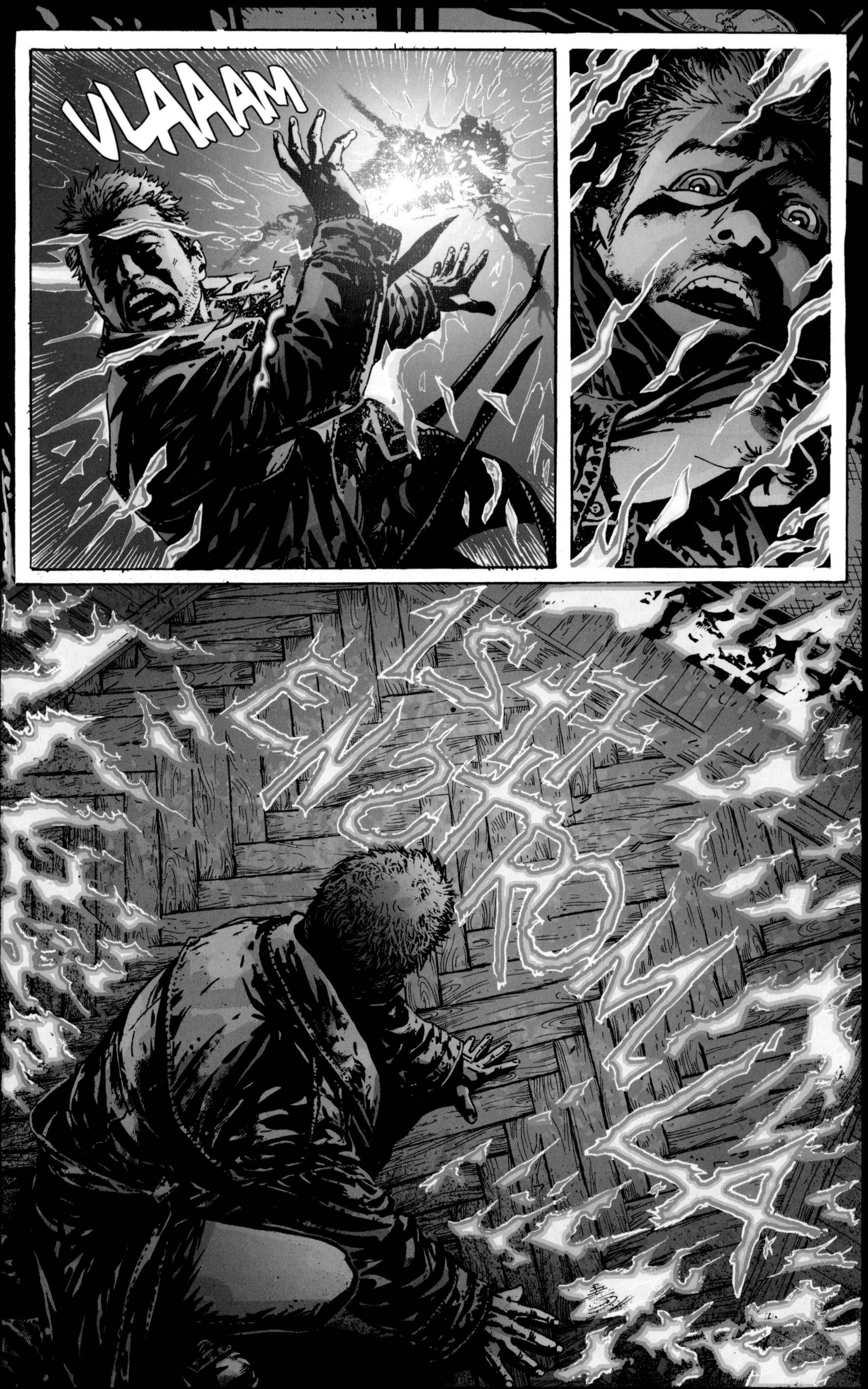
VLAAAM

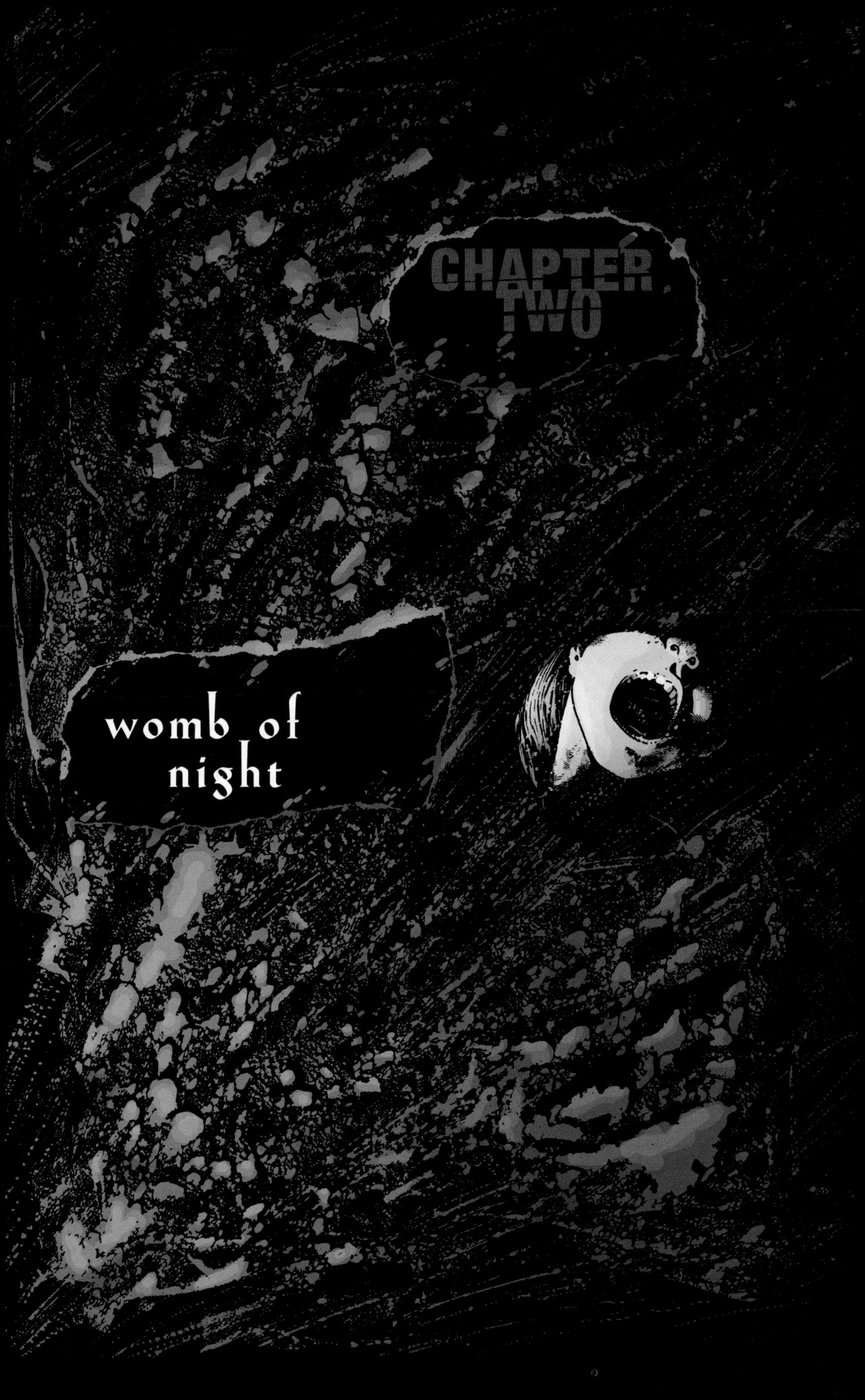
CHAPTER TWO
womb of night

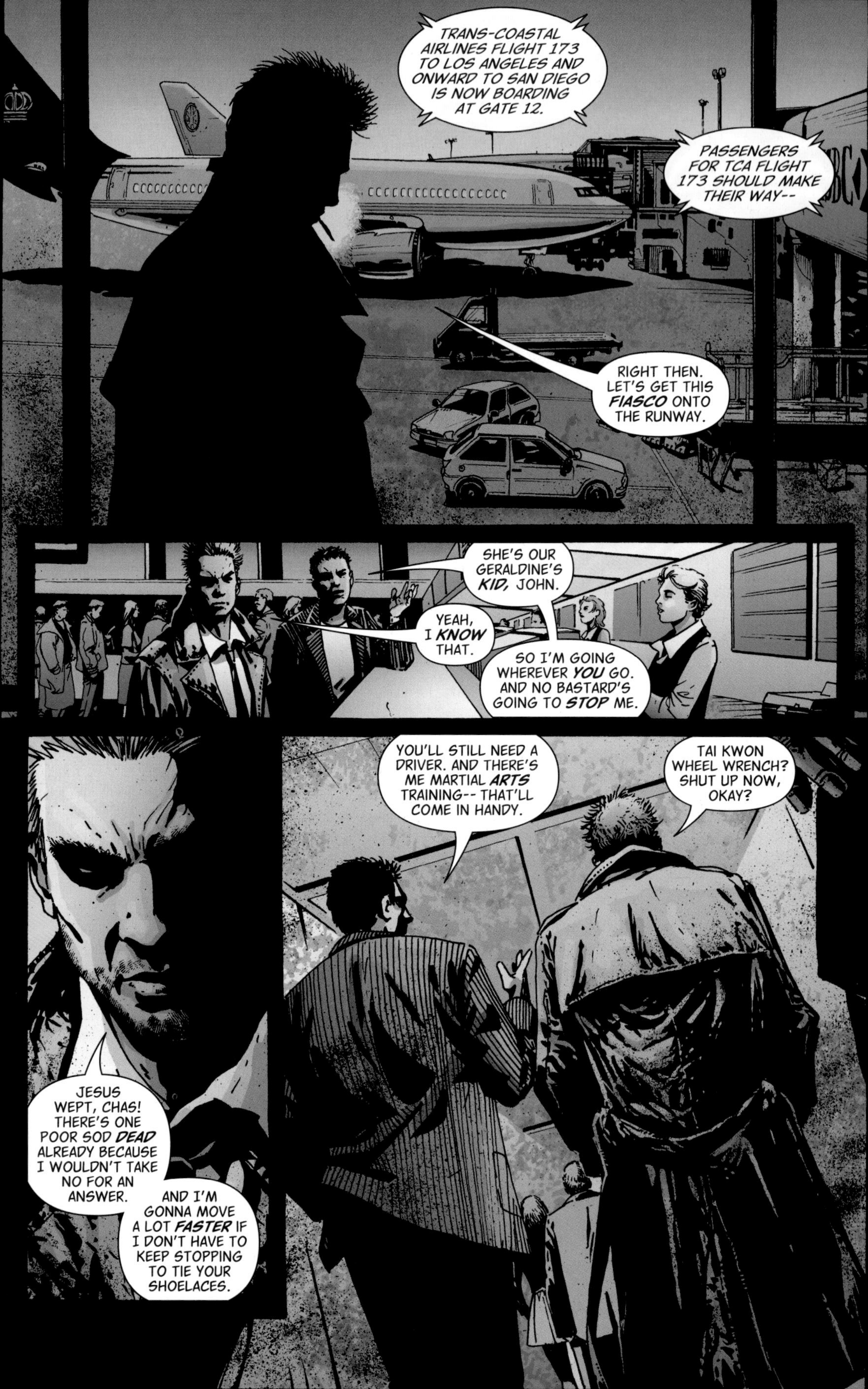

TRANS-COASTAL AIRLINES FLIGHT 173 TO LOS ANGELES AND ONWARD TO SAN DIEGO IS NOW BOARDING AT GATE 12.
PASSENGERS FOR TCA FLIGHT 173 SHOULD MAKE THEIR WAY--
RIGHT THEN. LET'S GET THIS FIASCO ONTO THE RUNWAY.
SHE'S OUR GERALDINE'S KID, JOHN.
YEAH, I KNOW THAT.
SO I'M GOING WHEREVER YOU GO. AND NO BASTARD'S GOING TO STOP ME.
YOU'LL STILL NEED A DRIVER. AND THERE'S ME MARTIAL ARTS TRAINING-- THAT'LL COME IN HANDY.
TAI KWON WHEEL WRENCH? SHUT UP NOW, OKAY?
JESUS WEPT, CHAS! THERE'S ONE POOR SOD DEAD ALREADY BECAUSE I WOULDN'T TAKE NO FOR AN ANSWER.
AND I'M GONNA MOVE A LOT FASTER IF I DON'T HAVE TO KEEP STOPPING TO TIE YOUR SHOELACES.

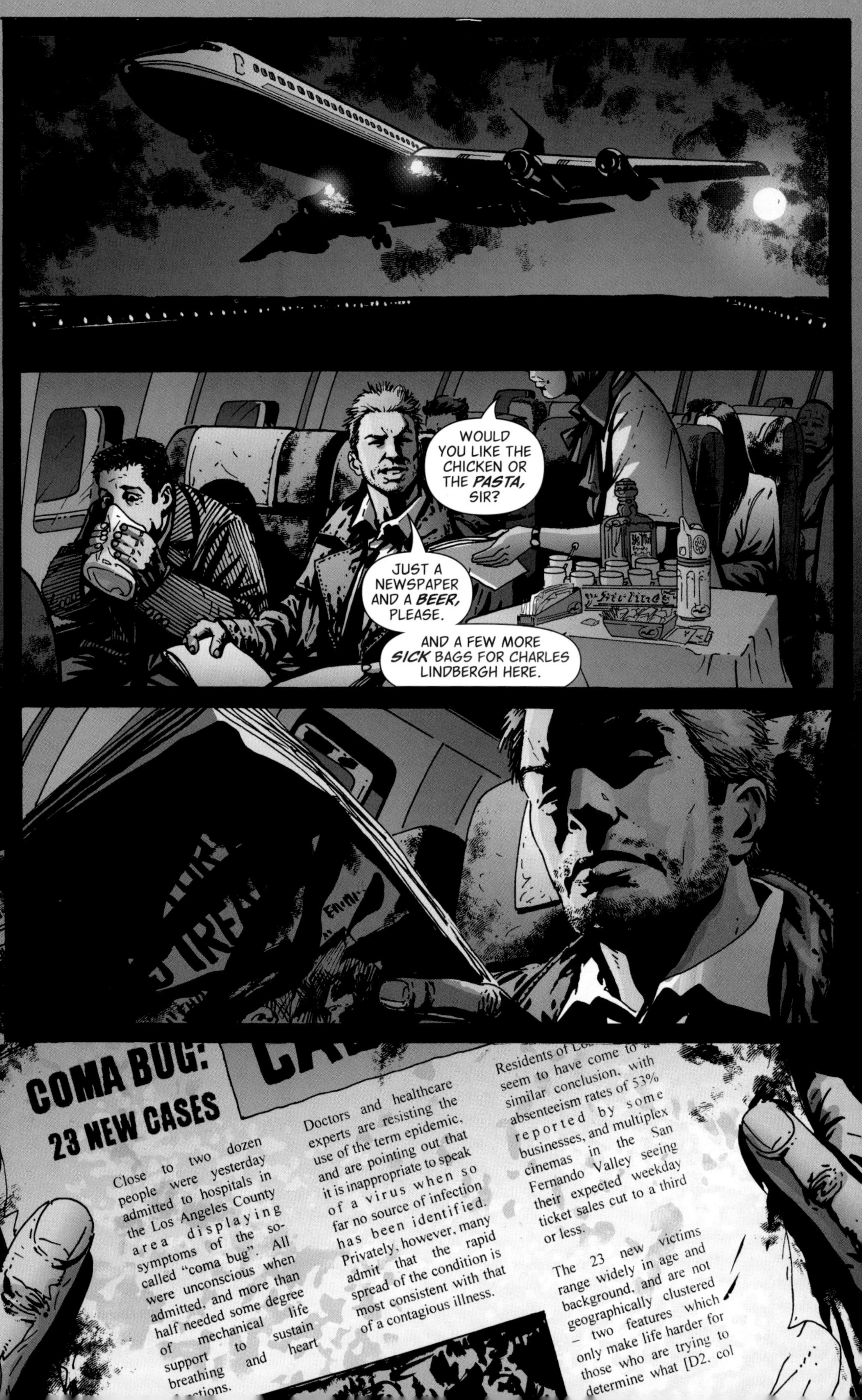

WOULD YOU LIKE THE CHICKEN OR THE *PASTA,* SIR?
JUST A NEWSPAPER AND A ***BEER,*** PLEASE.
AND A FEW MORE ***SICK*** BAGS FOR CHARLES LINDBERGH HERE.
COMA BUG: 23 NEW CASES
Close to two dozen people were yesterday admitted to hospitals in the Los Angeles County area displaying symptoms of the so-called "coma bug". All were unconscious when admitted, and more than half needed some degree of mechanical life support to sustain breathing and heart
Doctors and healthcare experts are resisting the use of the term epidemic, and are pointing out that it is inappropriate to speak of a virus when so far no source of infection has been identified. Privately, however, many admit that the rapid spread of the condition is most consistent with that of a contagious illness.
seem to have come to a similar conclusion, with absenteeism rates of 53% reported by some businesses, and multiplex cinemas in the San Fernando Valley seeing their expected weekday ticket sales cut to a third or less.
The 23 new victims range widely in age and background, and are not geographically clustered – two features which only make life harder for those who are trying to determine what [D2. col

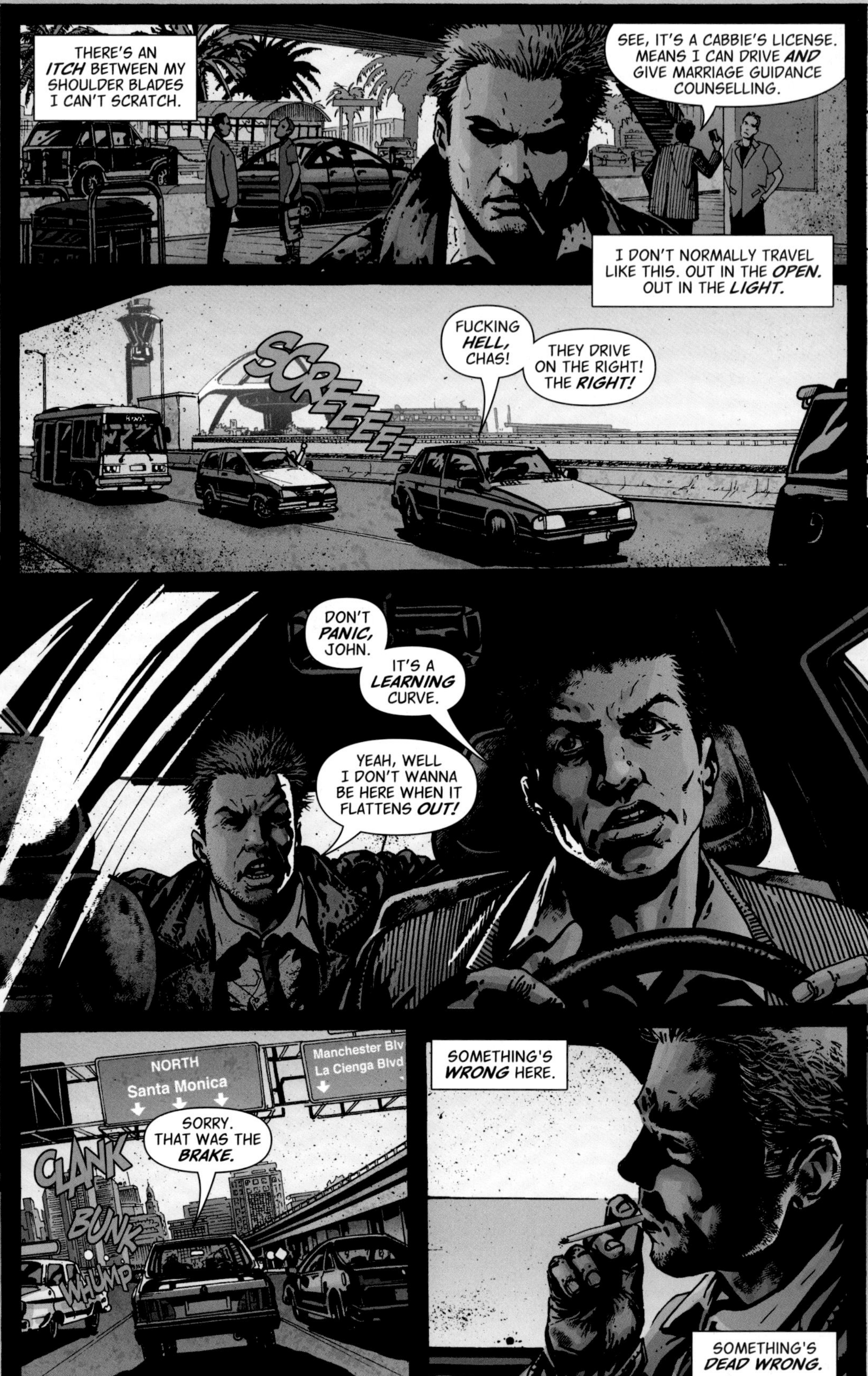
THERE'S AN ITCH BETWEEN MY SHOULDER BLADES I CAN'T SCRATCH.
SEE, IT'S A CABBIE'S LICENSE. MEANS I CAN DRIVE AND GIVE MARRIAGE GUIDANCE COUNSELLING.
I DON'T NORMALLY TRAVEL LIKE THIS. OUT IN THE OPEN. OUT IN THE LIGHT.
SCREEEEEE
FUCKING HELL, CHAS!
THEY DRIVE ON THE RIGHT! THE RIGHT!
DON'T PANIC, JOHN.
IT'S A LEARNING CURVE.
YEAH, WELL I DON'T WANNA BE HERE WHEN IT FLATTENS OUT!
NORTH
Santa Monica
Manchester Blvd
La Cienga Blvd
SORRY. THAT WAS THE BRAKE.
CLANK
BUNK
WHUMP
SOMETHING'S WRONG HERE.
SOMETHING'S DEAD WRONG.

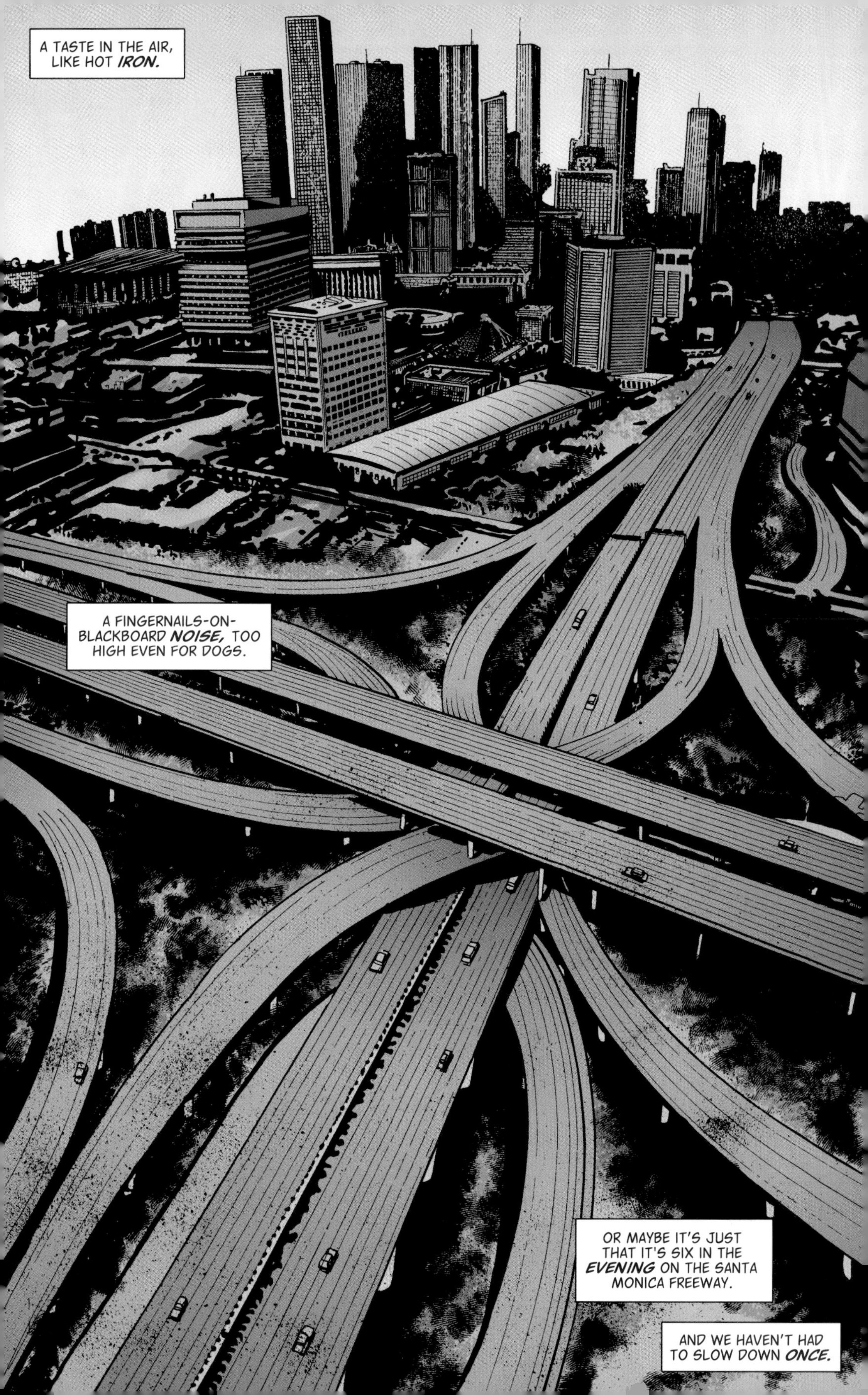
A TASTE IN THE AIR, LIKE HOT IRON.
A FINGERNAILS-ON-BLACKBOARD NOISE, TOO HIGH EVEN FOR DOGS.
OR MAYBE IT'S JUST THAT IT'S SIX IN THE EVENING ON THE SANTA MONICA FREEWAY.
AND WE HAVEN'T HAD TO SLOW DOWN ONCE.

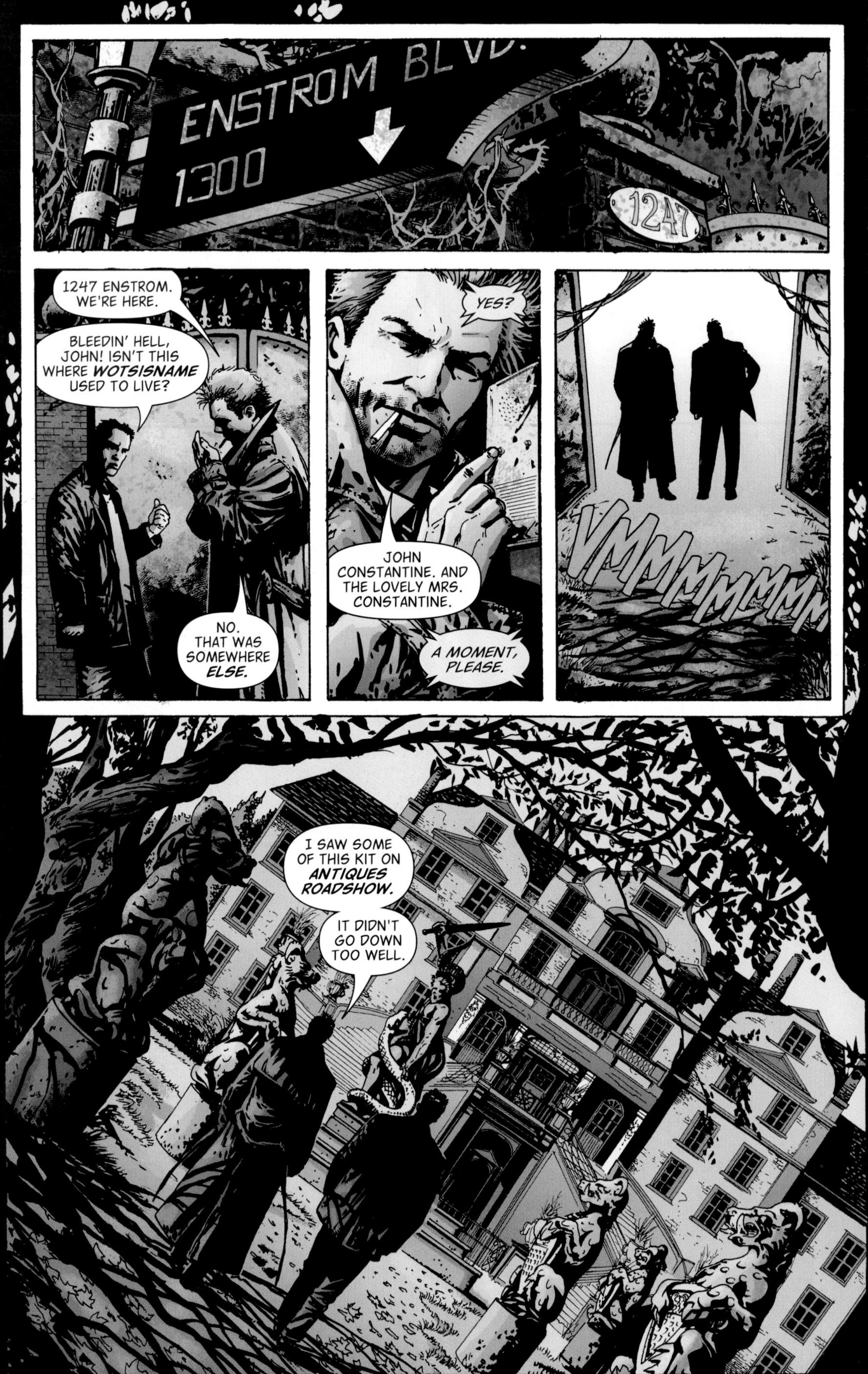
ENSTROM BLVD.
1300
1247
1247 ENSTROM. WE'RE HERE.
BLEEDIN' HELL, JOHN! ISN'T THIS WHERE **WOTSISNAME** USED TO LIVE?
NO. THAT WAS SOMEWHERE **ELSE.**
YES?
JOHN CONSTANTINE. AND THE LOVELY MRS. CONSTANTINE.
A MOMENT, PLEASE.
VMMMMMMMM
I SAW SOME OF THIS KIT ON **ANTIQUES ROADSHOW.**
IT DIDN'T GO DOWN TOO WELL.

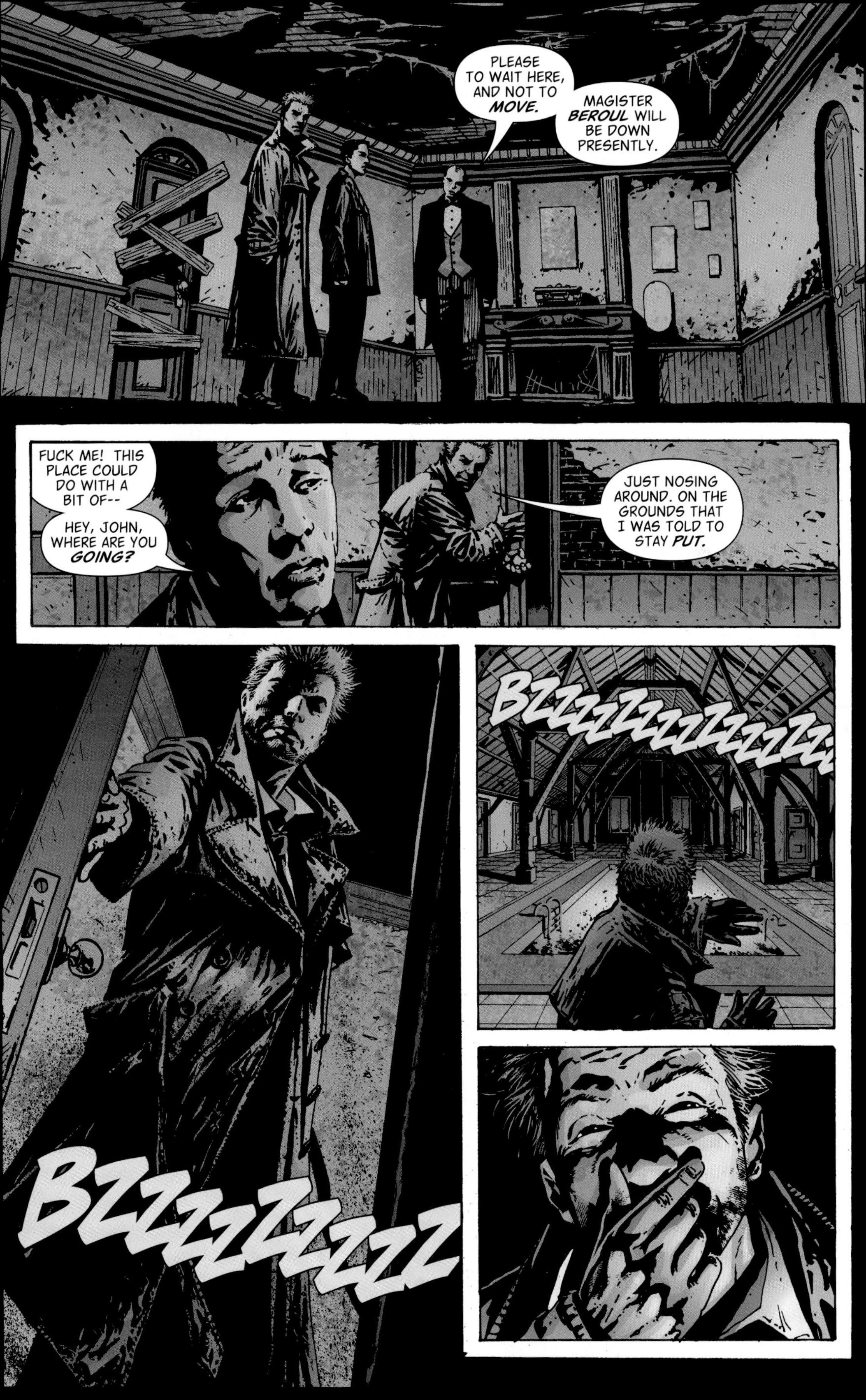
PLEASE TO WAIT HERE, AND NOT TO MOVE.
MAGISTER BEROUL WILL BE DOWN PRESENTLY.
FUCK ME! THIS PLACE COULD DO WITH A BIT OF--
HEY, JOHN, WHERE ARE YOU GOING?
JUST NOSING AROUND. ON THE GROUNDS THAT I WAS TOLD TO STAY PUT.
BZZZZZZZZZ
BZZZZZZZZZZZZZZ

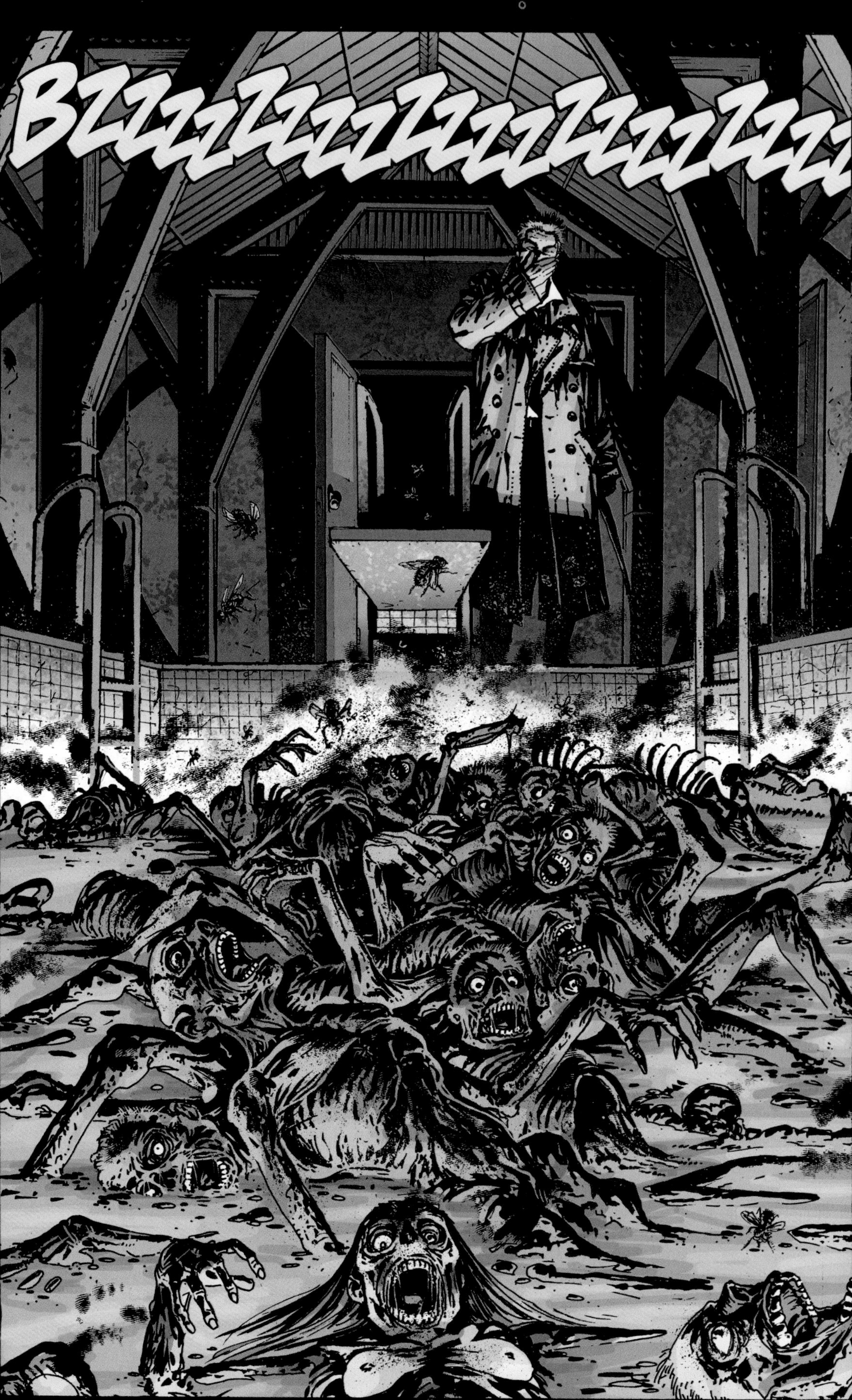
BZZzzZzzzZzzzZzzzZzzz

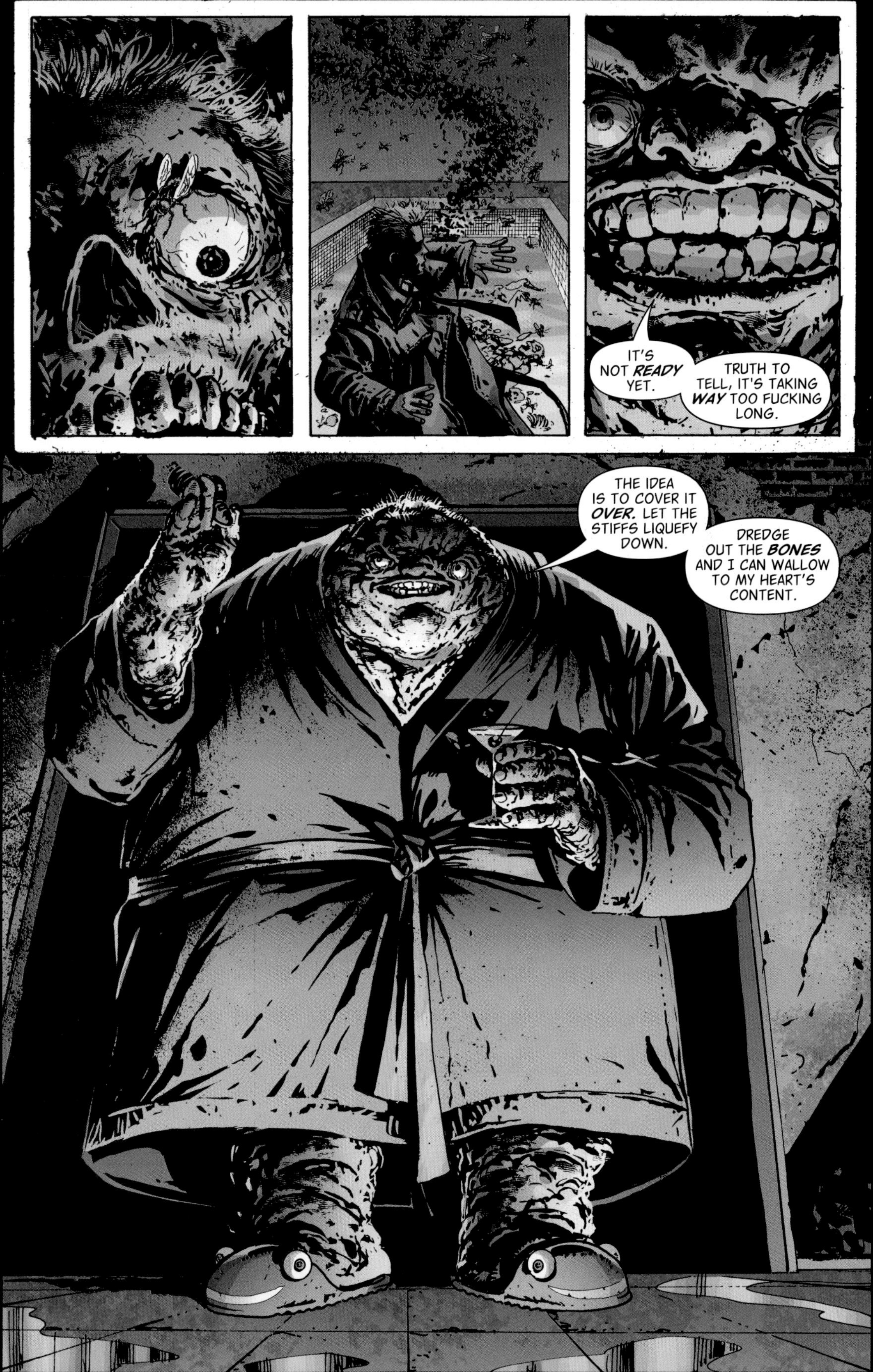
IT'S NOT READY YET.
TRUTH TO TELL, IT'S TAKING WAY TOO FUCKING LONG.
THE IDEA IS TO COVER IT OVER. LET THE STIFFS LIQUEFY DOWN.
DREDGE OUT THE BONES AND I CAN WALLOW TO MY HEART'S CONTENT.

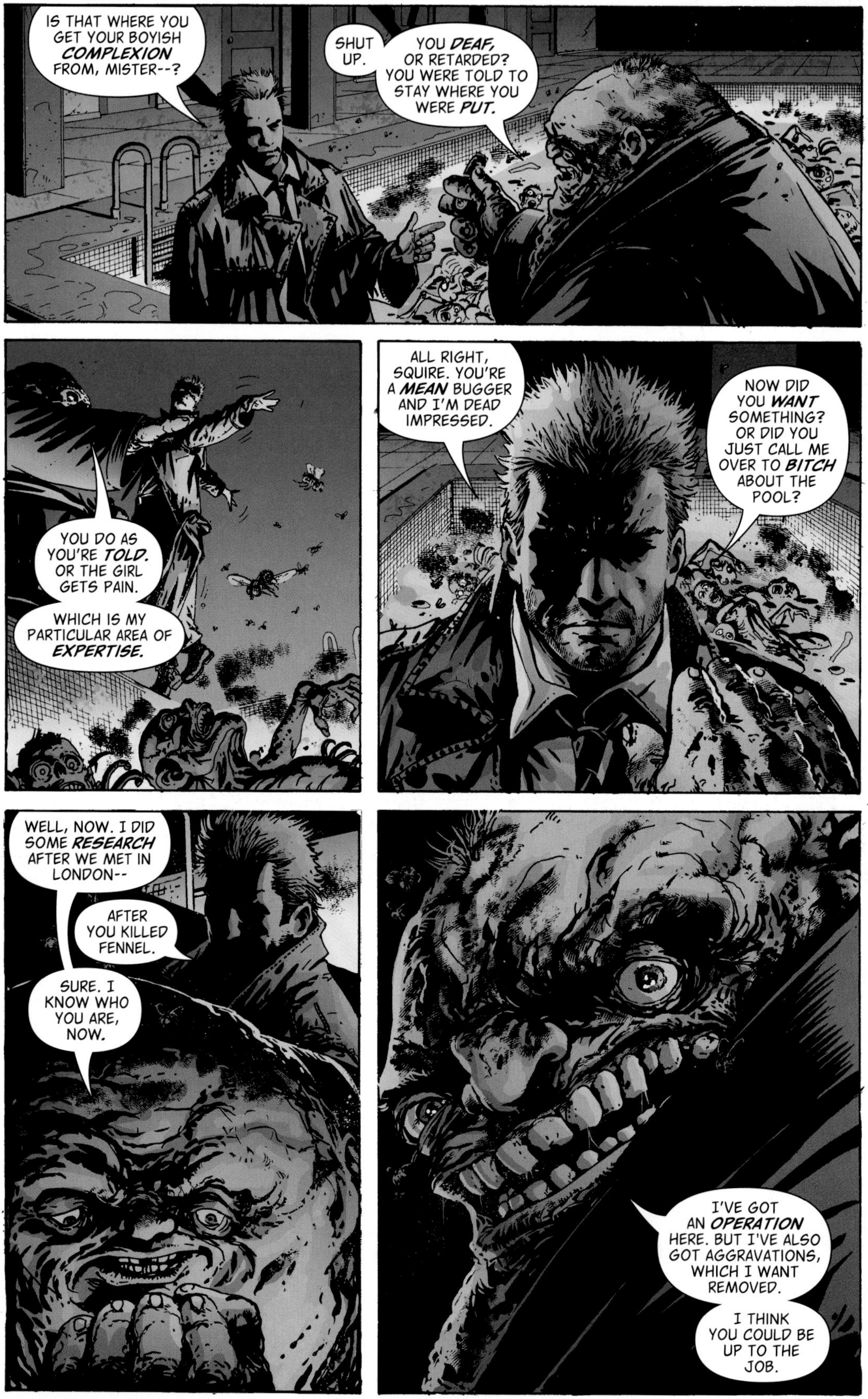
IS THAT WHERE YOU GET YOUR BOYISH COMPLEXION FROM, MISTER--?
SHUT UP.
YOU DEAF, OR RETARDED? YOU WERE TOLD TO STAY WHERE YOU WERE PUT.
YOU DO AS YOU'RE TOLD. OR THE GIRL GETS PAIN.
WHICH IS MY PARTICULAR AREA OF EXPERTISE.
ALL RIGHT, SQUIRE. YOU'RE A MEAN BUGGER AND I'M DEAD IMPRESSED.
NOW DID YOU WANT SOMETHING? OR DID YOU JUST CALL ME OVER TO BITCH ABOUT THE POOL?
WELL, NOW. I DID SOME RESEARCH AFTER WE MET IN LONDON--
AFTER YOU KILLED FENNEL.
SURE. I KNOW WHO YOU ARE, NOW.
I'VE GOT AN OPERATION HERE. BUT I'VE ALSO GOT AGGRAVATIONS, WHICH I WANT REMOVED.
I THINK YOU COULD BE UP TO THE JOB.

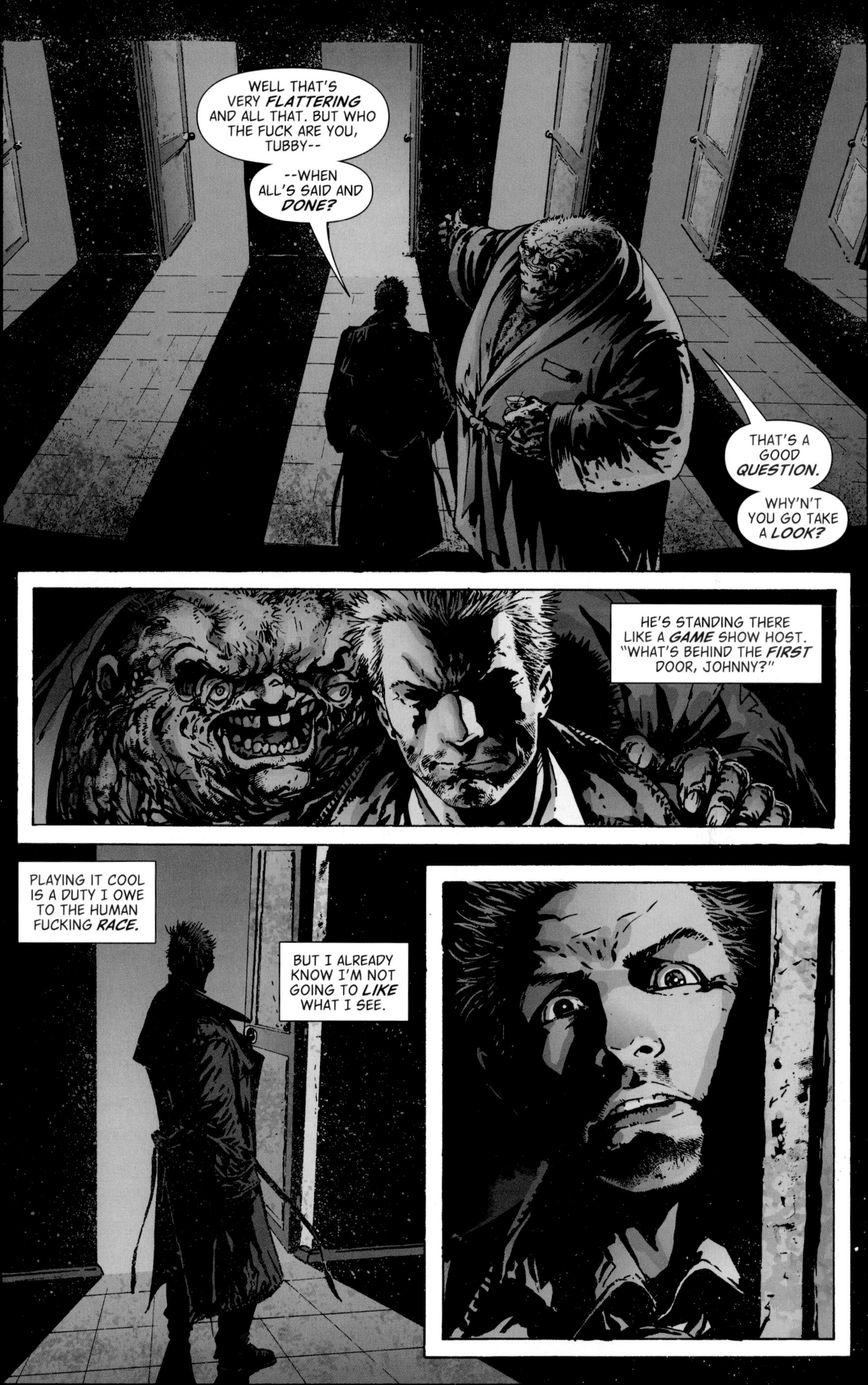

WELL THAT'S VERY FLATTERING AND ALL THAT. BUT WHO THE FUCK ARE YOU, TUBBY--
--WHEN ALL'S SAID AND DONE?
THAT'S A GOOD QUESTION.
WHY'N'T YOU GO TAKE A LOOK?
HE'S STANDING THERE LIKE A GAME SHOW HOST. "WHAT'S BEHIND THE FIRST DOOR, JOHNNY?"
PLAYING IT COOL IS A DUTY I OWE TO THE HUMAN FUCKING RACE.
BUT I ALREADY KNOW I'M NOT GOING TO LIKE WHAT I SEE.

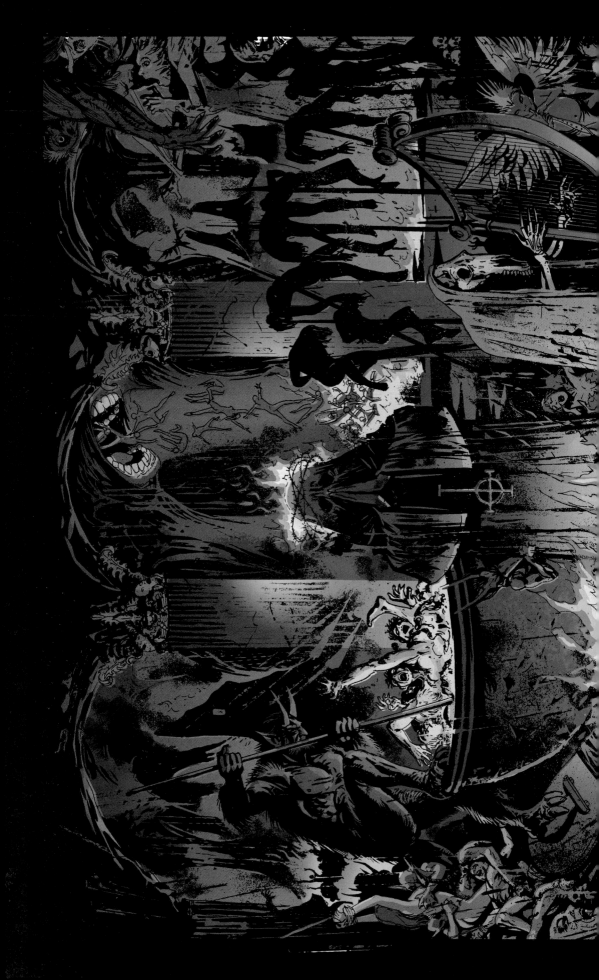

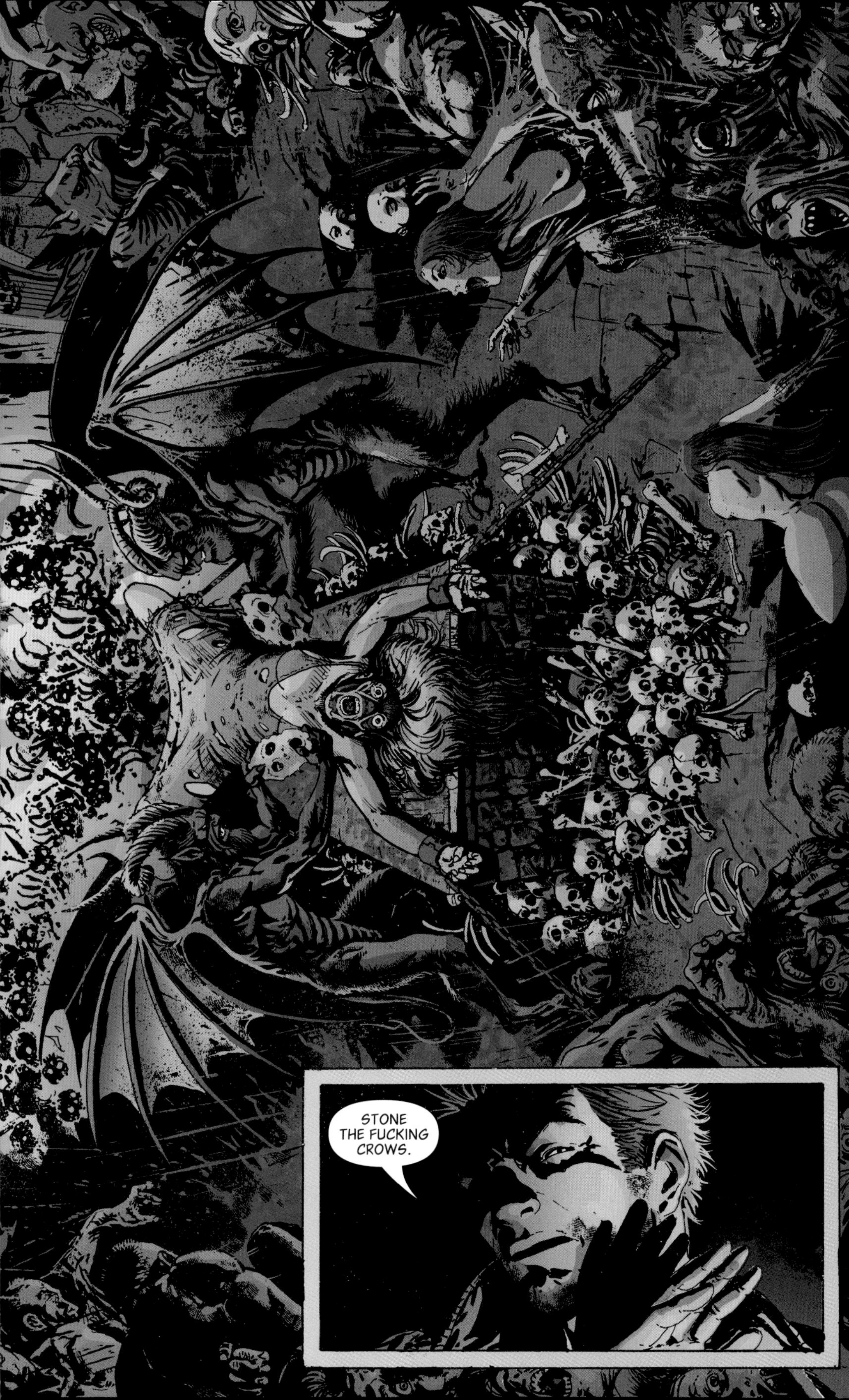
STONE THE FUCKING CROWS.

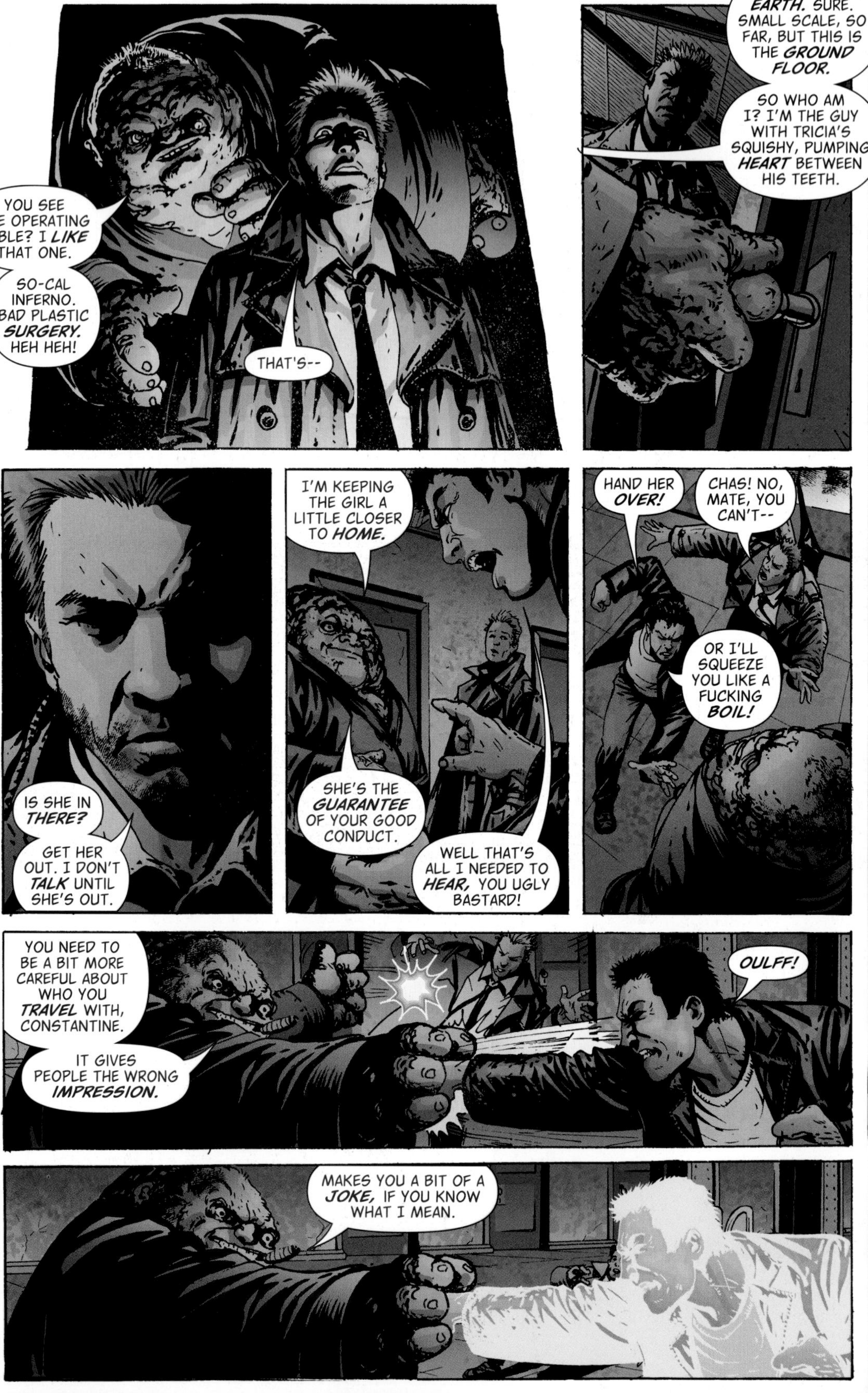
YOU SEE THE OPERATING TABLE? I LIKE THAT ONE.
SO-CAL INFERNO. BAD PLASTIC SURGERY. HEH HEH!
THAT'S--
--HELL ON EARTH. SURE. SMALL SCALE, SO FAR, BUT THIS IS THE GROUND FLOOR.
SO WHO AM I? I'M THE GUY WITH TRICIA'S SQUISHY, PUMPING HEART BETWEEN HIS TEETH.
IS SHE IN THERE?
GET HER OUT. I DON'T TALK UNTIL SHE'S OUT.
I'M KEEPING THE GIRL A LITTLE CLOSER TO HOME.
SHE'S THE GUARANTEE OF YOUR GOOD CONDUCT.
WELL THAT'S ALL I NEEDED TO HEAR, YOU UGLY BASTARD!
HAND HER OVER!
CHAS! NO, MATE, YOU CAN'T--
OR I'LL SQUEEZE YOU LIKE A FUCKING BOIL!
YOU NEED TO BE A BIT MORE CAREFUL ABOUT WHO YOU TRAVEL WITH, CONSTANTINE.
IT GIVES PEOPLE THE WRONG IMPRESSION.
OULFF!
MAKES YOU A BIT OF A JOKE, IF YOU KNOW WHAT I MEAN.

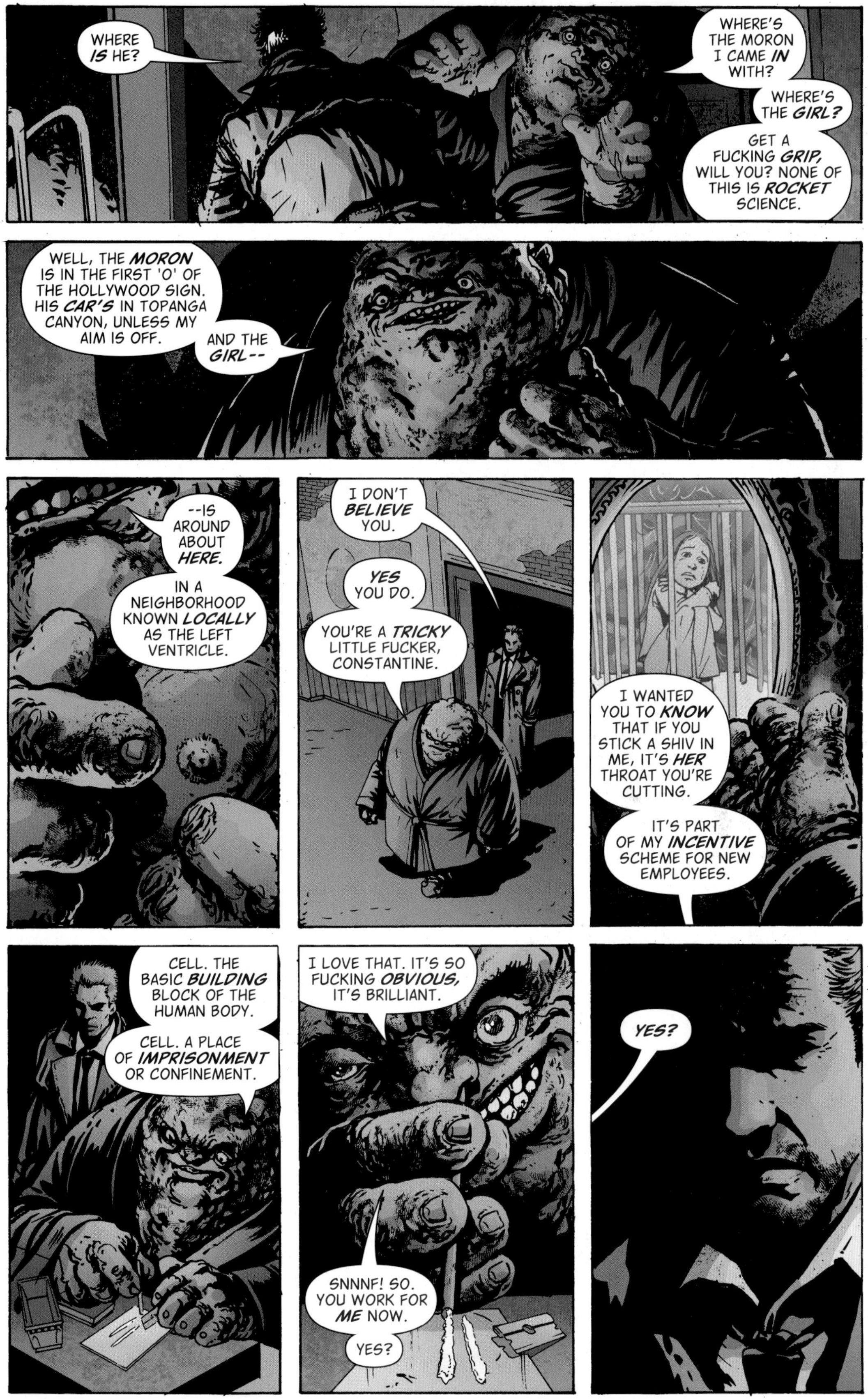
WHERE IS HE?
WHERE'S THE MORON I CAME IN WITH?
WHERE'S THE GIRL?
GET A FUCKING GRIP, WILL YOU? NONE OF THIS IS ROCKET SCIENCE.
WELL, THE MORON IS IN THE FIRST 'O' OF THE HOLLYWOOD SIGN. HIS CAR'S IN TOPANGA CANYON, UNLESS MY AIM IS OFF.
AND THE GIRL--
--IS AROUND ABOUT HERE.
IN A NEIGHBORHOOD KNOWN LOCALLY AS THE LEFT VENTRICLE.
I DON'T BELIEVE YOU.
YES YOU DO.
YOU'RE A TRICKY LITTLE FUCKER, CONSTANTINE.
I WANTED YOU TO KNOW THAT IF YOU STICK A SHIV IN ME, IT'S HER THROAT YOU'RE CUTTING.
IT'S PART OF MY INCENTIVE SCHEME FOR NEW EMPLOYEES.
CELL. THE BASIC BUILDING BLOCK OF THE HUMAN BODY.
CELL. A PLACE OF IMPRISONMENT OR CONFINEMENT.
I LOVE THAT. IT'S SO FUCKING OBVIOUS, IT'S BRILLIANT.
SNNNF! SO. YOU WORK FOR ME NOW.
YES?
YES?

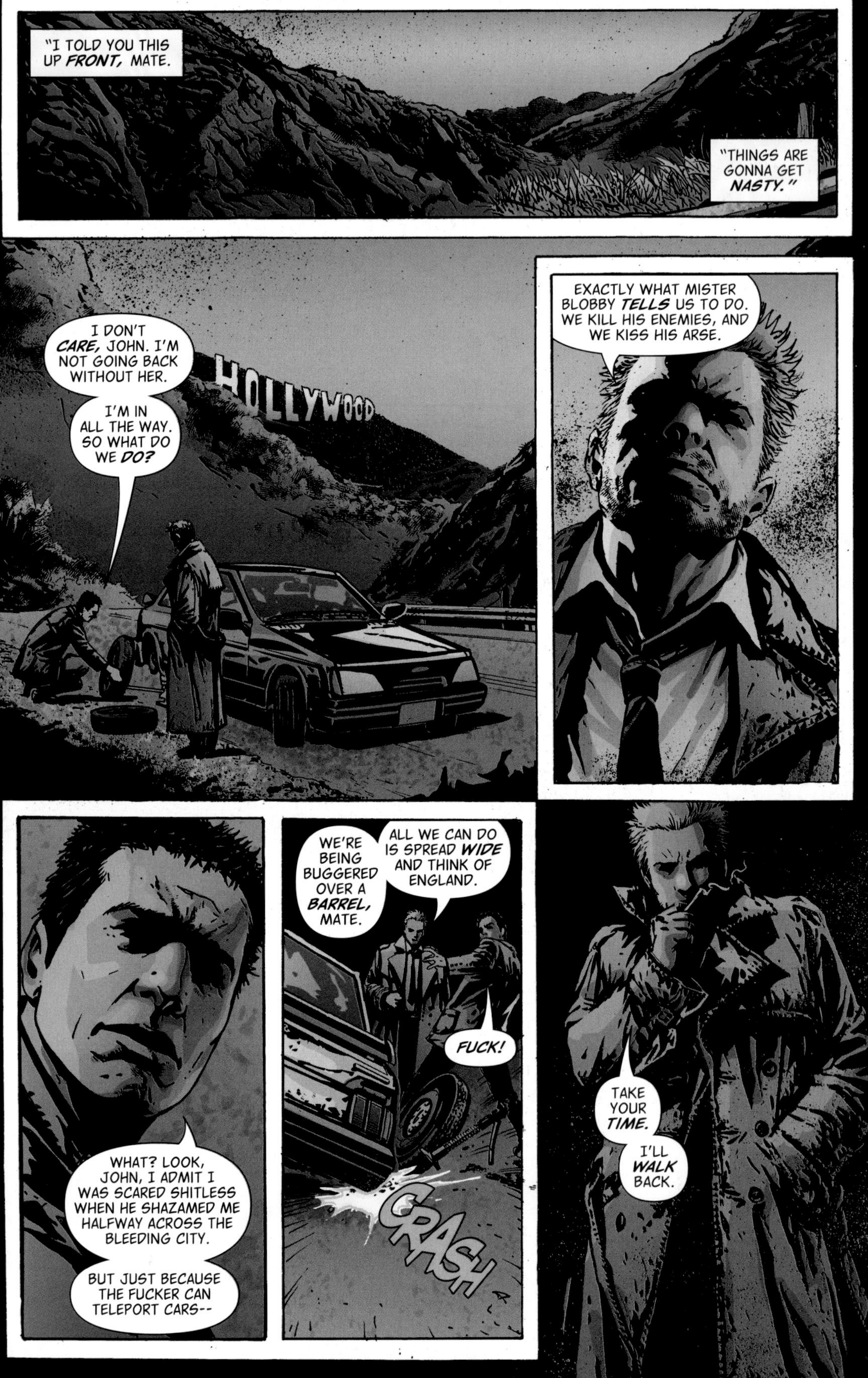
"I TOLD YOU THIS UP FRONT, MATE.
"THINGS ARE GONNA GET NASTY."
I DON'T CARE, JOHN. I'M NOT GOING BACK WITHOUT HER.
I'M IN ALL THE WAY. SO WHAT DO WE DO?
HOLLYWOOD
EXACTLY WHAT MISTER BLOBBY TELLS US TO DO. WE KILL HIS ENEMIES, AND WE KISS HIS ARSE.
WHAT? LOOK, JOHN, I ADMIT I WAS SCARED SHITLESS WHEN HE SHAZAMED ME HALFWAY ACROSS THE BLEEDING CITY.
BUT JUST BECAUSE THE FUCKER CAN TELEPORT CARS--
WE'RE BEING BUGGERED OVER A BARREL, MATE.
ALL WE CAN DO IS SPREAD WIDE AND THINK OF ENGLAND.
FUCK!
CRASH
TAKE YOUR TIME.
I'LL WALK BACK.

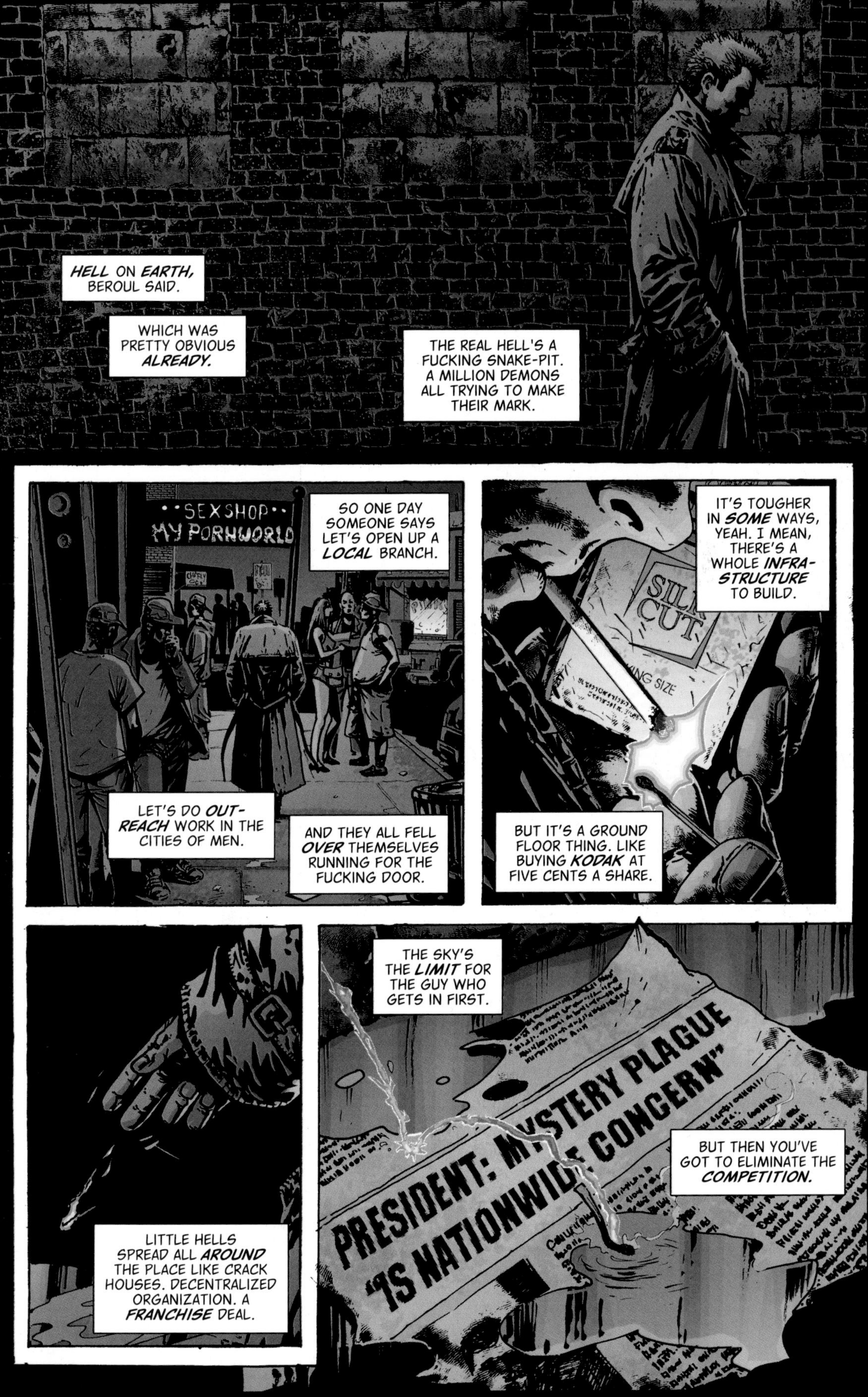
HELL ON EARTH, BEROUL SAID.
WHICH WAS PRETTY OBVIOUS ALREADY.
THE REAL HELL'S A FUCKING SNAKE-PIT. A MILLION DEMONS ALL TRYING TO MAKE THEIR MARK.
SEXSHOP
MY PORNWORLD
SO ONE DAY SOMEONE SAYS LET'S OPEN UP A LOCAL BRANCH.
LET'S DO OUT-REACH WORK IN THE CITIES OF MEN.
AND THEY ALL FELL OVER THEMSELVES RUNNING FOR THE FUCKING DOOR.
IT'S TOUGHER IN SOME WAYS, YEAH. I MEAN, THERE'S A WHOLE INFRA-STRUCTURE TO BUILD.
BUT IT'S A GROUND FLOOR THING. LIKE BUYING KODAK AT FIVE CENTS A SHARE.
LITTLE HELLS SPREAD ALL AROUND THE PLACE LIKE CRACK HOUSES. DECENTRALIZED ORGANIZATION. A FRANCHISE DEAL.
THE SKY'S THE LIMIT FOR THE GUY WHO GETS IN FIRST.
PRESIDENT: MYSTERY PLAGUE "IS NATIONWIDE CONCERN"
BUT THEN YOU'VE GOT TO ELIMINATE THE COMPETITION.

CHAPTER THREE

# blood of sacrifice

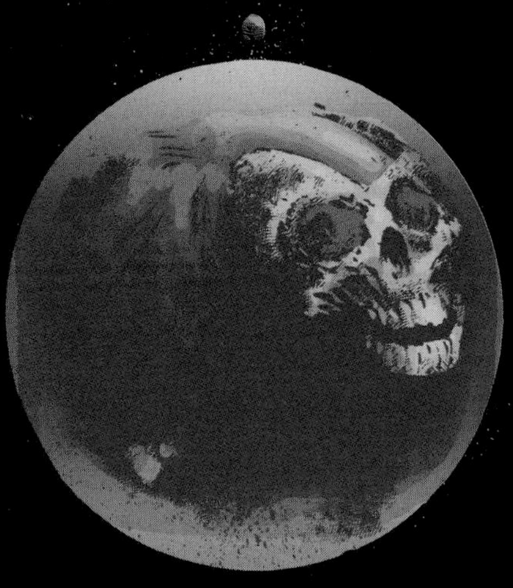

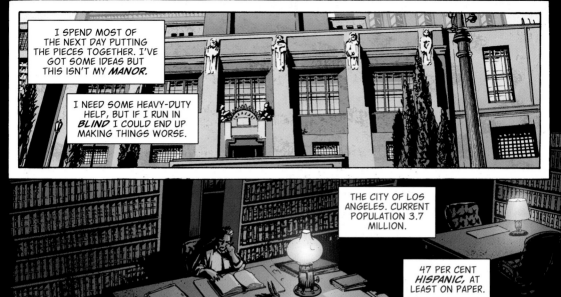

I SPEND MOST OF THE NEXT DAY PUTTING THE PIECES TOGETHER. I'VE GOT SOME IDEAS BUT THIS ISN'T MY *MANOR.*

I NEED SOME HEAVY-DUTY HELP, BUT IF I RUN IN *BLIND* I COULD END UP MAKING THINGS WORSE.

THE CITY OF LOS ANGELES. CURRENT POPULATION 3.7 MILLION.

47 PER CENT *HISPANIC,* AT LEAST ON PAPER.

THE AZTECS NEVER *GOT* THIS FAR UP THE COAST. BUT THE SPANISH EMPIRE THAT *SMASHED* THEM DID THE SAME JOB THAT WATER DOES ON A BURNING CHIP PAN.

IT SPREAD THE RELIGION OF *TENOCHTITLAN* THROUGH THE WHOLE OF CALIFORNIA, ALONG WITH A MILLION AND A HALF DISPLACED PEOPLE.

SO WHETHER YOU REMEMBER THE PAST OR FORGET IT, IT'S *STILL* PULLING YOUR STRINGS.

CATCH 22.

THAT'S *FUNNY,* IN A TWISTED WAY. REMINDS ME OF SOMETHING FREUD SAID.

FIRST YOU *ABSORB* WHAT YOU'VE CONQUERED, THEN YOU TURN INTO IT. AND OLD GODS LEARN NEW TRICKS IF THEY WANT TO *SURVIVE.*

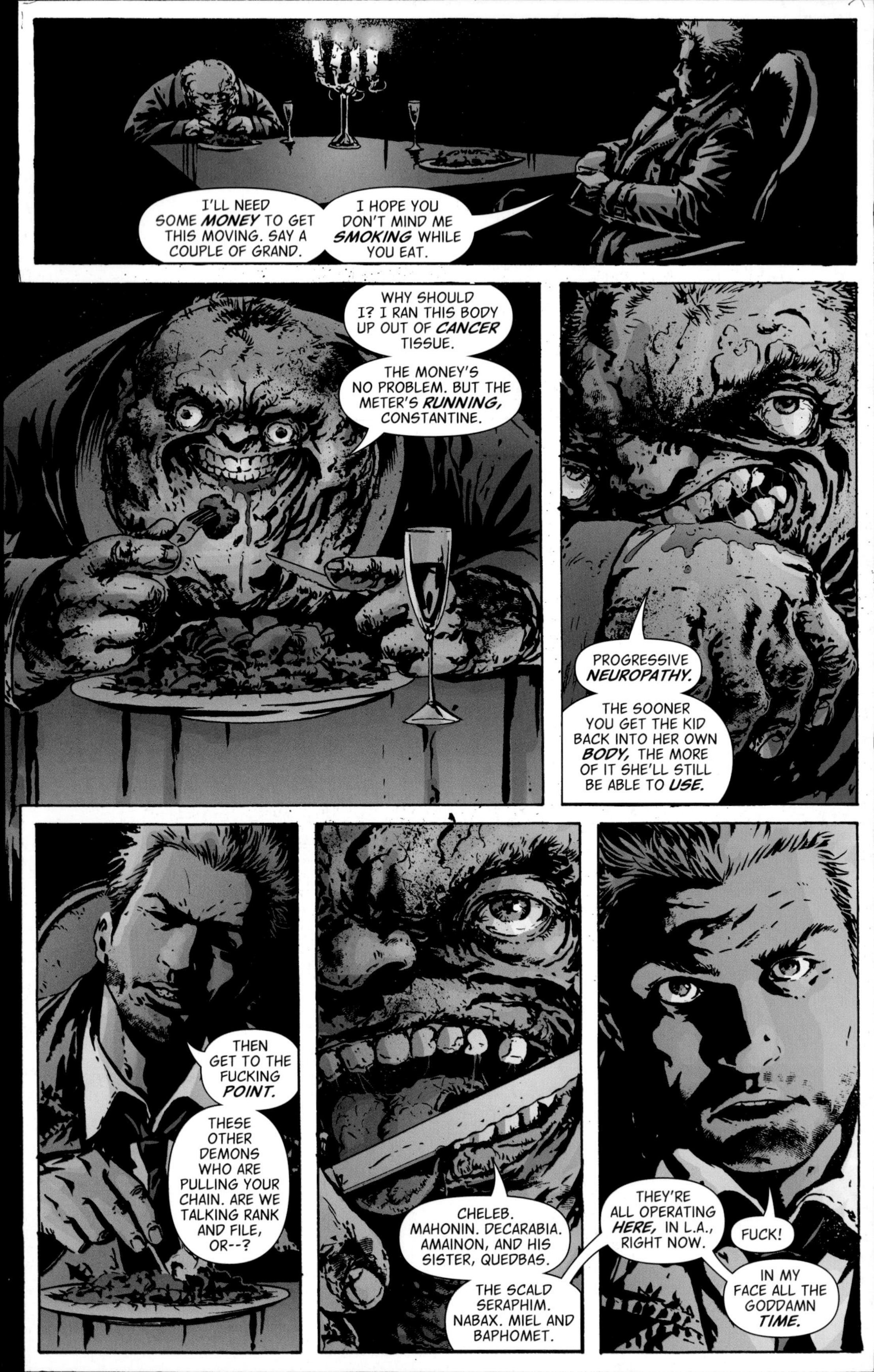
I HOPE YOU DON'T MIND ME SMOKING WHILE YOU EAT.
I'LL NEED SOME MONEY TO GET THIS MOVING. SAY A COUPLE OF GRAND.
WHY SHOULD I? I RAN THIS BODY UP OUT OF CANCER TISSUE.
THE MONEY'S NO PROBLEM. BUT THE METER'S RUNNING, CONSTANTINE.
PROGRESSIVE NEUROPATHY.
THE SOONER YOU GET THE KID BACK INTO HER OWN BODY, THE MORE OF IT SHE'LL STILL BE ABLE TO USE.
THEN GET TO THE FUCKING POINT.
THESE OTHER DEMONS WHO ARE PULLING YOUR CHAIN. ARE WE TALKING RANK AND FILE, OR--?
CHELEB. MAHONIN. DECARABIA. AMAINON, AND HIS SISTER, QUEDBAS.
THE SCALD SERAPHIM. NABAX. MIEL AND BAPHOMET.
THEY'RE ALL OPERATING HERE, IN L.A., RIGHT NOW.
FUCK!
IN MY FACE ALL THE GODDAMN TIME.

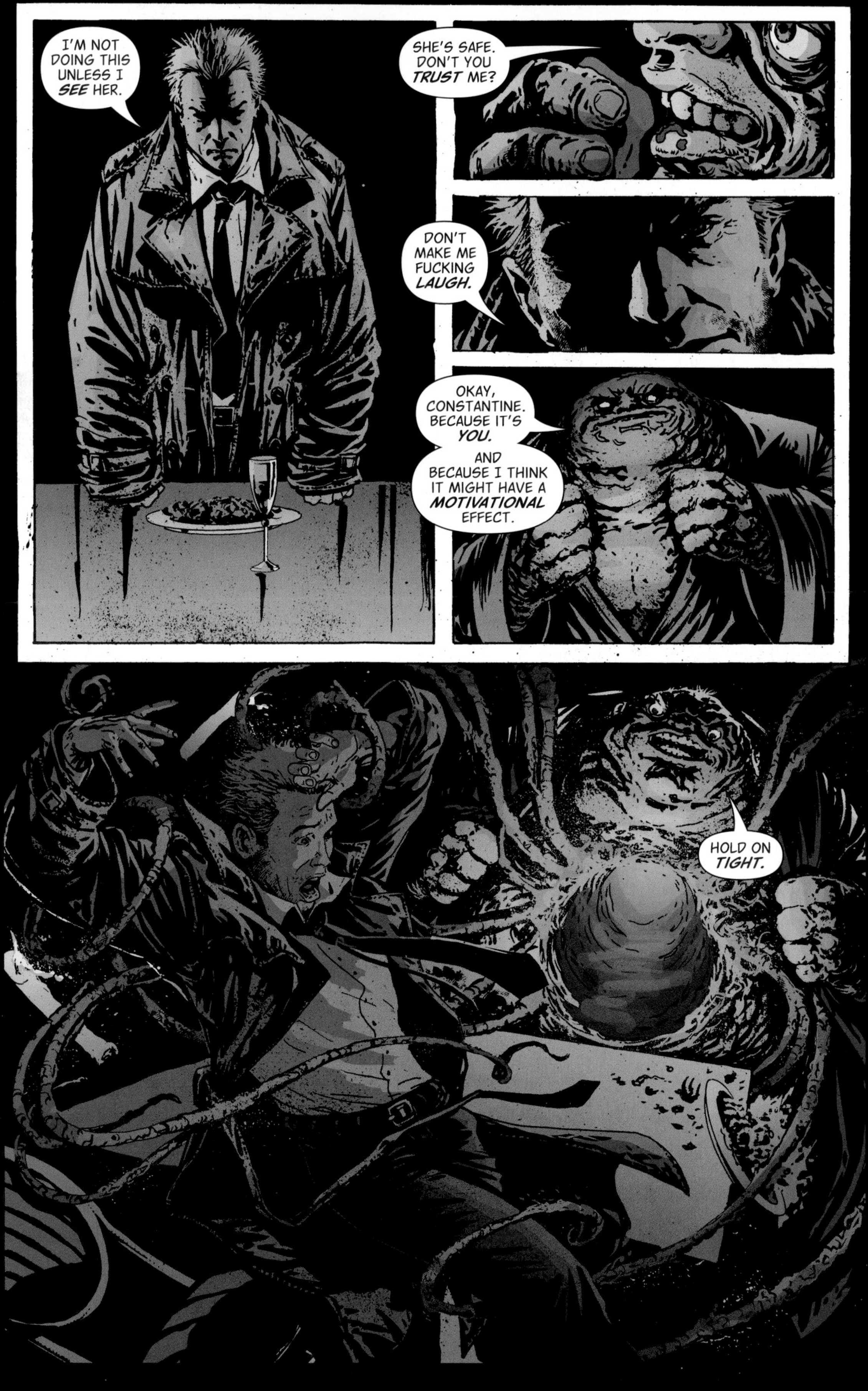

I'M NOT DOING THIS UNLESS I SEE HER.
SHE'S SAFE. DON'T YOU TRUST ME?
DON'T MAKE ME FUCKING LAUGH.
OKAY, CONSTANTINE. BECAUSE IT'S YOU.
AND BECAUSE I THINK IT MIGHT HAVE A MOTIVATIONAL EFFECT.
HOLD ON TIGHT.

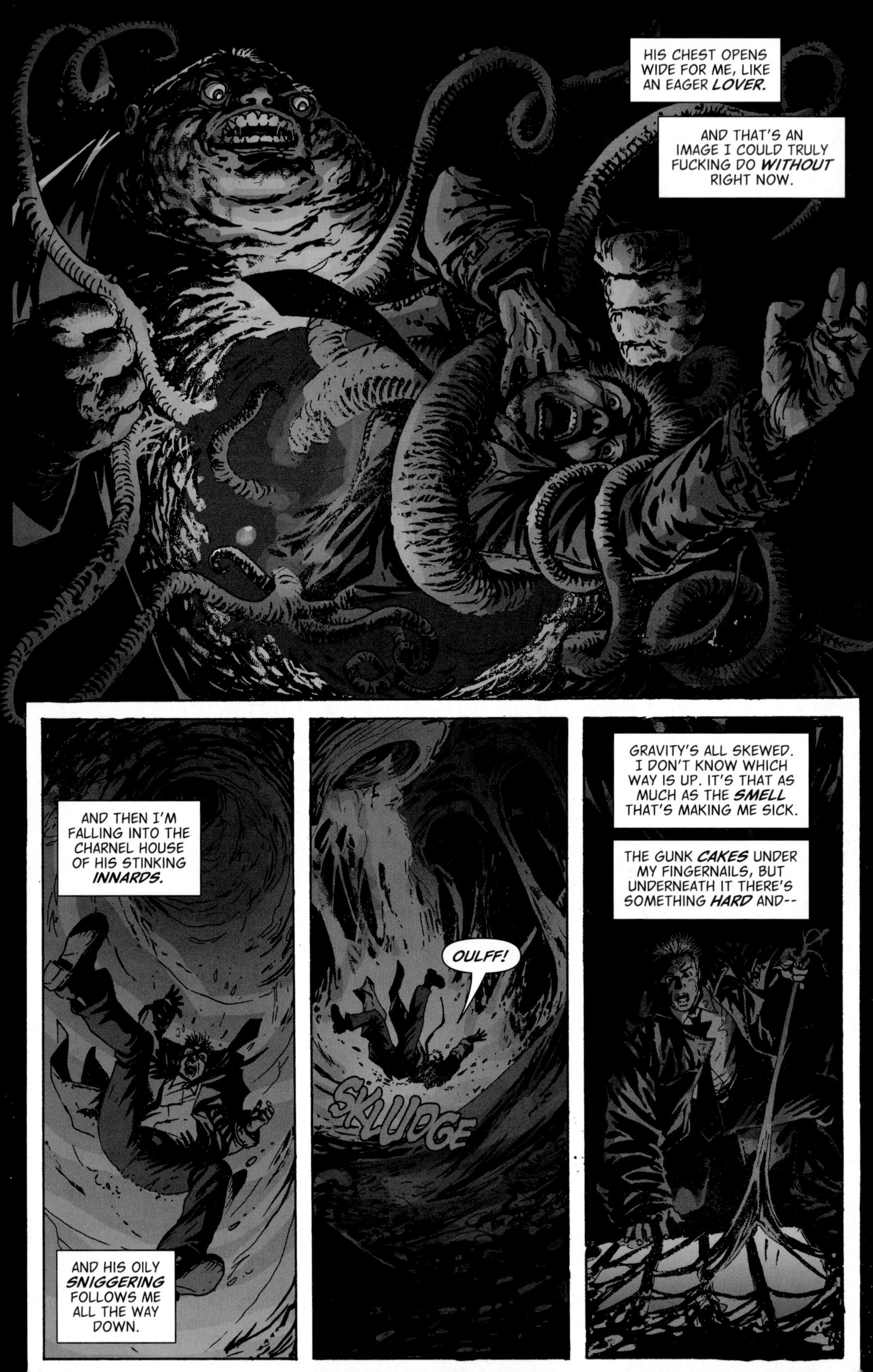
HIS CHEST OPENS WIDE FOR ME, LIKE AN EAGER *LOVER.*
AND THAT'S AN IMAGE I COULD TRULY FUCKING DO *WITHOUT* RIGHT NOW.
AND THEN I'M FALLING INTO THE CHARNEL HOUSE OF HIS STINKING *INNARDS.*
AND HIS OILY *SNIGGERING* FOLLOWS ME ALL THE WAY DOWN.
*OULFF!*
SKLUDGE
GRAVITY'S ALL SKEWED. I DON'T KNOW WHICH WAY IS UP. IT'S THAT AS MUCH AS THE *SMELL* THAT'S MAKING ME SICK.
THE GUNK *CAKES* UNDER MY FINGERNAILS, BUT UNDERNEATH IT THERE'S SOMETHING *HARD* AND--

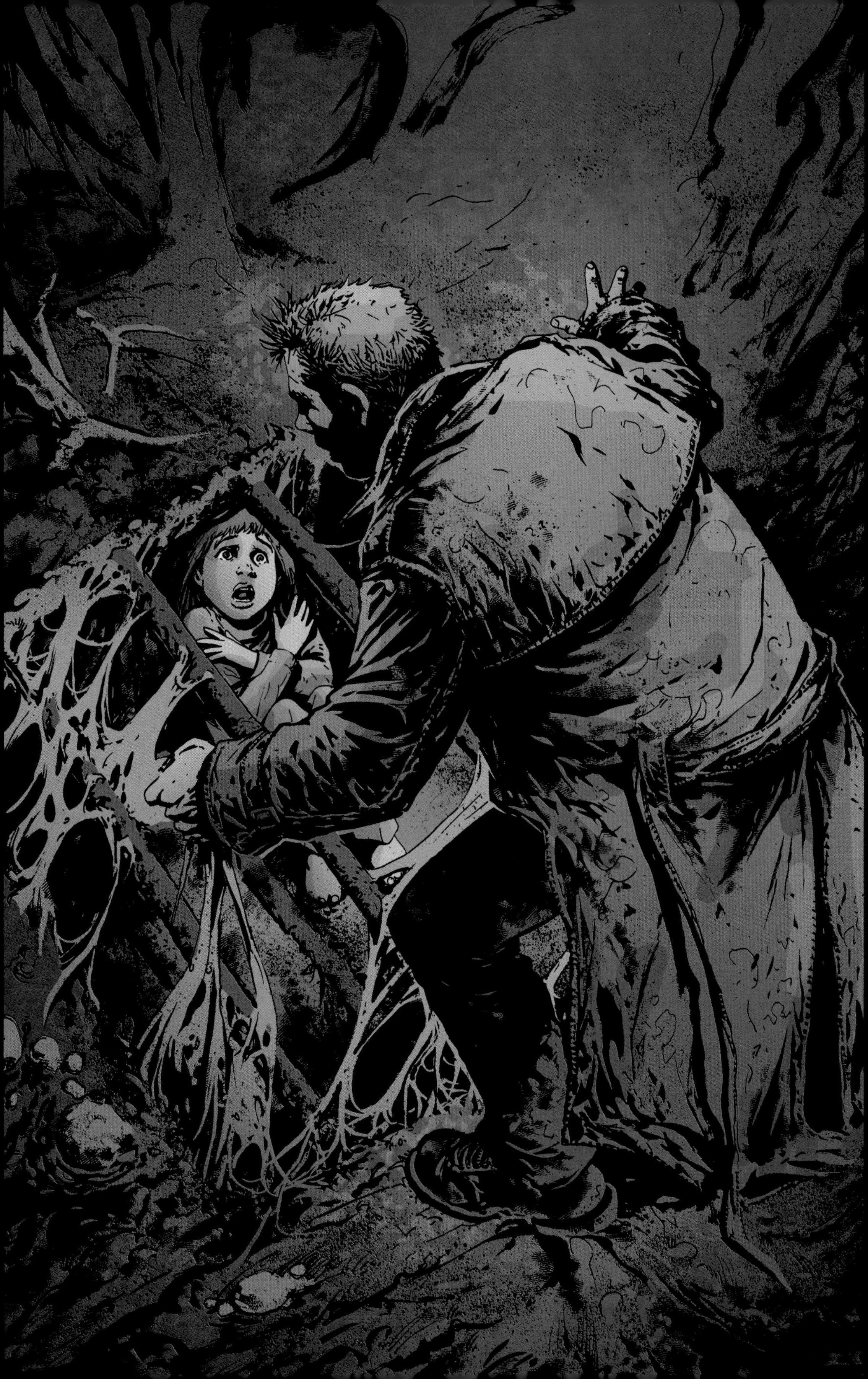

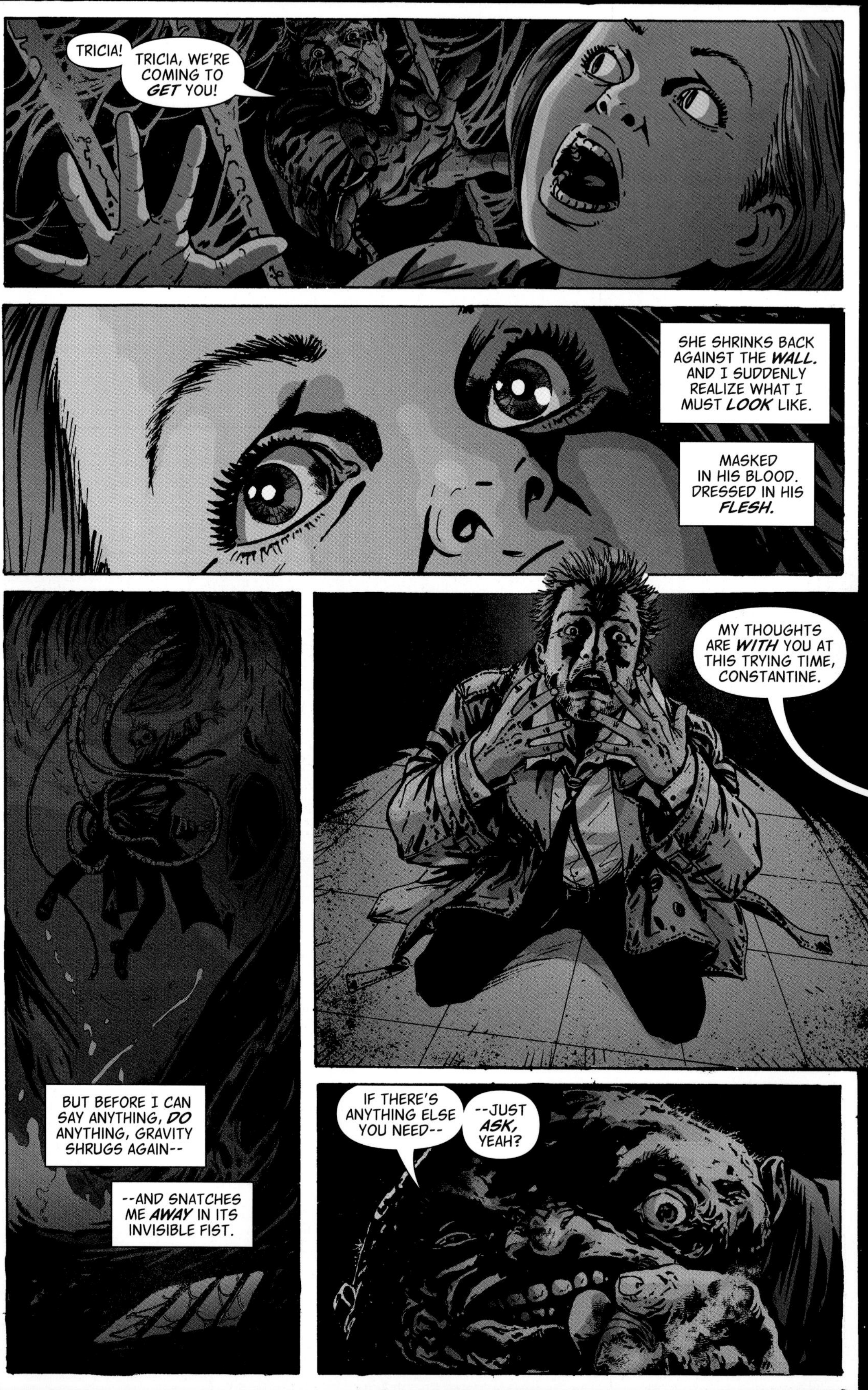
TRICIA!
TRICIA, WE'RE COMING TO GET YOU!
SHE SHRINKS BACK AGAINST THE WALL. AND I SUDDENLY REALIZE WHAT I MUST LOOK LIKE.
MASKED IN HIS BLOOD. DRESSED IN HIS FLESH.
MY THOUGHTS ARE WITH YOU AT THIS TRYING TIME, CONSTANTINE.
BUT BEFORE I CAN SAY ANYTHING, DO ANYTHING, GRAVITY SHRUGS AGAIN--
--AND SNATCHES ME AWAY IN ITS INVISIBLE FIST.
IF THERE'S ANYTHING ELSE YOU NEED--
--JUST ASK, YEAH?

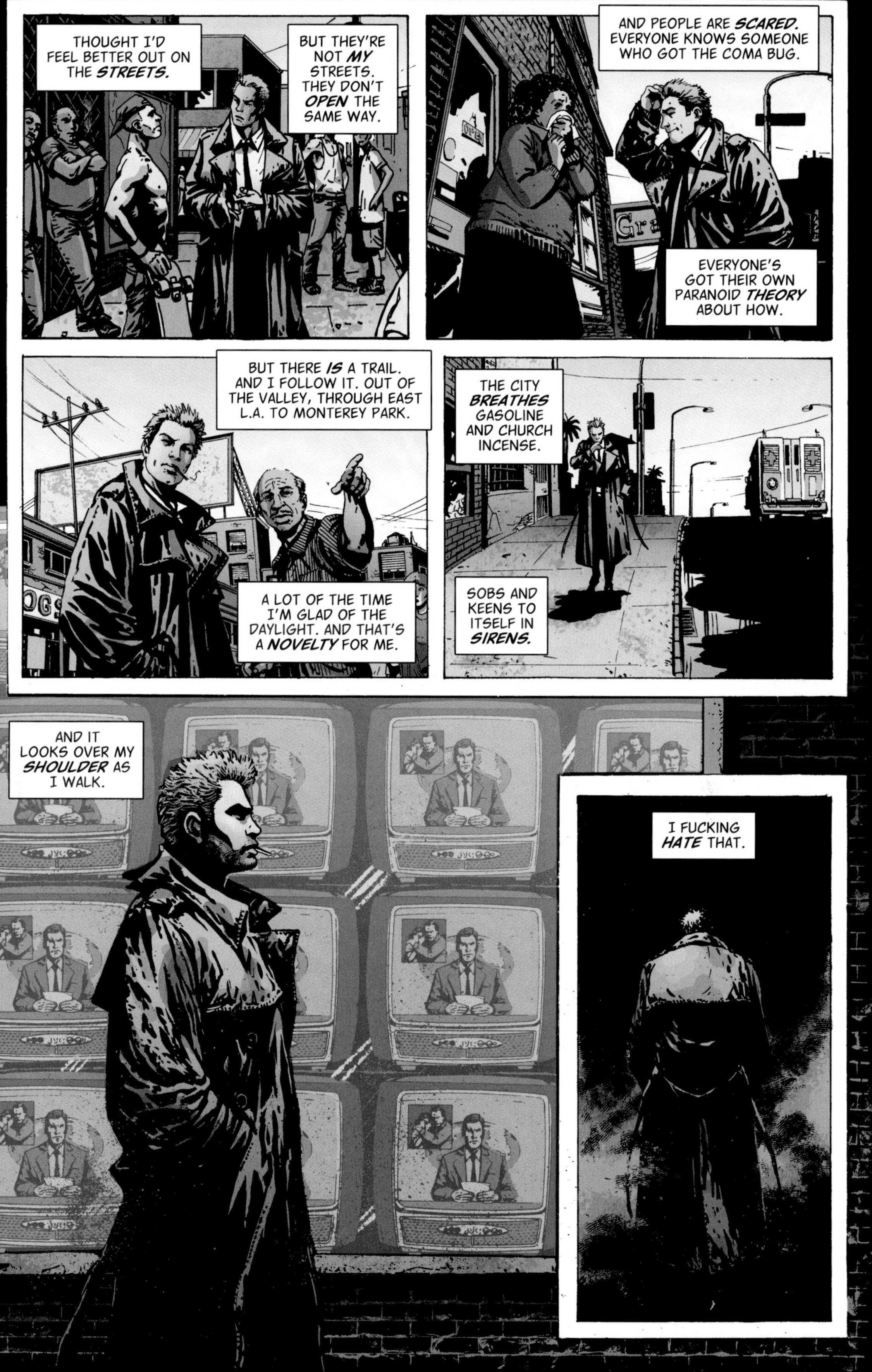
THOUGHT I'D FEEL BETTER OUT ON THE *STREETS.*
BUT THEY'RE NOT *MY* STREETS. THEY DON'T *OPEN* THE SAME WAY.
AND PEOPLE ARE *SCARED.* EVERYONE KNOWS SOMEONE WHO GOT THE COMA BUG.
OPEN
EVERYONE'S GOT THEIR OWN PARANOID *THEORY* ABOUT HOW.
BUT THERE *IS* A TRAIL. AND I FOLLOW IT. OUT OF THE VALLEY, THROUGH EAST L.A. TO MONTEREY PARK.
A LOT OF THE TIME I'M GLAD OF THE DAYLIGHT. AND THAT'S A *NOVELTY* FOR ME.
THE CITY *BREATHES* GASOLINE AND CHURCH INCENSE.
SOBS AND KEENS TO ITSELF IN *SIRENS.*
AND IT LOOKS OVER MY *SHOULDER* AS I WALK.
I FUCKING *HATE* THAT.

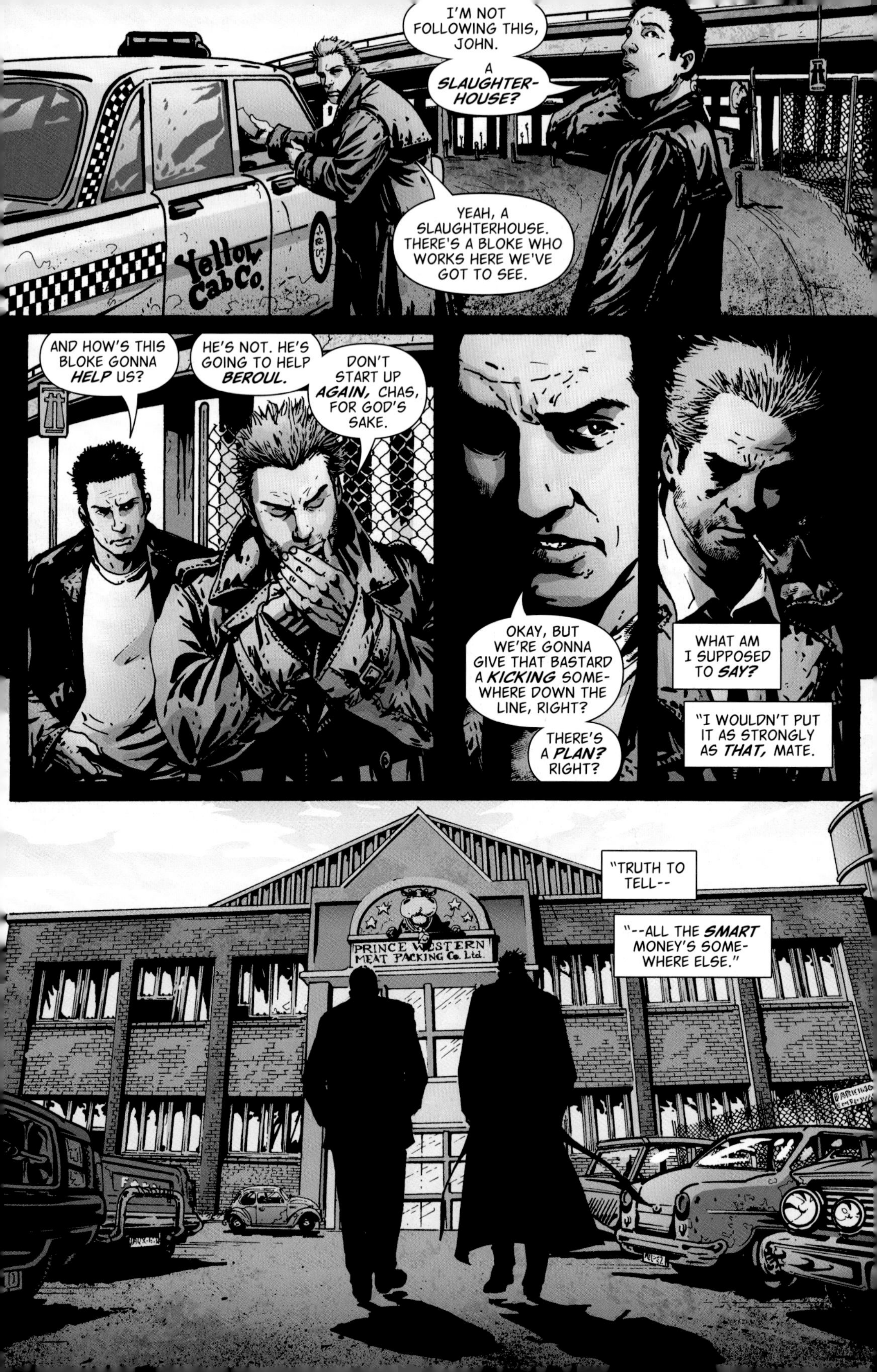
I'M NOT FOLLOWING THIS, JOHN.
A SLAUGHTER-HOUSE?
YEAH, A SLAUGHTERHOUSE. THERE'S A BLOKE WHO WORKS HERE WE'VE GOT TO SEE.
Yellow Cab Co.
AND HOW'S THIS BLOKE GONNA HELP US?
HE'S NOT. HE'S GOING TO HELP BEROUL.
DON'T START UP AGAIN, CHAS, FOR GOD'S SAKE.
OKAY, BUT WE'RE GONNA GIVE THAT BASTARD A KICKING SOME-WHERE DOWN THE LINE, RIGHT?
THERE'S A PLAN? RIGHT?
WHAT AM I SUPPOSED TO SAY?
"I WOULDN'T PUT IT AS STRONGLY AS THAT, MATE.
"TRUTH TO TELL--
"--ALL THE SMART MONEY'S SOME-WHERE ELSE."
PRINCE WESTERN MEAT PACKING Co. Ltd.

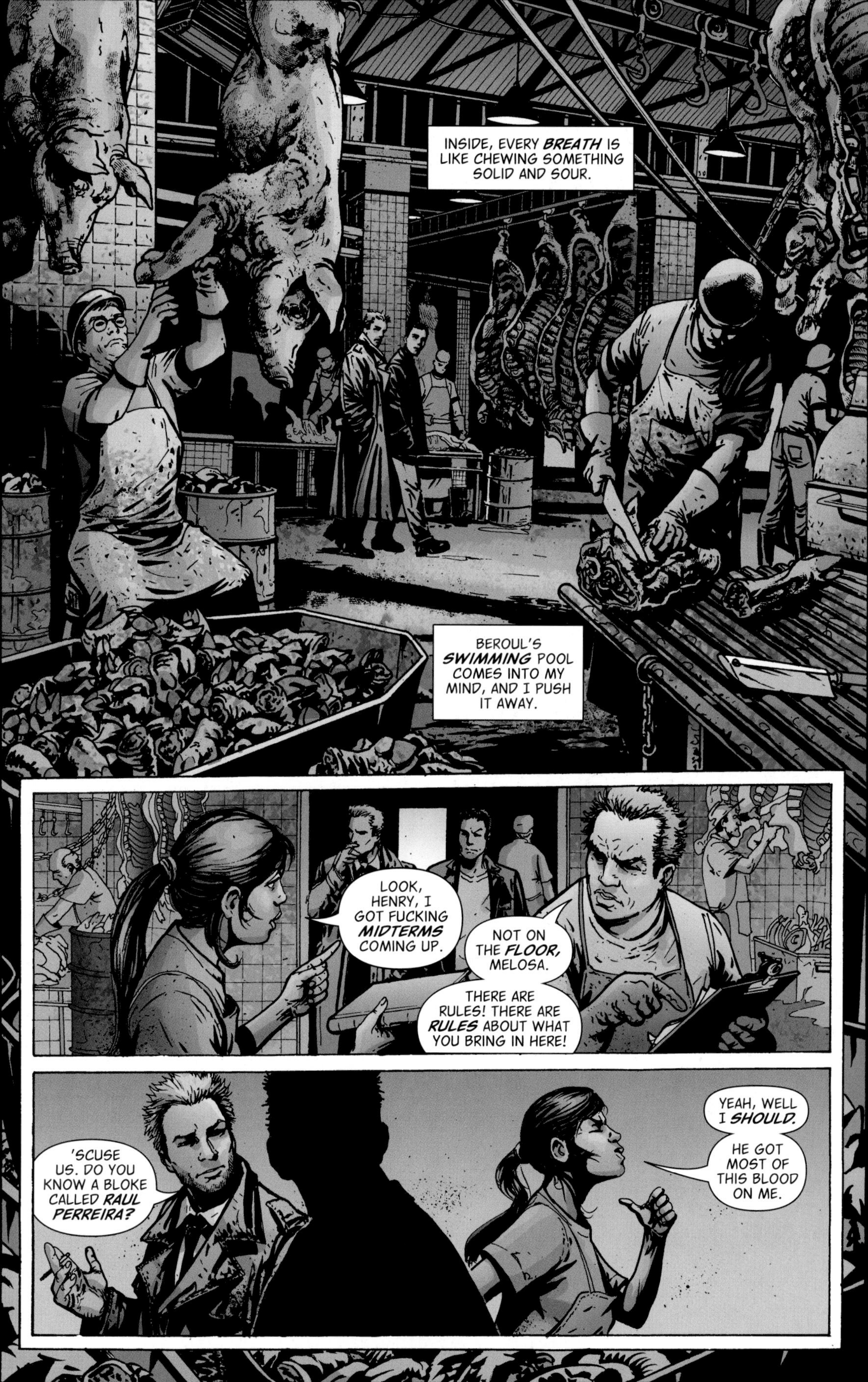
INSIDE, EVERY BREATH IS LIKE CHEWING SOMETHING SOLID AND SOUR.
BEROUL'S SWIMMING POOL COMES INTO MY MIND, AND I PUSH IT AWAY.
LOOK, HENRY, I GOT FUCKING MIDTERMS COMING UP.
NOT ON THE FLOOR, MELOSA.
THERE ARE RULES! THERE ARE RULES ABOUT WHAT YOU BRING IN HERE!
'SCUSE US. DO YOU KNOW A BLOKE CALLED RAUL PERREIRA?
YEAH, WELL I SHOULD.
HE GOT MOST OF THIS BLOOD ON ME.

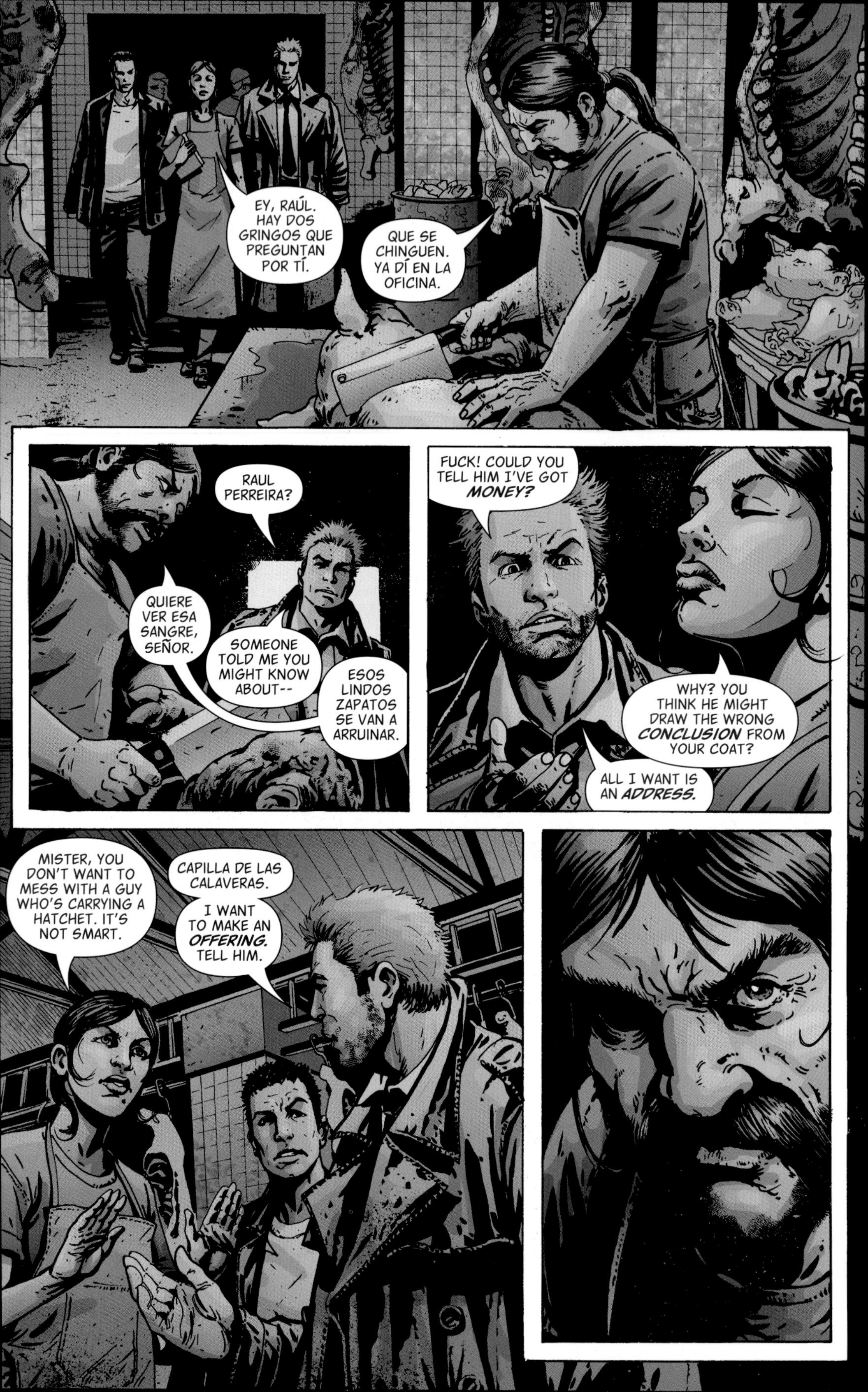
EY, RAÚL. HAY DOS GRINGOS QUE PREGUNTAN POR TÍ.
QUE SE CHINGUEN. YA DÍ EN LA OFICINA.
RAUL PERREIRA?
QUIERE VER ESA SANGRE, SEÑOR.
SOMEONE TOLD ME YOU MIGHT KNOW ABOUT--
ESOS LINDOS ZAPATOS SE VAN A ARRUINAR.
FUCK! COULD YOU TELL HIM I'VE GOT MONEY?
WHY? YOU THINK HE MIGHT DRAW THE WRONG CONCLUSION FROM YOUR COAT?
ALL I WANT IS AN ADDRESS.
MISTER, YOU DON'T WANT TO MESS WITH A GUY WHO'S CARRYING A HATCHET. IT'S NOT SMART.
CAPILLA DE LAS CALAVERAS.
I WANT TO MAKE AN OFFERING. TELL HIM.

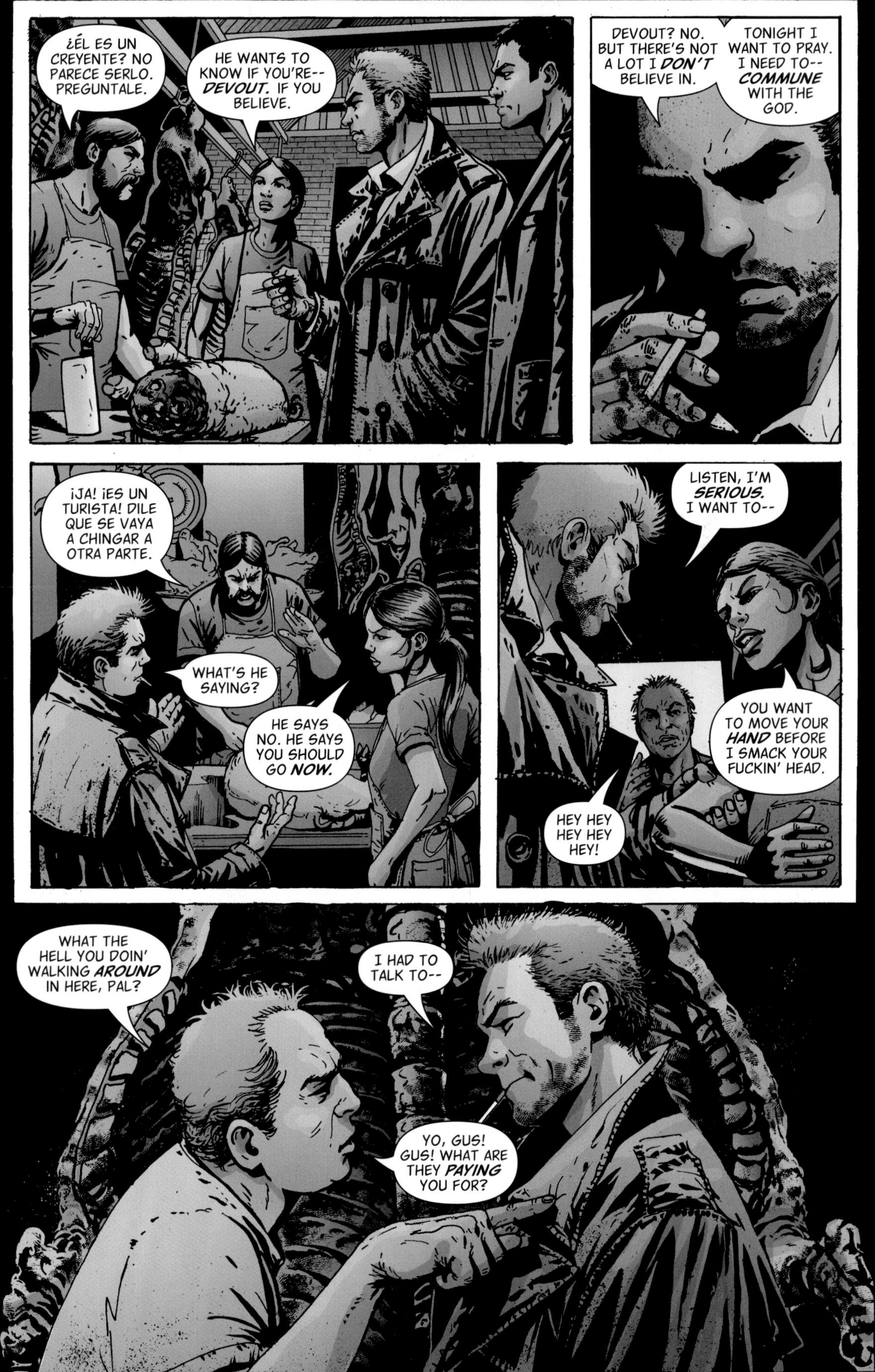
¿ÉL ES UN CREYENTE? NO PARECE SERLO. PREGUNTALE.
HE WANTS TO KNOW IF YOU'RE-- DEVOUT. IF YOU BELIEVE.
DEVOUT? NO. BUT THERE'S NOT A LOT I DON'T BELIEVE IN.
TONIGHT I WANT TO PRAY. I NEED TO-- COMMUNE WITH THE GOD.
¡JA! ¡ES UN TURISTA! DILE QUE SE VAYA A CHINGAR A OTRA PARTE.
WHAT'S HE SAYING?
HE SAYS NO. HE SAYS YOU SHOULD GO NOW.
LISTEN, I'M SERIOUS. I WANT TO--
YOU WANT TO MOVE YOUR HAND BEFORE I SMACK YOUR FUCKIN' HEAD.
HEY HEY HEY HEY HEY!
WHAT THE HELL YOU DOIN' WALKING AROUND IN HERE, PAL?
I HAD TO TALK TO--
YO, GUS! GUS! WHAT ARE THEY PAYING YOU FOR?

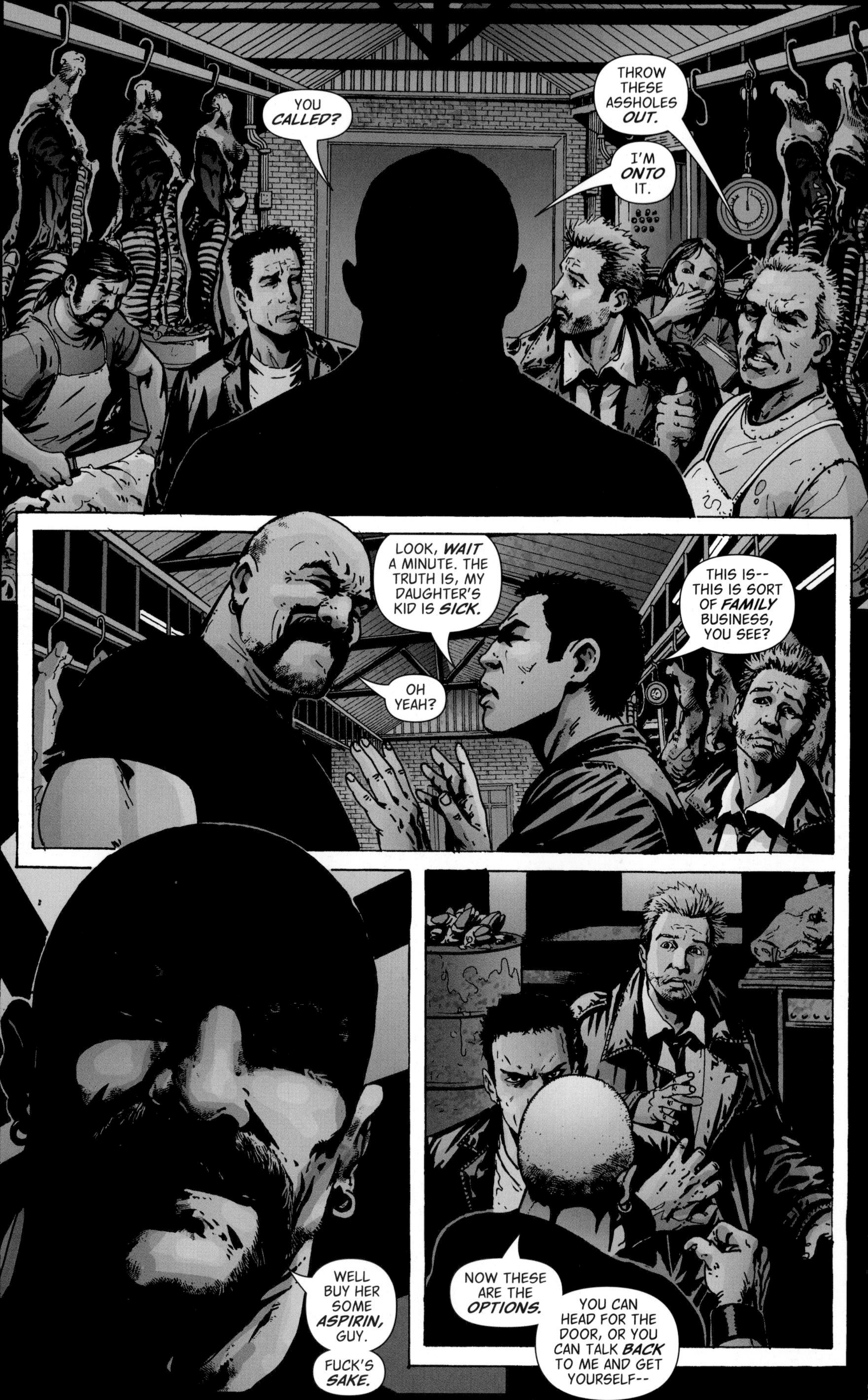
YOU CALLED?
THROW THESE ASSHOLES OUT.
I'M ONTO IT.
LOOK, WAIT A MINUTE. THE TRUTH IS, MY DAUGHTER'S KID IS SICK.
OH YEAH?
THIS IS-- THIS IS SORT OF FAMILY BUSINESS, YOU SEE?
WELL BUY HER SOME ASPIRIN, GUY.
FUCK'S SAKE.
NOW THESE ARE THE OPTIONS.
YOU CAN HEAD FOR THE DOOR, OR YOU CAN TALK BACK TO ME AND GET YOURSELF--

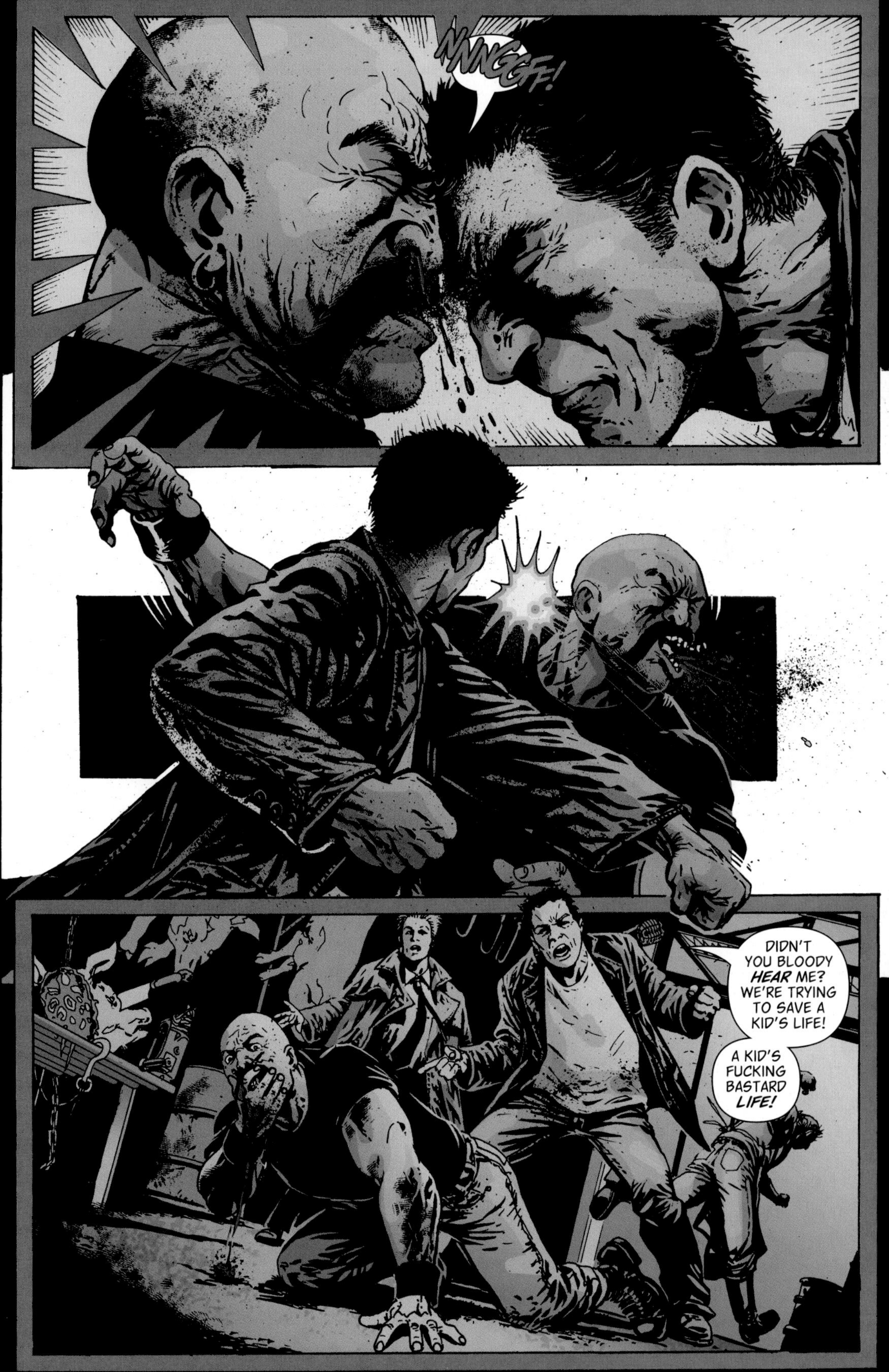
NNNGGFF!
DIDN'T YOU BLOODY HEAR ME? WE'RE TRYING TO SAVE A KID'S LIFE!
A KID'S FUCKING BASTARD LIFE!

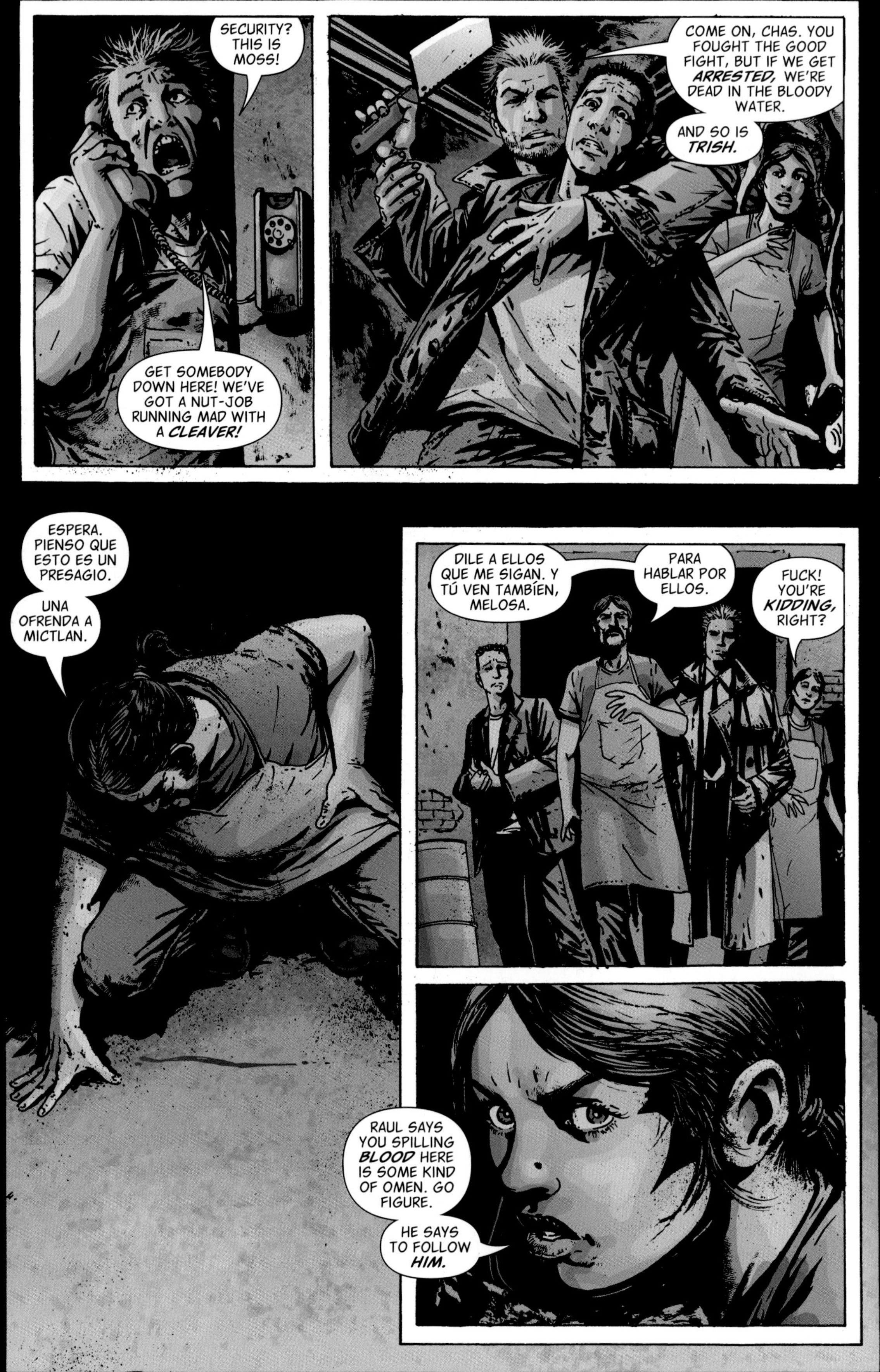
SECURITY? THIS IS MOSS!
GET SOMEBODY DOWN HERE! WE'VE GOT A NUT-JOB RUNNING MAD WITH A CLEAVER!
COME ON, CHAS. YOU FOUGHT THE GOOD FIGHT, BUT IF WE GET ARRESTED, WE'RE DEAD IN THE BLOODY WATER.
AND SO IS TRISH.
ESPERA. PIENSO QUE ESTO ES UN PRESAGIO.
UNA OFRENDA A MICTLAN.
DILE A ELLOS QUE ME SIGAN. Y TÚ VEN TAMBÍEN, MELOSA.
PARA HABLAR POR ELLOS.
FUCK! YOU'RE KIDDING, RIGHT?
RAUL SAYS YOU SPILLING BLOOD HERE IS SOME KIND OF OMEN. GO FIGURE.
HE SAYS TO FOLLOW HIM.

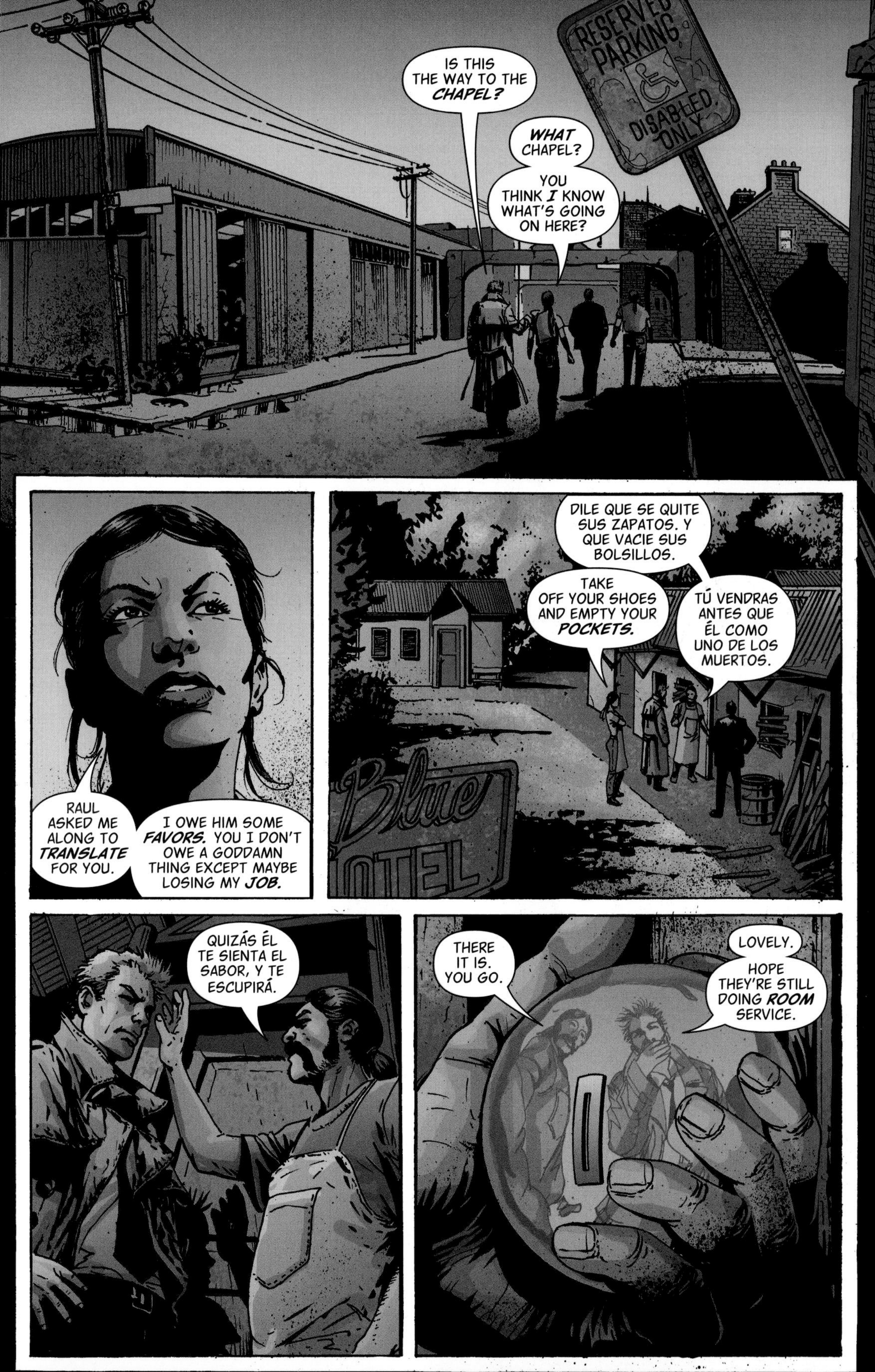
RESERVED PARKING
DISABLED ONLY
IS THIS THE WAY TO THE CHAPEL?
WHAT CHAPEL?
YOU THINK I KNOW WHAT'S GOING ON HERE?
RAUL ASKED ME ALONG TO TRANSLATE FOR YOU.
I OWE HIM SOME FAVORS. YOU I DON'T OWE A GODDAMN THING EXCEPT MAYBE LOSING MY JOB.
DILE QUE SE QUITE SUS ZAPATOS. Y QUE VACIE SUS BOLSILLOS.
TAKE OFF YOUR SHOES AND EMPTY YOUR POCKETS.
TÚ VENDRAS ANTES QUE ÉL COMO UNO DE LOS MUERTOS.
Blue
QUIZÁS ÉL TE SIENTA EL SABOR, Y TE ESCUPIRÁ.
THERE IT IS. YOU GO.
LOVELY.
HOPE THEY'RE STILL DOING ROOM SERVICE.

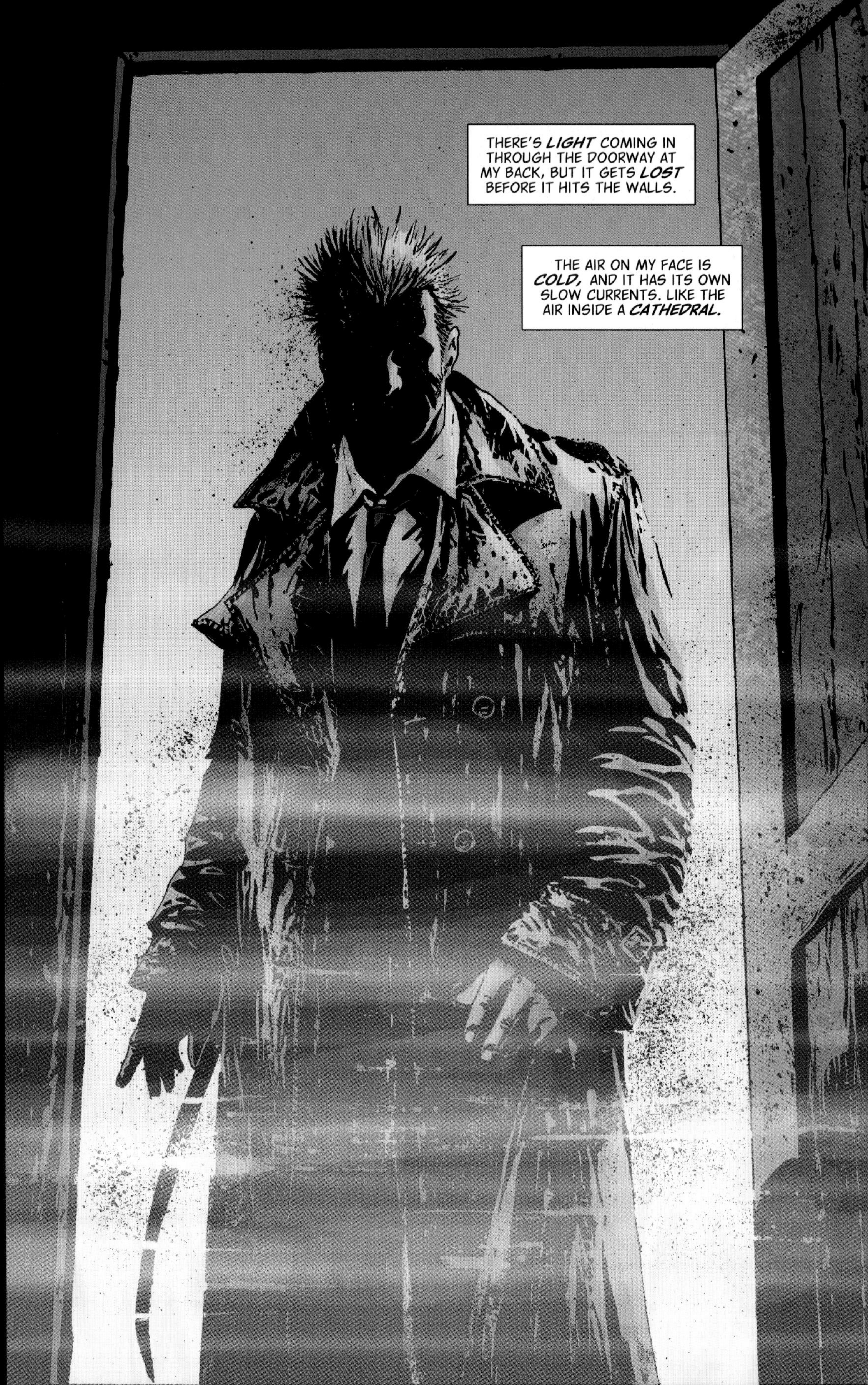
THERE'S *LIGHT* COMING IN THROUGH THE DOORWAY AT MY BACK, BUT IT GETS *LOST* BEFORE IT HITS THE WALLS.
THE AIR ON MY FACE IS *COLD,* AND IT HAS ITS OWN SLOW CURRENTS. LIKE THE AIR INSIDE A *CATHEDRAL.*

THEN THE DOOR SLAMS.

AND I'M *ALONE* IN THE DARK,

MY FRIEND SPILLED *BLOOD* FOR YOU BACK IN THE SLAUGHTERHOUSE. BUT THAT WAS AN *ACCIDENT*.

LOOK. I'M SPILLING MY OWN BLOOD NOW. TO SHOW *RESPECT*.

MICTLANTECUHTLI. GOD OF *BONES* AND OF THE GRAVE MOUTH AND OF ALL THAT *BEGINS* WHEN THE HEART STOPS.

I COME TO YOU AS A *SUPPLIANT*.

THANK YOU FOR LETTING ME COME INTO YOUR *HOUSE*.

THANK YOU FOR *HEARING* ME.

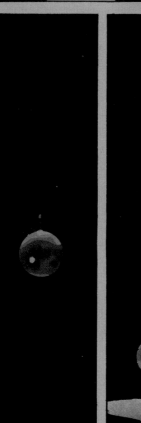

THAT IS BUT A *SMALL* FAVOR, MORTAL MAN.

LIAR. DEMON-SLAYER. LAUGHING MAGICIAN.

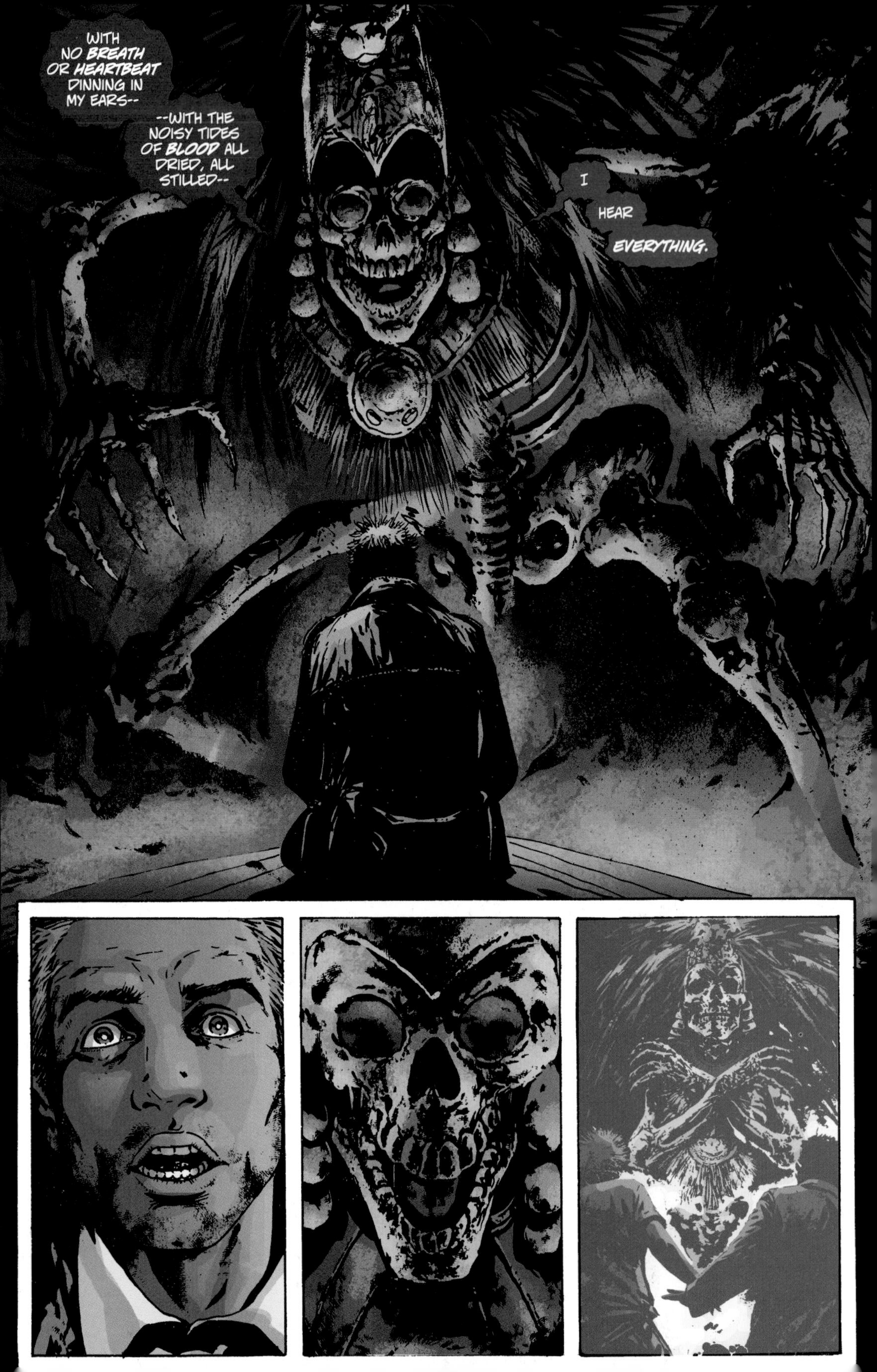
WITH NO BREATH OR HEARTBEAT DINNING IN MY EARS--
--WITH THE NOISY TIDES OF BLOOD ALL DRIED, ALL STILLED--
I HEAR EVERYTHING.

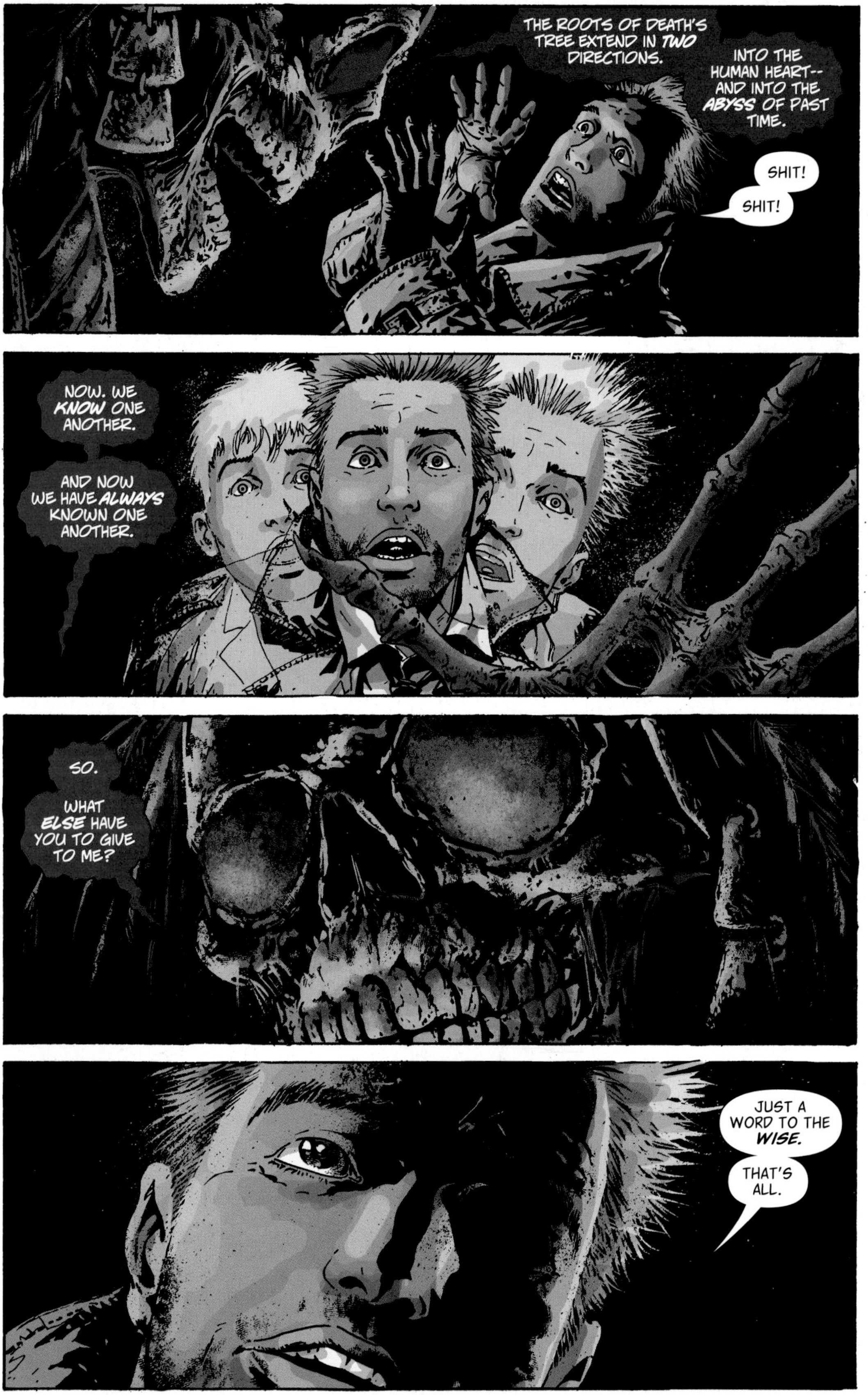
THE ROOTS OF DEATH'S TREE EXTEND IN TWO DIRECTIONS.
INTO THE HUMAN HEART-- AND INTO THE ABYSS OF PAST TIME.
SHIT!
SHIT!
NOW. WE KNOW ONE ANOTHER.
AND NOW WE HAVE ALWAYS KNOWN ONE ANOTHER.
SO.
WHAT ELSE HAVE YOU TO GIVE TO ME?
JUST A WORD TO THE WISE.
THAT'S ALL.

YOU WANNA *SMOKE?*

...

THANKS.

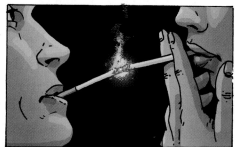

SO HEY.

YOU HIS *BODYGUARD,* OR WHAT?

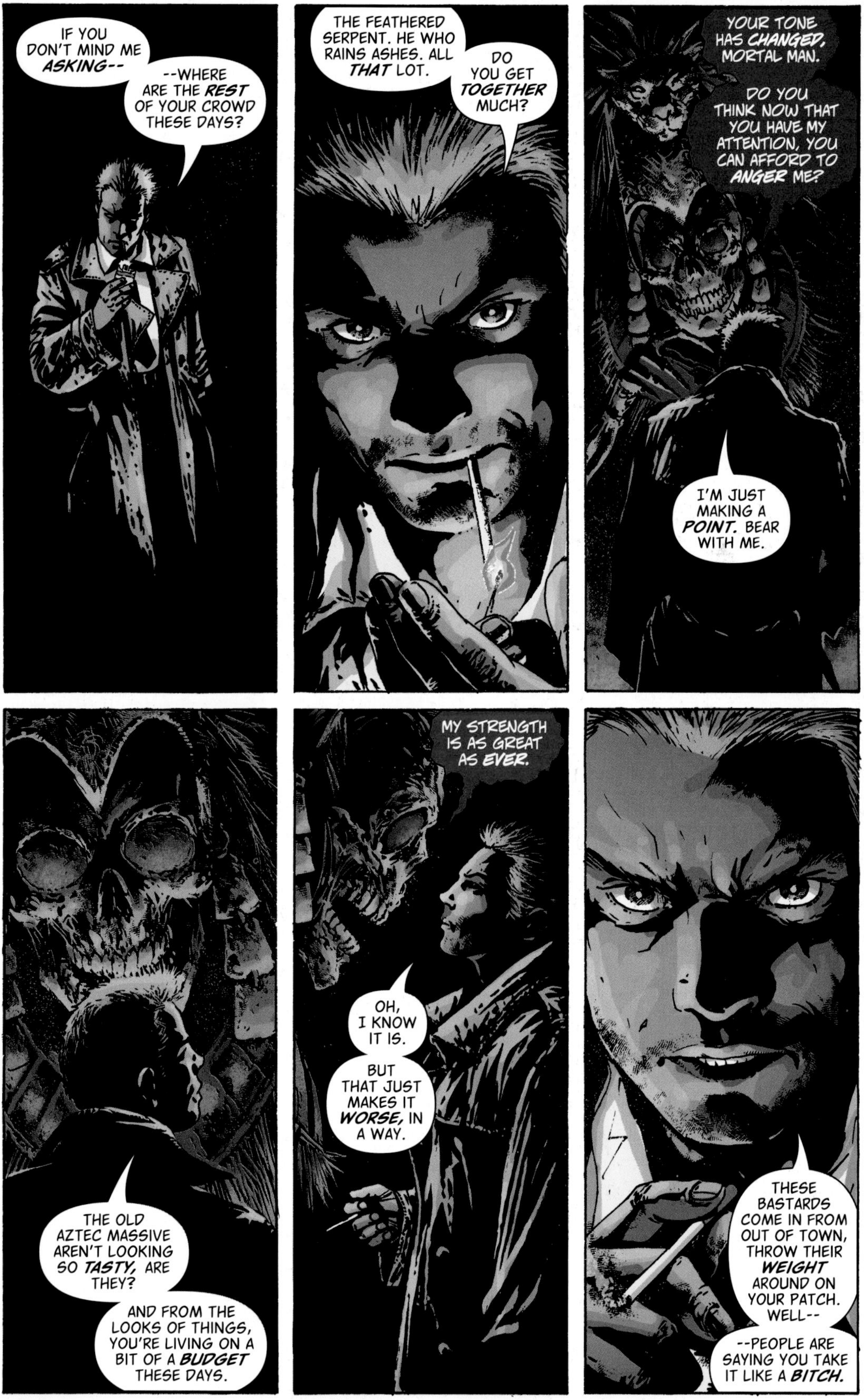
IF YOU DON'T MIND ME ASKING--
--WHERE ARE THE REST OF YOUR CROWD THESE DAYS?
THE FEATHERED SERPENT. HE WHO RAINS ASHES. ALL THAT LOT.
DO YOU GET TOGETHER MUCH?
YOUR TONE HAS CHANGED, MORTAL MAN.
DO YOU THINK NOW THAT YOU HAVE MY ATTENTION, YOU CAN AFFORD TO ANGER ME?
I'M JUST MAKING A POINT. BEAR WITH ME.
THE OLD AZTEC MASSIVE AREN'T LOOKING SO TASTY, ARE THEY?
AND FROM THE LOOKS OF THINGS, YOU'RE LIVING ON A BIT OF A BUDGET THESE DAYS.
MY STRENGTH IS AS GREAT AS EVER.
OH, I KNOW IT IS.
BUT THAT JUST MAKES IT WORSE, IN A WAY.
THESE BASTARDS COME IN FROM OUT OF TOWN, THROW THEIR WEIGHT AROUND ON YOUR PATCH. WELL--
--PEOPLE ARE SAYING YOU TAKE IT LIKE A BITCH.

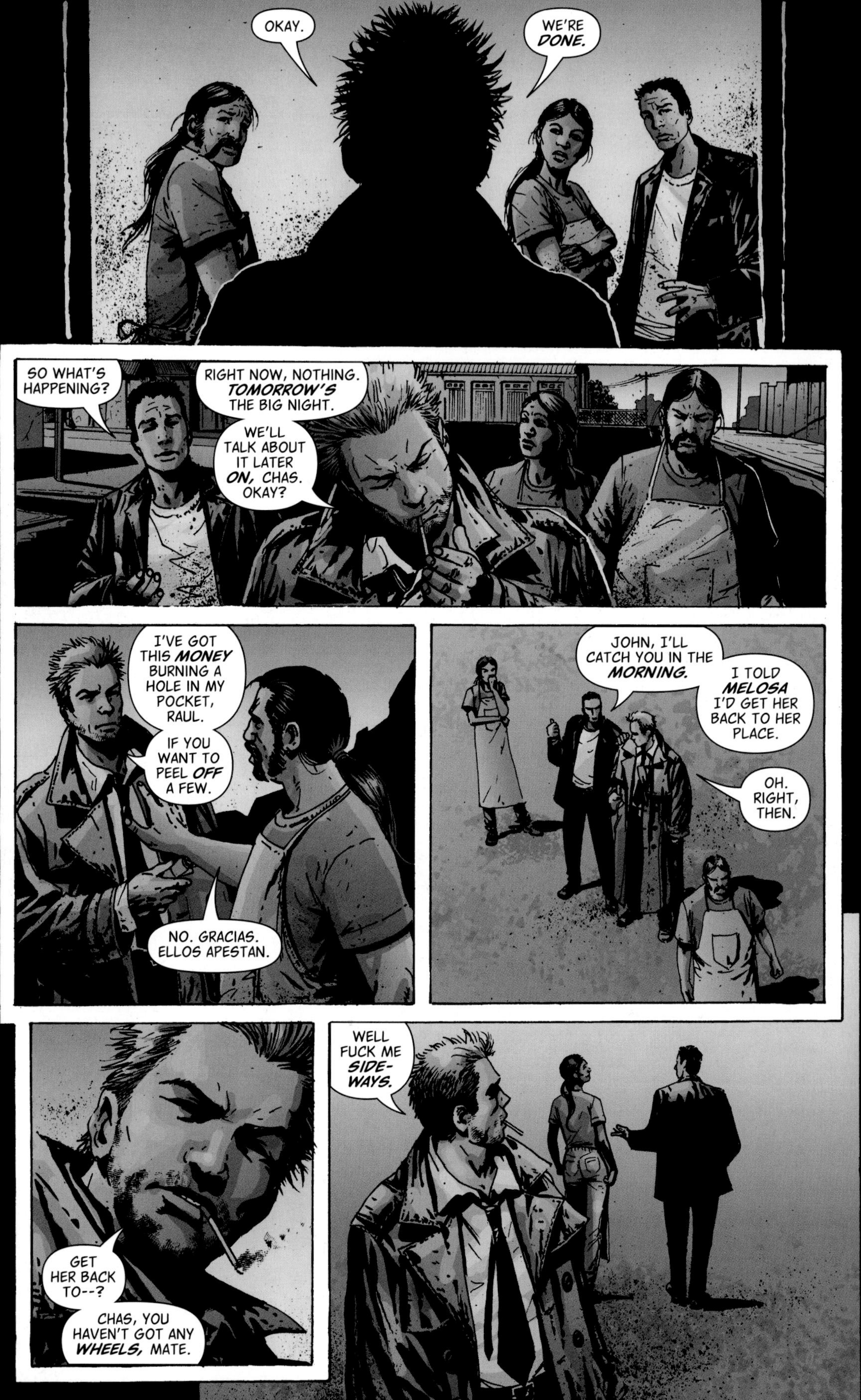
OKAY.
WE'RE *DONE.*
SO WHAT'S HAPPENING?
RIGHT NOW, NOTHING. *TOMORROW'S* THE BIG NIGHT.
WE'LL TALK ABOUT IT LATER *ON,* CHAS. OKAY?
I'VE GOT THIS *MONEY* BURNING A HOLE IN MY POCKET, RAUL.
IF YOU WANT TO PEEL *OFF* A FEW.
NO. GRACIAS. ELLOS APESTAN.
JOHN, I'LL CATCH YOU IN THE *MORNING.*
I TOLD *MELOSA* I'D GET HER BACK TO HER PLACE.
OH. RIGHT, THEN.
GET HER BACK TO--?
CHAS, YOU HAVEN'T GOT ANY *WHEELS,* MATE.
WELL FUCK ME *SIDE-WAYS.*

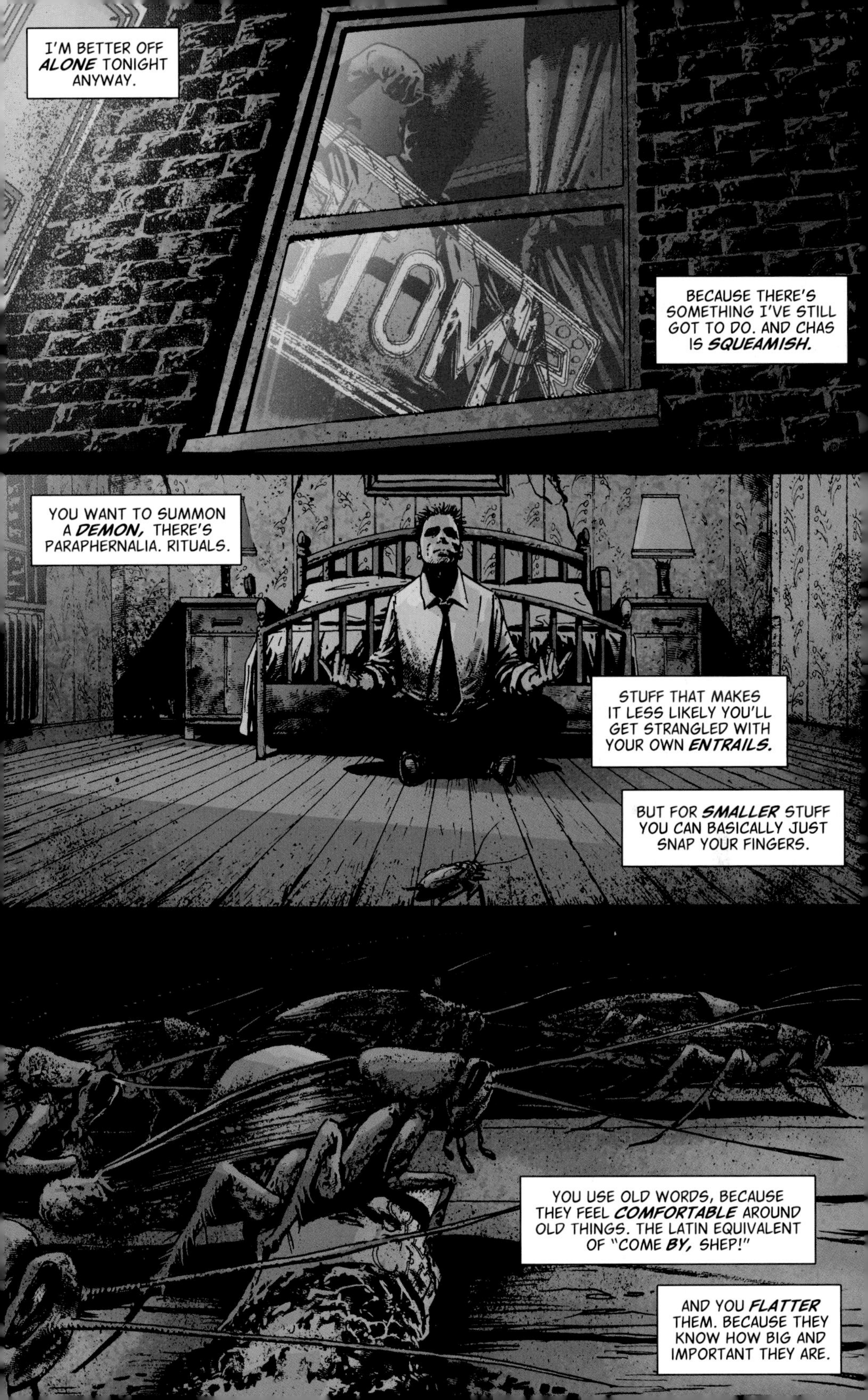
I'M BETTER OFF ALONE TONIGHT ANYWAY.
BECAUSE THERE'S SOMETHING I'VE STILL GOT TO DO. AND CHAS IS SQUEAMISH.
YOU WANT TO SUMMON A DEMON, THERE'S PARAPHERNALIA. RITUALS.
STUFF THAT MAKES IT LESS LIKELY YOU'LL GET STRANGLED WITH YOUR OWN ENTRAILS.
BUT FOR SMALLER STUFF YOU CAN BASICALLY JUST SNAP YOUR FINGERS.
YOU USE OLD WORDS, BECAUSE THEY FEEL COMFORTABLE AROUND OLD THINGS. THE LATIN EQUIVALENT OF "COME BY, SHEP!"
AND YOU FLATTER THEM. BECAUSE THEY KNOW HOW BIG AND IMPORTANT THEY ARE.

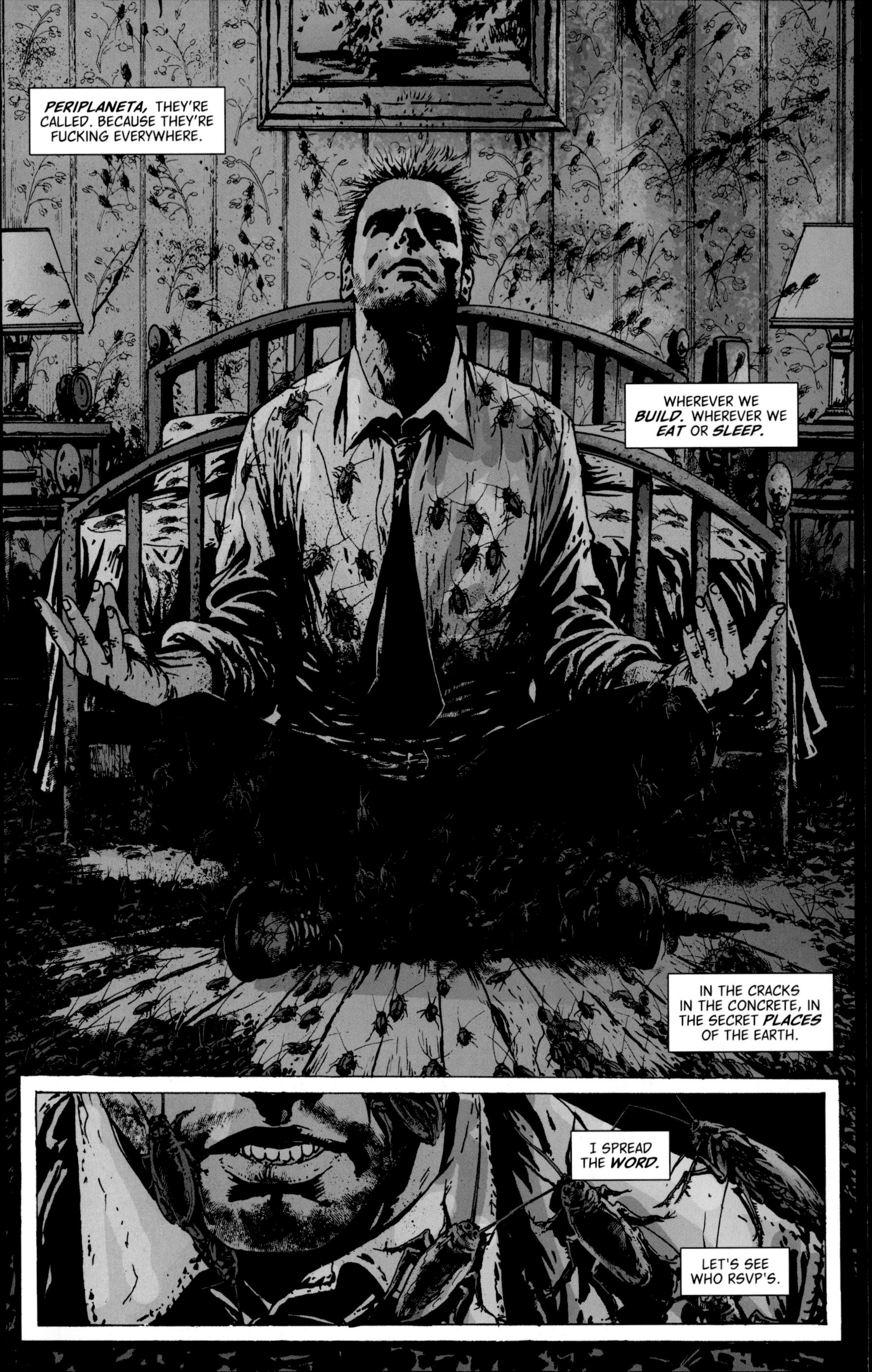
PERIPLANETA, THEY'RE CALLED. BECAUSE THEY'RE FUCKING EVERYWHERE.
WHEREVER WE BUILD. WHEREVER WE EAT OR SLEEP.
IN THE CRACKS IN THE CONCRETE, IN THE SECRET PLACES OF THE EARTH.
I SPREAD THE WORD.
LET'S SEE WHO RSVP'S.

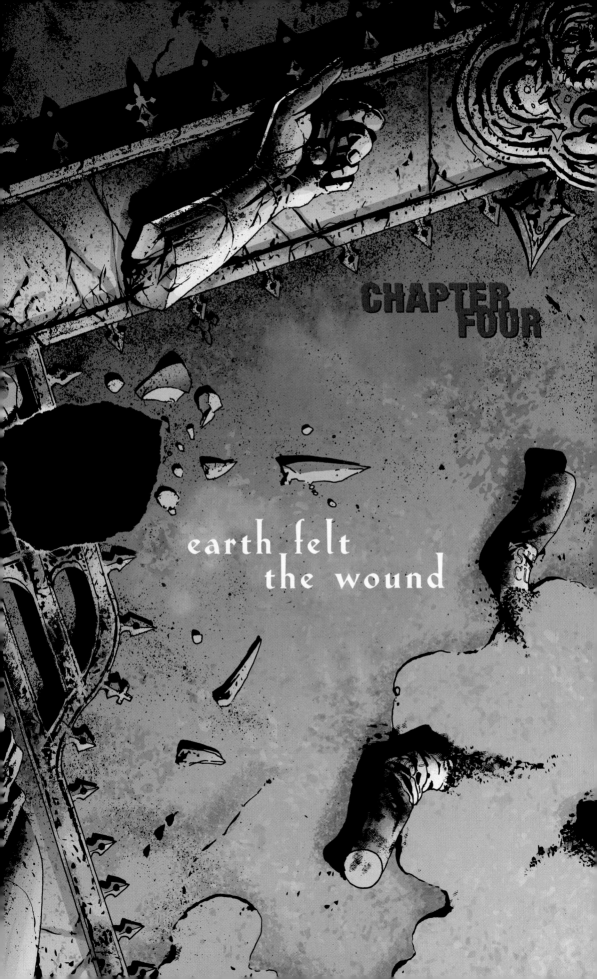

CHAPTER
FOUR

earth felt
the wound

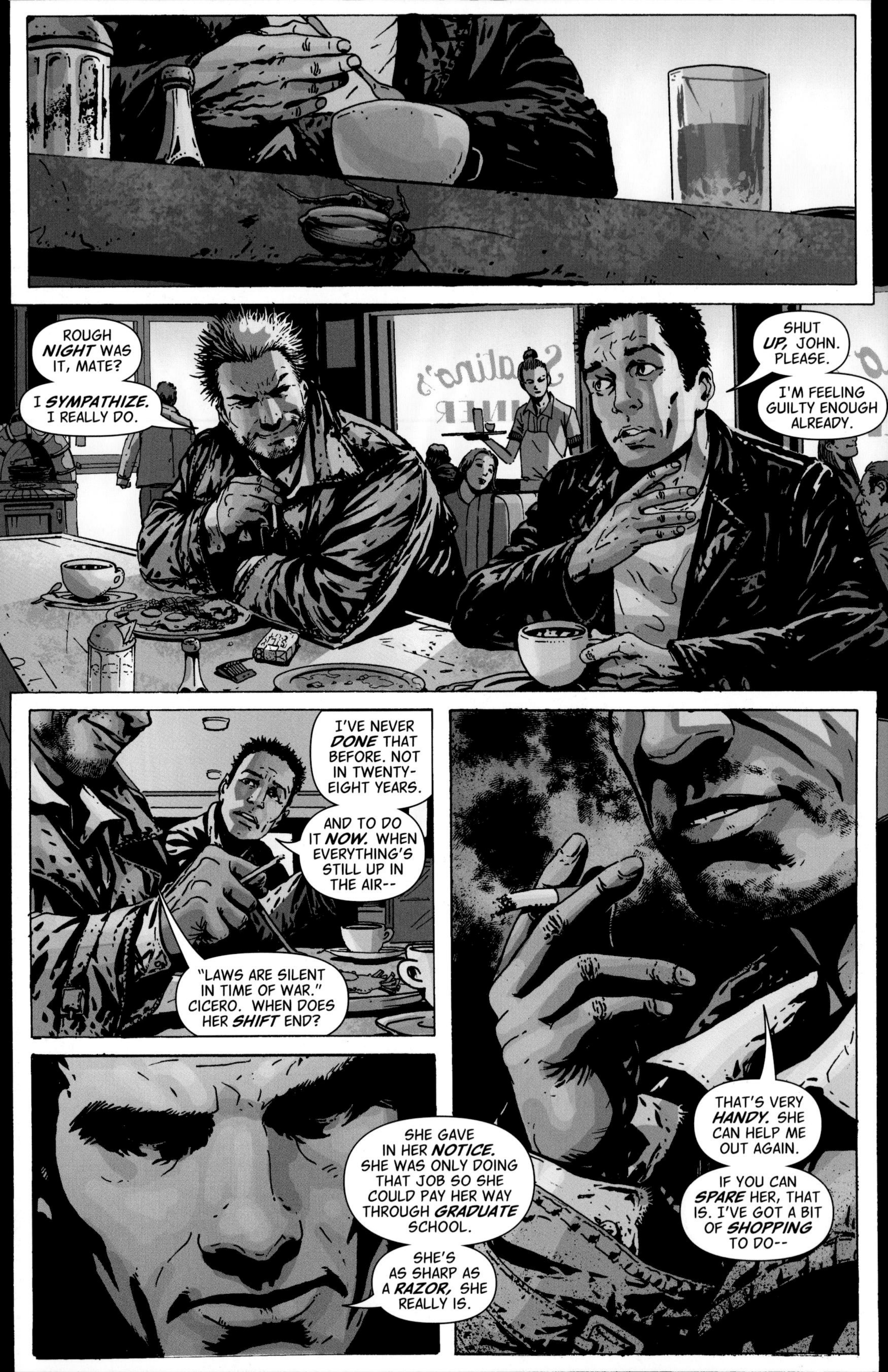

ROUGH NIGHT WAS IT, MATE?
I SYMPATHIZE. I REALLY DO.
SHUT UP, JOHN. PLEASE.
I'M FEELING GUILTY ENOUGH ALREADY.
I'VE NEVER DONE THAT BEFORE. NOT IN TWENTY-EIGHT YEARS.
AND TO DO IT NOW. WHEN EVERYTHING'S STILL UP IN THE AIR--
"LAWS ARE SILENT IN TIME OF WAR." CICERO. WHEN DOES HER SHIFT END?
SHE GAVE IN HER NOTICE. SHE WAS ONLY DOING THAT JOB SO SHE COULD PAY HER WAY THROUGH GRADUATE SCHOOL.
SHE'S AS SHARP AS A RAZOR, SHE REALLY IS.
THAT'S VERY HANDY. SHE CAN HELP ME OUT AGAIN.
IF YOU CAN SPARE HER, THAT IS. I'VE GOT A BIT OF SHOPPING TO DO--

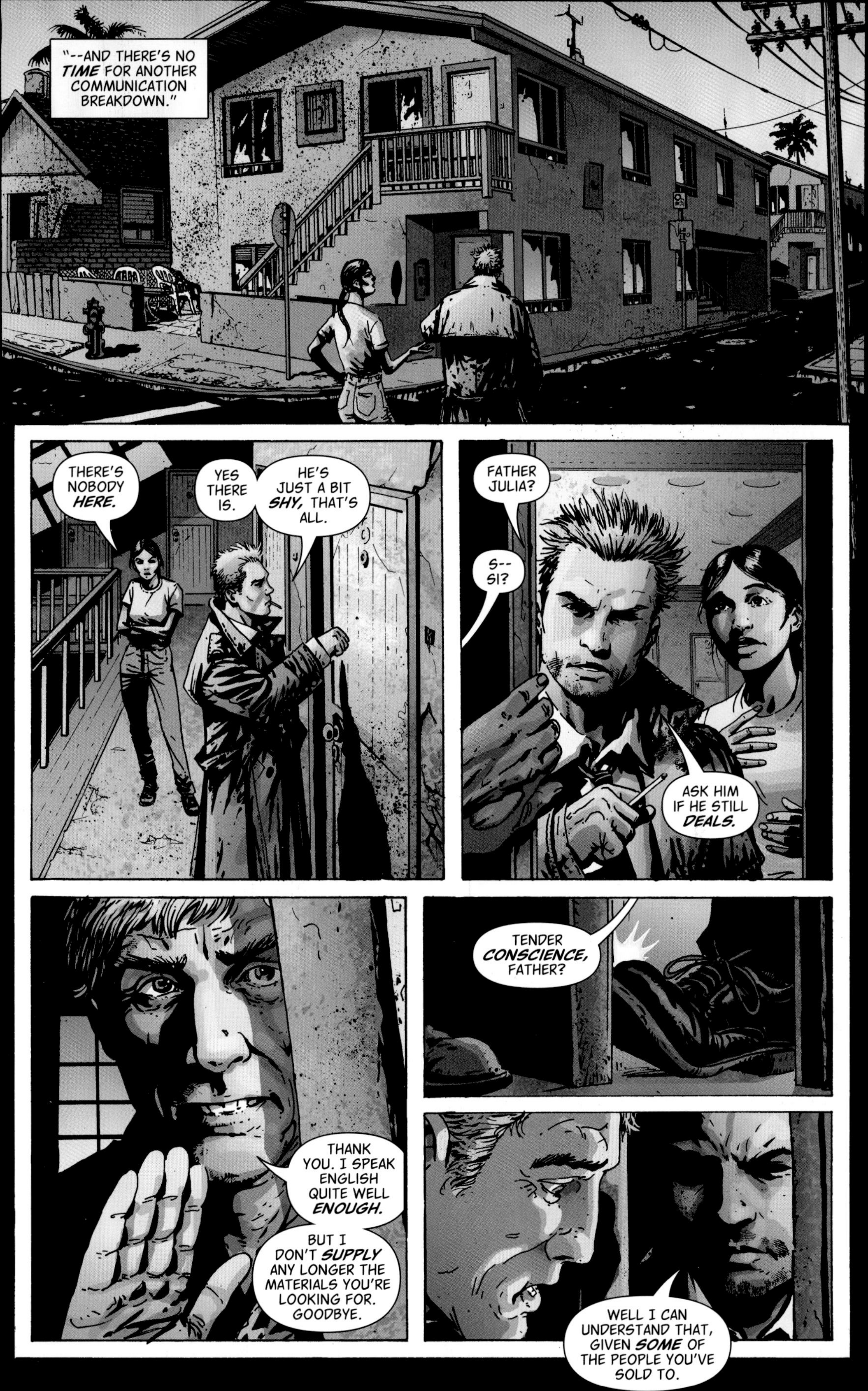
"--AND THERE'S NO TIME FOR ANOTHER COMMUNICATION BREAKDOWN."
THERE'S NOBODY HERE.
YES THERE IS.
HE'S JUST A BIT SHY, THAT'S ALL.
FATHER JULIA?
S-- SI?
ASK HIM IF HE STILL DEALS.
THANK YOU. I SPEAK ENGLISH QUITE WELL ENOUGH.
BUT I DON'T SUPPLY ANY LONGER THE MATERIALS YOU'RE LOOKING FOR. GOODBYE.
TENDER CONSCIENCE, FATHER?
WELL I CAN UNDERSTAND THAT, GIVEN SOME OF THE PEOPLE YOU'VE SOLD TO.

BUT IT'S A LUXURY YOU CAN'T *AFFORD* JUST NOW. THIS LADY BEHIND ME, SHE'S FROM THE L.A.P.D. PAROLE UNIT.

RESETTLEMENT OF *OFFENDERS.*

OH! B-- BUT I HAVEN'T-- NOT SINCE--

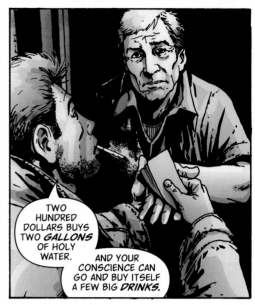

TWO HUNDRED DOLLARS BUYS TWO *GALLONS* OF HOLY WATER.

AND YOUR CONSCIENCE CAN GO AND BUY ITSELF A FEW BIG *DRINKS.*

YOU DID THAT VERY *WELL.*

THANKS, MELOSA.

YOU MUST HAVE HAD A LOT OF *PRACTICE* IN INTIMIDATING THE ELDERLY.

YEAH, BUT YOU'RE *WELL* AHEAD OF ME IN FUCKING MARRIED MEN.

IT'S ALL A QUESTION OF WHERE YOU DRAW THE *LINE,* ISN'T IT, LOVE?

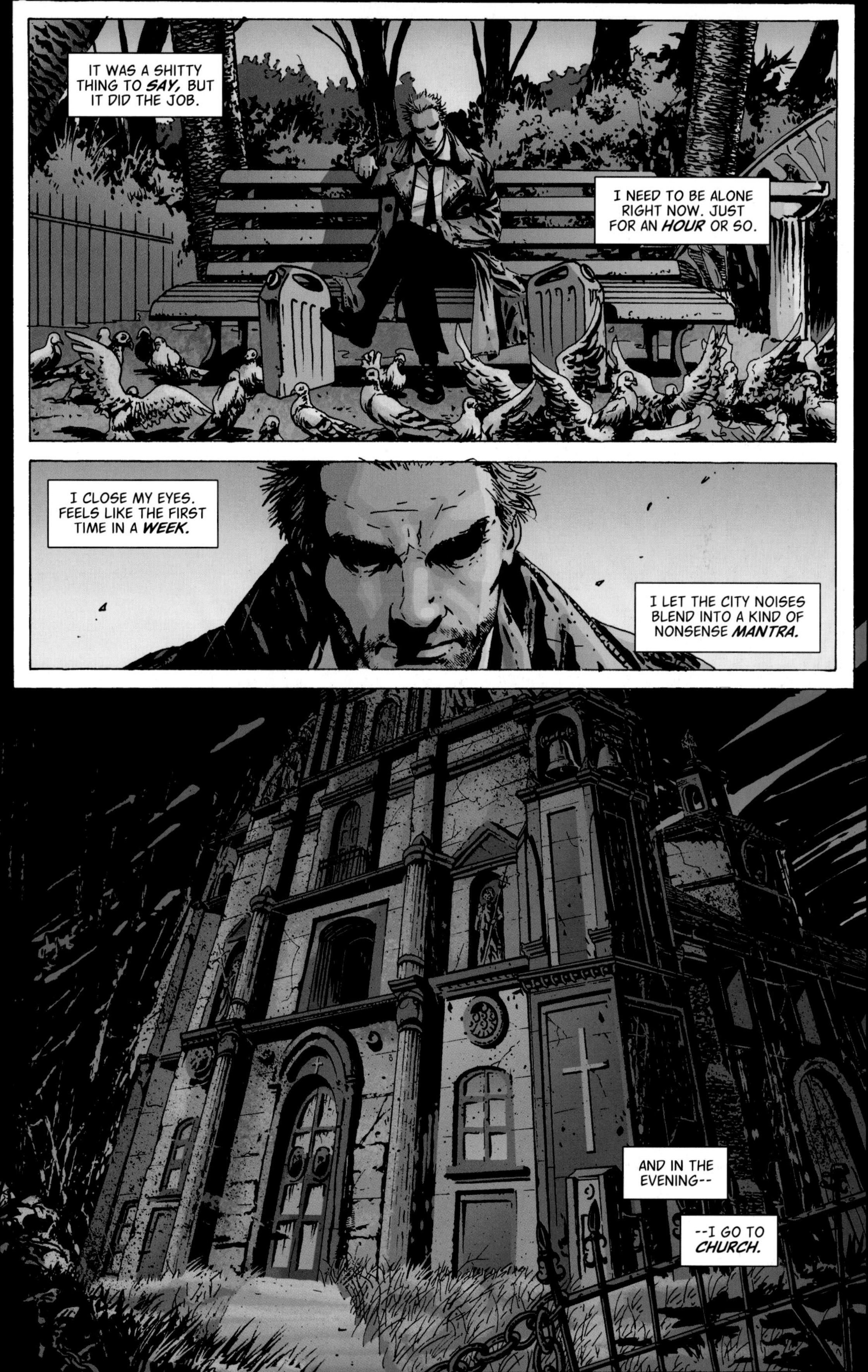
IT WAS A SHITTY THING TO *SAY,* BUT IT DID THE JOB.
I NEED TO BE ALONE RIGHT NOW. JUST FOR AN *HOUR* OR SO.
I CLOSE MY EYES. FEELS LIKE THE FIRST TIME IN A *WEEK.*
I LET THE CITY NOISES BLEND INTO A KIND OF NONSENSE *MANTRA.*
AND IN THE EVENING--
--I GO TO *CHURCH.*

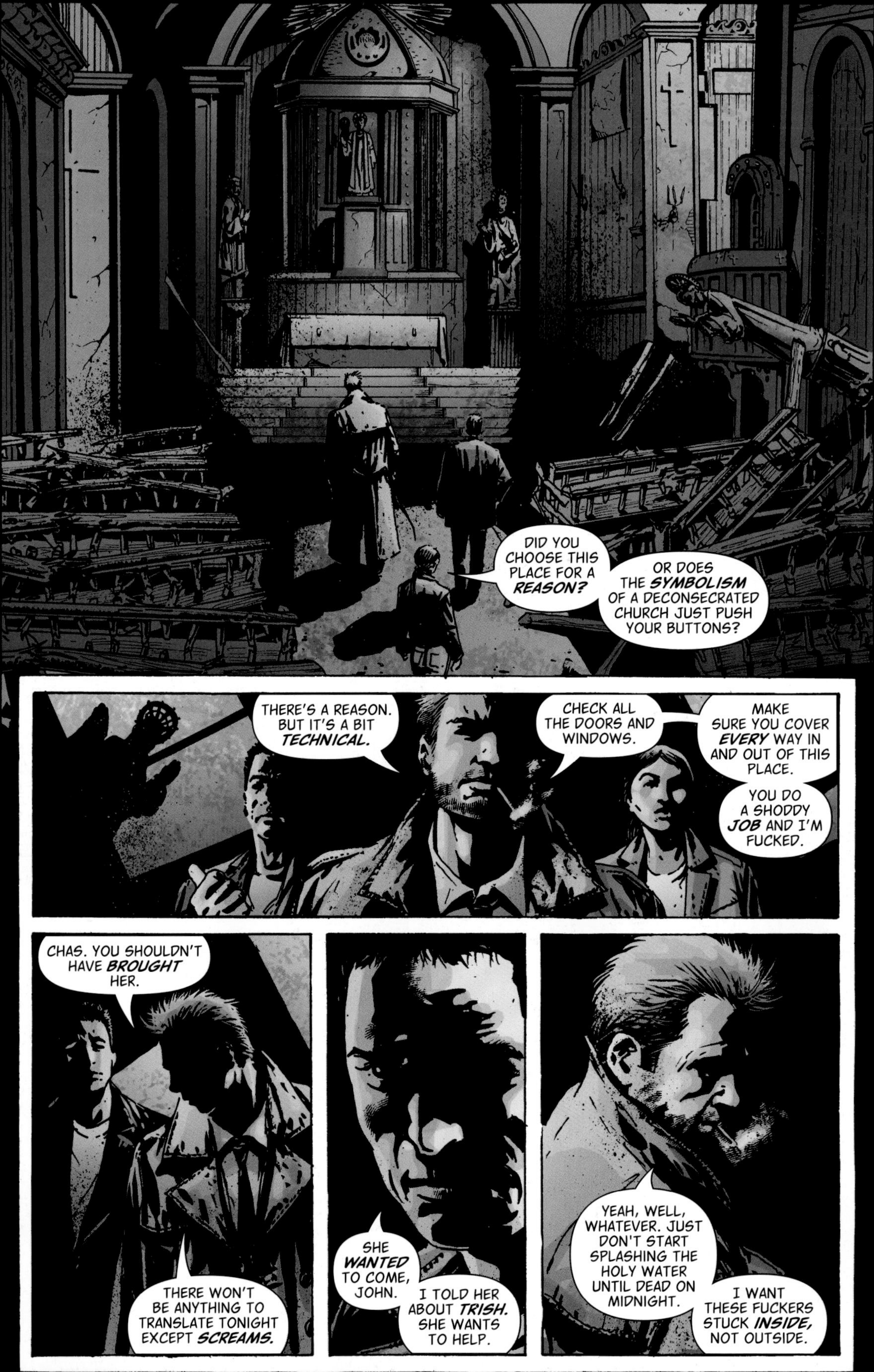
DID YOU CHOOSE THIS PLACE FOR A REASON?
OR DOES THE SYMBOLISM OF A DECONSECRATED CHURCH JUST PUSH YOUR BUTTONS?
THERE'S A REASON. BUT IT'S A BIT TECHNICAL.
CHECK ALL THE DOORS AND WINDOWS.
MAKE SURE YOU COVER EVERY WAY IN AND OUT OF THIS PLACE.
YOU DO A SHODDY JOB AND I'M FUCKED.
CHAS. YOU SHOULDN'T HAVE BROUGHT HER.
THERE WON'T BE ANYTHING TO TRANSLATE TONIGHT EXCEPT SCREAMS.
SHE WANTED TO COME, JOHN.
I TOLD HER ABOUT TRISH. SHE WANTS TO HELP.
YEAH, WELL, WHATEVER. JUST DON'T START SPLASHING THE HOLY WATER UNTIL DEAD ON MIDNIGHT.
I WANT THESE FUCKERS STUCK INSIDE, NOT OUTSIDE.

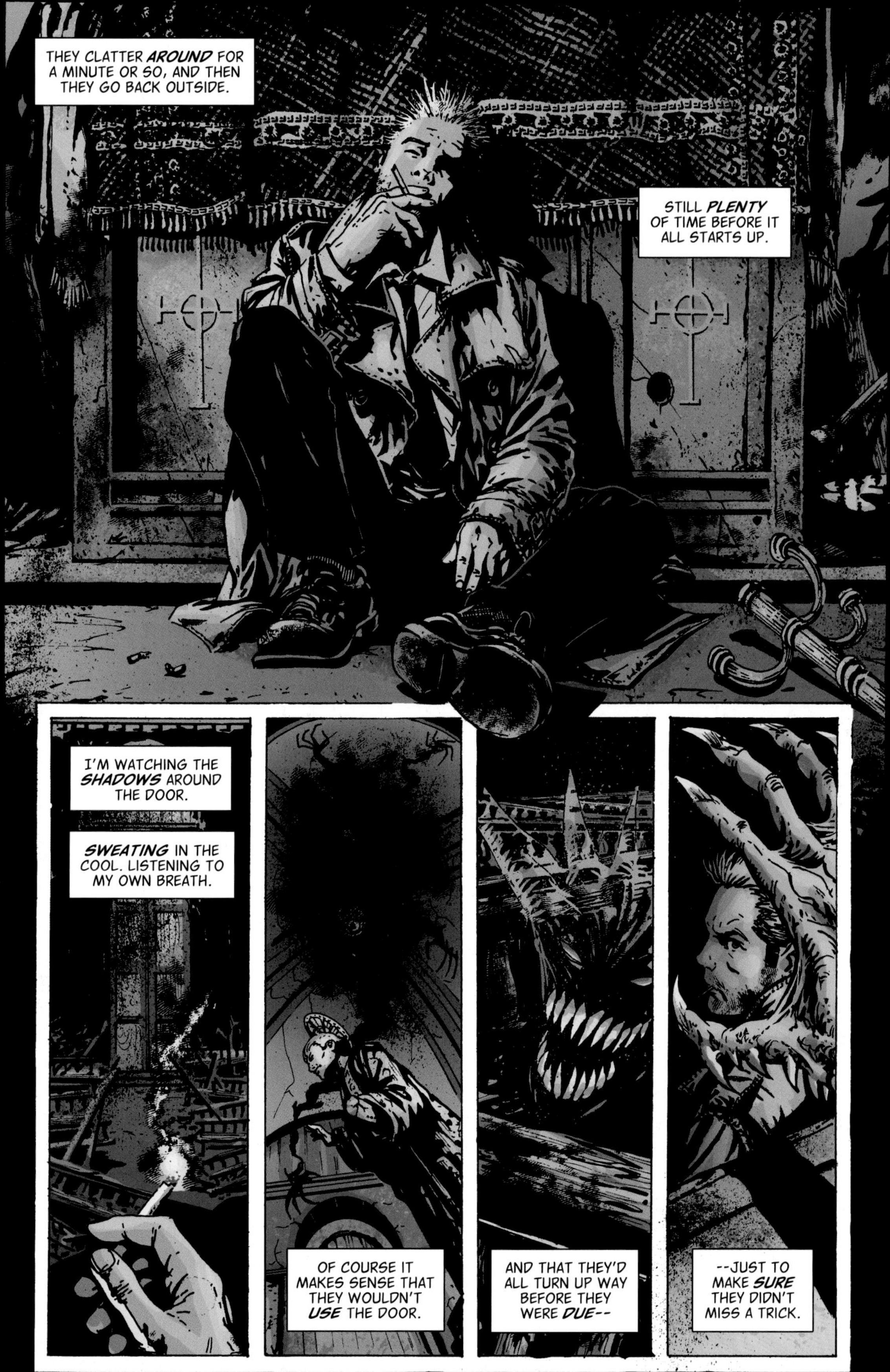
THEY CLATTER AROUND FOR A MINUTE OR SO, AND THEN THEY GO BACK OUTSIDE.
STILL PLENTY OF TIME BEFORE IT ALL STARTS UP.
I'M WATCHING THE SHADOWS AROUND THE DOOR.
SWEATING IN THE COOL. LISTENING TO MY OWN BREATH.
OF COURSE IT MAKES SENSE THAT THEY WOULDN'T USE THE DOOR.
AND THAT THEY'D ALL TURN UP WAY BEFORE THEY WERE DUE--
--JUST TO MAKE SURE THEY DIDN'T MISS A TRICK.

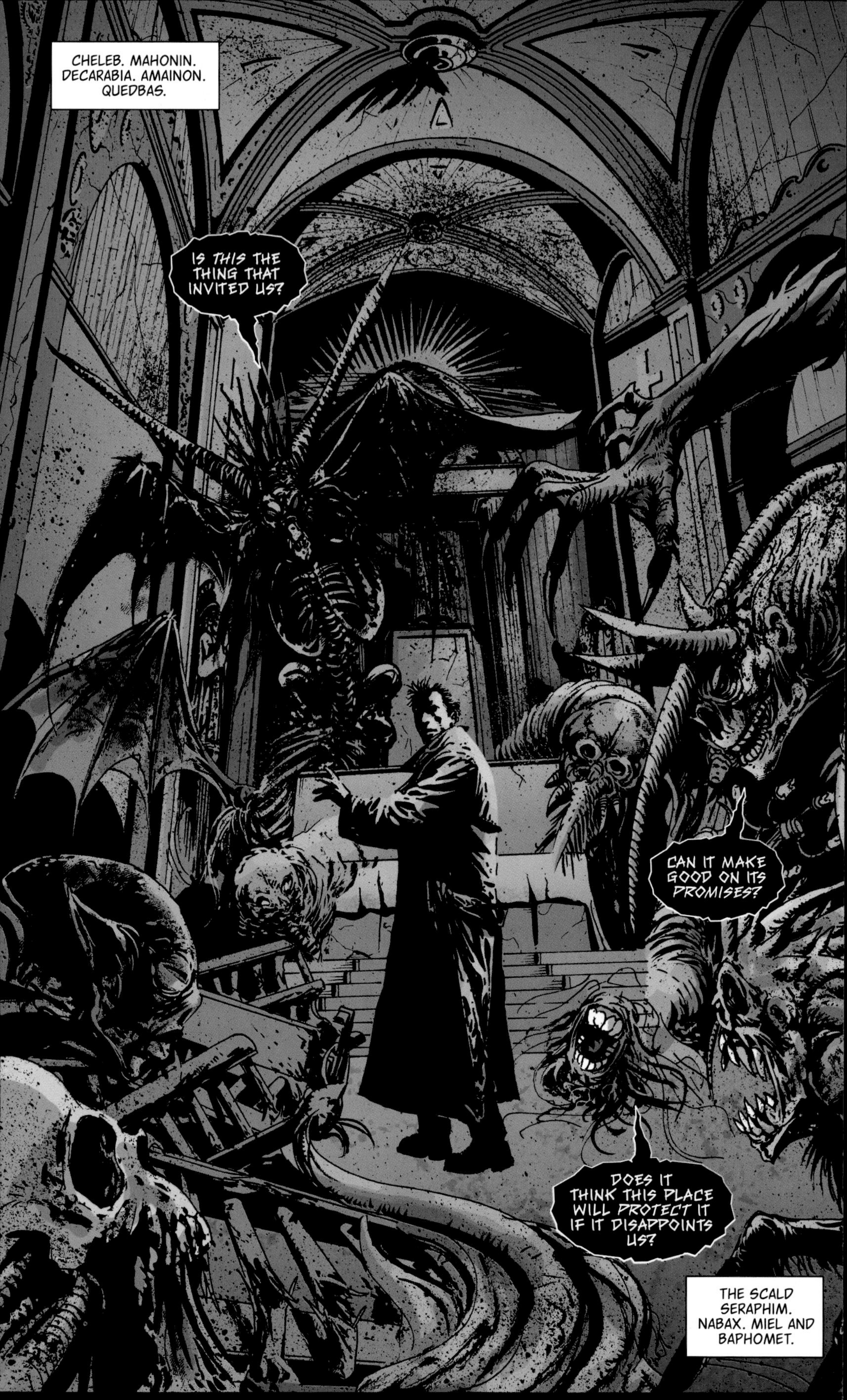
CHELEB. MAHONIN. DECARABIA. AMAINON. QUEDBAS.
IS *THIS* THE THING THAT INVITED US?
CAN IT MAKE GOOD ON ITS *PROMISES?*
DOES IT THINK THIS PLACE WILL *PROTECT* IT IF IT DISAPPOINTS US?
THE SCALD SERAPHIM. NABAX. MIEL AND BAPHOMET.

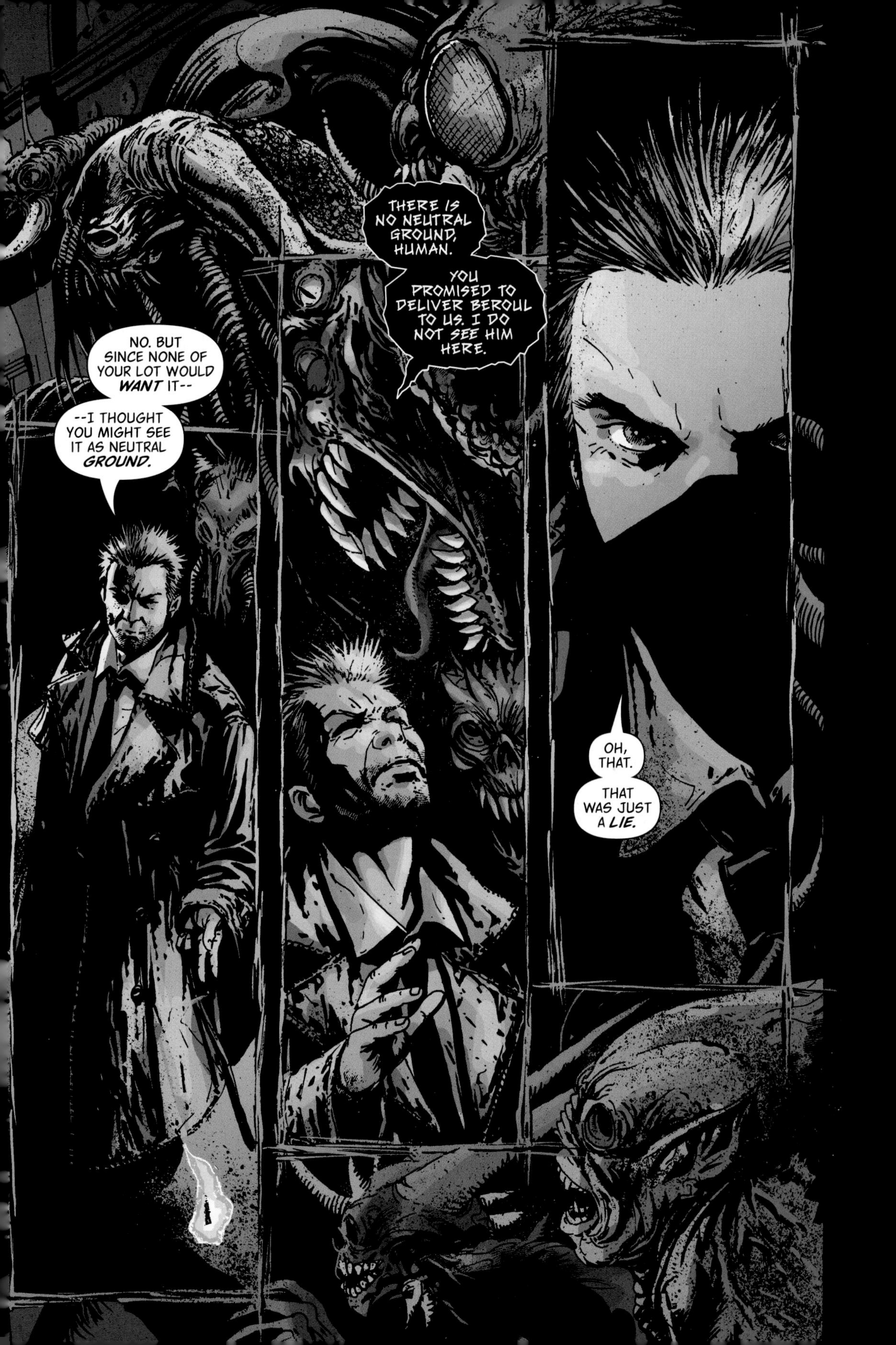
NO. BUT SINCE NONE OF YOUR LOT WOULD *WANT* IT--
--I THOUGHT YOU MIGHT SEE IT AS NEUTRAL *GROUND.*
THERE IS NO NEUTRAL GROUND, HUMAN.
YOU PROMISED TO DELIVER BEROUL TO US. I DO NOT SEE HIM HERE.
OH, THAT.
THAT WAS JUST A *LIE.*

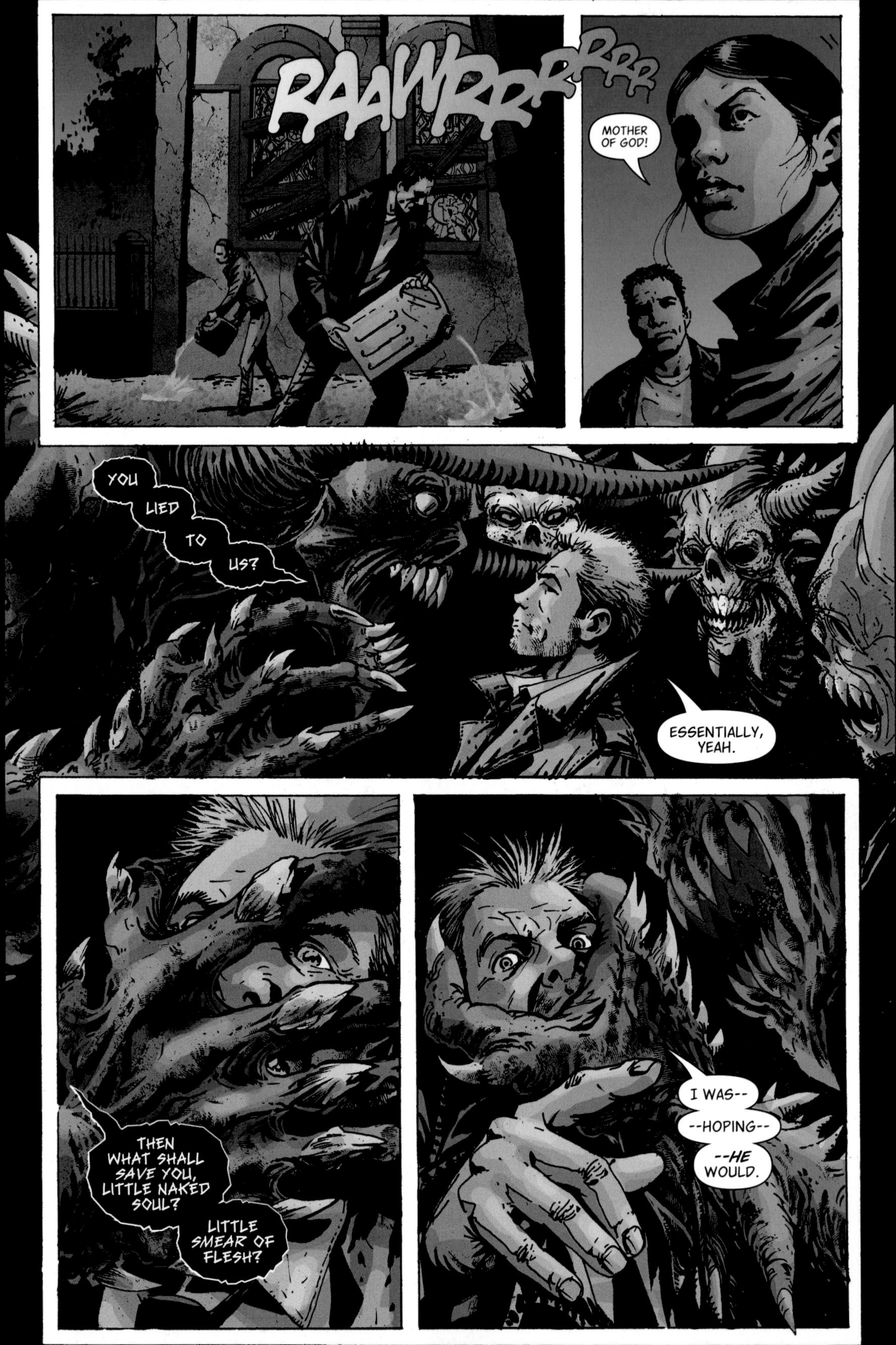
RAAWRRRRRR
MOTHER OF GOD!
YOU LIED TO US?
ESSENTIALLY, YEAH.
THEN WHAT SHALL SAVE YOU, LITTLE NAKED SOUL?
LITTLE SMEAR OF FLESH?
I WAS--
--HOPING--
--HE WOULD.

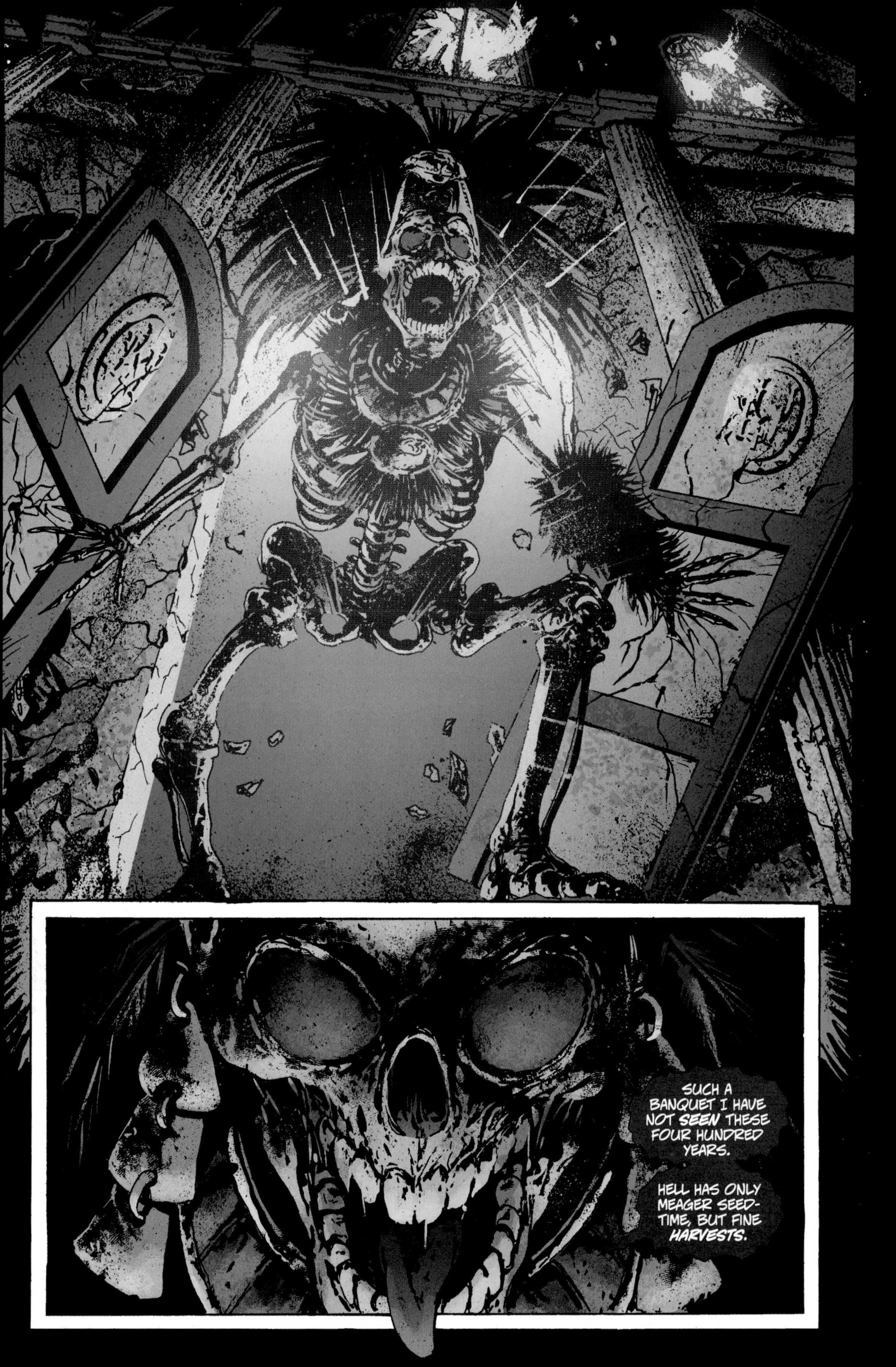
SUCH A BANQUET I HAVE NOT *SEEN* THESE FOUR HUNDRED YEARS.
HELL HAS ONLY MEAGER SEED-TIME, BUT FINE *HARVESTS*.

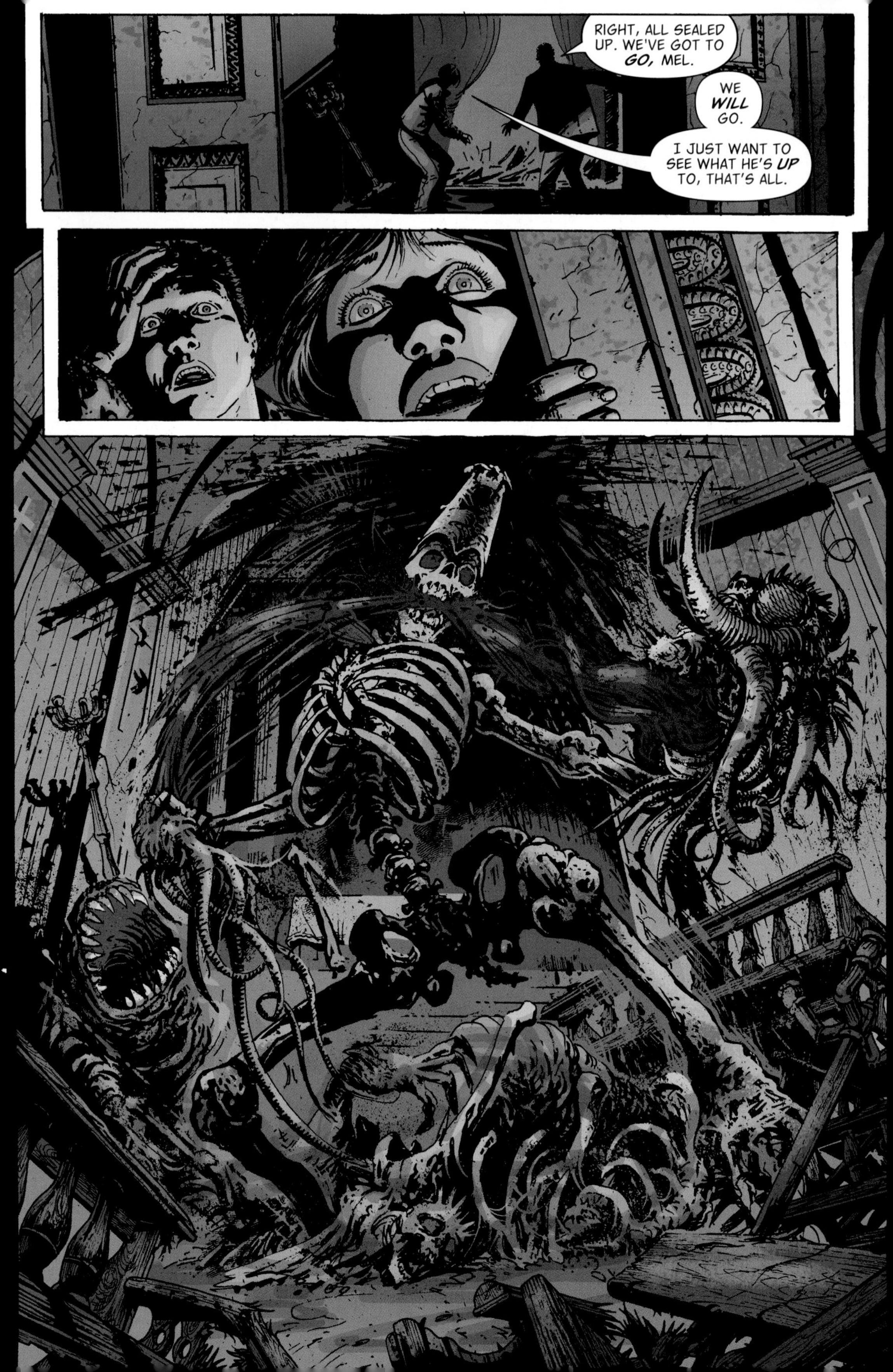
RIGHT, ALL SEALED UP. WE'VE GOT TO GO, MEL.
WE WILL GO.
I JUST WANT TO SEE WHAT HE'S UP TO, THAT'S ALL.

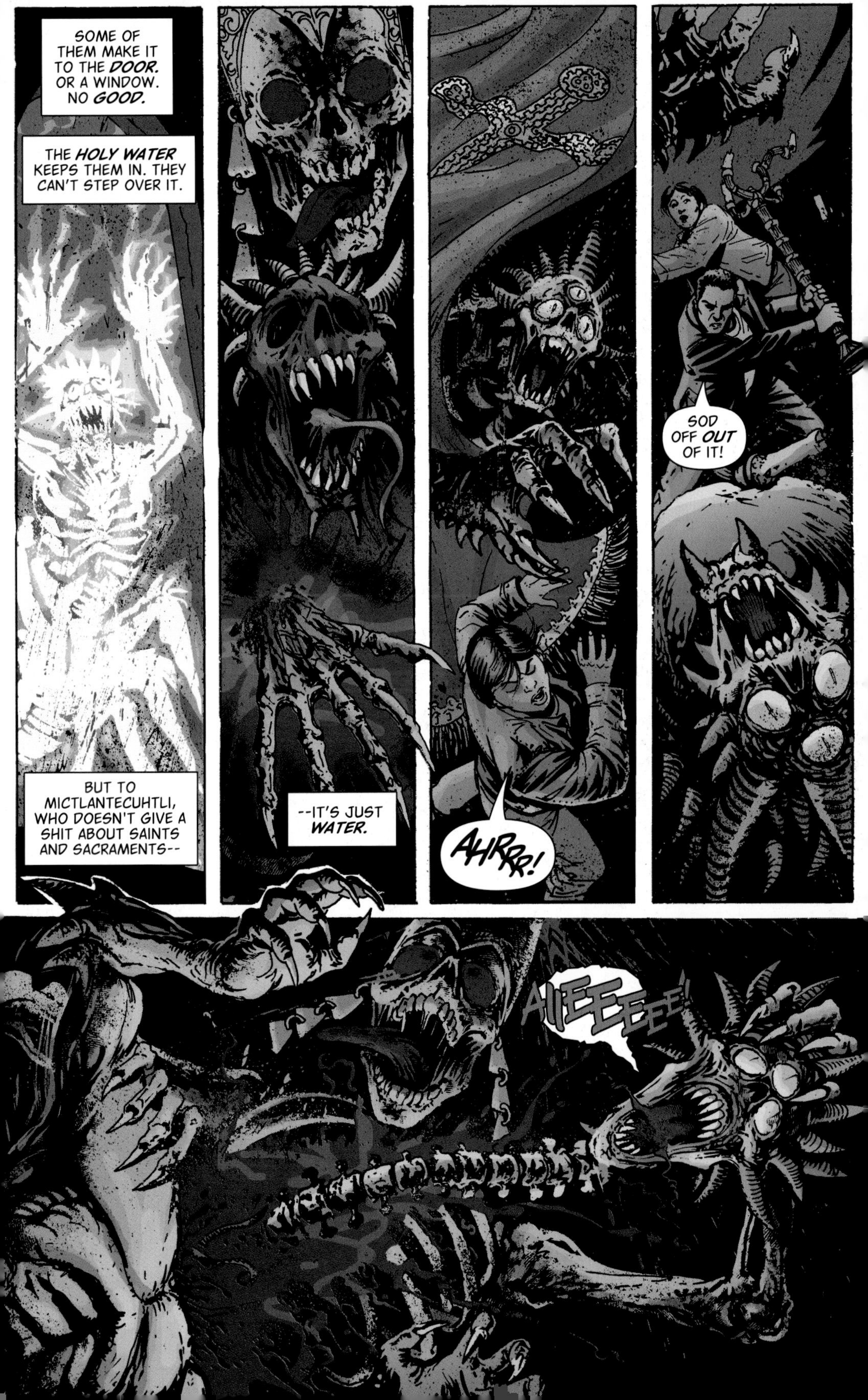

SOME OF THEM MAKE IT TO THE *DOOR.* OR A WINDOW. NO *GOOD.*
THE *HOLY WATER* KEEPS THEM IN. THEY CAN'T STEP OVER IT.
BUT TO MICTLANTECUHTLI, WHO DOESN'T GIVE A SHIT ABOUT SAINTS AND SACRAMENTS--
--IT'S JUST *WATER.*
AHRRR!
SOD OFF *OUT* OF IT!
AIIEEEEEE!

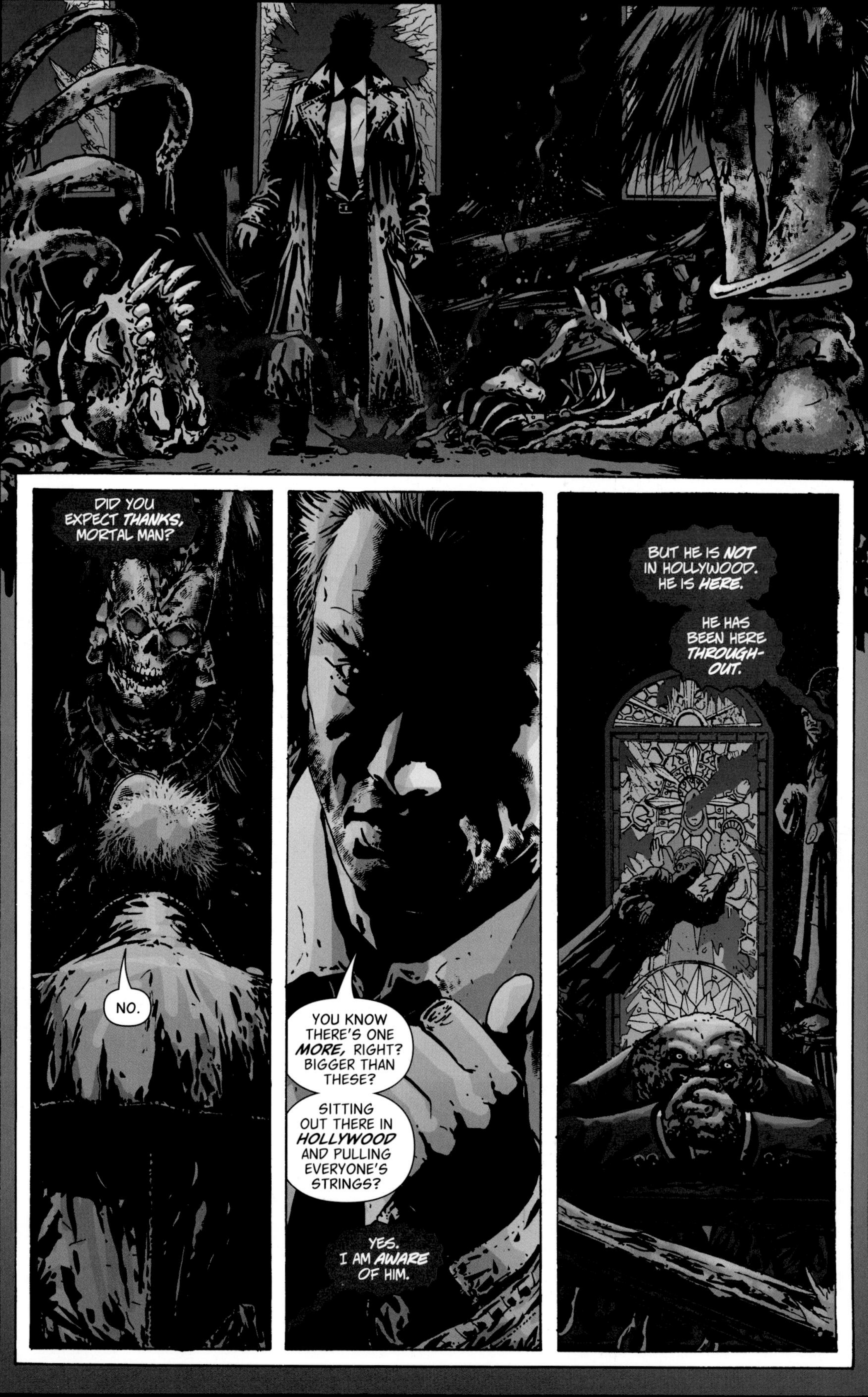
DID YOU EXPECT THANKS, MORTAL MAN?
NO.
YOU KNOW THERE'S ONE MORE, RIGHT? BIGGER THAN THESE?
SITTING OUT THERE IN HOLLYWOOD AND PULLING EVERYONE'S STRINGS?
YES. I AM AWARE OF HIM.
BUT HE IS NOT IN HOLLYWOOD. HE IS HERE.
HE HAS BEEN HERE THROUGH-OUT.

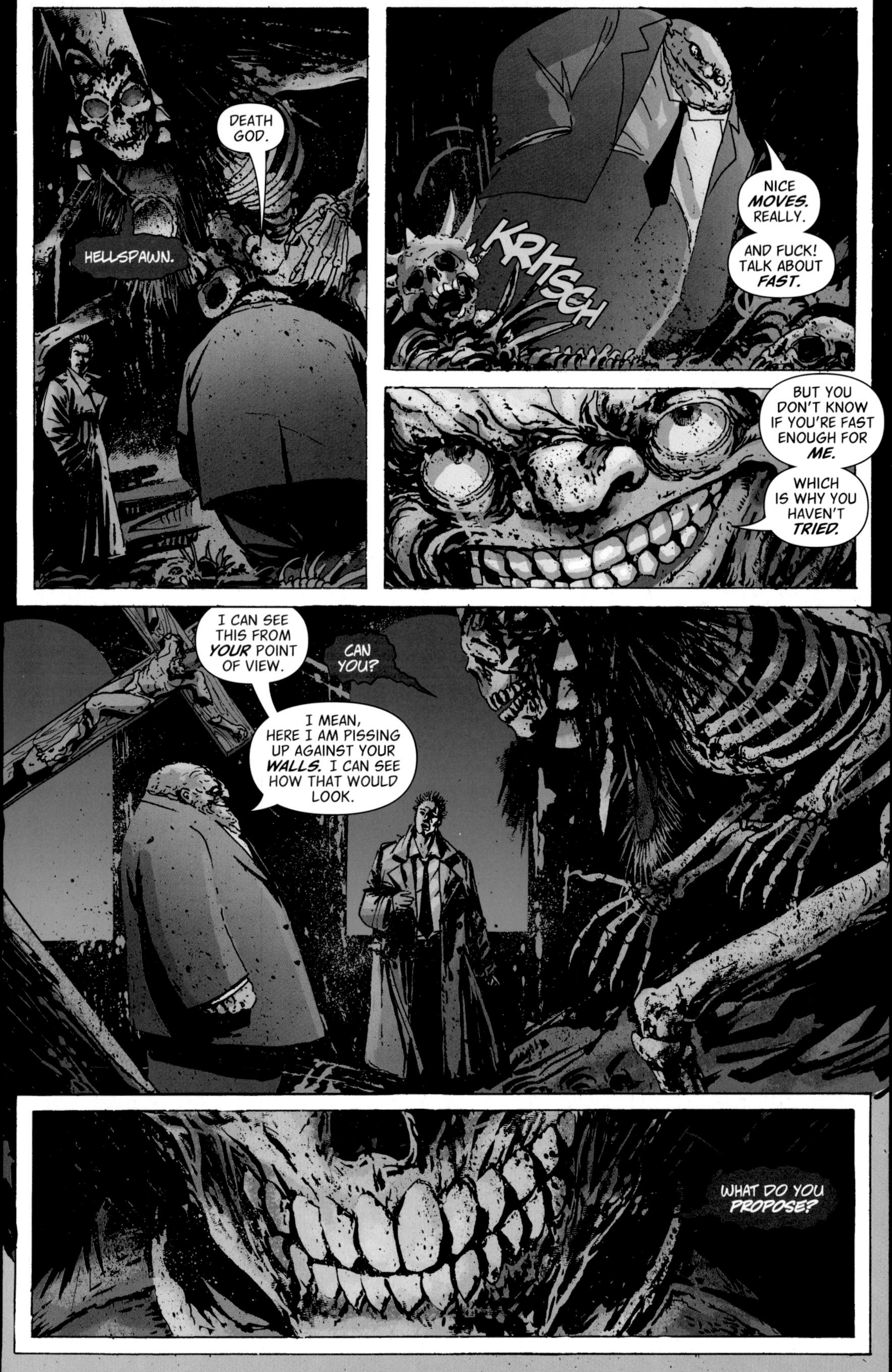
DEATH GOD.
HELLSPAWN.
KRITSCH
NICE MOVES. REALLY.
AND FUCK! TALK ABOUT FAST.
BUT YOU DON'T KNOW IF YOU'RE FAST ENOUGH FOR ME.
WHICH IS WHY YOU HAVEN'T TRIED.
I CAN SEE THIS FROM YOUR POINT OF VIEW.
CAN YOU?
I MEAN, HERE I AM PISSING UP AGAINST YOUR WALLS. I CAN SEE HOW THAT WOULD LOOK.
WHAT DO YOU PROPOSE?

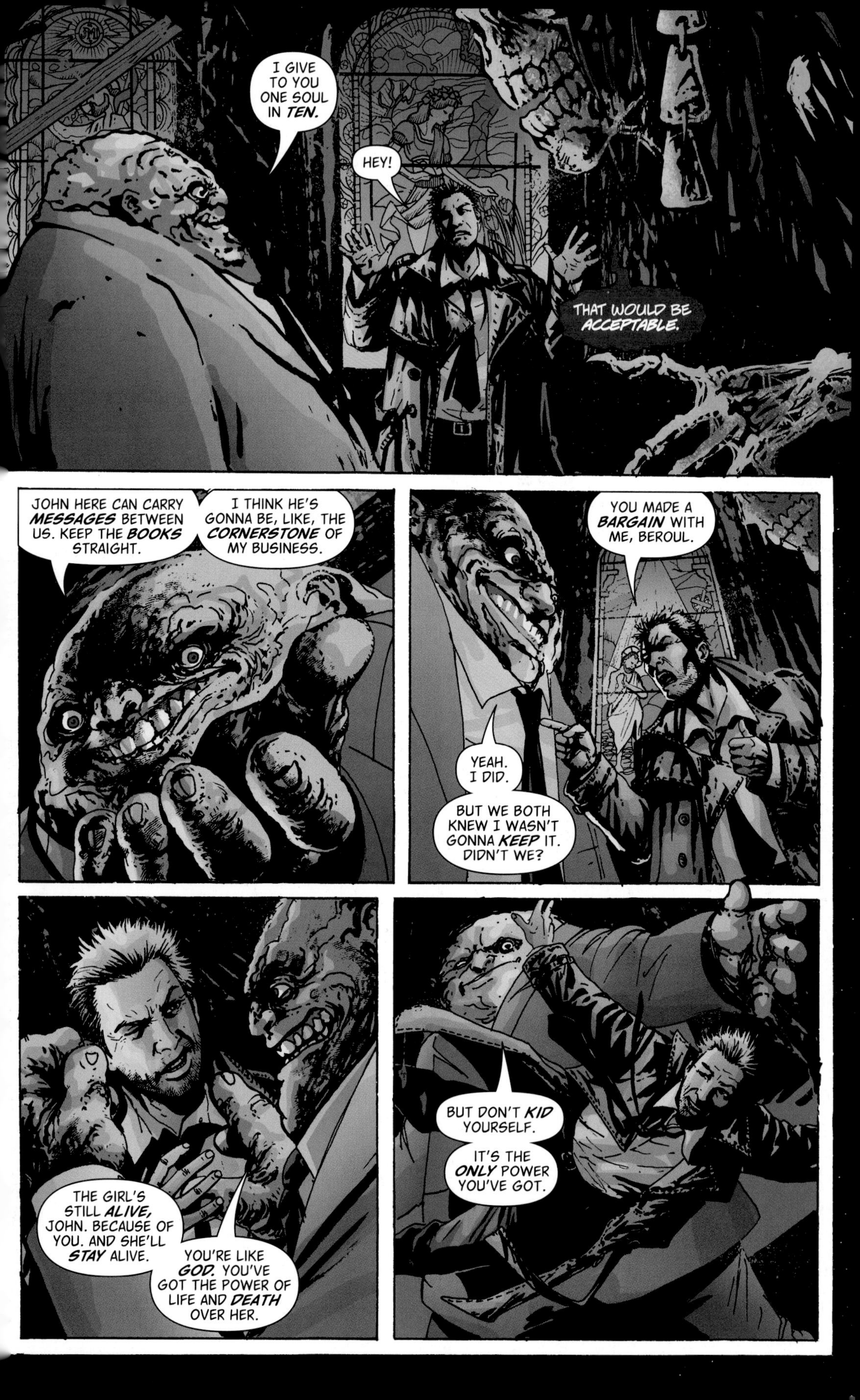
I GIVE TO YOU ONE SOUL IN TEN.
HEY!
THAT WOULD BE ACCEPTABLE.
JOHN HERE CAN CARRY MESSAGES BETWEEN US. KEEP THE BOOKS STRAIGHT.
I THINK HE'S GONNA BE, LIKE, THE CORNERSTONE OF MY BUSINESS.
YOU MADE A BARGAIN WITH ME, BEROUL.
YEAH. I DID.
BUT WE BOTH KNEW I WASN'T GONNA KEEP IT. DIDN'T WE?
THE GIRL'S STILL ALIVE, JOHN. BECAUSE OF YOU. AND SHE'LL STAY ALIVE.
YOU'RE LIKE GOD. YOU'VE GOT THE POWER OF LIFE AND DEATH OVER HER.
BUT DON'T KID YOURSELF.
IT'S THE ONLY POWER YOU'VE GOT.

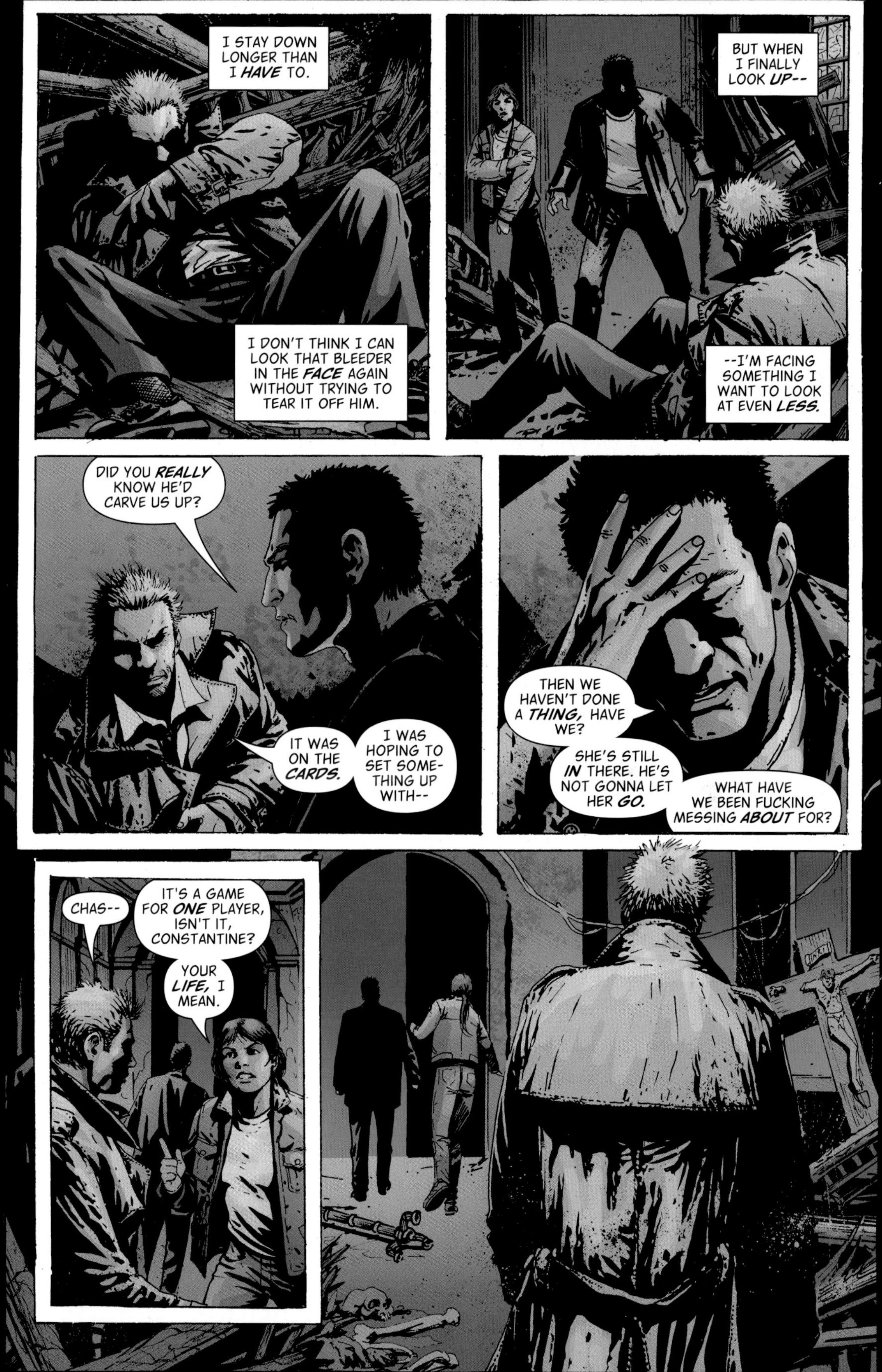
I STAY DOWN LONGER THAN I *HAVE* TO.
I DON'T THINK I CAN LOOK THAT BLEEDER IN THE *FACE* AGAIN WITHOUT TRYING TO TEAR IT OFF HIM.
BUT WHEN I FINALLY LOOK *UP*--
--I'M FACING SOMETHING I WANT TO LOOK AT EVEN *LESS.*
DID YOU *REALLY* KNOW HE'D CARVE US UP?
IT WAS ON THE *CARDS.*
I WAS HOPING TO SET SOME-THING UP WITH--
THEN WE HAVEN'T DONE A *THING,* HAVE WE?
SHE'S STILL *IN* THERE. HE'S NOT GONNA LET HER *GO.*
WHAT HAVE WE BEEN FUCKING MESSING *ABOUT* FOR?
CHAS--
IT'S A GAME FOR *ONE* PLAYER, ISN'T IT, CONSTANTINE?
YOUR *LIFE,* I MEAN.

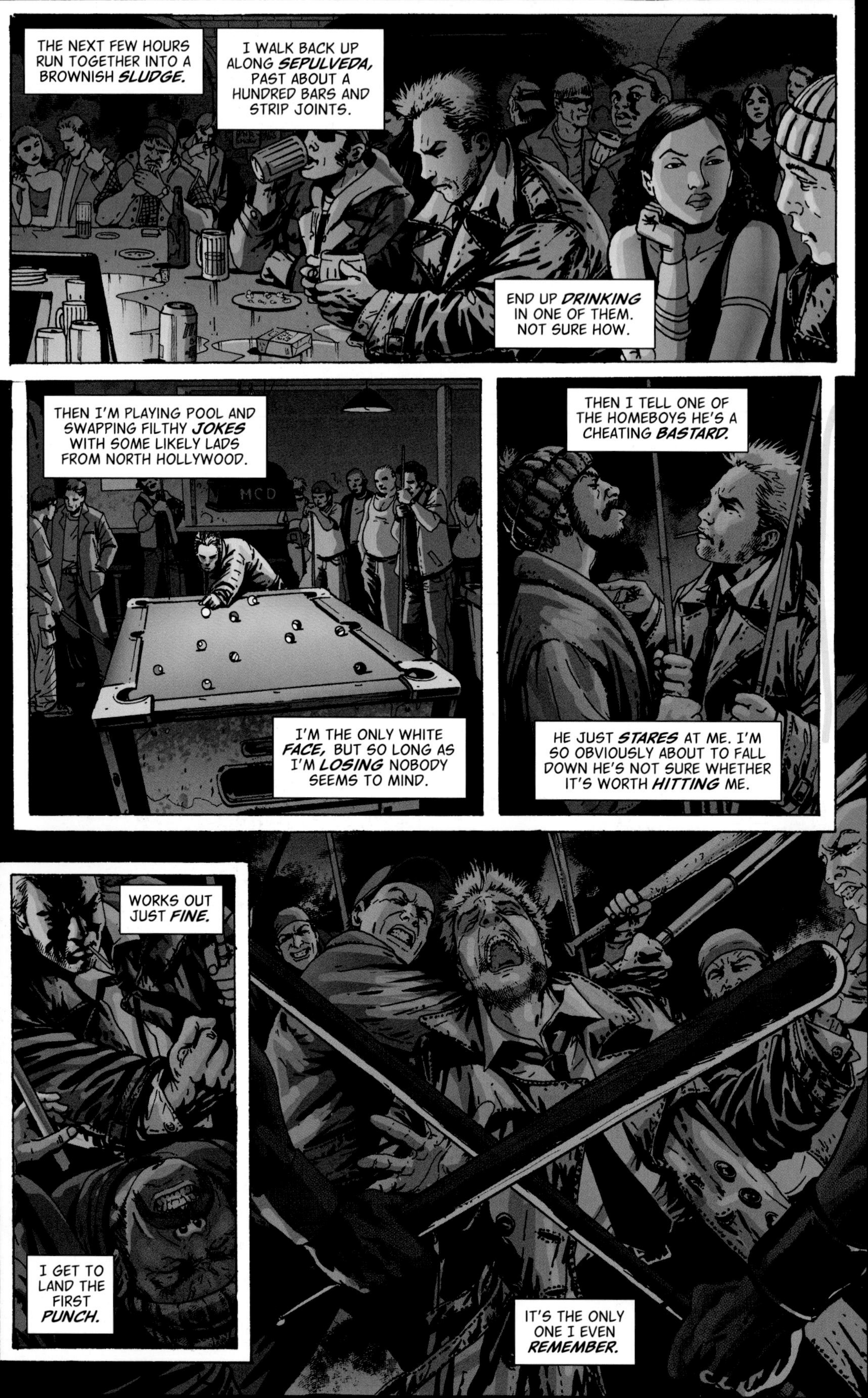
THE NEXT FEW HOURS RUN TOGETHER INTO A BROWNISH SLUDGE.
I WALK BACK UP ALONG SEPULVEDA, PAST ABOUT A HUNDRED BARS AND STRIP JOINTS.
END UP DRINKING IN ONE OF THEM. NOT SURE HOW.
THEN I'M PLAYING POOL AND SWAPPING FILTHY JOKES WITH SOME LIKELY LADS FROM NORTH HOLLYWOOD.
MCD
I'M THE ONLY WHITE FACE, BUT SO LONG AS I'M LOSING NOBODY SEEMS TO MIND.
THEN I TELL ONE OF THE HOMEBOYS HE'S A CHEATING BASTARD.
HE JUST STARES AT ME. I'M SO OBVIOUSLY ABOUT TO FALL DOWN HE'S NOT SURE WHETHER IT'S WORTH HITTING ME.
WORKS OUT JUST FINE.
I GET TO LAND THE FIRST PUNCH.
IT'S THE ONLY ONE I EVEN REMEMBER.

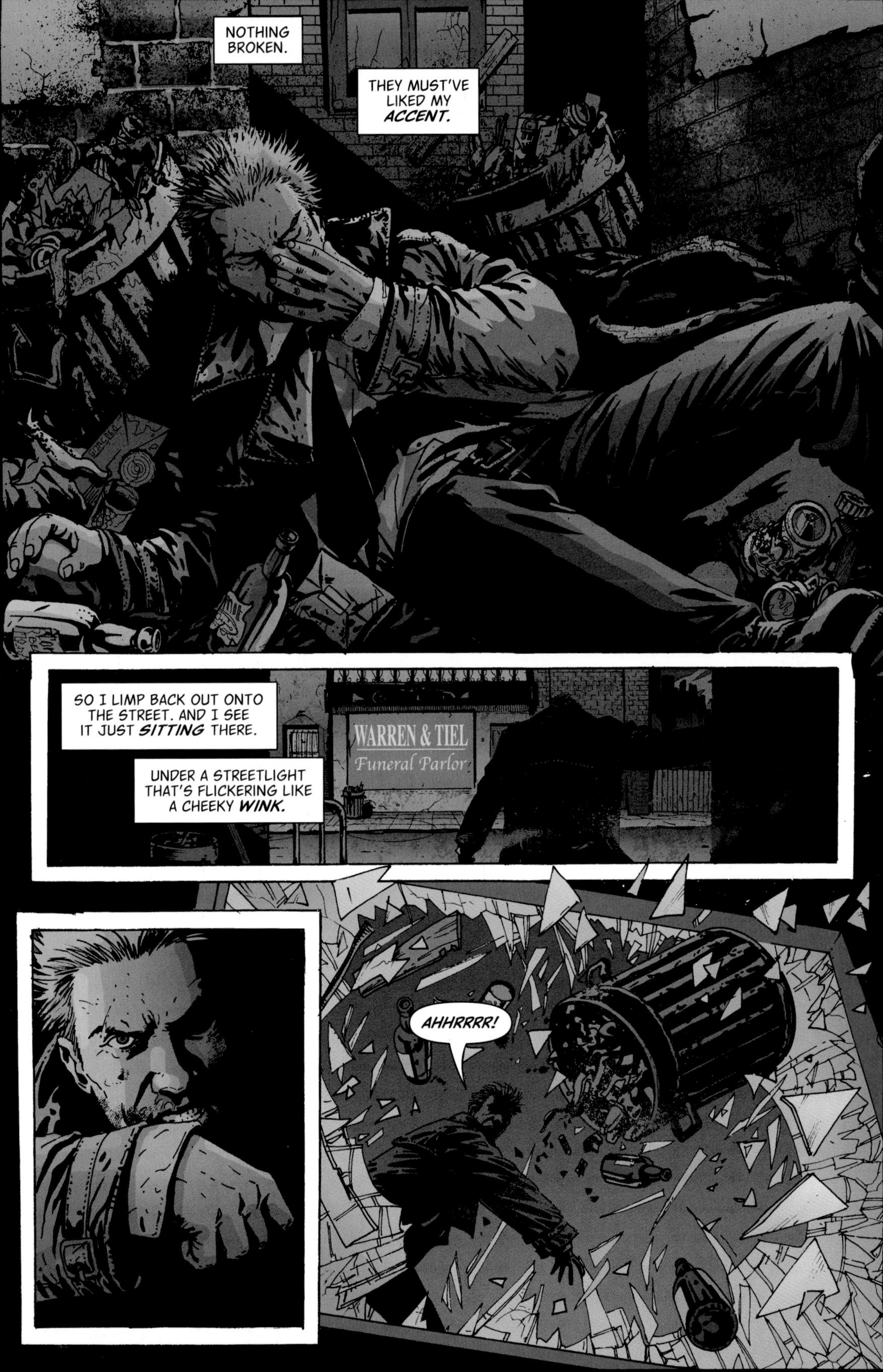
NOTHING BROKEN.
THEY MUST'VE LIKED MY ACCENT.
SO I LIMP BACK OUT ONTO THE STREET. AND I SEE IT JUST SITTING THERE.
WARREN & TIEL
Funeral Parlor
UNDER A STREETLIGHT THAT'S FLICKERING LIKE A CHEEKY WINK.
AHHRRRR!

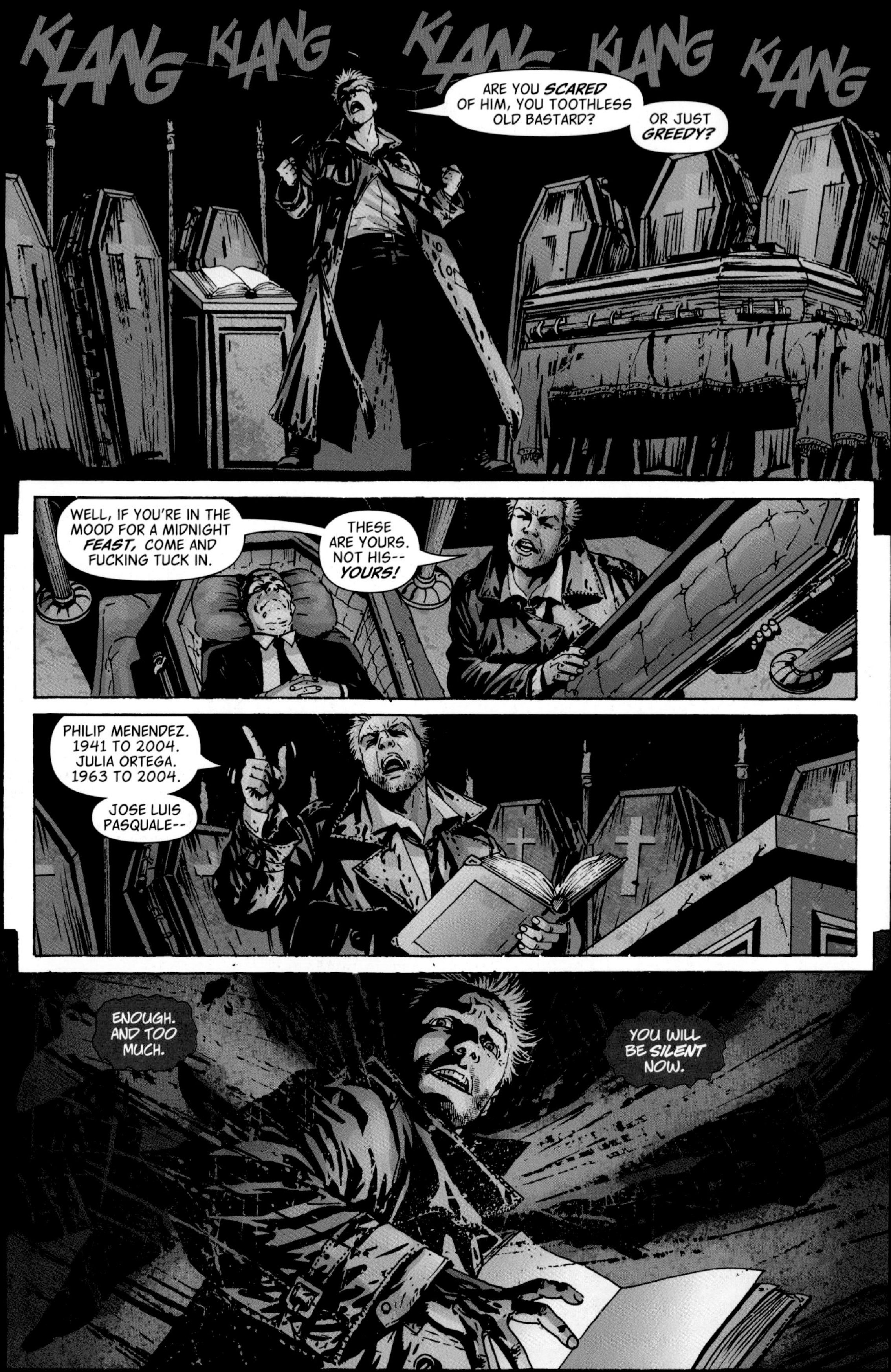
KLANG KLANG KLANG KLANG KLANG
ARE YOU SCARED OF HIM, YOU TOOTHLESS OLD BASTARD?
OR JUST GREEDY?
WELL, IF YOU'RE IN THE MOOD FOR A MIDNIGHT FEAST, COME AND FUCKING TUCK IN.
THESE ARE YOURS. NOT HIS-- YOURS!
PHILIP MENENDEZ. 1941 TO 2004. JULIA ORTEGA. 1963 TO 2004.
JOSE LUIS PASQUALE--
ENOUGH. AND TOO MUCH.
YOU WILL BE SILENT NOW.

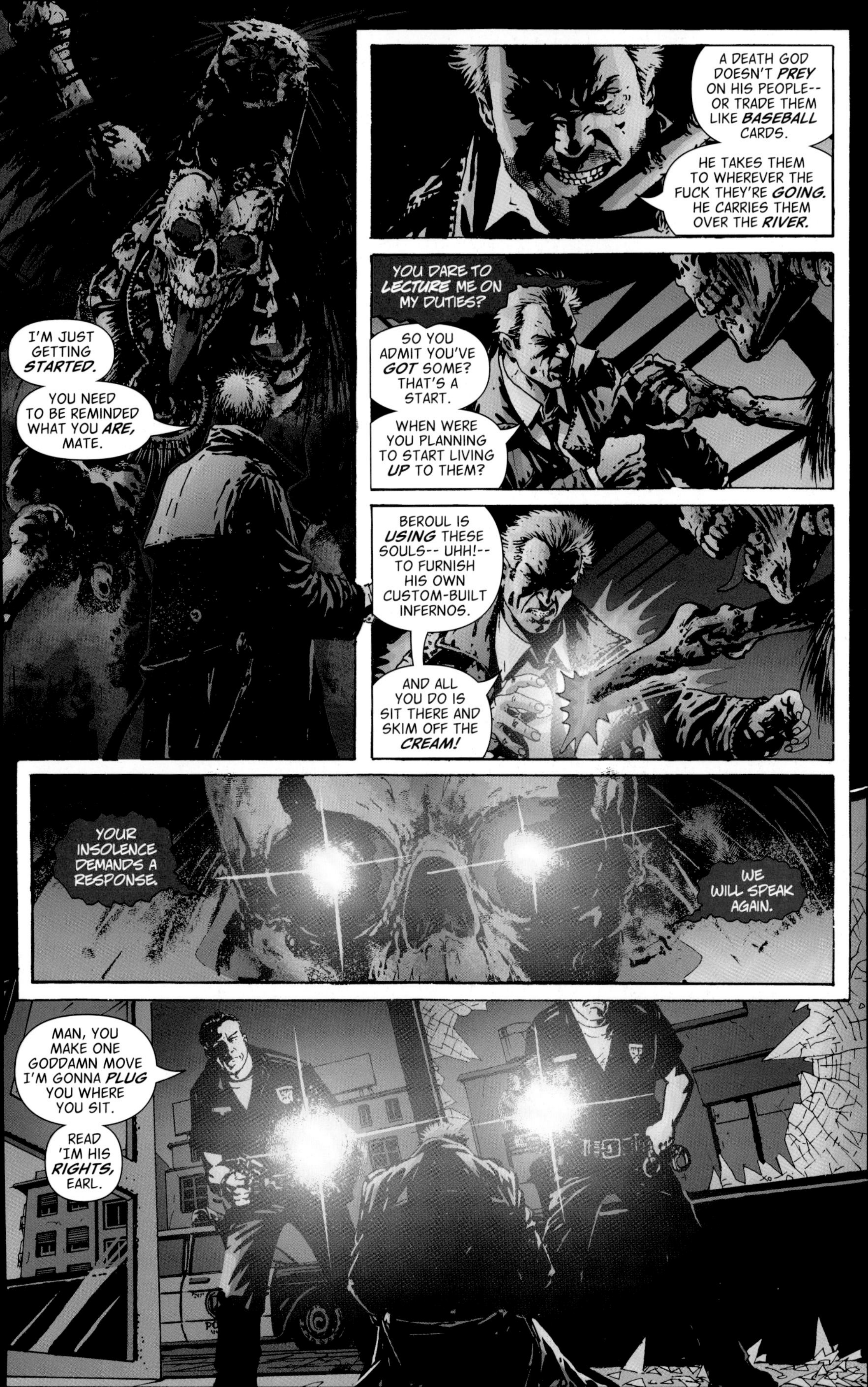

I'M JUST GETTING STARTED.
YOU NEED TO BE REMINDED WHAT YOU ARE, MATE.
A DEATH GOD DOESN'T PREY ON HIS PEOPLE-- OR TRADE THEM LIKE BASEBALL CARDS.
HE TAKES THEM TO WHEREVER THE FUCK THEY'RE GOING. HE CARRIES THEM OVER THE RIVER.
YOU DARE TO LECTURE ME ON MY DUTIES?
SO YOU ADMIT YOU'VE GOT SOME? THAT'S A START.
WHEN WERE YOU PLANNING TO START LIVING UP TO THEM?
BEROUL IS USING THESE SOULS-- UHH!-- TO FURNISH HIS OWN CUSTOM-BUILT INFERNOS.
AND ALL YOU DO IS SIT THERE AND SKIM OFF THE CREAM!
YOUR INSOLENCE DEMANDS A RESPONSE.
WE WILL SPEAK AGAIN.
MAN, YOU MAKE ONE GODDAMN MOVE I'M GONNA PLUG YOU WHERE YOU SIT.
READ 'IM HIS RIGHTS, EARL.

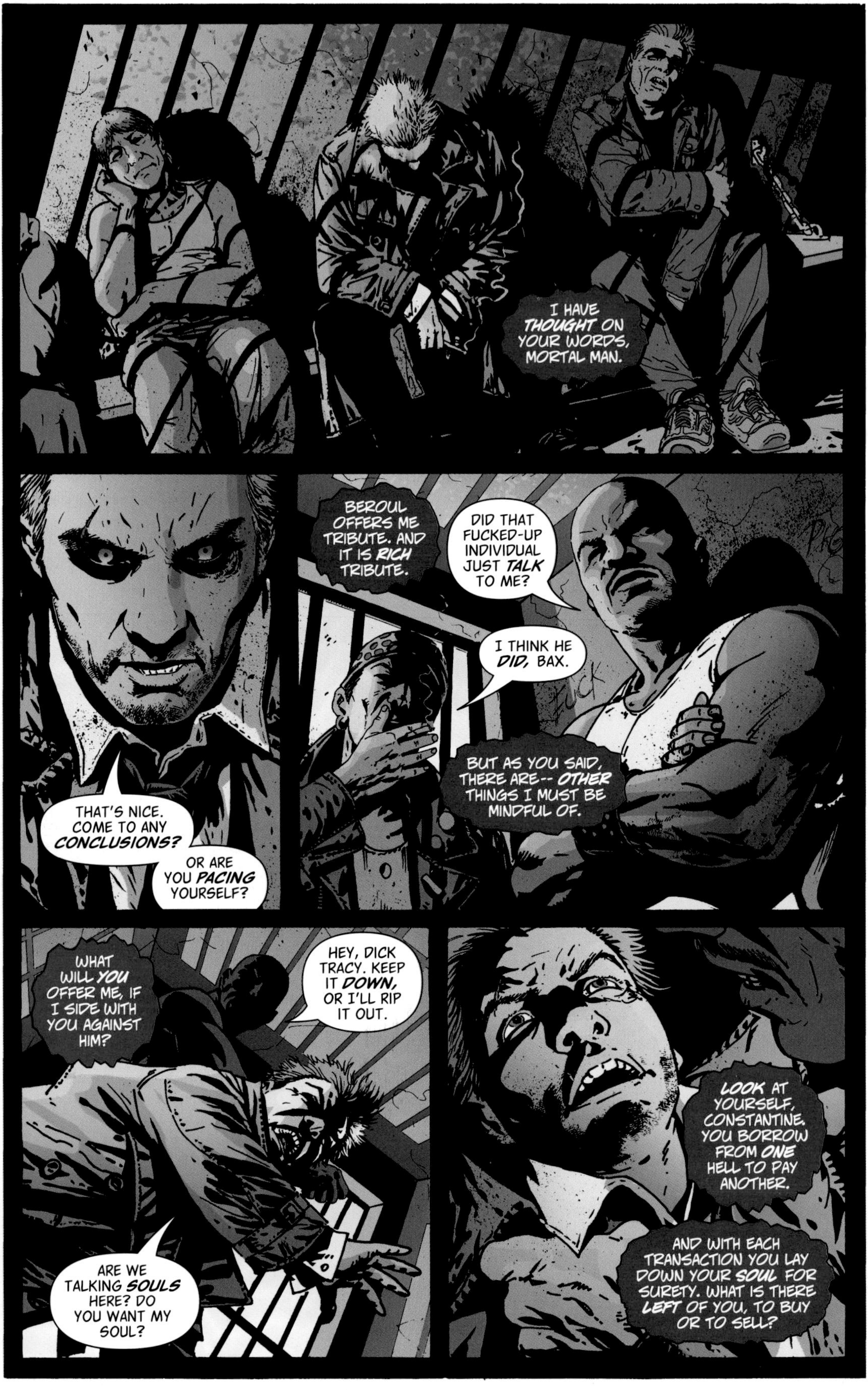
I HAVE THOUGHT ON YOUR WORDS, MORTAL MAN.
THAT'S NICE. COME TO ANY CONCLUSIONS?
OR ARE YOU PACING YOURSELF?
BEROUL OFFERS ME TRIBUTE. AND IT IS RICH TRIBUTE.
DID THAT FUCKED-UP INDIVIDUAL JUST TALK TO ME?
I THINK HE DID, BAX.
BUT AS YOU SAID, THERE ARE-- OTHER THINGS I MUST BE MINDFUL OF.
WHAT WILL YOU OFFER ME, IF I SIDE WITH YOU AGAINST HIM?
HEY, DICK TRACY. KEEP IT DOWN, OR I'LL RIP IT OUT.
ARE WE TALKING SOULS HERE? DO YOU WANT MY SOUL?
LOOK AT YOURSELF, CONSTANTINE. YOU BORROW FROM ONE HELL TO PAY ANOTHER.
AND WITH EACH TRANSACTION YOU LAY DOWN YOUR SOUL FOR SURETY. WHAT IS THERE LEFT OF YOU, TO BUY OR TO SELL?

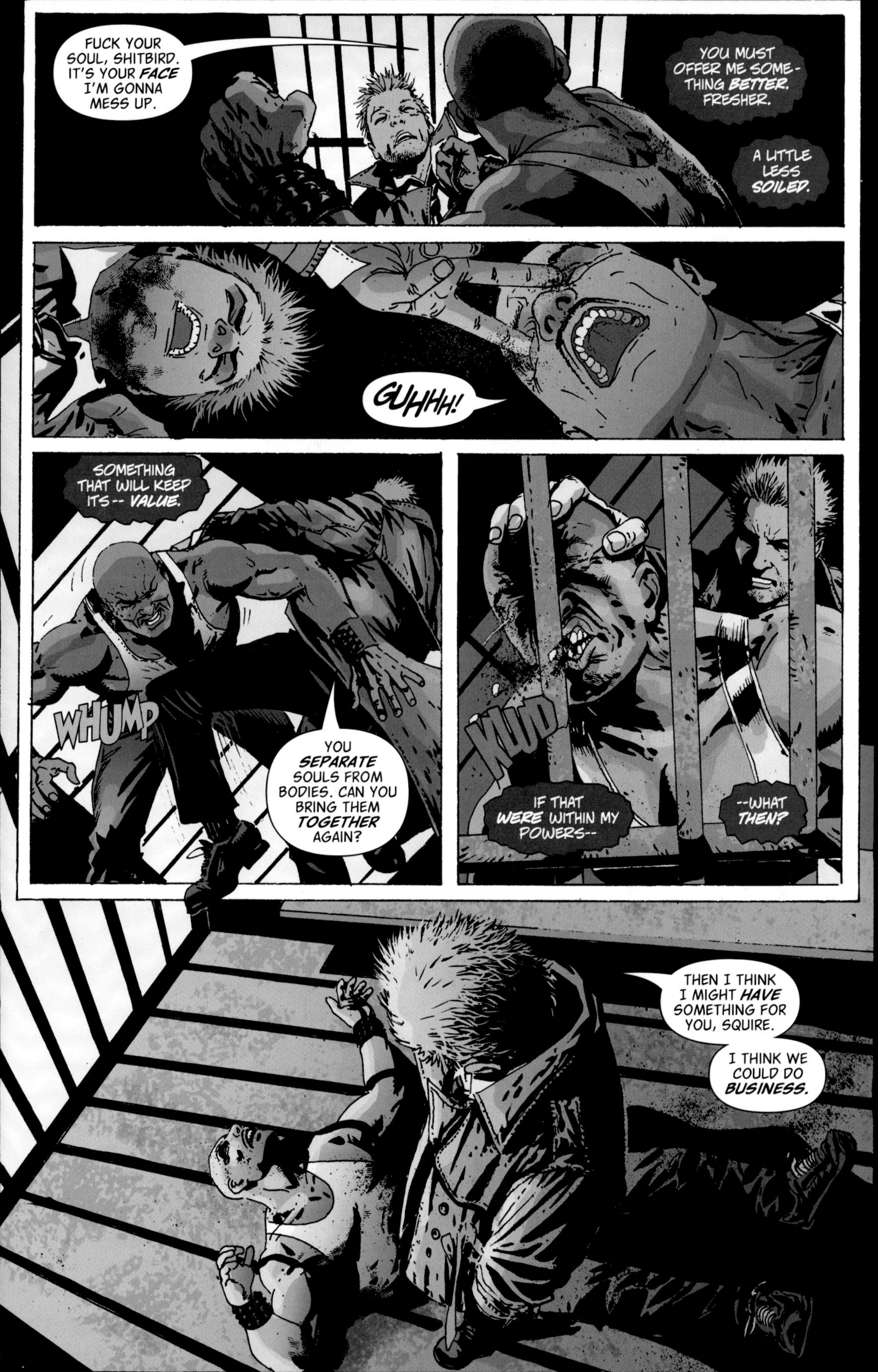
FUCK YOUR SOUL, SHITBIRD. IT'S YOUR *FACE* I'M GONNA MESS UP.
YOU MUST OFFER ME SOME-THING *BETTER*. FRESHER.
A LITTLE LESS *SOILED*.
GUHHH!
SOMETHING THAT WILL KEEP IT'S-- *VALUE*.
WHUMP
YOU *SEPARATE* SOULS FROM BODIES. CAN YOU BRING THEM *TOGETHER* AGAIN?
KUD
IF THAT *WERE* WITHIN MY POWERS--
--WHAT *THEN?*
THEN I THINK I MIGHT *HAVE* SOMETHING FOR YOU, SQUIRE.
I THINK WE COULD DO *BUSINESS*.

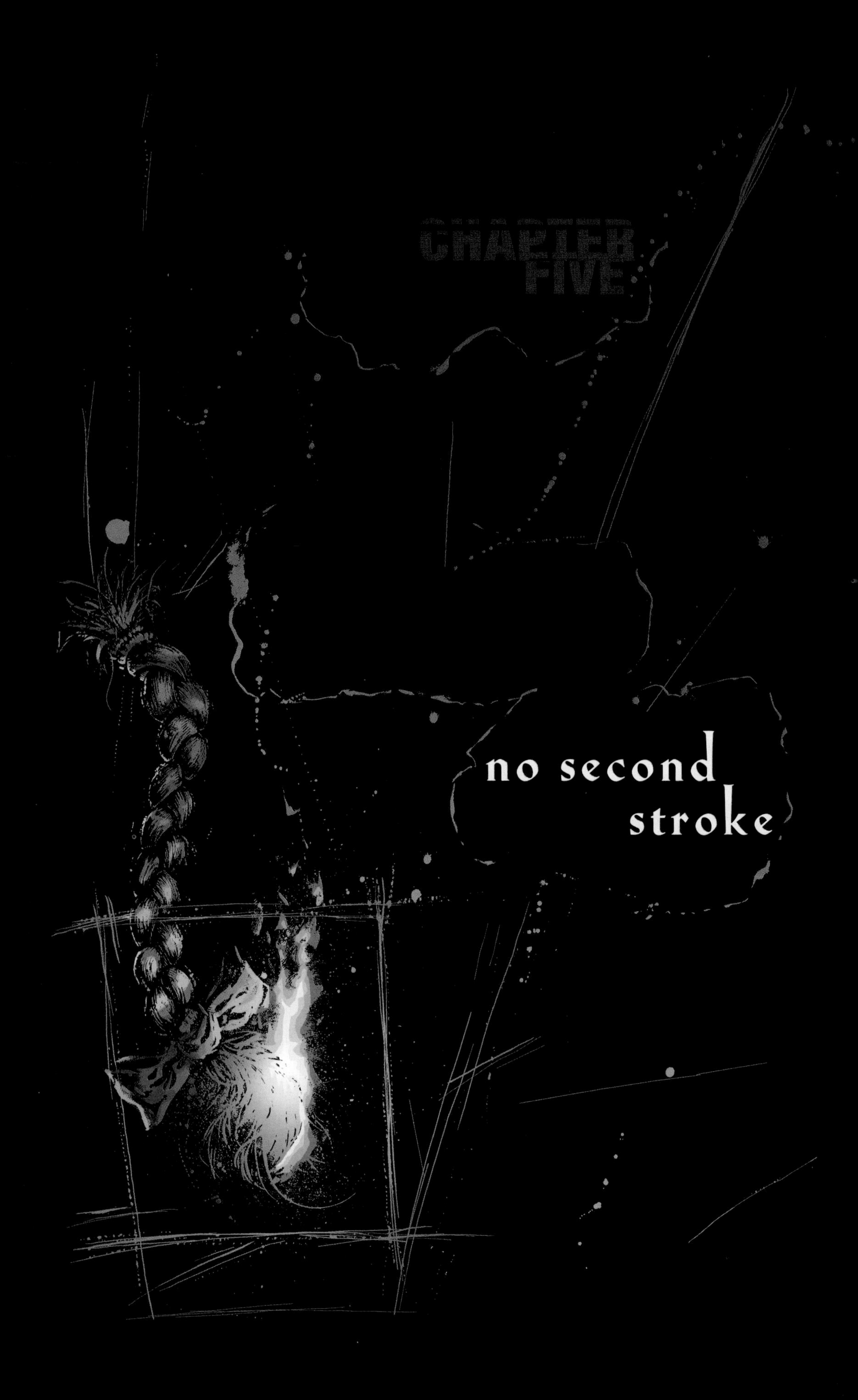
CHAPTER FIVE
no second stroke

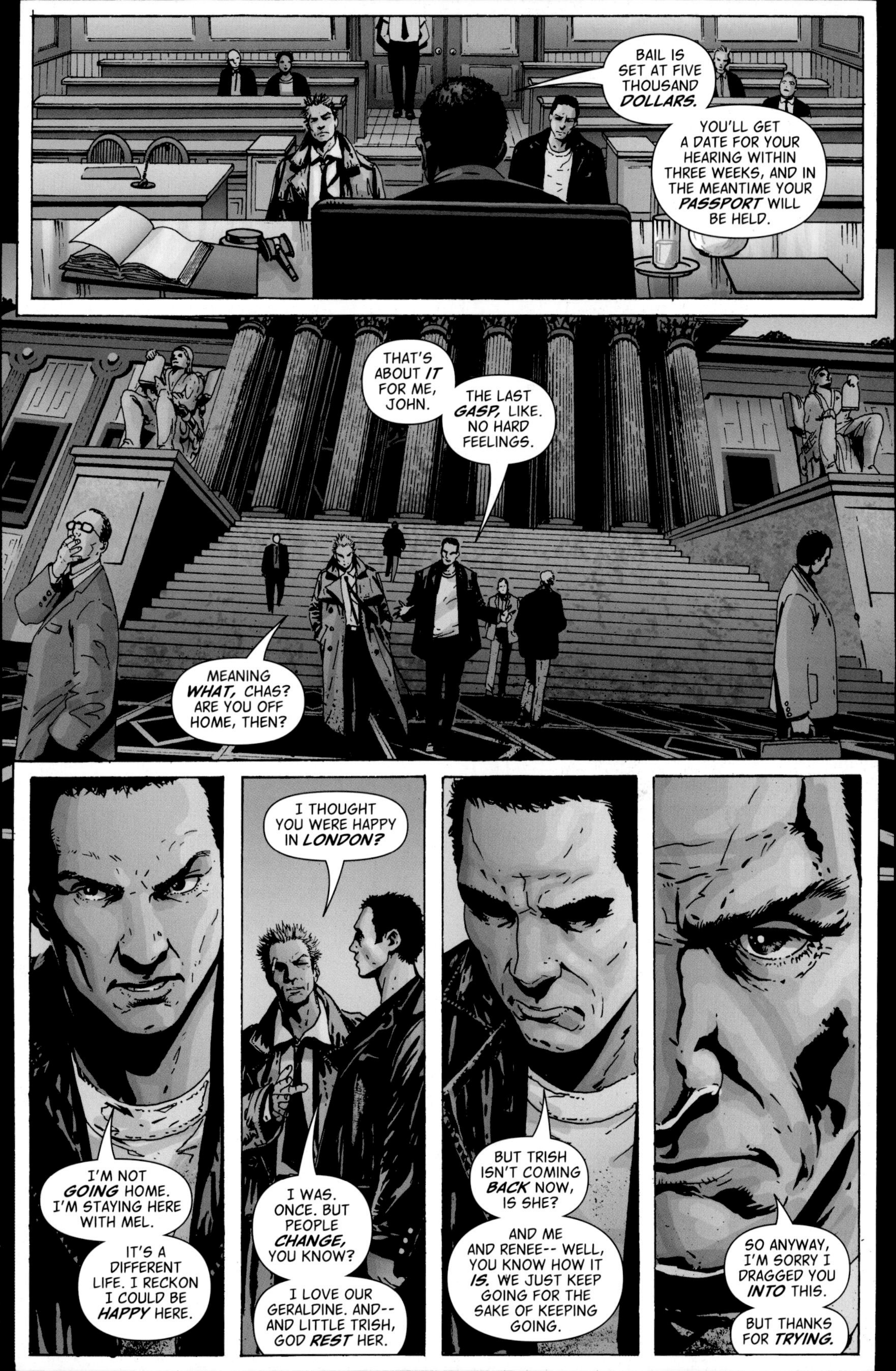
BAIL IS SET AT FIVE THOUSAND DOLLARS.
YOU'LL GET A DATE FOR YOUR HEARING WITHIN THREE WEEKS, AND IN THE MEANTIME YOUR PASSPORT WILL BE HELD.
THAT'S ABOUT IT FOR ME, JOHN.
THE LAST GASP, LIKE. NO HARD FEELINGS.
MEANING WHAT, CHAS? ARE YOU OFF HOME, THEN?
I'M NOT GOING HOME. I'M STAYING HERE WITH MEL.
IT'S A DIFFERENT LIFE. I RECKON I COULD BE HAPPY HERE.
I THOUGHT YOU WERE HAPPY IN LONDON?
I WAS. ONCE. BUT PEOPLE CHANGE, YOU KNOW?
I LOVE OUR GERALDINE. AND-- AND LITTLE TRISH, GOD REST HER.
BUT TRISH ISN'T COMING BACK NOW, IS SHE?
AND ME AND RENEE-- WELL, YOU KNOW HOW IT IS. WE JUST KEEP GOING FOR THE SAKE OF KEEPING GOING.
SO ANYWAY, I'M SORRY I DRAGGED YOU INTO THIS.
BUT THANKS FOR TRYING.

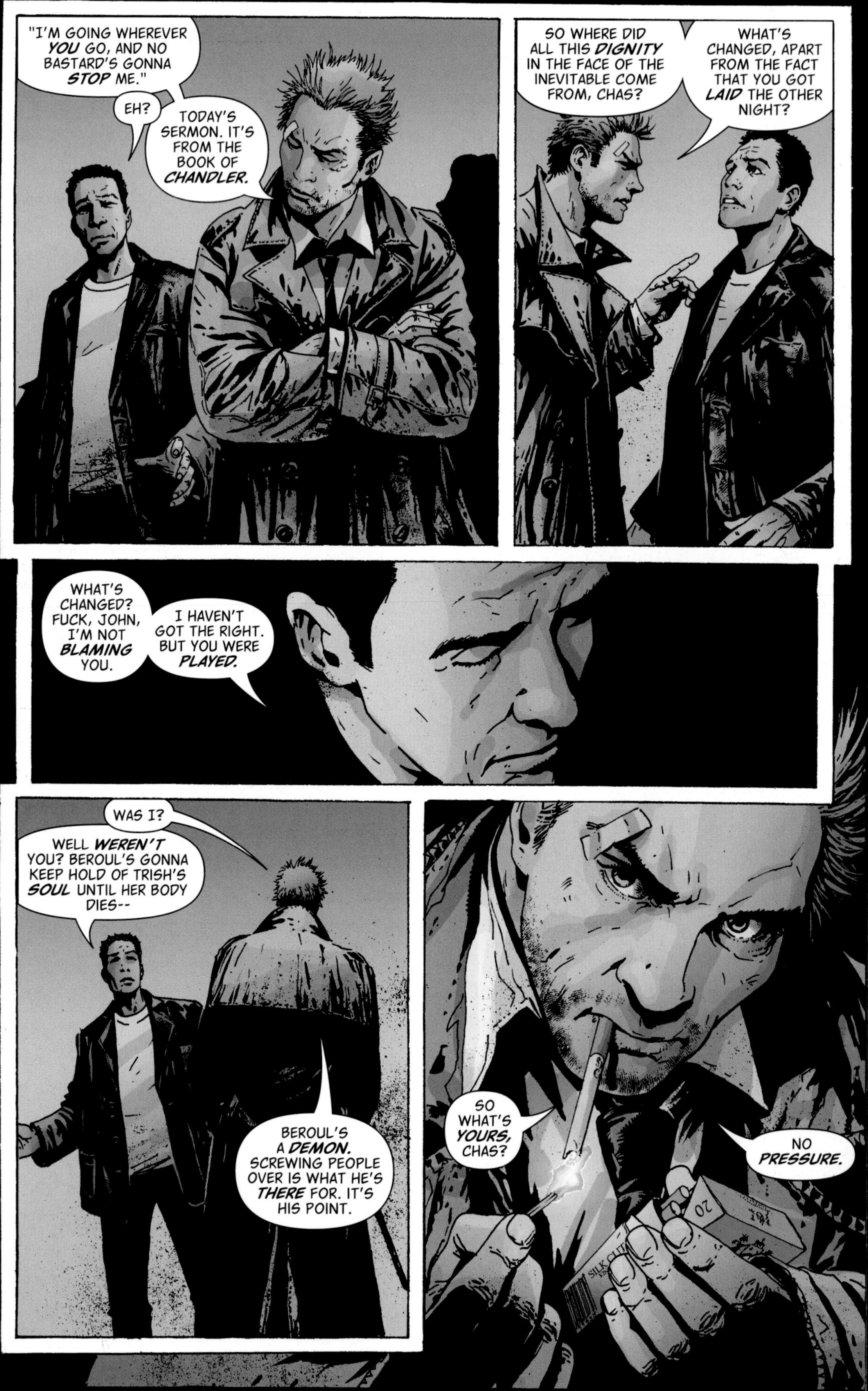
"I'M GOING WHEREVER YOU GO, AND NO BASTARD'S GONNA STOP ME."
EH?
TODAY'S SERMON. IT'S FROM THE BOOK OF CHANDLER.
SO WHERE DID ALL THIS DIGNITY IN THE FACE OF THE INEVITABLE COME FROM, CHAS?
WHAT'S CHANGED, APART FROM THE FACT THAT YOU GOT LAID THE OTHER NIGHT?
WHAT'S CHANGED? FUCK, JOHN, I'M NOT BLAMING YOU.
I HAVEN'T GOT THE RIGHT. BUT YOU WERE PLAYED.
WAS I?
WELL WEREN'T YOU? BEROUL'S GONNA KEEP HOLD OF TRISH'S SOUL UNTIL HER BODY DIES--
BEROUL'S A DEMON. SCREWING PEOPLE OVER IS WHAT HE'S THERE FOR. IT'S HIS POINT.
SO WHAT'S YOURS, CHAS?
NO PRESSURE.

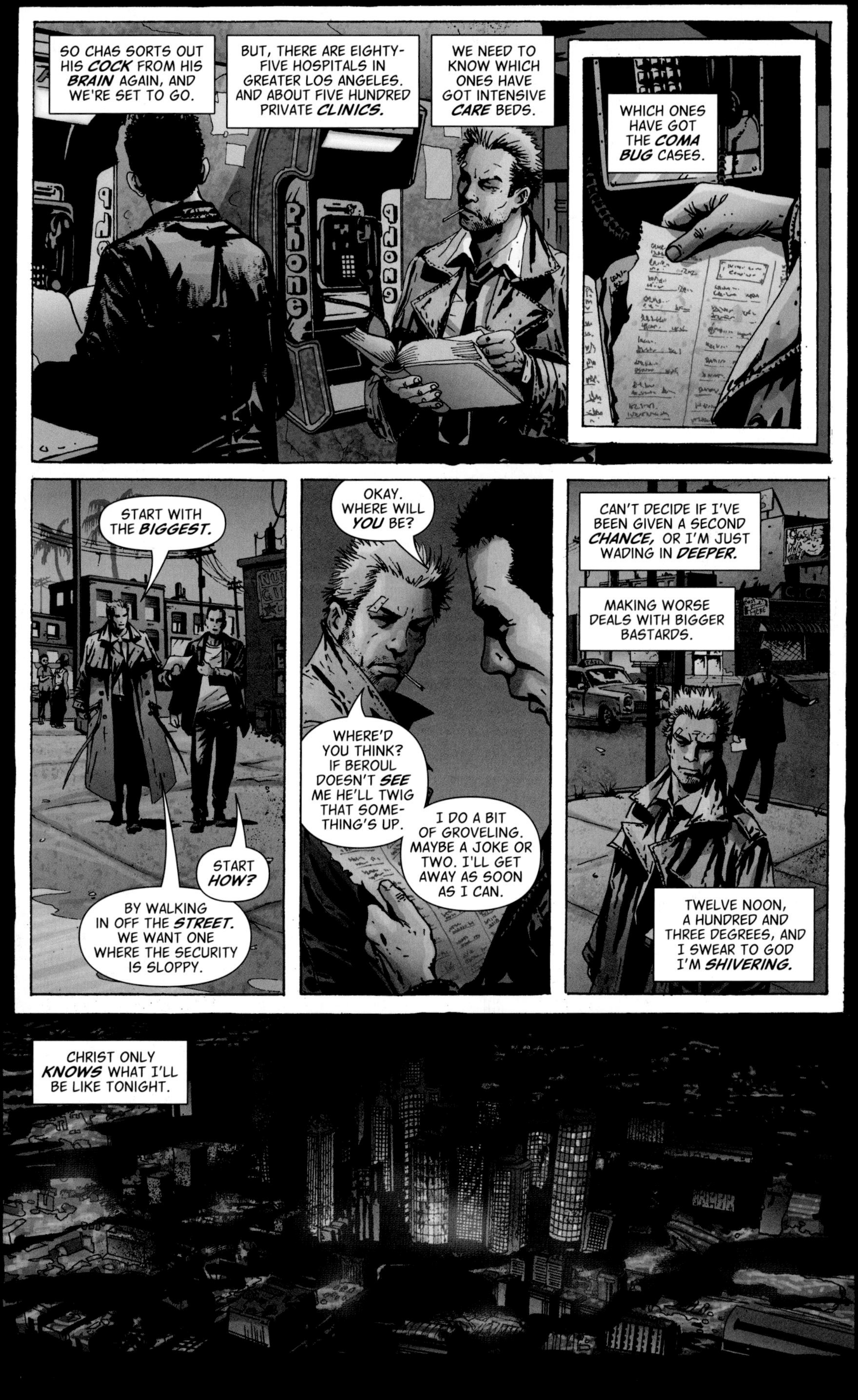
SO CHAS SORTS OUT HIS *COCK* FROM HIS *BRAIN* AGAIN, AND WE'RE SET TO GO.
BUT, THERE ARE EIGHTY-FIVE HOSPITALS IN GREATER LOS ANGELES. AND ABOUT FIVE HUNDRED PRIVATE *CLINICS.*
WE NEED TO KNOW WHICH ONES HAVE GOT INTENSIVE *CARE* BEDS.
WHICH ONES HAVE GOT THE *COMA BUG* CASES.
START WITH THE *BIGGEST.*
START *HOW?*
BY WALKING IN OFF THE *STREET.* WE WANT ONE WHERE THE SECURITY IS SLOPPY.
OKAY. WHERE WILL *YOU* BE?
WHERE'D YOU THINK? IF BEROUL DOESN'T *SEE* ME HE'LL TWIG THAT SOMETHING'S UP.
I DO A BIT OF GROVELING. MAYBE A JOKE OR TWO. I'LL GET AWAY AS SOON AS I CAN.
CAN'T DECIDE IF I'VE BEEN GIVEN A SECOND *CHANCE,* OR I'M JUST WADING IN *DEEPER.*
MAKING WORSE DEALS WITH BIGGER BASTARDS.
TWELVE NOON, A HUNDRED AND THREE DEGREES, AND I SWEAR TO GOD I'M *SHIVERING.*
CHRIST ONLY *KNOWS* WHAT I'LL BE LIKE TONIGHT.

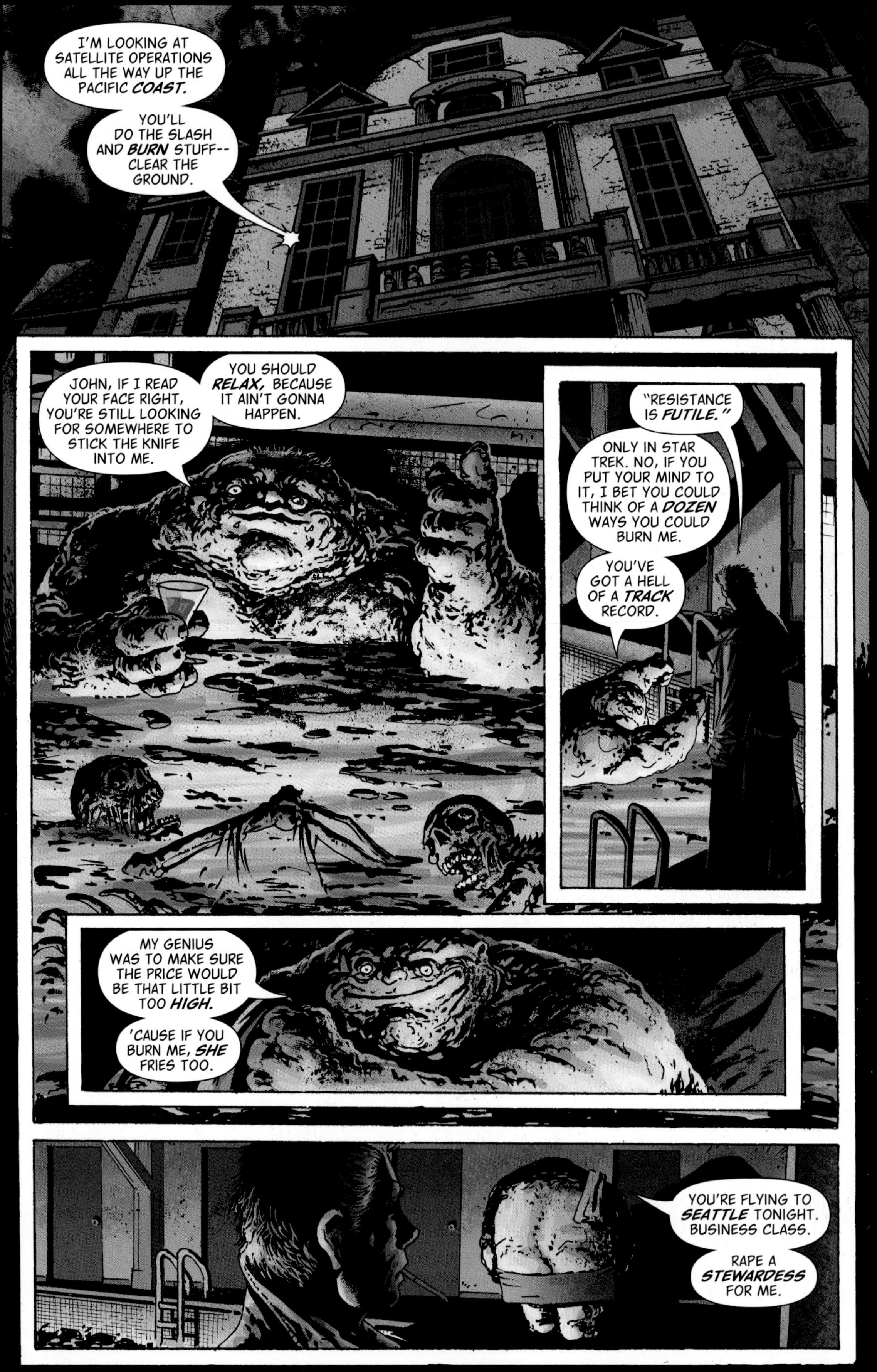
I'M LOOKING AT SATELLITE OPERATIONS ALL THE WAY UP THE PACIFIC COAST.
YOU'LL DO THE SLASH AND BURN STUFF-- CLEAR THE GROUND.
JOHN, IF I READ YOUR FACE RIGHT, YOU'RE STILL LOOKING FOR SOMEWHERE TO STICK THE KNIFE INTO ME.
YOU SHOULD RELAX, BECAUSE IT AIN'T GONNA HAPPEN.
"RESISTANCE IS FUTILE."
ONLY IN STAR TREK. NO, IF YOU PUT YOUR MIND TO IT, I BET YOU COULD THINK OF A DOZEN WAYS YOU COULD BURN ME.
YOU'VE GOT A HELL OF A TRACK RECORD.
MY GENIUS WAS TO MAKE SURE THE PRICE WOULD BE THAT LITTLE BIT TOO HIGH.
'CAUSE IF YOU BURN ME, SHE FRIES TOO.
YOU'RE FLYING TO SEATTLE TONIGHT. BUSINESS CLASS.
RAPE A STEWARDESS FOR ME.

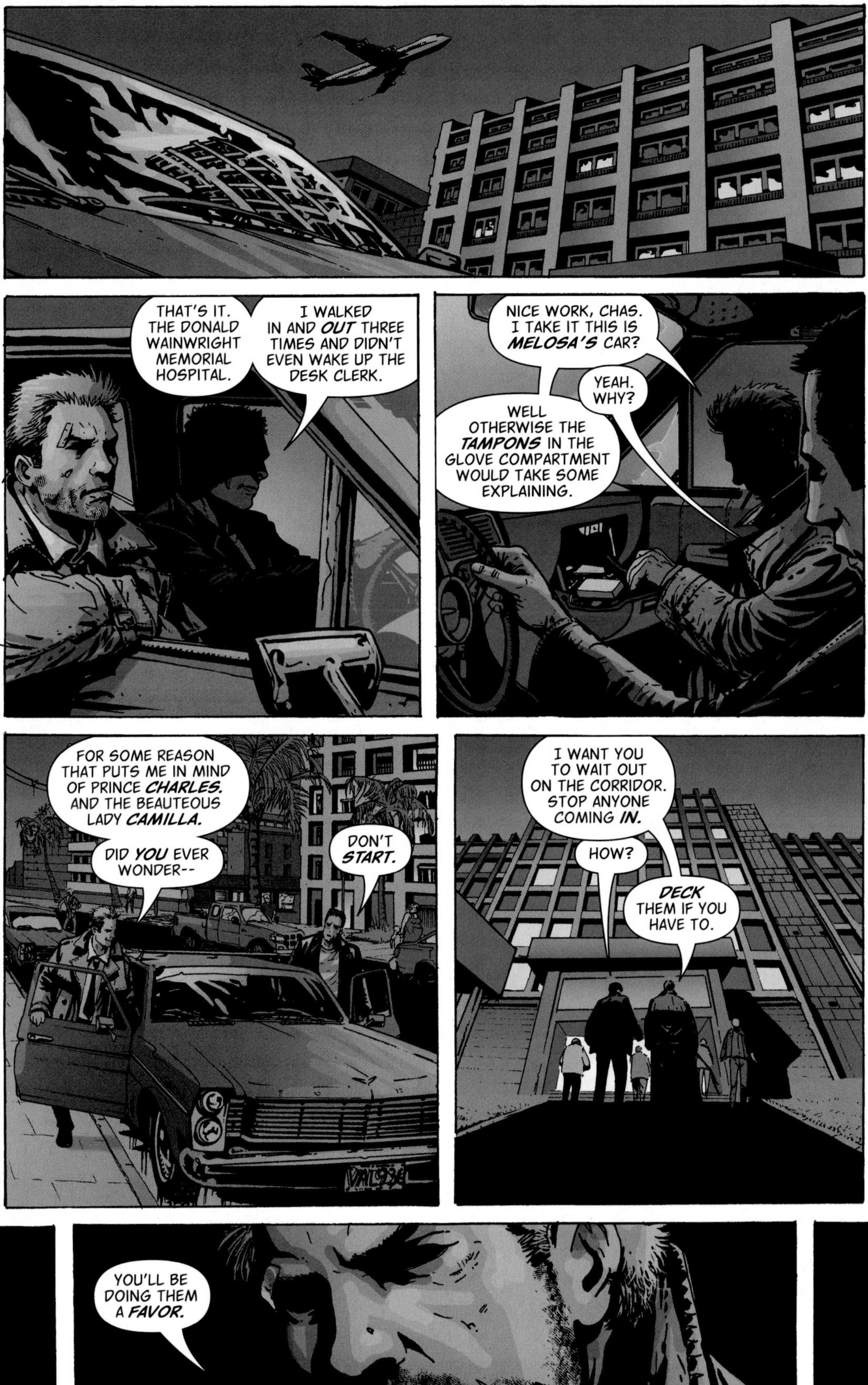
THAT'S IT. THE DONALD WAINWRIGHT MEMORIAL HOSPITAL.
I WALKED IN AND OUT THREE TIMES AND DIDN'T EVEN WAKE UP THE DESK CLERK.
NICE WORK, CHAS. I TAKE IT THIS IS MELOSA'S CAR?
YEAH. WHY?
WELL OTHERWISE THE TAMPONS IN THE GLOVE COMPARTMENT WOULD TAKE SOME EXPLAINING.
FOR SOME REASON THAT PUTS ME IN MIND OF PRINCE CHARLES. AND THE BEAUTEOUS LADY CAMILLA.
DID YOU EVER WONDER--
DON'T START.
I WANT YOU TO WAIT OUT ON THE CORRIDOR. STOP ANYONE COMING IN.
HOW?
DECK THEM IF YOU HAVE TO.
YOU'LL BE DOING THEM A FAVOR.

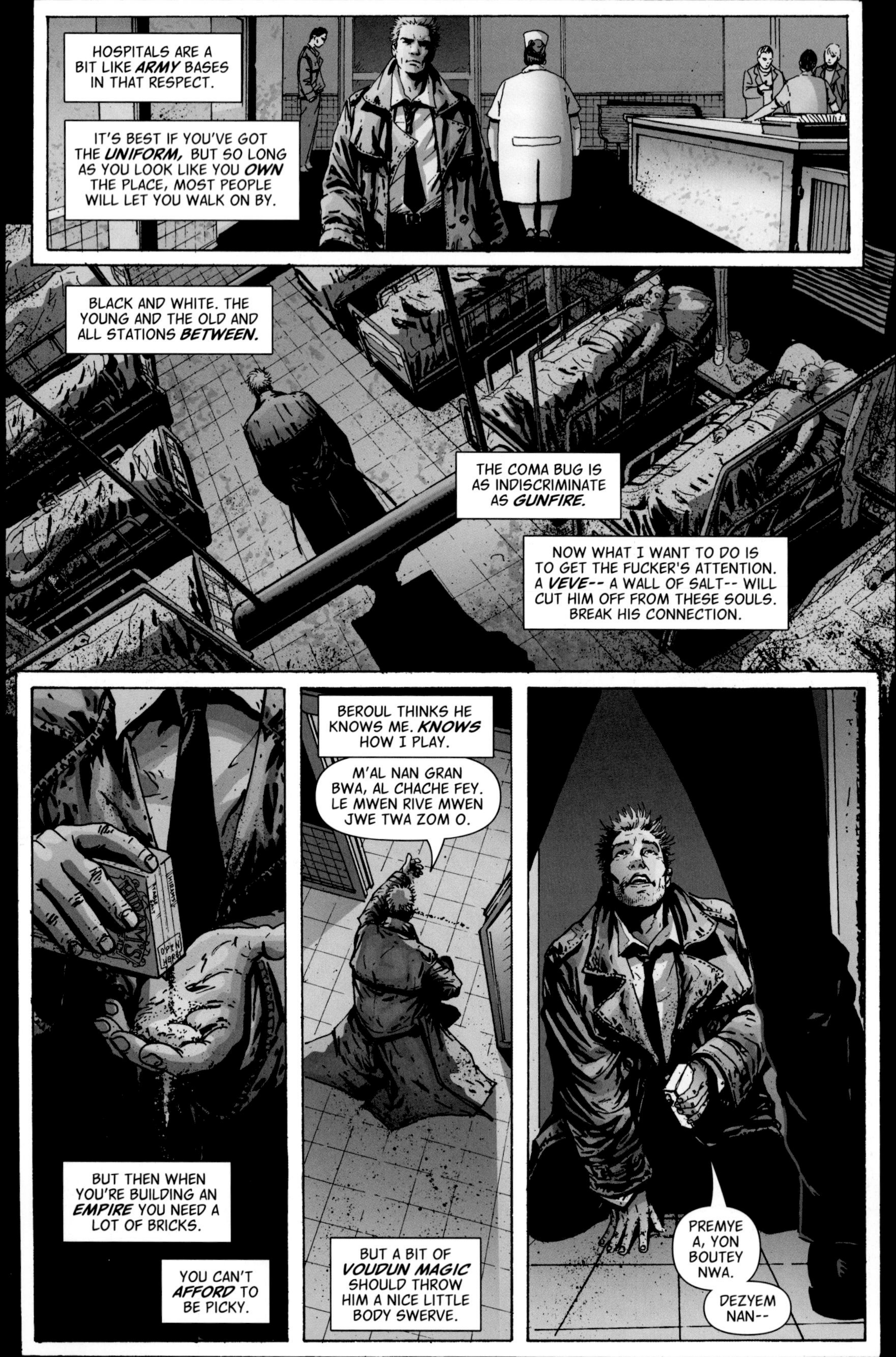
HOSPITALS ARE A BIT LIKE ARMY BASES IN THAT RESPECT.
IT'S BEST IF YOU'VE GOT THE UNIFORM, BUT SO LONG AS YOU LOOK LIKE YOU OWN THE PLACE, MOST PEOPLE WILL LET YOU WALK ON BY.
BLACK AND WHITE. THE YOUNG AND THE OLD AND ALL STATIONS BETWEEN.
THE COMA BUG IS AS INDISCRIMINATE AS GUNFIRE.
NOW WHAT I WANT TO DO IS TO GET THE FUCKER'S ATTENTION. A VEVE-- A WALL OF SALT-- WILL CUT HIM OFF FROM THESE SOULS. BREAK HIS CONNECTION.
BUT THEN WHEN YOU'RE BUILDING AN EMPIRE YOU NEED A LOT OF BRICKS.
YOU CAN'T AFFORD TO BE PICKY.
BEROUL THINKS HE KNOWS ME. KNOWS HOW I PLAY.
M'AL NAN GRAN BWA, AL CHACHE FEY. LE MWEN RIVE MWEN JWE TWA ZOM O.
BUT A BIT OF VOUDUN MAGIC SHOULD THROW HIM A NICE LITTLE BODY SWERVE.
PREMYE A, YON BOUTEY NWA.
DEZYEM NAN--

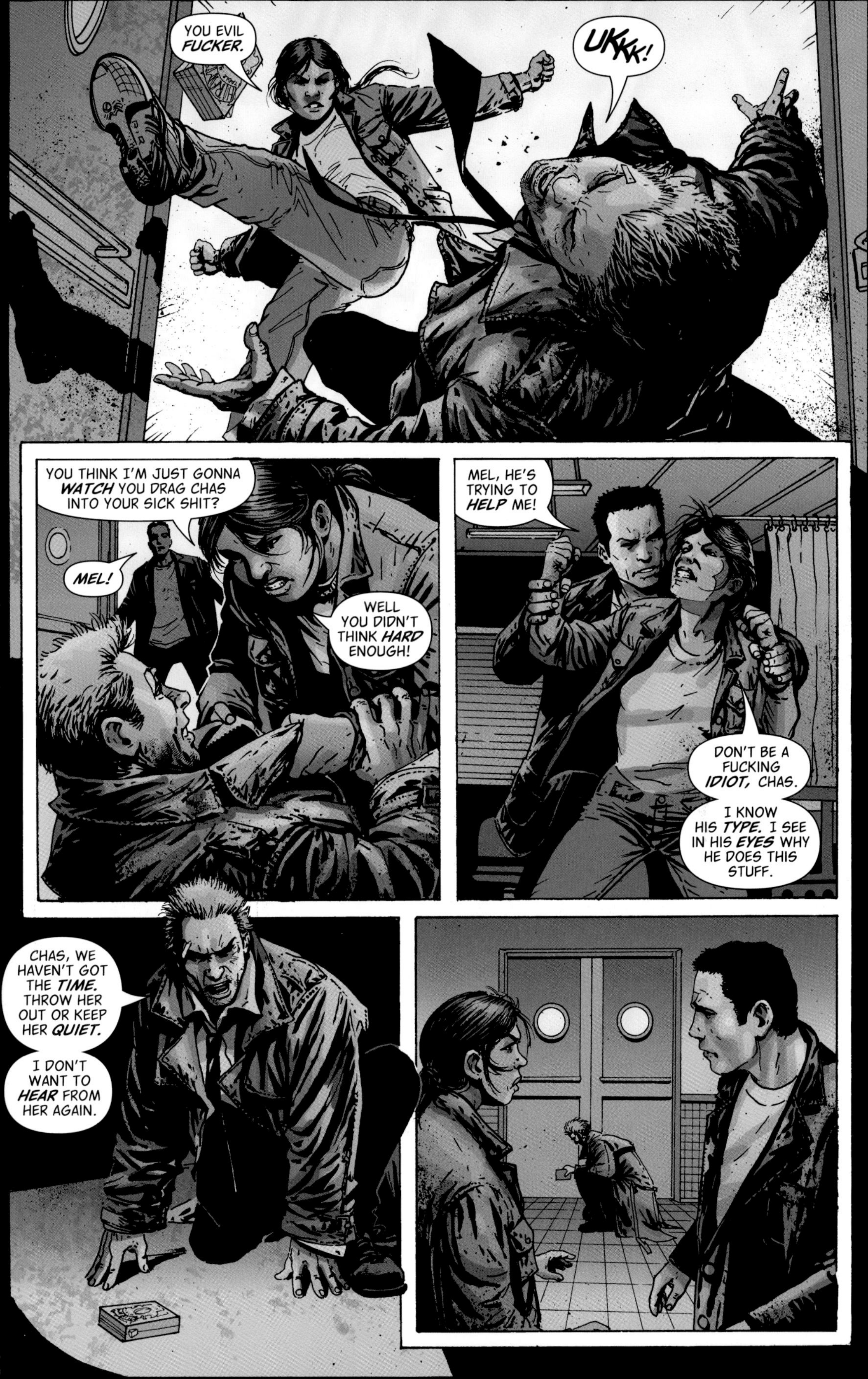
YOU EVIL FUCKER.
UKKK!
YOU THINK I'M JUST GONNA WATCH YOU DRAG CHAS INTO YOUR SICK SHIT?
MEL!
WELL YOU DIDN'T THINK HARD ENOUGH!
MEL, HE'S TRYING TO HELP ME!
DON'T BE A FUCKING IDIOT, CHAS.
I KNOW HIS TYPE. I SEE IN HIS EYES WHY HE DOES THIS STUFF.
CHAS, WE HAVEN'T GOT THE TIME. THROW HER OUT OR KEEP HER QUIET.
I DON'T WANT TO HEAR FROM HER AGAIN.

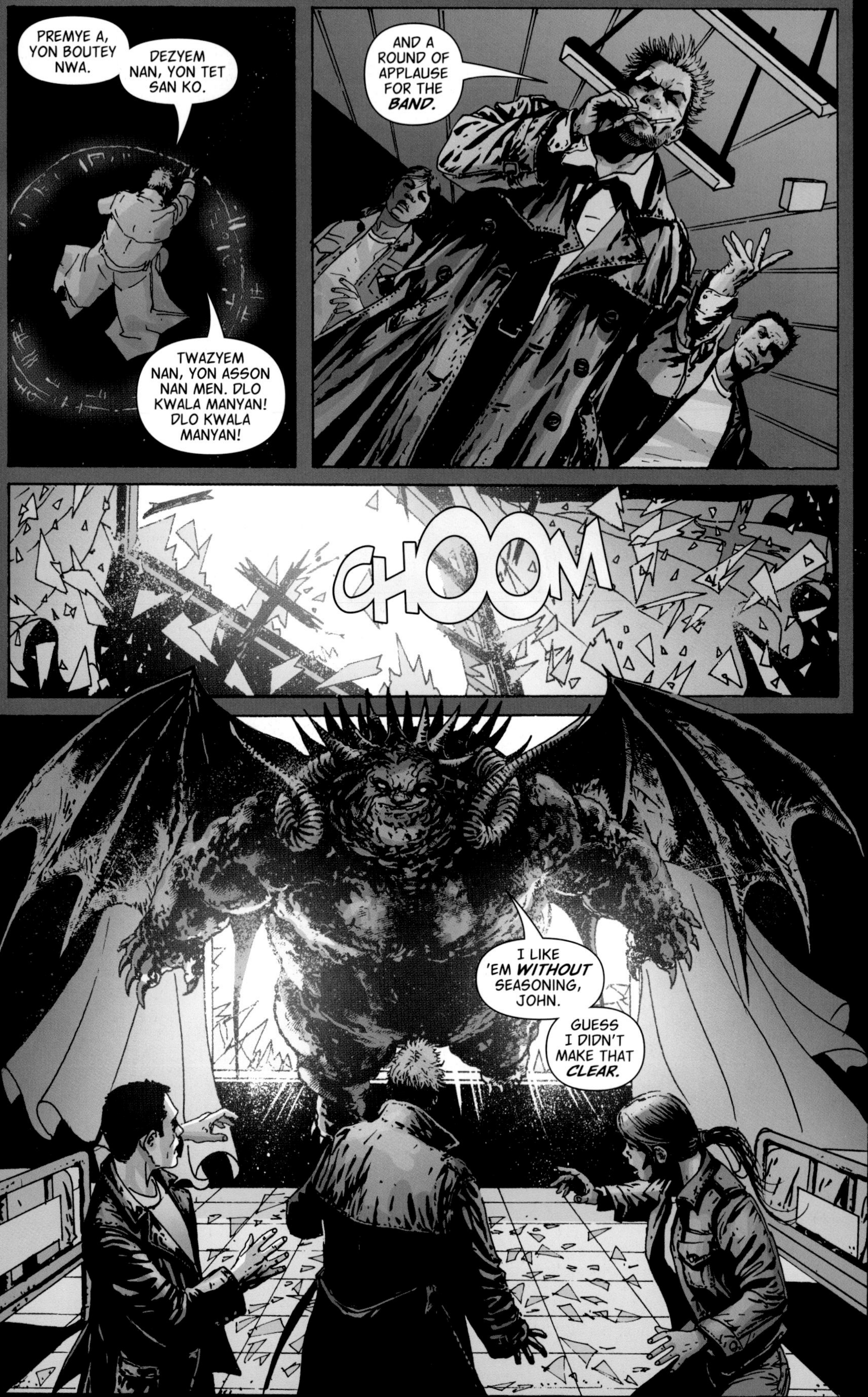
PREMYE A, YON BOUTEY NWA.
DEZYEM NAN, YON TET SAN KO.
TWAZYEM NAN, YON ASSON NAN MEN. DLO KWALA MANYAN! DLO KWALA MANYAN!
AND A ROUND OF APPLAUSE FOR THE *BAND.*
CHOOM
I LIKE 'EM *WITHOUT* SEASONING, JOHN.
GUESS I DIDN'T MAKE THAT *CLEAR.*

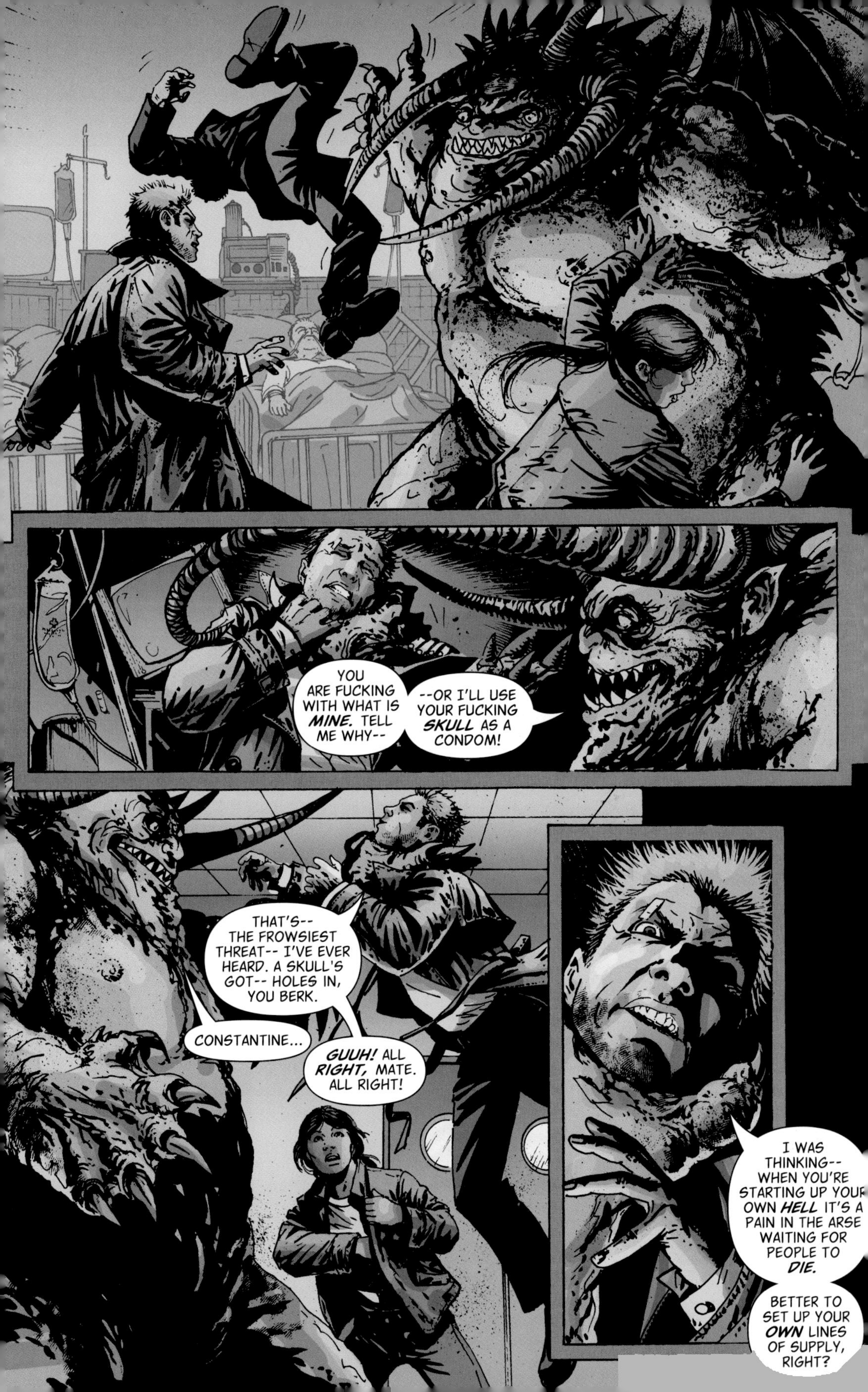
YOU ARE FUCKING WITH WHAT IS MINE. TELL ME WHY--
--OR I'LL USE YOUR FUCKING SKULL AS A CONDOM!
THAT'S-- THE FROWSIEST THREAT-- I'VE EVER HEARD. A SKULL'S GOT-- HOLES IN, YOU BERK.
CONSTANTINE...
GUUH! ALL RIGHT, MATE. ALL RIGHT!
I WAS THINKING-- WHEN YOU'RE STARTING UP YOUR OWN HELL IT'S A PAIN IN THE ARSE WAITING FOR PEOPLE TO DIE.
BETTER TO SET UP YOUR OWN LINES OF SUPPLY, RIGHT?

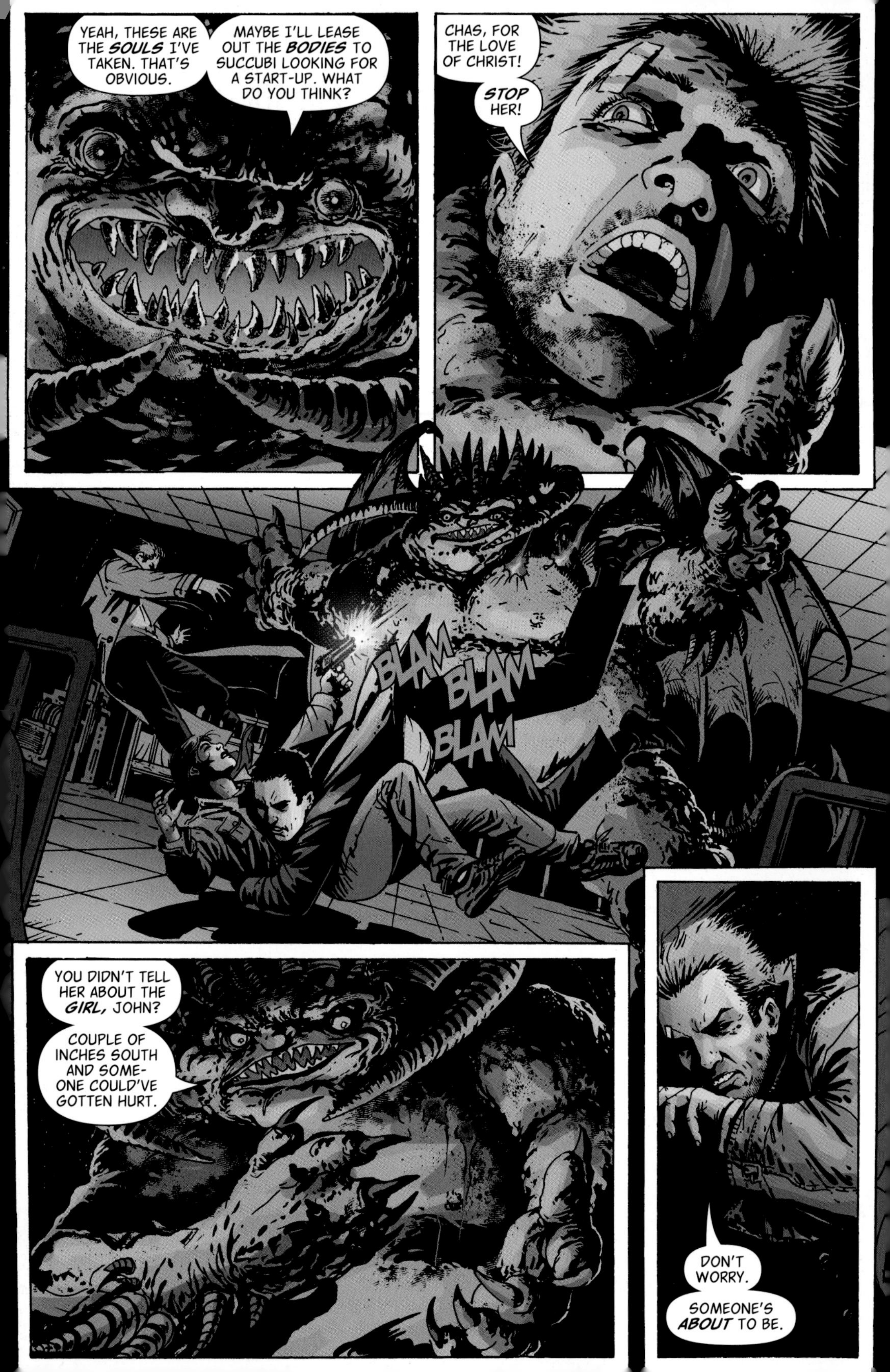
YEAH, THESE ARE THE SOULS I'VE TAKEN. THAT'S OBVIOUS.
MAYBE I'LL LEASE OUT THE BODIES TO SUCCUBI LOOKING FOR A START-UP. WHAT DO YOU THINK?
CHAS, FOR THE LOVE OF CHRIST!
STOP HER!
BLAM
BLAM
BLAM
YOU DIDN'T TELL HER ABOUT THE GIRL, JOHN?
COUPLE OF INCHES SOUTH AND SOME-ONE COULD'VE GOTTEN HURT.
DON'T WORRY.
SOMEONE'S ABOUT TO BE.

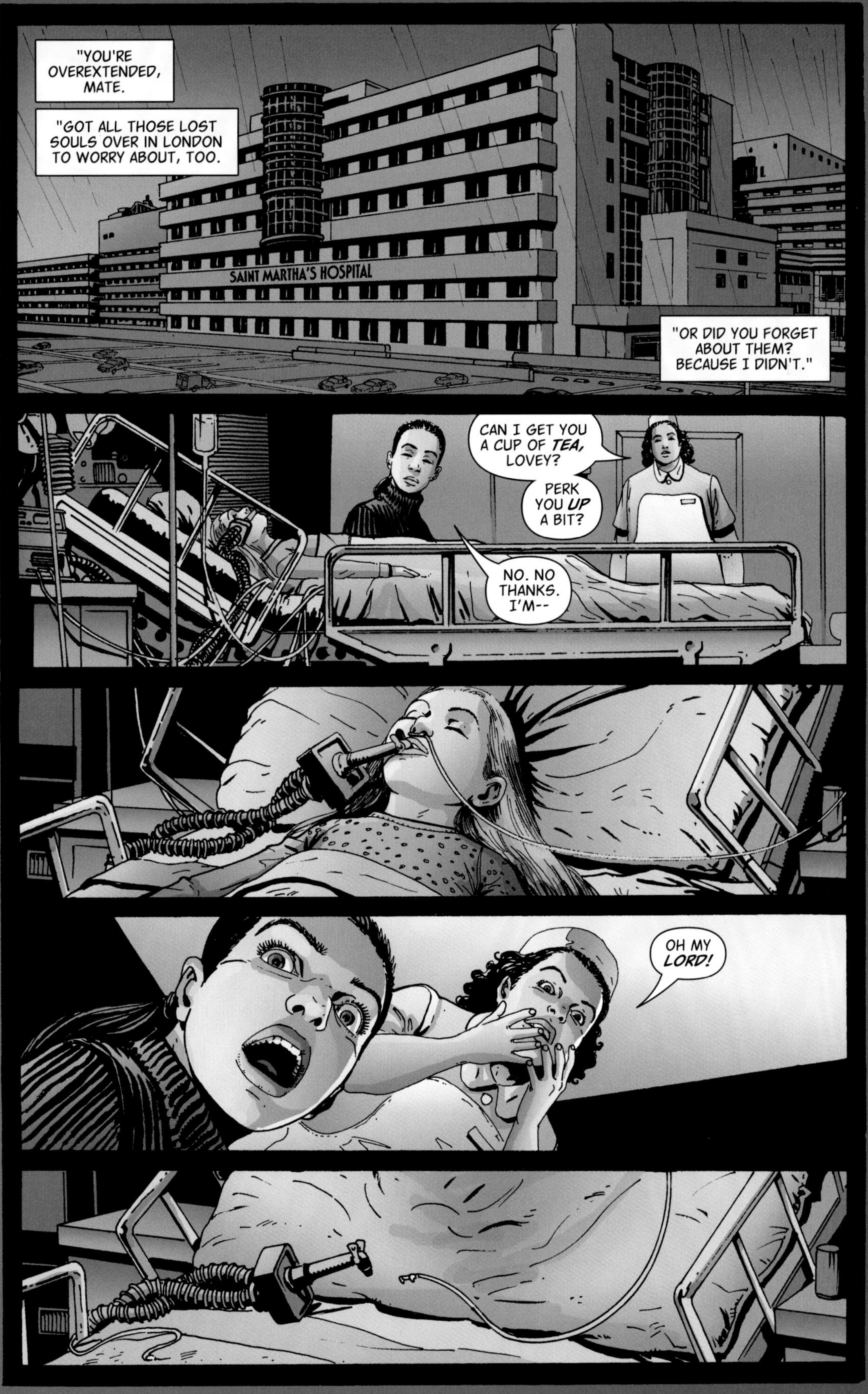
"YOU'RE OVEREXTENDED, MATE.
"GOT ALL THOSE LOST SOULS OVER IN LONDON TO WORRY ABOUT, TOO.
SAINT MARTHA'S HOSPITAL
"OR DID YOU FORGET ABOUT THEM? BECAUSE I DIDN'T."
CAN I GET YOU A CUP OF *TEA,* LOVEY?
PERK YOU *UP* A BIT?
NO. NO THANKS. I'M--
OH MY *LORD!*

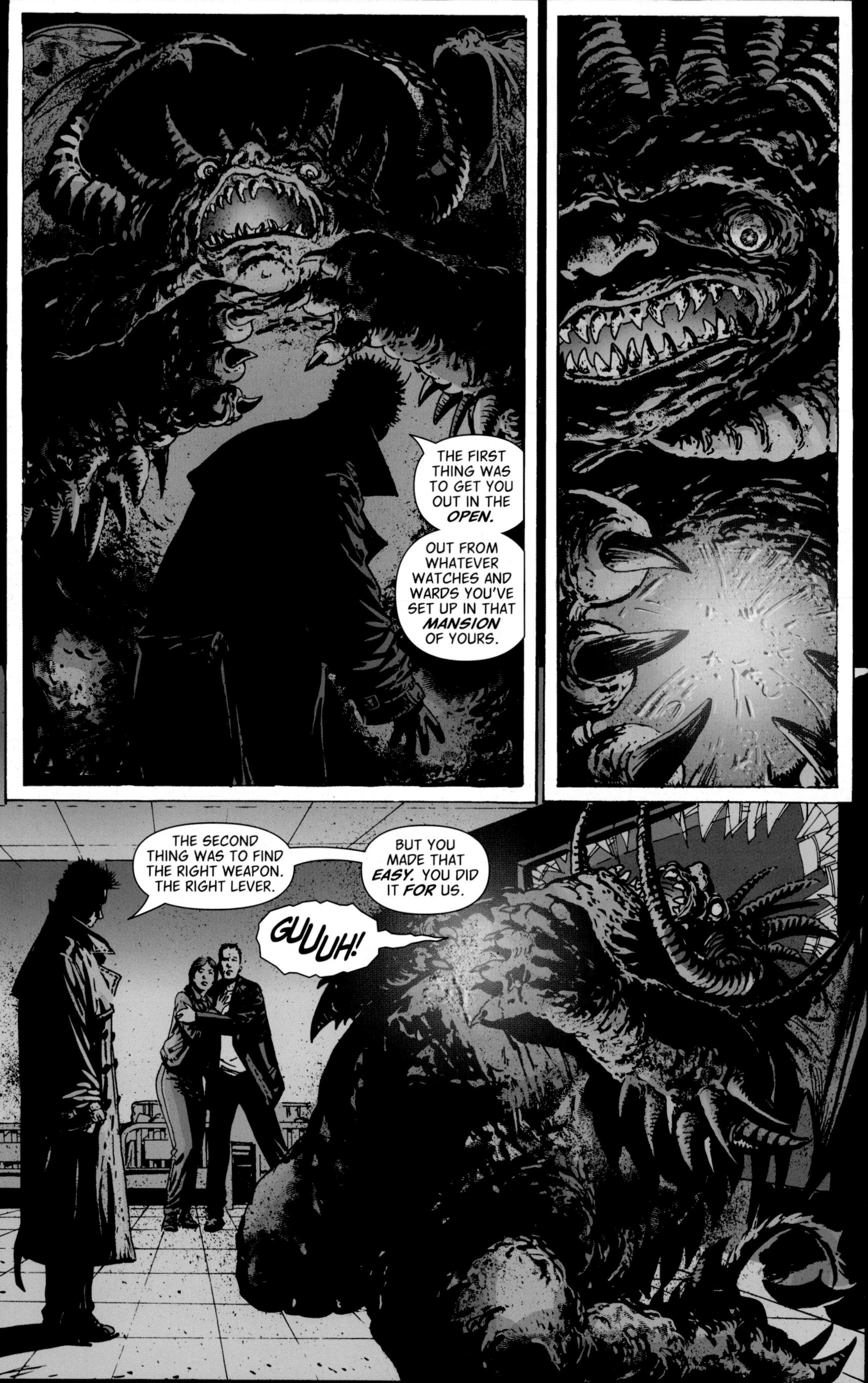
THE FIRST THING WAS TO GET YOU OUT IN THE *OPEN.*
OUT FROM WHATEVER WATCHES AND WARDS YOU'VE SET UP IN THAT *MANSION* OF YOURS.
THE SECOND THING WAS TO FIND THE RIGHT WEAPON. THE RIGHT LEVER.
BUT YOU MADE THAT *EASY.* YOU DID IT *FOR* US.
GUUUH!

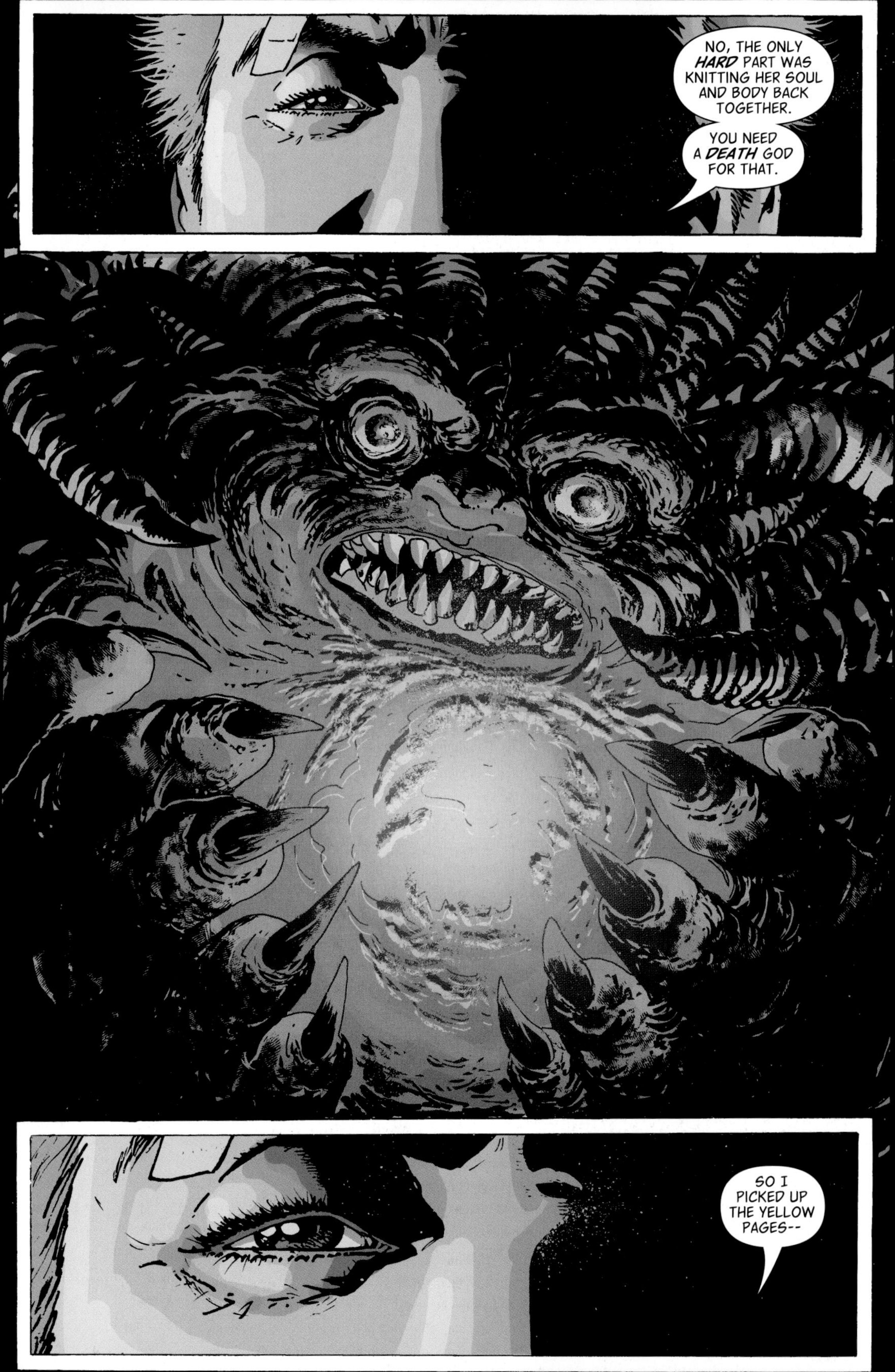
NO, THE ONLY HARD PART WAS KNITTING HER SOUL AND BODY BACK TOGETHER.
YOU NEED A DEATH GOD FOR THAT.
SO I PICKED UP THE YELLOW PAGES--

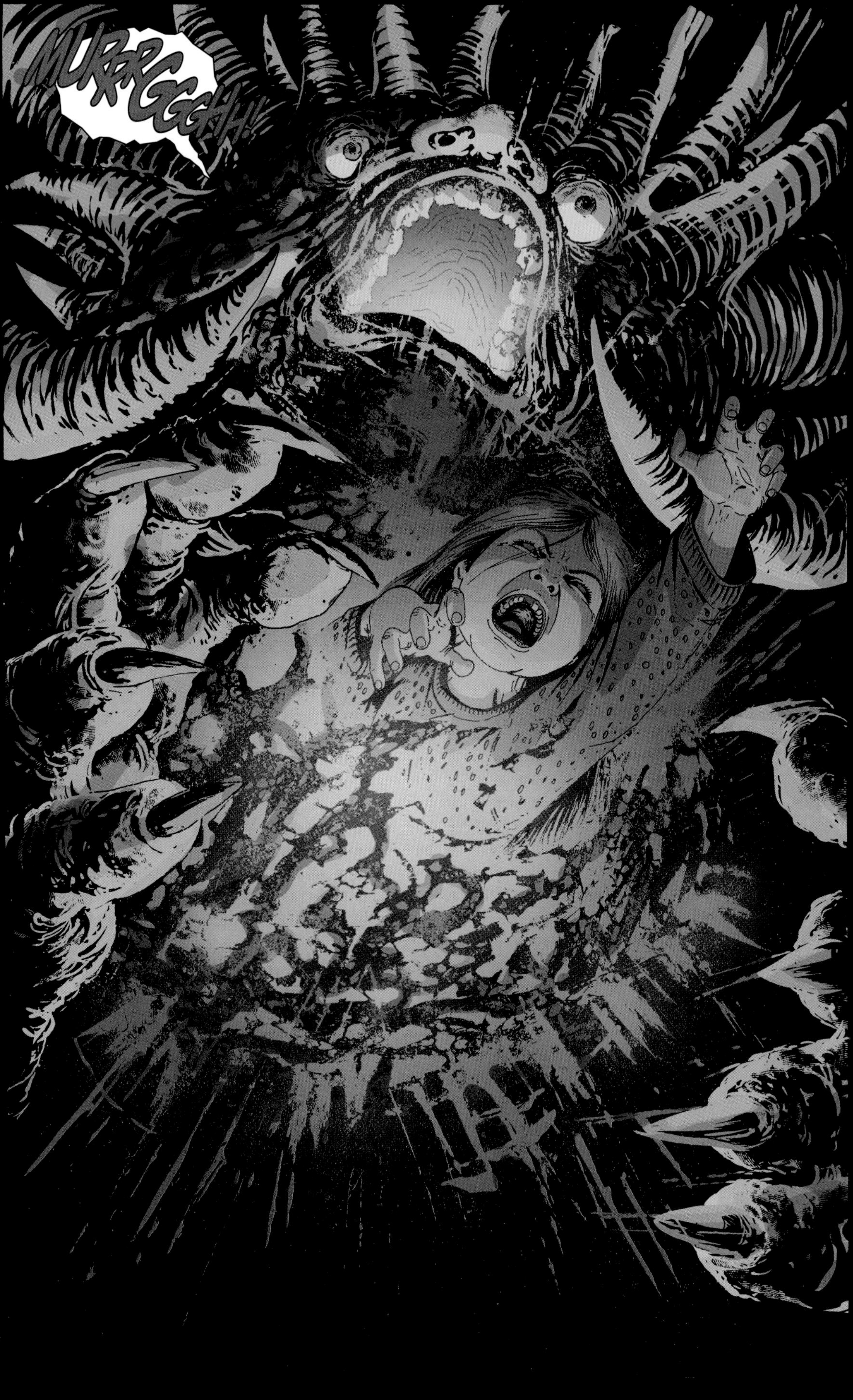
MURRRGGGHH!

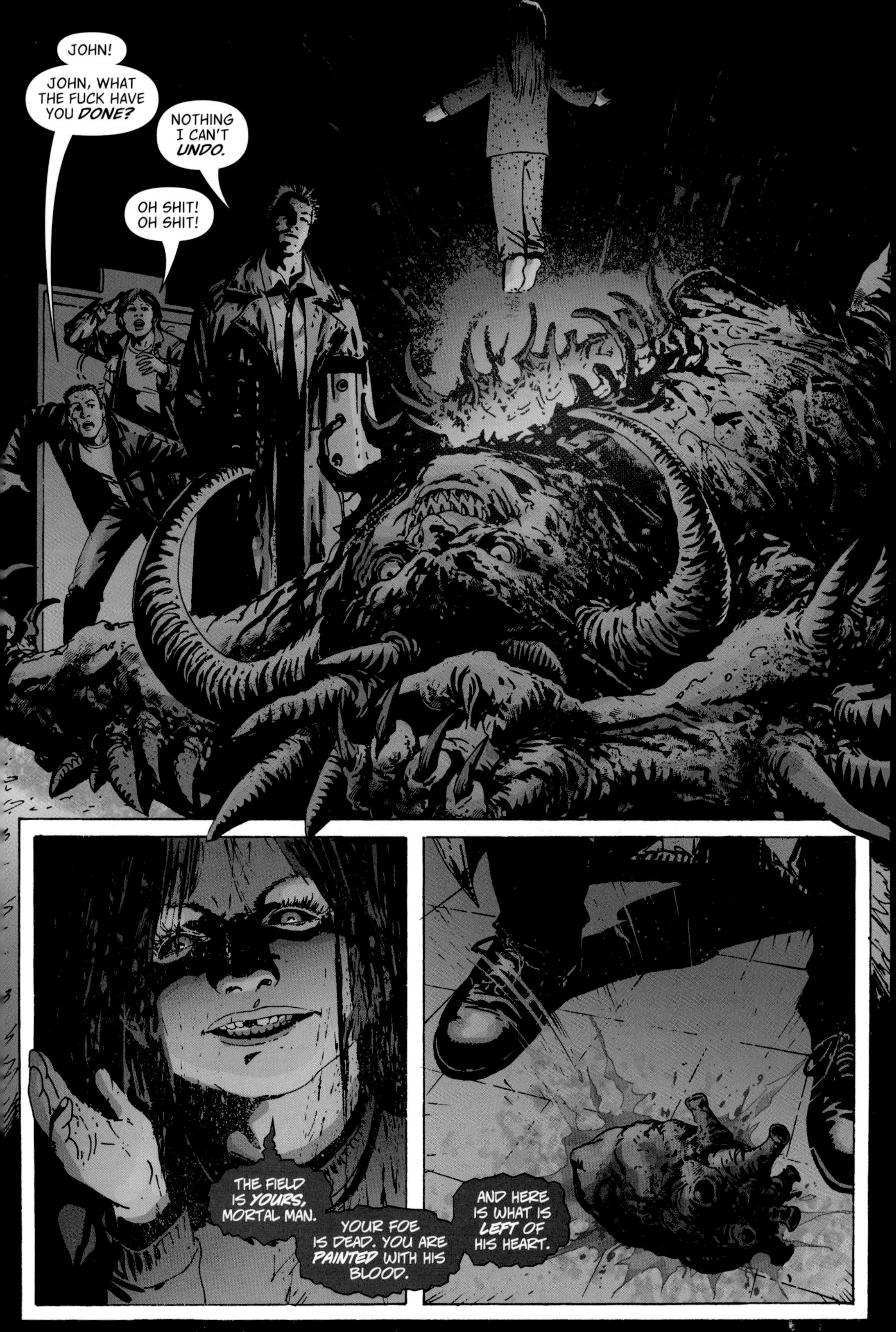
JOHN!
JOHN, WHAT THE FUCK HAVE YOU DONE?
NOTHING I CAN'T UNDO.
OH SHIT! OH SHIT!
THE FIELD IS YOURS, MORTAL MAN.
YOUR FOE IS DEAD. YOU ARE PAINTED WITH HIS BLOOD.
AND HERE IS WHAT IS LEFT OF HIS HEART.

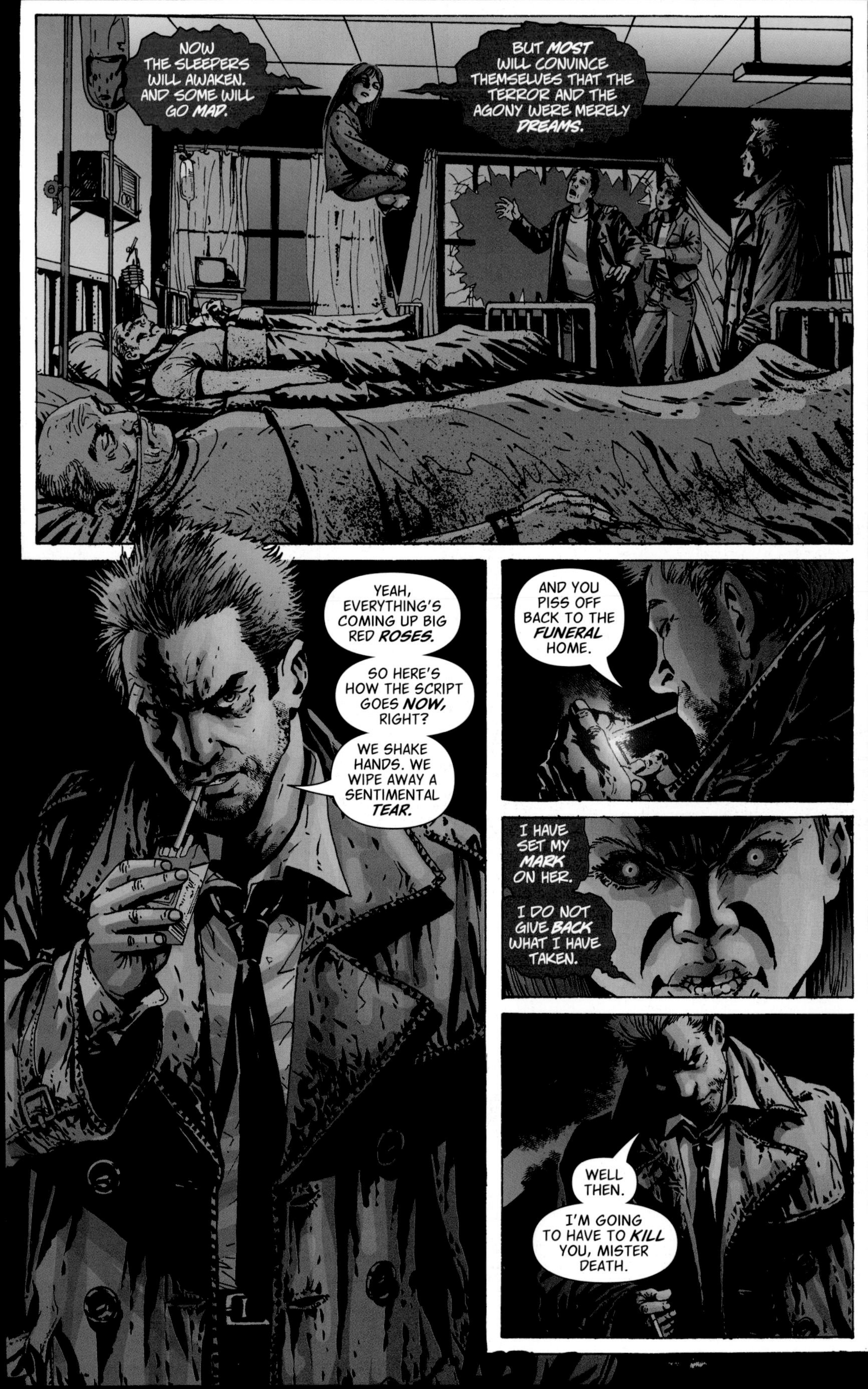
NOW THE SLEEPERS WILL AWAKEN. AND SOME WILL GO MAD.
BUT MOST WILL CONVINCE THEMSELVES THAT THE TERROR AND THE AGONY WERE MERELY DREAMS.
YEAH, EVERYTHING'S COMING UP BIG RED ROSES.
SO HERE'S HOW THE SCRIPT GOES NOW, RIGHT?
WE SHAKE HANDS. WE WIPE AWAY A SENTIMENTAL TEAR.
AND YOU PISS OFF BACK TO THE FUNERAL HOME.
I HAVE SET MY MARK ON HER.
I DO NOT GIVE BACK WHAT I HAVE TAKEN.
WELL THEN.
I'M GOING TO HAVE TO KILL YOU, MISTER DEATH.

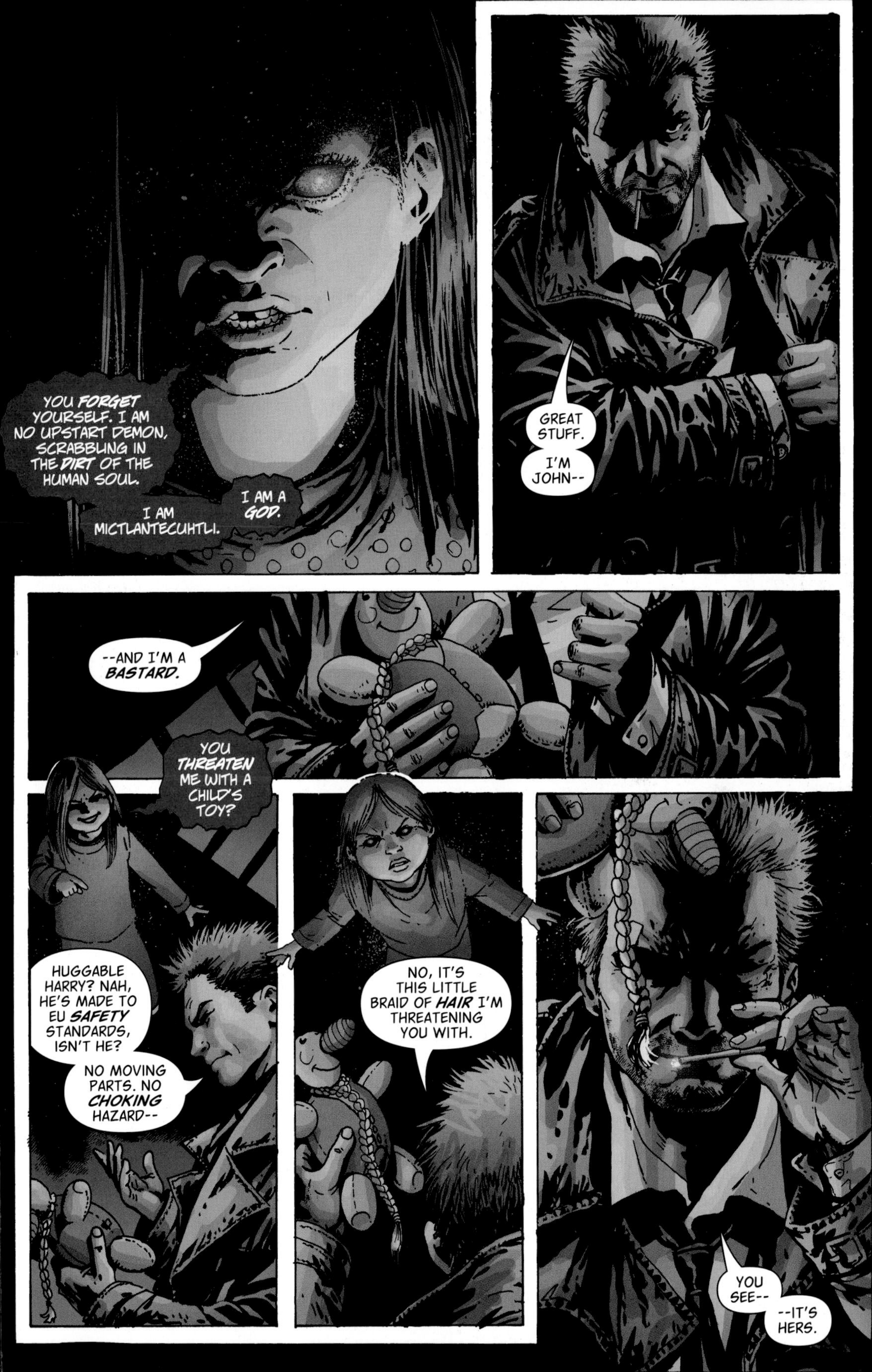
YOU FORGET YOURSELF. I AM NO UPSTART DEMON, SCRABBLING IN THE DIRT OF THE HUMAN SOUL.
I AM MICTLANTECUHTLI.
I AM A GOD.
GREAT STUFF.
I'M JOHN--
--AND I'M A BASTARD.
YOU THREATEN ME WITH A CHILD'S TOY?
HUGGABLE HARRY? NAH, HE'S MADE TO EU SAFETY STANDARDS, ISN'T HE?
NO MOVING PARTS. NO CHOKING HAZARD--
NO, IT'S THIS LITTLE BRAID OF HAIR I'M THREATENING YOU WITH.
YOU SEE--
--IT'S HERS.

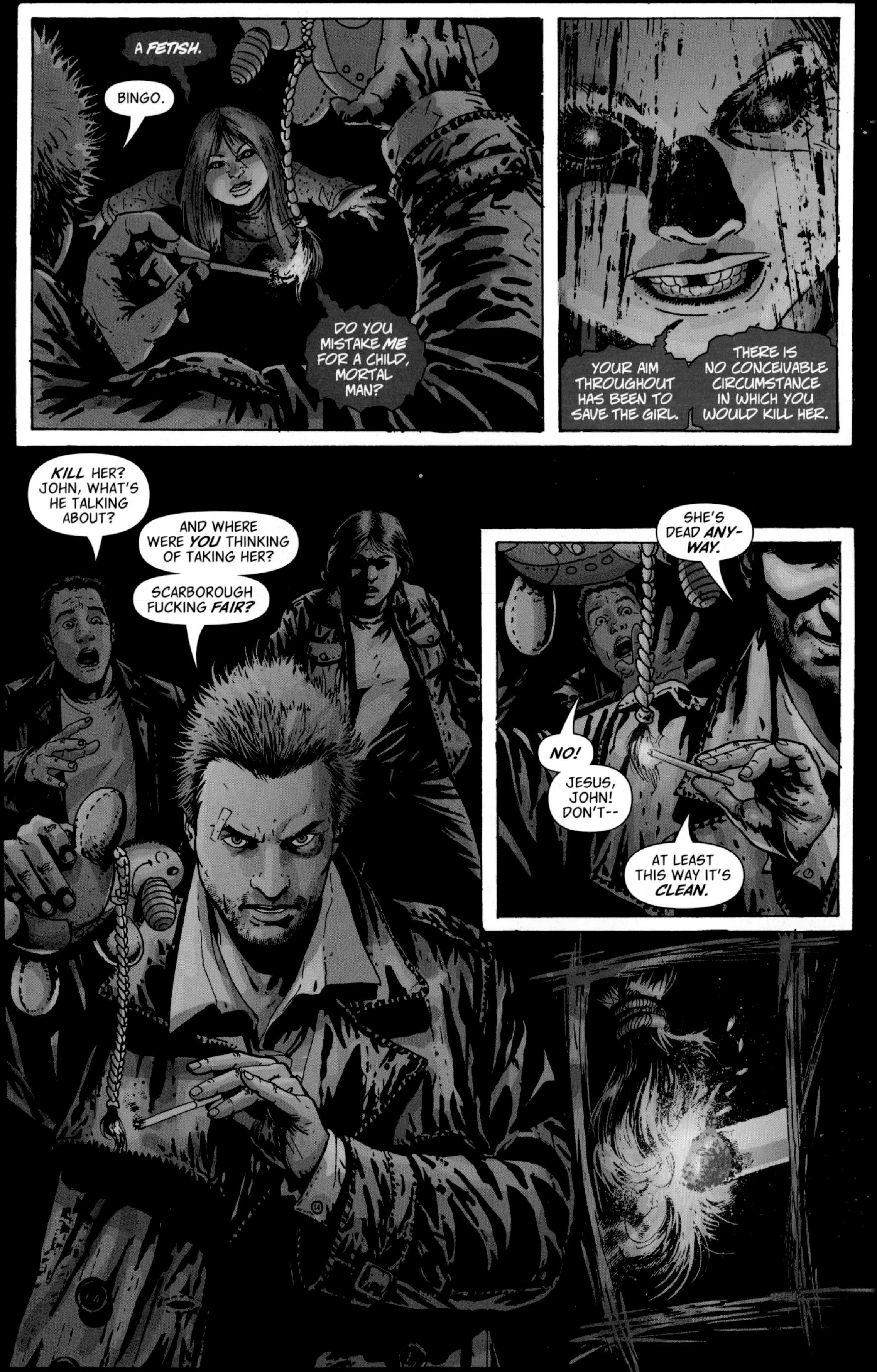
A FETISH.
BINGO.
DO YOU MISTAKE ME FOR A CHILD, MORTAL MAN?
YOUR AIM THROUGHOUT HAS BEEN TO SAVE THE GIRL.
THERE IS NO CONCEIVABLE CIRCUMSTANCE IN WHICH YOU WOULD KILL HER.
KILL HER? JOHN, WHAT'S HE TALKING ABOUT?
AND WHERE WERE YOU THINKING OF TAKING HER?
SCARBOROUGH FUCKING FAIR?
SHE'S DEAD ANYWAY.
NO!
JESUS, JOHN! DON'T--
AT LEAST THIS WAY IT'S CLEAN.

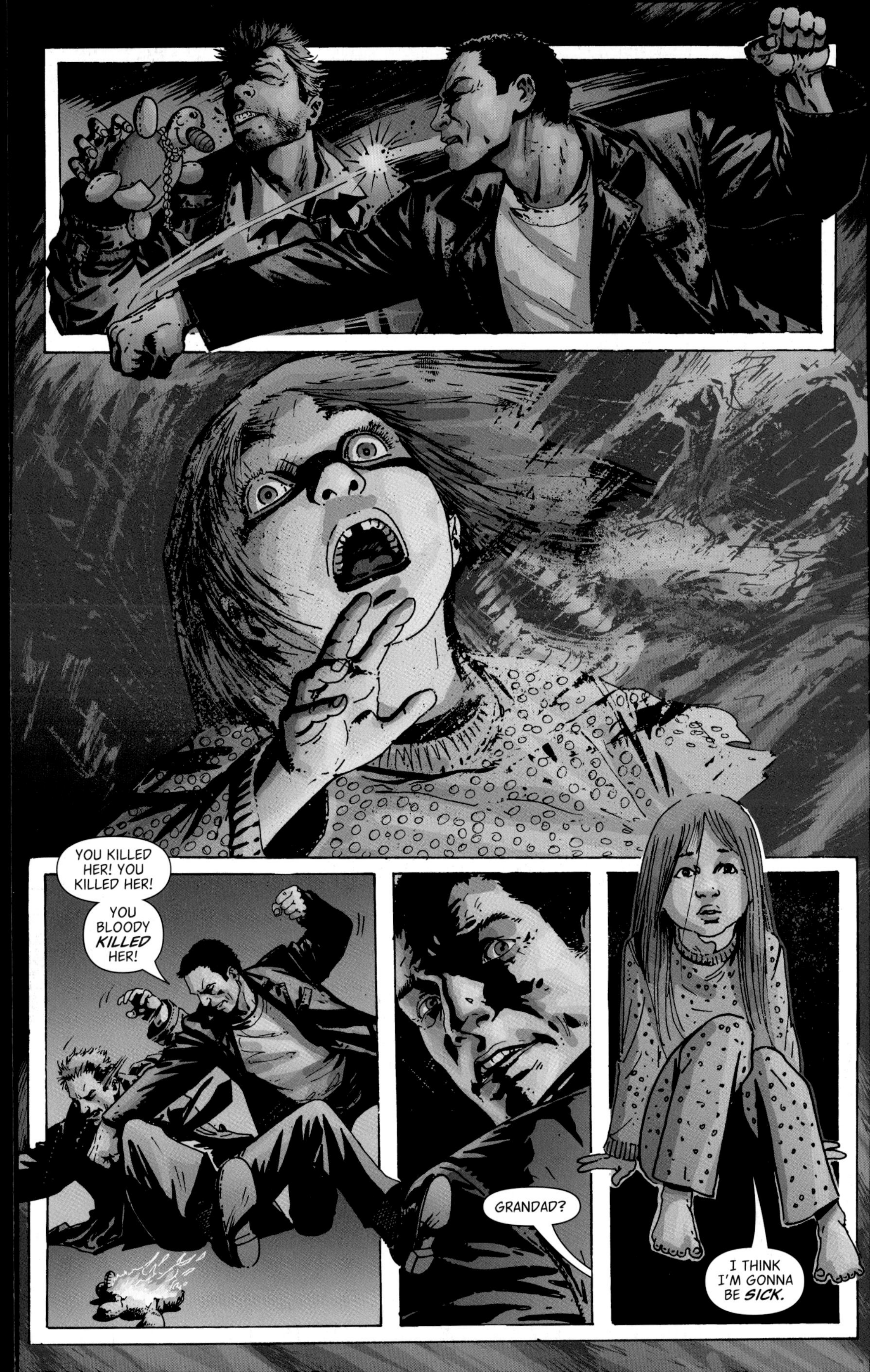
YOU KILLED HER! YOU KILLED HER!
YOU BLOODY KILLED HER!
GRANDAD?
I THINK I'M GONNA BE SICK.

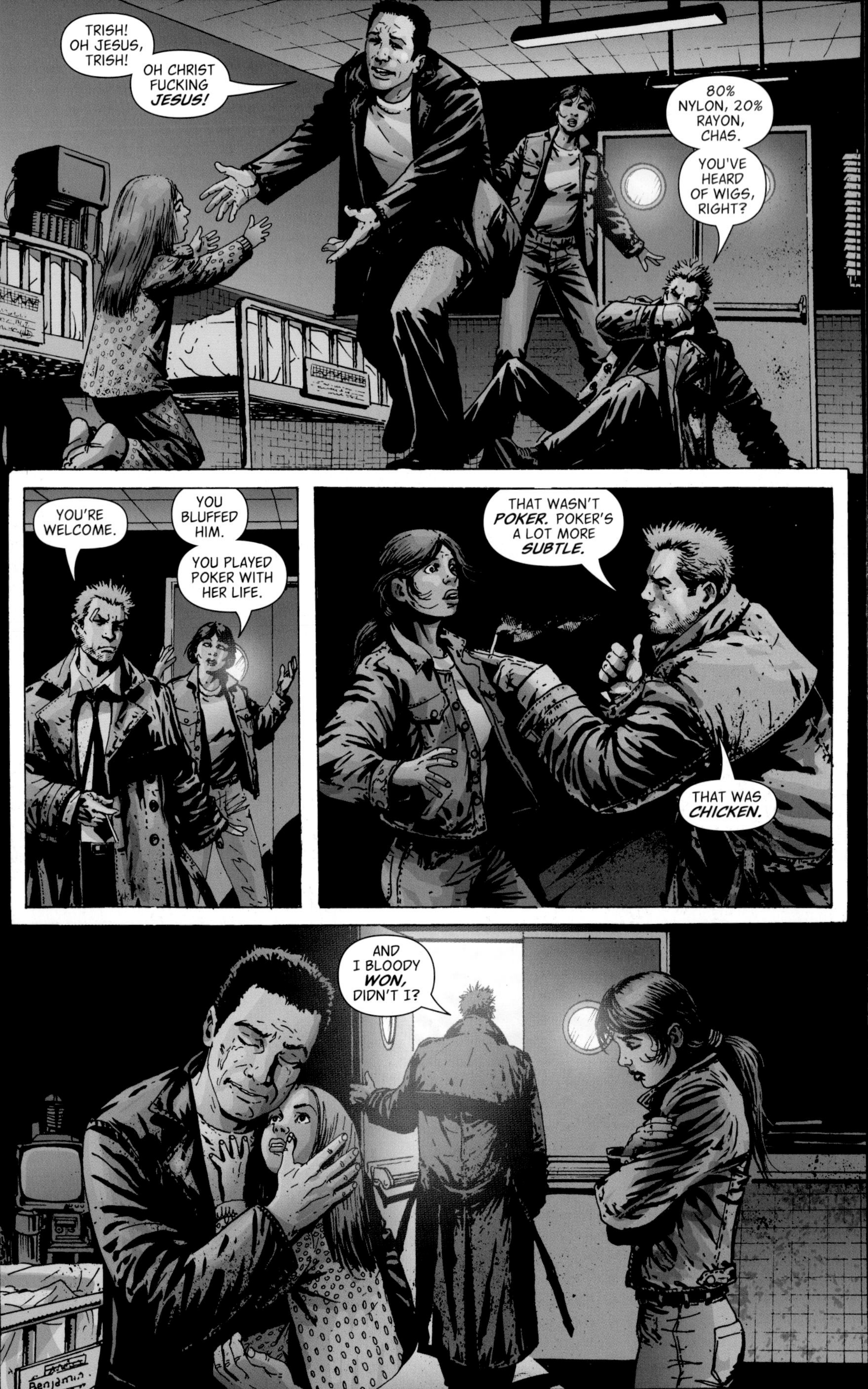
TRISH! OH JESUS, TRISH!
OH CHRIST FUCKING ***JESUS!***
80% NYLON, 20% RAYON, CHAS.
YOU'VE HEARD OF WIGS, RIGHT?
YOU'RE WELCOME.
YOU BLUFFED HIM.
YOU PLAYED POKER WITH HER LIFE.
THAT WASN'T ***POKER.*** POKER'S A LOT MORE ***SUBTLE.***
THAT WAS ***CHICKEN.***
AND I BLOODY ***WON,*** DIDN'T I?

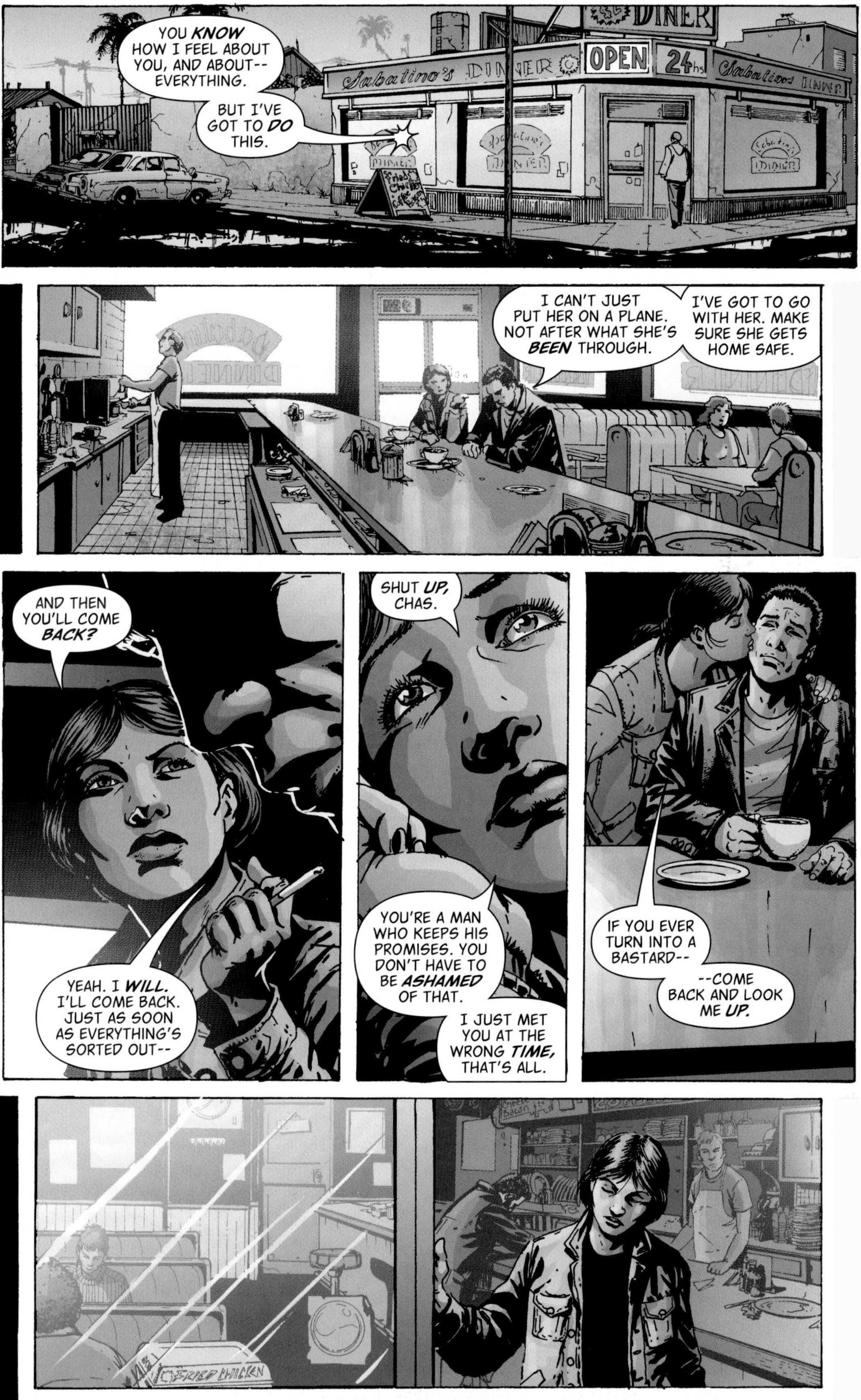
DINER
OPEN
24hs
Sabatino's DINNER
YOU KNOW HOW I FEEL ABOUT YOU, AND ABOUT-- EVERYTHING.
BUT I'VE GOT TO DO THIS.
I CAN'T JUST PUT HER ON A PLANE. NOT AFTER WHAT SHE'S BEEN THROUGH.
I'VE GOT TO GO WITH HER. MAKE SURE SHE GETS HOME SAFE.
AND THEN YOU'LL COME BACK?
YEAH. I WILL. I'LL COME BACK. JUST AS SOON AS EVERYTHING'S SORTED OUT--
SHUT UP, CHAS.
YOU'RE A MAN WHO KEEPS HIS PROMISES. YOU DON'T HAVE TO BE ASHAMED OF THAT.
I JUST MET YOU AT THE WRONG TIME, THAT'S ALL.
IF YOU EVER TURN INTO A BASTARD--
--COME BACK AND LOOK ME UP.
FRIED CHICKEN

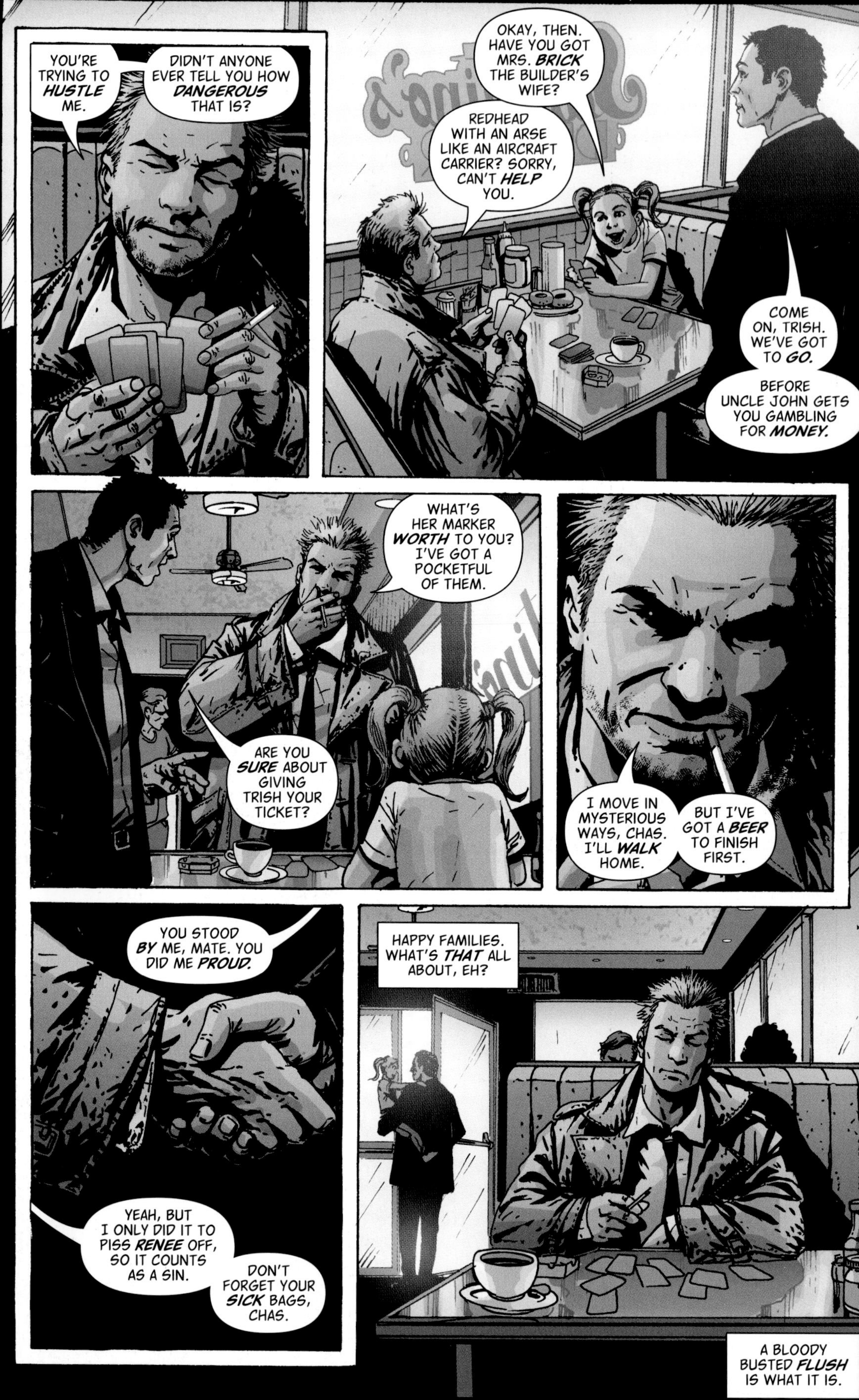
YOU'RE TRYING TO HUSTLE ME.
DIDN'T ANYONE EVER TELL YOU HOW DANGEROUS THAT IS?
OKAY, THEN. HAVE YOU GOT MRS. BRICK THE BUILDER'S WIFE?
REDHEAD WITH AN ARSE LIKE AN AIRCRAFT CARRIER? SORRY, CAN'T HELP YOU.
COME ON, TRISH. WE'VE GOT TO GO.
BEFORE UNCLE JOHN GETS YOU GAMBLING FOR MONEY.
WHAT'S HER MARKER WORTH TO YOU? I'VE GOT A POCKETFUL OF THEM.
ARE YOU SURE ABOUT GIVING TRISH YOUR TICKET?
I MOVE IN MYSTERIOUS WAYS, CHAS. I'LL WALK HOME.
BUT I'VE GOT A BEER TO FINISH FIRST.
YOU STOOD BY ME, MATE. YOU DID ME PROUD.
YEAH, BUT I ONLY DID IT TO PISS RENEE OFF, SO IT COUNTS AS A SIN.
DON'T FORGET YOUR SICK BAGS, CHAS.
HAPPY FAMILIES. WHAT'S THAT ALL ABOUT, EH?
A BLOODY BUSTED FLUSH IS WHAT IT IS.

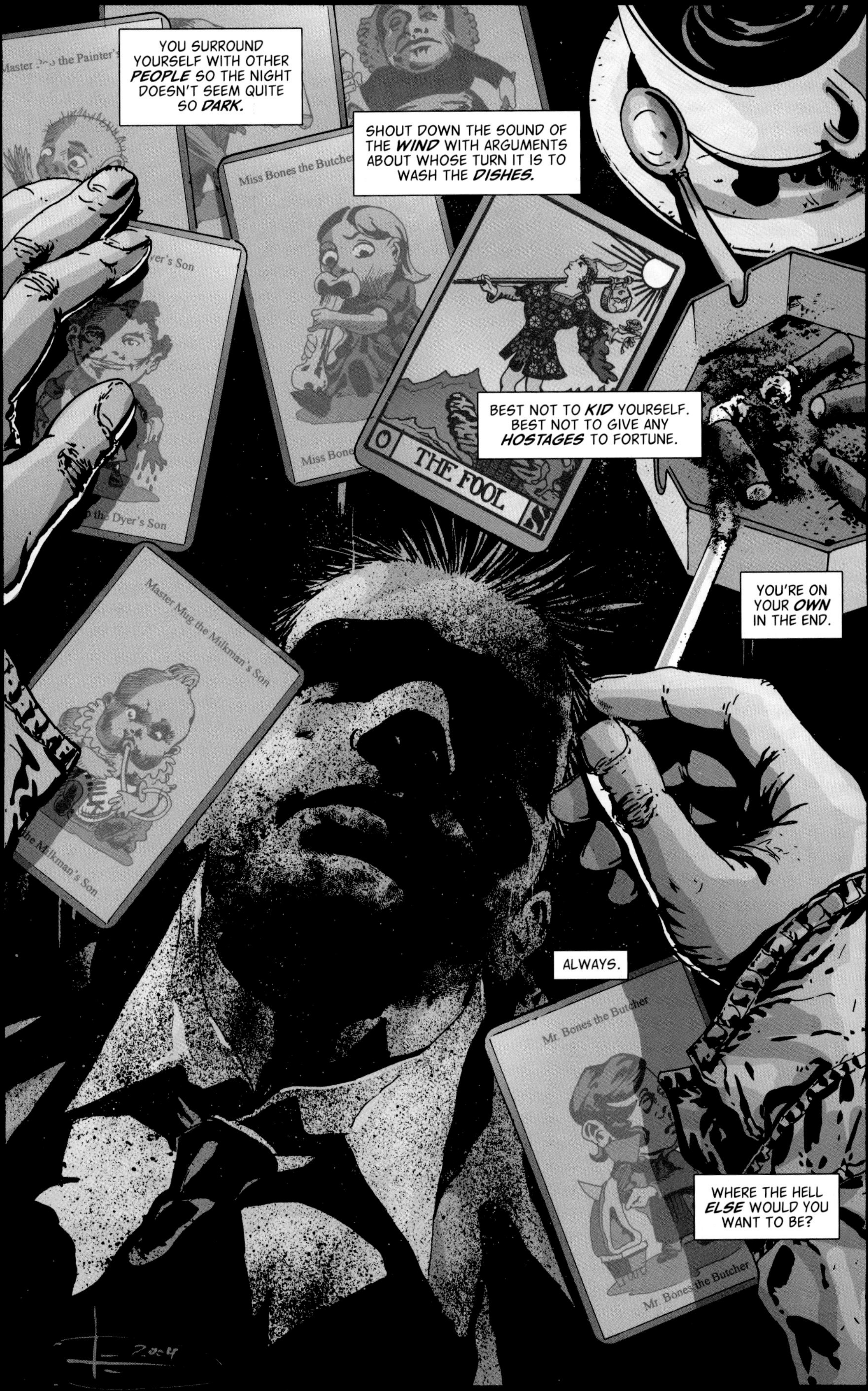
YOU SURROUND YOURSELF WITH OTHER *PEOPLE* SO THE NIGHT DOESN'T SEEM QUITE SO *DARK.*
SHOUT DOWN THE SOUND OF THE *WIND* WITH ARGUMENTS ABOUT WHOSE TURN IT IS TO WASH THE *DISHES.*
Miss Bones the Butcher
THE FOOL
BEST NOT TO *KID* YOURSELF. BEST NOT TO GIVE ANY *HOSTAGES* TO FORTUNE.
Master Mug the Milkman's Son
YOU'RE ON YOUR *OWN* IN THE END.
ALWAYS.
Mr. Bones the Butcher
WHERE THE HELL *ELSE* WOULD YOU WANT TO BE?
Mr. Bones the Butcher

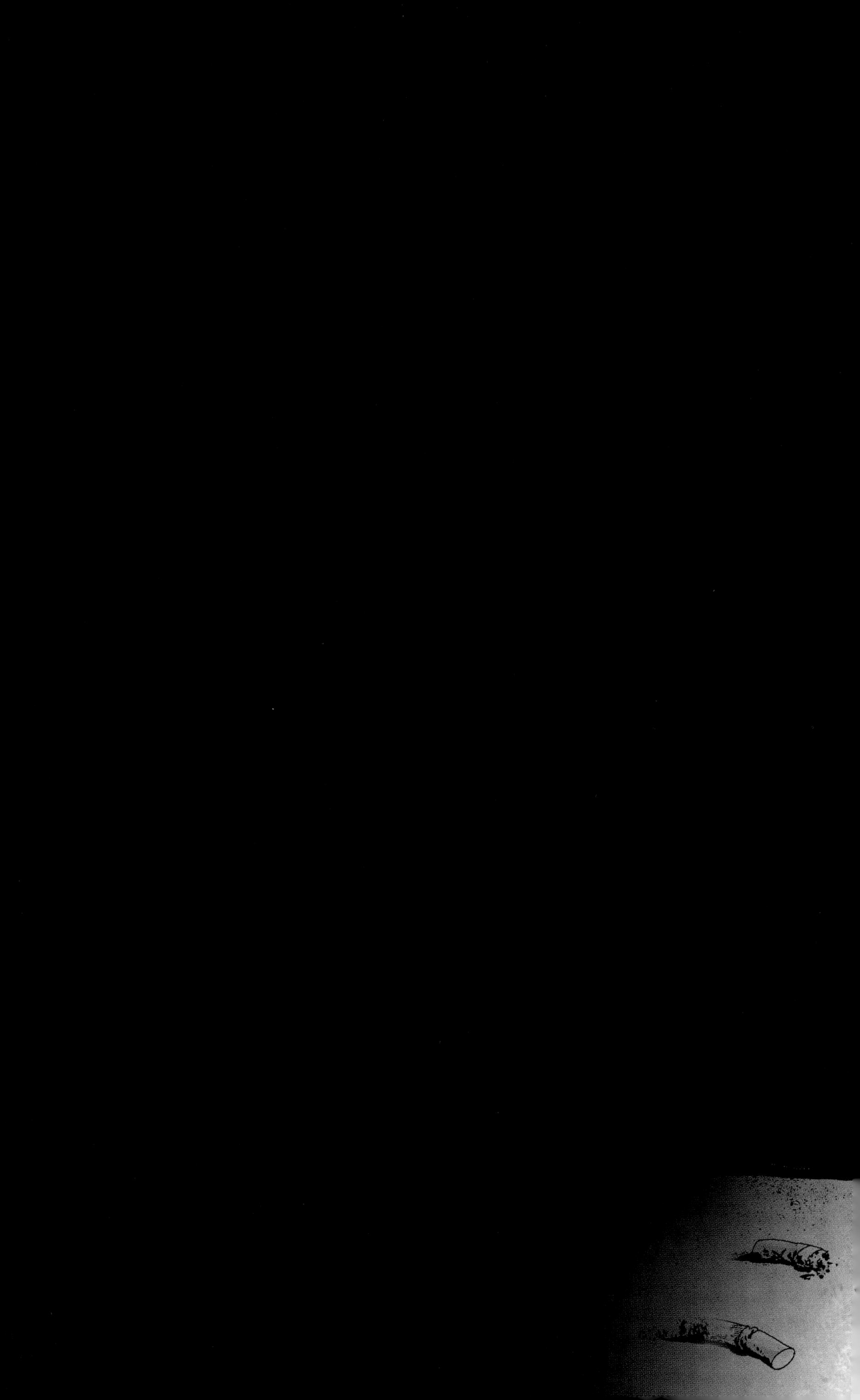

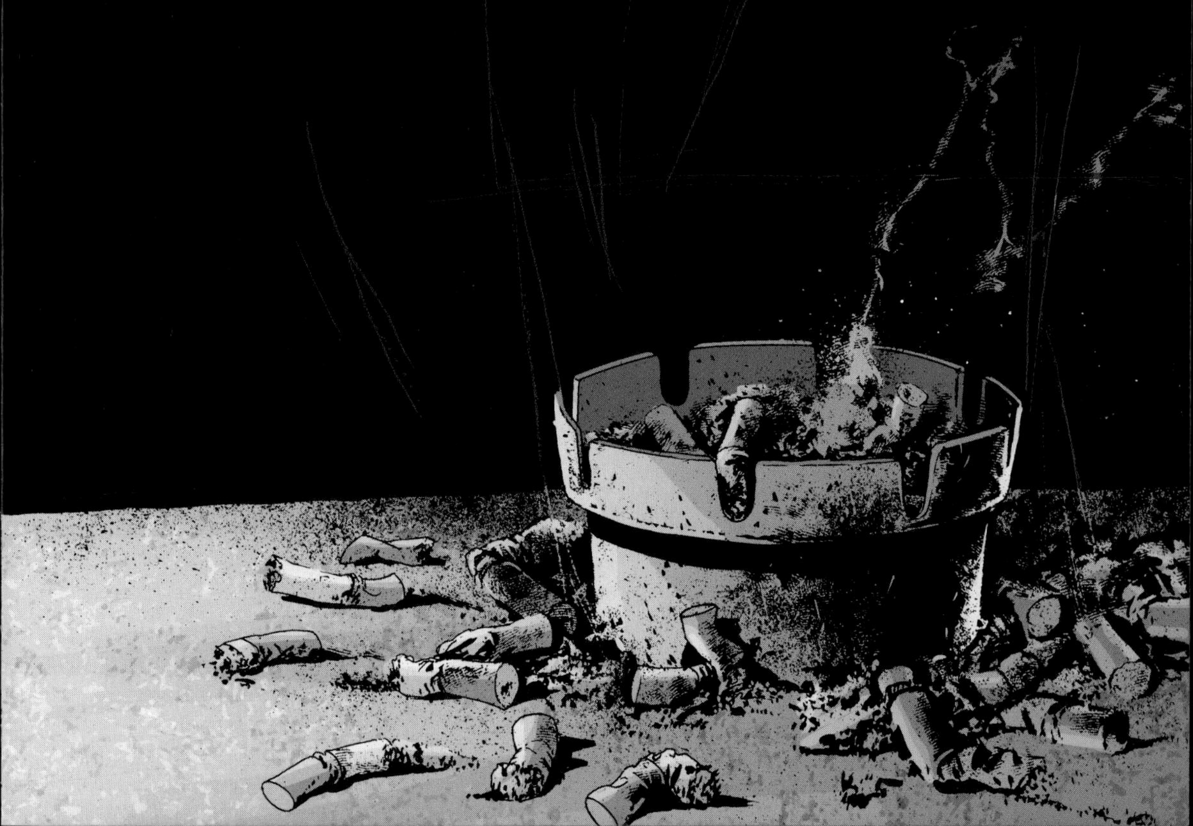

MIKE CAREY lives in London with his family which
now includes a cat—a fact which puzzles him because
he doesn't have the faintest idea where she came from.
He's been writing comics for 15 years, starting with
the UK anthology title *Toxic!*, now deceased. In fact,
he worked for quite a few companies that have died since.
Pretty suspicious, when you think about it.

His credits include LUCIFER, HELLBLAZER and
MY FAITH IN FRANKIE for DC/Vertigo comics, and
*Inferno* from Titan books. He looks fairly normal, up to a
point. Just don't remove the bracelet from his
left arm, or walk widdershins around him under a full moon.

Or buy him a drink.

LEONARDO MANCO was born in the coastal
city of Mar del Plata, Argentina, in 1971, and now
resides in Buenos Aires. He started his career when he
was 19 years old, and in 1991 made his stateside
debut at Marvel Comics with *Hellstorm: Prince of Lies*.
He has since then continued working for the American
market, pencilling and inking such titles as *Blaze of
Glory, Apache Skies, Doom, Nick Fury/Captain America*
for Marvel, and BATMAN, which opened the doors of
DC Comics for him.

Manco recently became the ongoing monthly artist on
HELLBLAZER for DC/Vertigo, which he states is
"one of my greatest artistic passions." Another of his
passions is watching his son, Augusto, grow, and take
him for rides on endless highways to visit strange and
exciting places. The problem is his son is able to return
to reality, but Leo… well, he can't.

ZYLONOL STUDIO was formed in 1996 by Lee Loughridge. Based in Savannah, Georgia, Zylonol has worked
on hundreds of titles over the past 10 years. Current titles include DC/Vertigo's HELLBLAZER, Y: THE LAST MAN,
HUMAN TARGET, ANGELTOWN and THE LOSERS.

# JOHN CONSTANTINE

## "...Con man, joker, thief...Magus."

JOHN CONSTANTINE is as complex and fascinating figure as there comes: the most powerful magician of comics' modern age, his life has been blighted by sorrow, pain and death.

Born in Liverpool, England into harsh, working class conditions, Constantine was an unwanted child. His father, Thomas, in fact tried to induce John's abortion, resulting instead in the death of John's mother, Mary Anne. Unjustly held responsible by his father, Constantine was subjected to a torturous childhood and, consequently, found release in magic (HLB #31, "Mourning of the Magician").

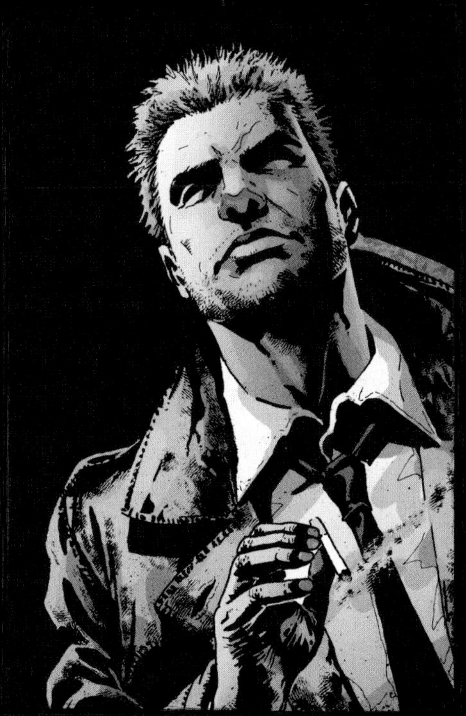

Rebelling against his dysfunctional family life, Constantine ran away to London. Instantly drawn to the emergent punk scene of the late seventies — identifying via his working class Socialist background with its anti-establishment call-to-arms — John eventually formed a punk band called Mucous Membrane, with an old school friend from Liverpool, Gary Lester.

As Constantine's magic skills developed, he found himself embroiled in a terrifying series of encounters with the forces of darkness, at times facing down the finest Hell has to offer with characteristic Scouse flippancy. Often this has led to disaster, as one of his earliest experiences in Newcastle demonstrated. Botching an attempt to summon a demon, Constantine condemned a young girl, Astra Logue, to Hell and barely escaped with his own life (HLB #11, "A Taste of Things to Come").

John's subsequent two-year stint in the Ravenscar sanitarium did little to dissuade him from magic, nor have subsequent episodes in which the casualties of his indiscretions have been those closest to his heart. And while he has had a string of love interests, they nearly always end up getting buried — often quite literally — in his deadly wake. Chas Chandler, his sometimes driver and all-times best mate, is one of the only real constants in his otherwise solitary life.

Despite being weighed down with the baggage of his past mistakes, Constantine soldiers on. He's stared down demons and serial killers — from the First of the Fallen to the King of the Vampires. He's even condemned part of his soul to Hell — and managed to get it back. All because of his astonishing nerve, attitude, and amazing capacity for self-belief.

Constantine has undergone several significant upheavals in his life — the discovery of the Golden Boy, the twin brother he'd murdered in the womb (HLB #39, "The Hanged Man"), a battle against cancer (HLB #41-46, "Dangerous Habits"), his attempt to thwart a seemingly unstoppable global apocalypse (HLB #189-193, "Staring at the Wall") — but the real Constantine always returns: the con man, the joker, the thief, the Magus. And what keeps him going through all this is his insatiable appetite for magic — at whatever the cost.

First appearance: SAGA OF THE SWAMP THING #37.

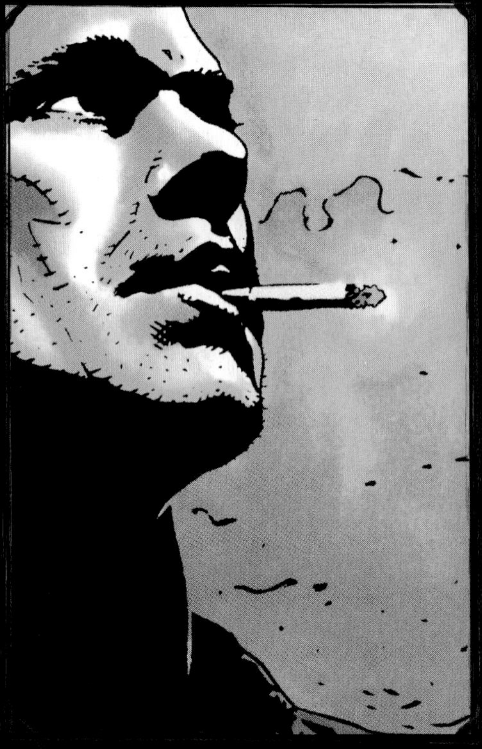

# STRAIGHT TO HELL

A true story: In 1986, the English comics vriter Alan Moore sat down at a table in a small café in Vestminster, London, just a short walk from the Houses of Parliament and Big Ben. As he tucked into a round of sandwiches in this unremarkable London café, Moore ooked up to see a man in a suit and rumpled trench coat valk in through the door. The man winked conspiratorially at Moore, smiled, then disappeared into another part of he café. It was an instance of fiction intruding on the real vorld, of fantasy made flesh — and Moore was left reeling from the experience. He'd just been "Constantined."

At that point in his career, Moore had cemented his status as one of the preeminent comics writers with a number of highly acclaimed series to his name, including SAGA OF THE SWAMP THING, his revisionist reworking of Len Wein and Bernie Wrightson's horror title for DC Comics. A vast, lyrical and imaginative series that chronicled the extraordinary adventures of an earth elemental born from the death of doctor Alec Holland in the swamps of Louisiana, SWAMP THING addressed complex themes with a fierce intelligence that stood in sharp contrast to the traditional superhero fare characteristic of the time.

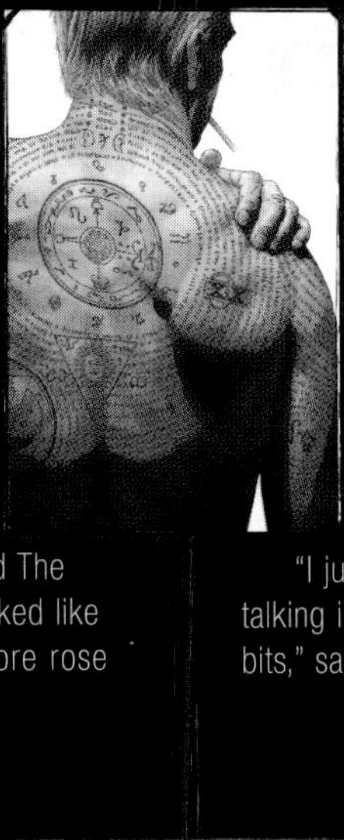

One of Moore's many memorable creations in the pages of SWAMP THING was a Machiavellian, chain-smoking magician from England called John Constantine, whose dramatic debut in S.O.T.S.T. #37, in June 1985, heralded the start of Moore's ambitious "American Gothic" storyline. Moore created Constantine at the behest of his collaborators on S.O.T.S.T., artists John Totleben and Steve Bissette. Both fans of the British New Wave band The Police, they wanted to draw a character who looked like the group's bassist and vocalist, Sting, and Moore rose to the challenge.

As Moore told *Wizard* magazine in November, 1993, "I have an idea that most of the mystics in comics are generally older people, very austere, very proper, very middle class in a lot of ways. They are not at all functional on the street. It struck me that it might be interesting for once to do an almost blue-collar warlock. Somebody who was streetwise, working class and from a different background than the standard run of comic book mystics. Constantine started to grow out of that."

By 1986, within a year of his first appearance, this sly, sinister yet deeply charismatic figure with an alluringly mysterious past had developed from a simple extra into a notable character in his own right. As Neil Gaiman, who would occasionally write Constantine over the years, recalls, "I remember asking Alan the first time I met him whether Constantine would survive till the end of 'American Gothic.' He seemed too cool a character to kill."

1986 was a watershed year for the comics industry. The popularity of WATCHMEN, Moore's sweeping reinvention of the superhero genre, THE DARK KNIGHT RETURNS, Frank Miller's ultra-violent take on the Batman myth, and *Maus*, Art Spiegelman's Pulitzer Prize-winning tale of survivors from Hitler's concentration camps, alerted publishers to the potential for similar "adult" comics. This was not lost on SWAMP THING editor Karen Berger, who began to examine the possibilities of originating more comic books along comparable lines. Although she claims there was "no great defining moment when we decided to do a Constantine book," Berger suspected early on that Constantine had enough appeal to carry his own title. Berger relates, "He had real stage presence and an aura of mystery around him, and we felt we could expand upon, but not give away the story of this guy."

The writer to whom this task fell was another Briton — Jamie Delano. Delano had come to comics in 1984, writing *Captain Britain* and contributing stories to *Doctor Who Monthly,* both for Marvel UK. Along with artist John Ridgway, Delano laid the foundations for Constantine which remain in place to this day, transforming a supporting character into the fully-fledged star capable of carrying his own series. Delano created a world and a life beyond the Louisiana bayou for Constantine: he elaborated on his origins, identifying his place of birth as Liverpool, he gave him a family — sister Cheryl, niece Gemma, father Thomas — and established his base of operations as London, Constantine's adopted home.

"I just sit down and start the characters walking and talking in my head and hope I write down the entertaining bits," says Delano. "It's always a tricky strategy, and for a first major series, probably particularly foolhardy. With any other character I would probably have fallen flat on my face and been trampled into oblivion by the press of cooler-headed talents behind me, but Constantine seemed to come naturally."

Says Berger, "We took the approach, as we do for all of our books, that the writer really has to understand the character. If half of what the writer develops on the character never sees print, the character still has to have a history — it should be fully realized." HELLBLAZER made its debut with a January 1988 cover date (Clive Barker had already nabbed their intended title for the series, Hellraiser). Delano's two-part opening story drew the reader into John's sallow, poisonous world, as Constantine set out to defeat a hunger demon roaming New York due to the folly of an old friend, Gary Lester. Delano immediately established some of the series' prime attributes and characters: the introduction of Chas, the first appearance of the ghosts of John's dead friends, and through the eventual fate of Lester, Constantine's worrying habit of sacrificing his friends for the cause. The dramatic impact of these would be felt over time, but for now — along with the Satchmo Hawkins column Delano penned for the first two issues — they offered tantalizing insights into John's character and past.

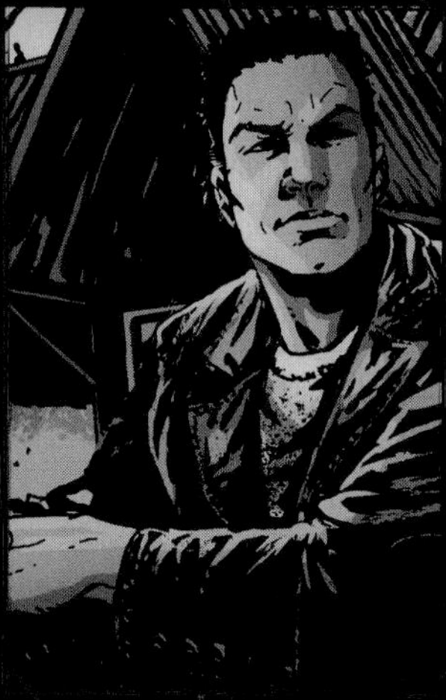

Over the first year, Delano outlined John's family and personal history in more detail. Readers met his sister and niece, Cheryl and Gemma, when they were imperiled by the Damnation Army, and finally learned the true horror of the events at Newcastle, alluded to since Constantine's earliest appearances in SWAMP THING. In issue #11, aptly titled "A Taste of Things to Come," Delano flashed back to 1978, when Constantine condemned a nine-year-old girl to Hell through his own recklessness and inexperience. The story highlighted the tragedy in his past, reinforced him as a flawed anti-hero, and gave him a new depth.

"But even if it hadn't been Newcastle," says Gaiman, "he would have done something like Newcastle, because that's the kind of person he is. He's John Constantine, after all."

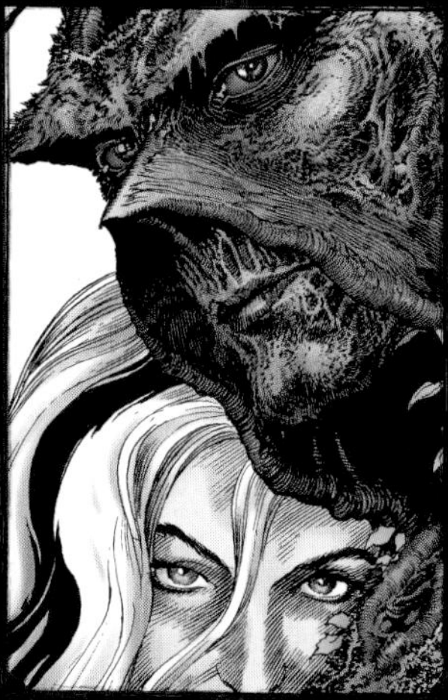

The story raised pointed questions, notably: why does Constantine return to magic, despite the harm it causes? Delano answers: "Because the world is fucking boring, remorseless and inevitable. Because he's a junkie, and no price is too much to pay when you need to feel that rush of possibility scream through your veins. Because he's scared of dying."

Driven by his interests in "politics, the human condition and the 'magic' inherent in the subconscious mind," Delano refused to just sit back and simply tell horror stories. He wrote scathing satire, metaphysical fever dreams and domestic dramas, and with equal vigor tackled racism, Vietnam, government conspiracies and environmental politics. Along the way, Delano returned more frequently to Constantine's formative years, using the past to explore Constantine's motives and behavior even further.

"I like 'Dead Boy's Heart' (HLB #35) and 'In Another Part of Hell' (HLB #84)," says Delano, "particularly because both those stories seem to offer us glimpses of a younger, more vulnerable John Constantine, in contrast to the 'veiled complexity' which confuses our perceptions of the older man."

Berger agrees, "For a character who has this mysterious, enigmatic aura, it's pretty rewarding when you can peek behind the curtain. I still feel there's a lot about Constantine that I don't know, but I don't think he'd be as strong a character if we didn't know some of the details of his past."

Delano's final story was "The Magus" (HLB #40), a climactic, metaphysical journey inside Constantine, where he finally met his twin and the two became integrated. It signaled the end of the defining run on the series, though Delano would write Constantine again, unable to get the bastard off his back. Delano concludes, "John is a man constantly driven to live up to his expectations, at the same time undermined by the knowledge that failure is inevitable and laughing himself shitless at the ridiculous spectacle of his struggle."

Delano's successor on the series was Belfast-born writer Garth Ennis, then a virtual unknown outside the UK, where he had written for *2000AD* and its short-lived sister publication, *Crisis*. It was one series for Crisis, called "True Faith," which caught the attention of HELLBLAZER's departing editor, Berger.

"I liked the fact that Garth dealt with such a controversial subject in such a human way," she says. "Garth is a very effective writer in terms of character portrayal, the ease with which he writes people. He's got a great ear for dialogue, and an ability to write people, to make them sound like someone that you know."

"I liked the 'ordinary bloke' aspect of Constantine," admits Ennis. "With HELLBLAZER, I could write a monthly comic featuring a normal, non-superpowered or costumed character who moved in a recognizable world, with realistic motivation and moral behavior. His reactions would be those of a mortal, vulnerable man — and the fact that he was a bit of a bastard helped."

For his dramatic, six-part debut storyline, "Dangerous Habits" (HLB #41-#46) in 1991, Ennis reinforced Constantine's mortality by giving him terminal lung cancer. It was a long way from the psychological horrors Delano had visited upon Constantine, and the raw intensity and considerable humanity displayed in the story became the chief characteristics of Ennis' run. "Dangerous Habits" also introduced two pivotal characters to Constantine's world: the First of the Fallen and Kit Ryan.

"With the First, I wanted to give Constantine an unbeatable, terrifying adversary that would mean certain doom to him, and to create an archvillain of irredeemable, absolute bastardy," notes Ennis. "None of that he's-not-all-bad crap here, thank you."

If the First was Constantine's ultimate enemy, Kit was his true love. "Kit was supposed to be the one woman who could see through Constantine," says Ennis. "She would take none of his shit and put up with none of the danger he foists on those closest to him. Having seen him at his weakest and most vulnerable, his usual 'act' would be laughable to her."

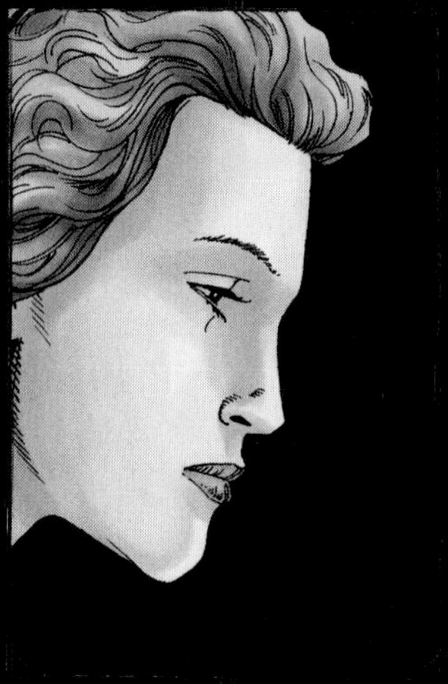

Ennis brought a distinctive, earthy voice to HELLBLAZER. He gave John an active social life, upping Chas' role in the series from mere gopher to regular drinking partner and occasional sidekick, while much of John's relationship with Kit took place either in bed or down the pub. This added a new dimension to Constantine, giving him a more personable, down-to-earth demeanor as he swore, drank and laughed the time away with his mates. A rake at the gates of Hell, indeed.

Ennis' led the reader deep into Constantine's life, though, pulling him from one emotional extreme to the other in his relationship with Kit, which remains one of the series' all-time highlights. John loved Kit, but his inability to keep the one promise he made to her — to leave her out of his magic — doomed their relationship.

Devastated, Constantine slid into self-pity and alcoholism. He lived rough on the streets of London, begging for money and food — a pitiful shadow of his former self. This was Constantine as he'd never been seen before: stripped of his charm and magic, a tragic, broken man. If the readers felt any pangs of sympathy for him after Kit's departure, they were swiftly reminded exactly what a manipulative bastard Constantine is as he prepared for his final showdown with the Devil. One by one, Constantine pulled in all the favors he was owed, cruelly exploiting friends and contacts to ensure his own survival — at whatever the cost.

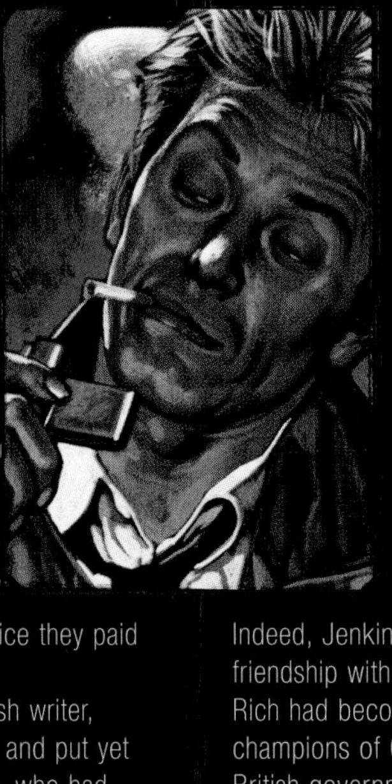

"He's a junkie for magic," says Ennis. "I always think it's kind of funny that Constantine purports to be some kind of socialist/left winger in his politics, when his actual personal politics are those of the addict: ruthless, willing to sacrifice whoever and whatever it takes to get what he needs. He pays lip service to the idea of regretting the human cost of his dabbling, but that wears thinner and thinner as he heads for 50."

By the end of Ennis' run, the streets of London were awash with the blood of John's fallen comrades. It was the ultimate price they paid for knowing John Constantine.

Ennis' formal successor was another British writer, Paul Jenkins, who took over the title in 1995 and put yet another unique spin on the character. Jenkins, who had previously worked as an editor on titles like Dave McKean's *Cages* and Moore's *Big Numbers,* made the move to writing with the encouragement of then-HELLBLAZER editor, the late Lou Stathis. In his first major story line, "Critical Mass" (HLB #92-#96), Jenkins resolved a number of loose ends — in particular the fates of the First of the Fallen and Astra, the young girl Constantine had sent to Hell all those years ago in Newcastle — which signified the direction he wanted the series to take.

"One loose end I felt needed resolving was Constantine's alcoholism. One minute he's got a serious drink problem, then suddenly he's a casual drinker, which in my experience doesn't happen very often," says Jenkins. "So with 'Critical Mass' I said to the reader 'Look, here's all the things Constantine's been, here's who he is and where he is,' and through a contrivance of the story I took all the bits of Constantine I wasn't interested in, shoved them in a homunculus and sent that off to Hell, leaving me with the bits of Constantine I wanted to write about."

Significantly, Jenkins had Constantine confront his past. In a powerful 100th issue, Constantine was taken to Hell by the Devil for a reunion with his dead father. Constantine learned that his father had forced his mother to have an abortion when she was pregnant with John, the shock of which killed her. It was a horrifying revelation, shedding new light on John's already troubled relationship with his father: Constantine hadn't been wanted, he hadn't even been loved. It's no wonder he'd been drawn to magic and the escape it offered from the real world.

Jenkins continued to develop his version of Constantine. With his bad half in Hell, Constantine seemed to mellow and assume a new sense of responsibility. "Constantine is a great person," says Jenkins. "He won't suffer fools gladly, he won't be shat on. He doesn't care if it's the ultimate fascist like the First of the Fallen or some other little fascist who wants to kick some ghost out of a house, he rails against them equally. He tries to pretend that he's a mean, heartless bastard, but the way I saw it was that nobody's just one color, there has to be another side to him."

Subsequently, this new-look Constantine embarked on his first serious relationship since Kit, with an American journalist, Dani Wright. He became socially active again, mixing with old friends from his punk days, memorably Rich Eldridge (based on Jenkins' own brother), his girlfriend Michelle and their son, Syder. Indeed, Jenkins' own concerns emerged as Constantine's friendship with Rich & Co. grew. Like a lot of old punks, Rich had become involved with crusty techno travelers, champions of Green politics and primary targets of the British government's Criminal Justice Bill. Jenkins dovetailed these issues of personal liberty and environmentalism into an exploration of English myth, with Constantine visiting lost magical kingdoms and meeting legendary figures like King Arthur and Merlin.

"When I was growing up in Dorset, my family lived on a Roman road, and about half a mile away from our house was an ancient burial site," reveals Jenkins. "My mum used to say things like 'If you listen to it at midnight, you can hear the fairies playing,' and I used to go into the woods at night with the guy who I wrote into HELLBLAZER as Tom, the Jesus figure, and feed badgers. So I saw magic every day as a child, I became accustomed to it as part of the land."

With Jenkins' final story arc, "How To Play With Fire" (HLB #125-#128), Constantine's transformation was complete. For once, there were no scenes of terrible bloodshed; Constantine's friends walked safely away. John had sold his soul to ensure their safety. Jenkins proved there was another side to John, one capable of compassion — and making the ultimate sacrifice himself.

After Jenkins, Ennis returned briefly to the title for "Son of Man" (HLB #129-#133), a five-part story which delved even deeper into Constantine's relationship with the beleaguered Chas. Then Warren Ellis, British writer of TRANSMETROPOLITAN, was approached to pen the series. As with his predecessors, Ellis brought out a different side in the magician — one darker, more cruel and sinister.

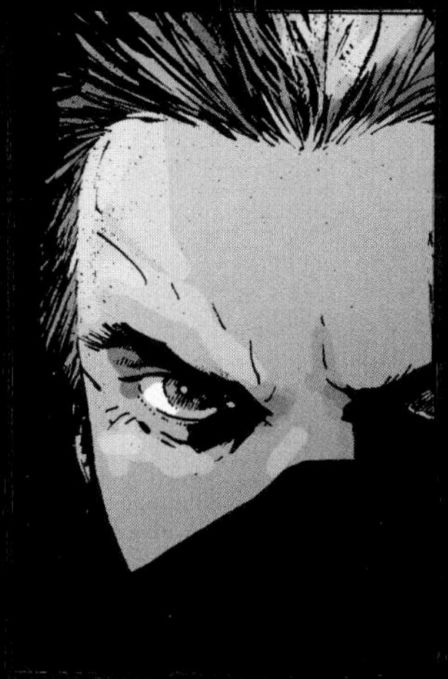

"Warren went back and made the book a real, true horror title, whereas I think Paul's run had got more into the magical aspect of Constantine," says Berger. "Warren grounded him again in London, sent him back to the dark, filthy world where Jamie had put him at the start of the book, and pitted him against, in most cases, a singular adversary. He narrowed the focus a little bit more, brought Constantine back to a microcosm."

During Ellis' run he focused on a symbiotic relationship between Constantine and London, drawing on the city's grim and lengthy magical past for inspiration.

"London and magic, for me, are all tangled up together: both have undeniable glamour, both can kick free a sense of wonder, and both can very easily be ugly and pretty fucking stupid-looking," explains Ellis. "It amused me to take a walk round it all, from the sad bastards to the genuinely scary people, from a pretty face in Soho to a dead body in Spitalfields. And speaking of dead bodies, there's a certain strain of British crime fiction that's not been seen in American comics, a kind of murder writing that's blacker and sadder than [James] Ellroy. Derek Raymond's 'Factory' novels are the obvious touchstone, brutal things without a chink of light in them. A very English kind of urban fiction, a perfect fit with John Constantine's world of shabby magic."

Ellis immersed Constantine in London's secret history — from ritualistic murder to unsettling revelations concerning the origins of the British monarchy. The old bastard, it seemed, had come home. However, Ellis left the series prematurely after only ten issues with issue #143, after encountering problems with a controversial story that dealt with children and gun violence, a topic that cut too close to home in the aftermath of the Columbine shootings.

Following in Ellis' footsteps was the series' first American writer, Brian Azzarello, who brought to HELLBLAZER the same hard-boiled intensity that characterizes his other ongoing Vertigo series, 100 BULLETS. Electing to remove Constantine from his natural environment, Azzarello's initial story arc, "Hard Time" (HLB #146-#150), found John sentenced to 35 years in a maximum-security prison somewhere in America. Playing one side off against another with consummate skill, the slippery Constantine swiftly engineered his freedom, before setting off on a road trip round the States — with customarily unpleasant results.

"John's a spiritual grifter, a con man working a psychological shell game," proposes Azzarello. "You may be certain where that pea is, but the only certainty is you know where it is if he lets you. It's this control — or illusion of control — that lies at the heart of the character. He may not be one step ahead of the game, but he makes you think he is."

"Brian made John more of a manipulator again, back to the twinkle in the eye, the more unpredictable nature," says Berger. "He's not as dark as, say, during Warren's run. He's cheekier, but still very much the bastard. Brian's take is definitely closer to Alan [Moore]'s vision of the character."

During Azzarello's controversial stint on HELLBLAZER, Constantine had managed to travel across America, encountering urban legends, Neo-Nazi militias and underground sex clubs along the way. However, when the book was handed back to another English writer—namely current scribe Mike Carey—Constantine found himself back home in Liverpool, reuniting with his family, friends and old haunts. However, wherever Constantine goes, trouble always follows, and under Carey's run, John has had to save his niece, Gemma, from an evil sorcerer in "Red Sepulchre" (HLB #177-180), thwart Armageddon in "Staring at the Wall" (HLB #198-193), and try to defeat three of his "children" sired with a dubious shape-shifting demon in "Happy Families" (HLB #200).

With over 200 issues under his belt, Constantine still manages to maintain his status as one of the most complex and fascinating characters in comics — a man with a tragic, blood-soaked past, whose behavior is ambiguous at the best of times, and terrifying at the worst. He's one of the truly great anti-heroes comics will ever know. "Flawed, smart, funny, and cool," says Gaiman. "He's also a dickheaded, stubborn idiot, who causes nothing but doom and misery for his loved ones and friends."

"[We all] have the secret desire to walk the walk, fuck with the immensely powerful and not worry about any comeback, and never be stuck for a line," adds Garth Ennis on John's continued popularity. "And girls. They fancy him." •

# THE HELLBLAZER LIBRARY

**14 definitive collections showcasing comic's mystical anti-hero and his journeys through hell and back.**

VERTIGO
CONSTANTINE
HELLBLAZER
ORIGINAL SINS
Jamie Delano
John Ridgway
Alfredo Alcala

### 1: ORIGINAL SINS

(Jamie Delano/John Ridgway/Alfredo Alcala)

The volume that introduces John Constantine, master manipulator of black magic, and chronicles the inescapable nightmares that threaten his closest friends and loved ones.

HELLBLAZER
DANGEROUS HABITS

### 2: DANGEROUS HABITS

(Garth Ennis/Will Simpson)

Constantine succumbs to terminal lung cancer and heads off to Hell to make a deal for his life. However, he soon discovers that dying might be the least of his problems.

JOHN CONSTANTINE
VERTIGO
HELLBLAZER
fear and loathing
Garth Ennis Steve Dillon

### 3: FEAR AND LOATHING

(Garth Ennis/Steve Dillon)

Constantine must dissuade his young niece, Gemma, from following in his troubled footsteps, engineer the fall from heaven, and cope with an upcoming birthday.

JOHN CONSTANTINE
HELLBLAZER
TAINTED LOVE
GARTH ENNIS•STEVE DILLON

### 4: TAINTED LOVE

(Garth Ennis/Steve Dillon)

John loses the love of his life and, in turn, chooses life on the streets. There, he meets a vicious vampire cult and revisits the scene of one of his earlier—and tragic—encounters with the black arts.

JOHN CONSTANTINE
HELLBLAZER
DAMNATION'S FLAME

### 5: DAMNATION'S FLAME

(Garth Ennis/Steve Dillon/William Simpson/Peter Snejbjerg)

Still distraught over losing his girlfriend, John goes to New York City, where his body takes abuse on the streets, and his mind is taken hostage in Hell.

VERTIGO
HELLBLAZER
RAKE at the
GATES of HELL
Garth Ennis
Steve Dillon

### 6: RAKE AT THE GATES OF HELL

(Garth Ennis/Steve Dillon)

Looking for revenge after being tricked by Constantine, Satan again confronts Constantine in hopes of destroying him once and for all. Meanwhile, Constantine's actions inadvertently cause a series of violent race riots.

VERTIGO
JOHN CONSTANTINE
HELLBLAZER
Garth Ennis John Higgins
SON of MAN

**7: SON OF MAN**
(Garth Ennis/John Higgins)
Constantine must put right a series of unfortunate events, including his best mate, Chas Chandler, being wrongly accused of killing a mob boss and stopping an undead child from unleashing unimaginable evil on the world.

VERTIGO
WARREN ELLIS JOHN HIGGINS
HAUNTED

**8: HAUNTED**
(Warren Ellis/John Higgins)
In this tale of retribution, Constantine hunts the killer of a past love. When the killer makes the unfortunate mistake of exposing himself to the Hellblazer, John soon teaches him a lesson in revenge not soon forgotten.

VERTIGO
HELLBLAZER
Hard Time
BRIAN AZZARELLO
RICHARD CORBEN

**9: HARD TIME**
(Brian Azzarello/Richard Corben)
Framed for a murder he didn't commit, Constantine is sentenced to 35 years in a maximum security prison in America. However, using his wits and mastery of black magic, he soon climbs the ranks to become top dog of his new, horrible environment.

VERTIGO
HELLBLAZER
GOOD INTENTIONS
Brian Azzarello
Marcelo Frusin

**10: GOOD INTENTIONS**
(Brian Azzarello/Marcelo Frusin)
In small town Doglick, West Virginia, Constantine must survive two brothers intent on killing him and a legendary demonic wild boar with a blind bloodlust.

VERTIGO
HELLBLAZER
FREEZES OVER

**11: FREEZES OVER**
(Brian Azzarello/Marcelo Frusin)
Held hostage by a blizzard, an urban legend known as the "Iceman" and three desperate gunmen, Constantine must gamble with his life in order to save a group of innocent hostages.

VERTIGO
JOHN CONSTANTINE
HELLBLAZER
HIGHWATER
Brian Azzarello Marcelo Frusin
Giuseppe Camuncoli Cameron Stewart

**12: HIGHWATER**
(Brian Azzarello/Marcelo Frusin/Giuseppe Camuncoli/Cameron Stewart)
Constantine tours the dark side of America's sunny Pacific Coast, infiltrating a white supremacists' camp and an underground sex club.

VERTIGO
CONSTANTINE
HELLBLAZER
SETTING SUN
Warren Ellis
Frank Teran
Tim Bradstreet
Javier Pulido
James Romberger
Marcelo Frusin

**13: SETTING SUN**
(Warren Ellis/Various)
Four short stories follow Constantine encountering a psychotic murderer, the "crib" of the miscarried antichrist and a wandering spirit of a Japanese torture "doctor."

VERTIGO
CONSTANTINE
HELLBLAZER
RARE CUTS

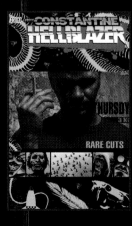

**14: RARE CUTS**
(Jamie Delano/Grant Morrison/Garth Ennis/Sean Phillips/David Lloyd)
A collection of controversial stories, never before collected until now.

# CONTENTS

# Foreword by the Bishop of Truro

The Board for Social Responsibility set up its working party on homosexual relationships in the circumstances described by its chairman, the Bishop of Gloucester, in his introduction. The working party reported to us in the summer of 1978 and it was first considered by the Board in October. Since then we have engaged in careful discussion within the Board, with two objectives. First, to determine our own corporate reaction as a Board to the working party's findings and presentation, before taking a decision on publication. Secondly, to consider whether, in the event that we published it, any other material should be attached to the report, to indicate the views of members of the Board and as an indication of the status and authority of the working party's report. The Board has decided to publish the report of the working party as Part I of this document, together with the principal critical comments made on it within the Board as Part II.

As for the status of the report, it is important to recognise that the Board has not adopted the working party's report or endorsed its contents. Consequently publication in no way commits the Church of England or the Board to them. Responsibility for its final report (Part I of this document) lies solely with the working party which produced it, although we are grateful for the opportunity of consultation at a draft stage. That report is theirs and not ours.

To publish the report of the working party in this way is to recognise that diverse attitudes to homosexuality exists within the Board, reflecting a similar diversity within the Church of England, which therefore makes it impossible to contemplate a definitive statement at this moment. The question of homosexuality raises questions to do with the authority of Scripture and the Church's tradition. Because of this, we do not think that the Church of England is yet ready to declare its mind on the subject of homosexuality. However, we do believe that the report and the attached critical comments can make an important contribution to the process of forming the mind of the Church. We therefore envisage a period during which widespread discussion takes place on the issues raised in this document. Before the General Synod seeks to consider these issues, the Board will look at ways of helping the Synod in that task, in the light of the discussion of the present document in the Church at large.

The Board appreciates that many readers of the report will find it disturbing and ask why it has been published. It should first be said emphatically that the fact that the fresh study of a subject questions received truths is

# Homosexual Relationships

## A Contribution to Discussion

CIO PUBLISHING
CHURCH HOUSE, DEAN'S YARD, LONDON SW1.

ISBN 0 7151 6555 0

Published for the General Synod Board for Social Responsibility
by the Church Information Office 1979

Printed in England by The Wickham Press Ltd., Blackfen Road, Sidcup, Kent.

not in itself sufficient reason for deciding not to make the results of that study public. The weight of Christian teaching against all homosexual acts, and the general testimony of Scripture, however, are such that any official body, such as the Board for Social Responsibility, must carefully consider whether to publish a report which questions that teaching. Many homosexuals have in the past and today given up opportunities for sexual relationships in obedience to Christian teaching; the Church must avoid any possibility of the deduction being drawn, from a reassessment of homosexuality, that they have made an unnecessary sacrifice. Nevertheless the views expressed in the working party's report are held by members of the Church of England; they need to be weighed and assessed if the Church of England is corporately to arrive at a right judgment in the matter.

The Board itself was deeply divided about the report, some members supporting its general approach and conclusions, others dissenting from them. Several members of the Board, among them some who sympathise with the conclusions of the report, would question the methods of exegesis and argument used to reach them. In addition some members regret particular omissions in a report which undertakes the redirection of Christian thinking in a most sensitive area of personal relationships. The Board was faced with a dilemma: either, by refusing to publish, to incur the odium of suppressing a serious piece of work; or by publishing, to appear to accept methods of exegesis and argument which must invite criticism.

We have decided to publish the report, with a statement of the main criticisms voiced within the Board. The 1978 Lambeth Conference spoke of 'the need for deep and dispassionate study of the question . . . which would take seriously both the teaching of Scripture and the results of scientific and medical research.' Other Churches are already engaged on that study. In 1975 the Roman Catholic Church issued a Declaration on Certain Questions concerning Sexual Ethics, which dealt *inter alia* with homosexuality. Pastoral guidelines for Roman Catholic clergy in respect of homosexuality are, we understand, in preparation. This year a report on Human Sexuality has been presented to the Methodist Conference; this includes a section on homosexuality. There is an increasing challenge to the Church's traditional teaching coming from a number of theologians in different Churches who have written on this subject, and their contributions need to be evaluated. The working party's report, and the criticisms of it expressed by members of the Board, both reflect views held among members of the Church of England; these views must be taken into account in any further study which may take place.

We realise that the criticisms of the report which have been made in the Board will not commend themselves to the working party. But we believe it would be irresponsible of us not to publish them along with the report. The Board has the primary duty of making information and advice available to the General Synod. We therefore draw attention to Part II of this document containing some Board members' criticisms of the biblical and theological sections of the report, since it is Parts I and II together which constitute the material we submit to the Synod as a contribution to its discussions. It should be noted that certain members of the Board have felt unable to accept Part II because, although intended as a statement of the critical views expressed in the Board, it does not contain a reasoned and positive statement of the Church's traditional viewpoint. Most members of the Board hold that to do this would be tantamount to writing another report.

We are aware that the members of the working party had an extremely difficult task to discharge. We should like to thank all of them, and in particular the Chairman, the Bishop of Gloucester, for their long and hard labour on our behalf.

✠ GRAHAM TRURON:
Chairman of the Board
for Social Responsibility

*July* 1979

# PART I

# The Working Party's Report

# The Working Party

The Rt Rev. John Yates, Bishop of Gloucester (*Chairman*)

The Rev. Canon R. Askew, Principal of Salisbury and Wells Theological College

The Rev. Canon P. R. Baelz, Canon of Christ Church and Regius Professor of Moral and Pastoral Theology in the University of Oxford

The Rev. C. R. Bryant, Society of St John the Evangelist

The Rev. Canon P. E. Coleman, Director of Ordination Training in the Diocese of Bristol and Canon Residentiary of Bristol Cathedral

Dr M. J. Courtenay, General Practitioner and Chief Medical Adviser to the Advisory Council for the Church's Ministry

Mrs J. Davies, Lecturer in Personal Relationships, Inner London Education Authority

The Rev. M. Day, Member of the Anglican Chaplaincy to the Universities in London

J. D. McClean, Professor of Law at the University of Sheffield

B. G. Mitchell, Nolloth Professor of the Philosophy of the Christian Religion and Fellow of Oriel College, Oxford

Miss J. Pelham, Principal Medical Social Worker, Booth Hall Children's Hospital, Manchester

The Rev. Canon J. R. Porter, Professor of Theology at the University of Exeter

The Rev. D. Wainwright, Deputy Secretary to the Board for Social Responsibility (*Secretary*)

# *Preface*

In February 1974 the Board for Social Responsibility considered a request, contained in a letter from the Conference of Principals of Theological Colleges, for a study to be made of the theological, social, pastoral and legal aspects of homosexuality. The Board agreed to this request and a Working Party, whose report this is, was set up.

The last official published document from the Church of England on the subject had been the evidence submitted to the Wolfenden Committee on Homosexual Offences and Prostitution by the Church of England Moral Welfare Council. This evidence was published under the title *Sexual Offenders and Social Punishment* and proceeded largely from the pen of the Rev. Dr Sherwin Bailey, whose book *Homosexuality and the Western Christian Tradition* has come to be regarded as a standard work on the subject. The major argument of the evidence, which found indirect expression in the report of the Wolfenden Committee, was based on a distinction between the concepts of sin and crime. Although homosexual acts were sinful, nevertheless, when performed between consenting adults in private, they should not be the concern of the criminal law.

It was clear to the Working Party from the outset that no adequate consideration of homosexuality could be divorced from a consideration of human sexuality as a whole. Even if such an undertaking were beyond its scope, nevertheless it must take into account the understanding afforded by the human sciences of the nature and importance of sexuality in the various patterns of human relationships, and at the same time work towards a Christian appraisal of sexuality in general and of its genital expression in particular.

The Working Party commenced its work in September 1974, and met on 27 occasions including three residential meetings. During the early part of its life, most of its time was spent in receiving both oral and written evidence from a wide variety of individuals and organizations. This dealt with those aspects of homosexuality which were covered by the terms of reference of the Working Party. The evidence was received in a number of ways. Some people met or corresponded with the Secretary. Others submitted written evidence which was distributed to the Working Party. Yet others were invited to meet the Working Party to submit oral evidence. A list of acknowledgements appears at the end of the Report. To all those who by their advice or discussion have given help the Working Party is grateful.

At the same time a number of papers were written by members of the Working Party dealing with the issues raised for the Church, and these papers form the basis of the Report itself. The earlier chapters are

3

evidential in character and reflect the Working Party's understanding of the social, medical and biblical material. The remaining chapters grapple with the theological, ethical, legal and pastoral problems which this evidence raises.

It may help to avoid misunderstanding if we say something about the method which the Working Party adopted. Some readers of the Report may turn immediately to the later sections in which we argue in favour of some modification of the traditional Christian position. They may then be tempted to imagine that, despite the order in which the sections of the Report appear, the medical and biblical section were framed in the light of the later argument, or even composed in order to justify it.

That is not so. The Working Party attempted to discover and assess the medical evidence as objectively as it could and to set down what seemed to be the facts of the matter, whether the facts were to the liking of all its members or not. We approached the biblical material in the same way. Our job here, however, was not merely to report but also to interpret, given the medical facts as we now understand them to be, the insights of biblical scholarship and the authority accorded to the Scriptures in the Anglican tradition. In so interpreting we have not brushed aside what the Bible has to say about sexuality: we have indeed taken great pains to interpret it rightly. On the other hand we have not felt bound simply to repeat its every utterance. Accepting its authority as witness to the ways of God with men, and listening carefully to its teachings, we have at the same time laid claim, under the guidance of the Holy Spirit, to a liberty of judgement in discerning what God is saying to us here and now, whether it be something old or something new. In following such a method, whatever the merits of our conclusions, we believe that we have continued in the main-stream of Anglican theology.

Any discussion of human sexuality, let alone homosexuality, is bound to provoke strong feelings. While this may be inevitable, the Working Party offers its Report to the Board for Social Responsibility, and through the Board to the Church, as a contribution towards a fuller understanding not only of the needs of homosexual men and women, but also of the question which they raise for society as a whole.

The Working Party would like to express its thanks to the Rev. David Wainwright, Deputy Secretary to the Board, who acted as Secretary to the Working Party.

Our Report is unanimous.

✠ JOHN GLOUCESTER
*Chairman of the Working Party*

*July* 1978

4

# 1

# The Social Setting of Homosexuality

1. We live at a time in which people's interest in sexuality is not only intense but also explicit and overt. A symptom of this state of affairs is the popular assumption that more or less everybody is sexually active. It is widely assumed, for example, that any two people living together will inevitably engage in genital activity. Too often, the deeper questions about the nature of human relationships, including friendship, are swept aside by this over-riding interest, even though in many relationships genital activity may not occur, or, if it does, may be of only secondary importance.

2. Current attitudes towards sexuality include an interest in sexual minorities. Their existence and position in society have been a matter of especial public attention since the Report of the Wolfenden Committee in 1957 and the passing of the Sexual Offences Act 1967. As a result of that legislation homosexual acts between consenting male adults ceased, within certain safeguards, to be subject to legal penalties. The main safeguards were that the age of consent was deemed to be twenty-one, the age of majority at that time, that privacy was observed, that coercion or prostitution in any form was banned, and that homosexual acts by members of the Armed Forces and of the Merchant Navy remained illegal. The last provision was intended to safeguard security and to protect men who were living in all-male communities. The Act does not apply to Scotland or Northern Ireland, where male homosexual acts in all circumstances remained illegal. By contrast, homosexual acts between women are not subject to legal restriction.

3. When we consider the decade since the Act, we are able to see how some things are changing. It has been possible, for example, for homosexuality to be treated more openly in the press, on television and in the cinema. Not only have there been articles and programmes which set out to inform, but also interviews permitting individuals to talk freely about their own sexual behaviour. In general, programmes about homosexuality have introduced the debate in more reasoned terms. Some have detected a more sympathetic general response when men and women in public life have suffered in their careers because of the accusations of homosexual affairs in the past. Again, Churches and other bodies now study homosexuality in terms of a possible change of moral attitudes in society and

not simply in terms of possible cure or the need of counselling. These changes will be assessed differently by different people. To some they will represent a very marked change of climate: to others the shift will appear far less pronounced. Increased awareness, however, and more frank discussion have not always been accurately informed. Many people are confused and identify all homosexuality with paedophilia so that homosexuals are believed to be men who corrupt little boys. Nor has greater discussion always led to greater understanding and sympathy. Instead attitudes have increasingly tended to polarize: not only support for homosexual people but also hostility towards them has become more stridently articulated. Where extremes proliferate, a judicious view of the situation is more difficult to achieve.

## TWO AREAS OF UNCERTAINTY

4. Public discussion has tended to conceal two areas of uncertainty in our contemporary understanding of homosexuality, quite apart from the major question of its cause. First, to whom are we referring? Many homosexual people, contrary to popular belief, are indistinguishable in appearance and behaviour from the rest of the community. If, as is widely asserted, one person in twenty is predominantly homosexual, then members of homophile organizations and other self-declared homosexuals make up only a small proportion of the total number. We know very little about the majority of homosexual men and women, though we suspect that many suffer considerably because they feel unable to declare their sexual preferences.

5. Secondly, there is uncertainty about the range of people's sexual feelings and the extent to which they may change during any individual's lifetime. One of the best known pieces of research, the Kinsey Report[1]*, refers to a *scale* of homosexual involvement during the subject's lifetime. This reveals that for many people sexual preference is not a matter of stark alternatives, but is to be found somewhere on a continuum between an exclusive preference for sexual relationships with one's own sex, and an equally exclusive preference for sexual relationships with the opposite sex.

6. For a man or woman who is predominantly or exclusively homosexual there is a double problem: that of accepting his or her homosexuality, and that of deciding whether this self-knowledge shall be made public, the process increasingly known as 'coming out'. While some members of the homophile movement have stressed the responsibility of homosexuals to 'come out', the Working Party has been made aware of the pressures on many homosexuals to 'pass for straight' and requiring such sexual relationships as they may engage in to be secret, fleeting and impersonal.

*All notes appear at the end of the report.

There is a weight of human hostility which makes the whole process of self-revelation involved in 'coming out' difficult and painful.

7.   An example of such difficulty is to be seen in the number of homosexual men and women who have married.   Many have done so, and have been advised to do so, in the hope that they will be 'cured' of their homosexuality.   Some have been able to adjust, and their marriages have remained stable because of the rich quality of their personal relationships. Others have discovered a strong attraction to another person of the same sex and have realized that this new relationship holds out a hope for love and personal growth which their marriage could never possess. Others, more especially married men, have been driven to pursue a series of clandestine relationships and impersonal encounters in public lavatories and elsewhere, where the risk of prosecution and subsequent disgrace is high. Homosexual women who are married and have a family are faced with an especially acute problem.   If the marriage breaks up and the wife subsequently enters into a homosexual partnership, it is unlikely that she will be awarded the custody of the children should the husband contest her claim.

## HOMOPHILE AND OTHER ORGANIZATIONS

8.   It is worth recalling that in 1952 the Church of England Moral Welfare Council initiated a study programme on the problem of homosexuality, and its subsequent report, together with that of the Howard League for Penal Reform, influenced the Government in appointing the Wolfenden Committee.   After that Committee reported, the Church Assembly debated the recommendation concerning the change in the law and approved it. In 1958 the Homosexual Law Reform Society was formed with the support of some senior churchmen, including Dr Mortimer, the then Bishop of Exeter.   Since the passing of the 1967 Act a large number of homophile organizations have appeared.   Most of these organizations have developed three emphases in their activities.   They have sought to educate the general public about the homosexual condition and its implications for the work of the caring professions.   They have sought to be supportive of homosexuals and to provide counselling help and a degree of social organization.   They have sought to initiate further reform: while before 1967 they advocated the removal of sanctions from homosexual acts, they now campaign for the removal of other restrictions on homosexual behaviour which discriminate against homosexuals over against heterosexuals.

9.   The largest homophile organization is the *Campaign for Homosexual Equality* (CHE).   This is based in Manchester and grew out of the North West Homosexual Law Reform Association of the nineteen-sixties.   CHE employs paid staff, holds an annual conference which is attended by about

2,000 people, and organizes itself into local groups. Its main campaigning preoccupation is with the reform of the law relating to sexual offences, but it has also established in some areas a counselling and befriending agency named *Friend,* an activity which is duplicated by several other organizations, mainly in the London area.

10. The *Albany Trust,* based in London, has a wider interest in psychosexual problems in general, and has been concerned in counselling as well as in the education of the public. A third kind of activity is exemplified by a smaller organization, *Integroup,* based on a Unitarian church in North London, which attempts to bring together an integrated group of homosexual and heterosexual people with the hope of reaching a deeper understanding of human sexuality. Gay Societies and the National Union of Students' Gay Rights Campaign are to be found in the universities and colleges; like other student bodies, their fortunes vary from year to year. Lastly, we mention, as instances, groups for Gay Social Workers and Probation Officers, *Gaycon* (for members of the Conservative Party) and 'gay' groups within trade unions such as **NALGO**; these exist as homophile groups with special interests. Inevitably, the style of work of some of the homophile organizations has changed and has come to resemble that of other campaigning organizations in the community. This has resulted in an increased self-confidence.

11. At this point it is worth noting that some homophile organizations, such as the National Organization of Lesbians, exist solely for women. Female homosexuality, or lesbianism, cannot be completely subsumed under a discussion of homosexuality which is expressed mainly in male terms. Dr Charlotte Wolff[2] has sought to demonstrate the special origins and qualities of lesbianism, believing it to be rooted in a woman's greater capacity for 'bisexuality', and finding expression in a highly aesthetic sensibility and a more intense emotionality. In social terms, lesbians have often identified as much with the Women's Movement as with the homophile element. Many have expressed their anger at what they believe to be a double discrimination: discrimination against them both as women and as lesbians. The anger of an active minority at what they saw as lack of concern by their male counterparts was expressed at the 1975 National Conference of the Campaign for Homosexual Equality where there was a female invasion of the conference platform. Any adequate consideration of female homosexuality must therefore take account of those elements which identify more with the feminist than with the homophile cause.

12. The change in social attitudes has found expression in the Churches in an increased theological questioning of the traditional position[3] and in the formation of specifically Christian homophile organizations, of which the best known are the *Gay Christian Movement, Quest* (RC), the *Open*

*Church Group* and *Reach*. These exist to inform and educate their fellow Christians and to offer supportive help to Christians who are homosexual. They overlap considerably both in membership and in objectives with other homophile organizations.

13.   Not all organizations active in this field, it should be noted, are homophile organizations.   The *Nationwide Festival of Light* has consistently expressed its vigorous opposition to the acceptance of homosexual behaviour as a morally acceptable means of sexual expression.   It has made available in support of its position such documents as the report of the Anglican Archdiocese of Sydney as well as issuing its own pamphlets,[4] and gives practical advice to homosexuals.


IMPRESSIONS OF HOSTILITY

14.   Alongside the growth of homophile organizations and the movement of some opinion towards a more tolerant attitude to sexual minorities, there remains, as has already been noted, a strong element of hostility towards the homosexual, who may experience hostility and prejudice on account of his sexual orientation.   In extreme cases there may be outbreaks of 'queer-bashing'.

15.   An example of an apparent growth in hostility is to be found in attitudes towards lesbian partnerships.   In the past, the fact that two women were living together attracted little attention.   Now, however, the growth of the feminist movement and the sexual liberation of women have produced in some people feelings of aggression towards lesbians; for example, women engaged in telephone counselling services for homosexuals have reported an increased number of obscene telephone calls from men. The present sexual climate, with its challenge to the traditional concept of marriage and of the sexual roles of men and women, may well have elicited such a response.

16.   The term 'prejudice' has in popular usage come to possess an emotive and derogatory meaning, and for this reason the Working Party has been reluctant to use it.   Where it is used in this report, it is intended to refer to an inability to judge any aspect of a person's life apart from his or her homosexuality.   Even the use of the word 'homosexual' as a noun, though at times inevitable, can suggest a stereotype and encourage prejudice in this sense.   Prejudice is a word which must be used with caution.   To be a victim of prejudice needs to be distinguished from the experience of alienation and rejection which may come to any member of a minority living in a society which does not cater for his needs.   The undeclared homosexual may feel out of place in a society in which the heterosexual married couple is seen as the basic and most important unit.   He may

9

forget that he shares this experience with other groups of people such as widows, who are all too often excluded from the patterns of social life of the majority.

17. The emergence of homosexual clubs and the overt use of public houses as meeting places by the homosexual community has led to some expressions of hostility from the public. Sometimes these take the form of complaints, and may lead to intervention by the police.

18. The Working Party is aware of the desire of minorities to have meeting places where they can relax and feel able to be themselves. It is also aware that homophile organizations can have difficulty in finding a regular venue for their meetings, as well as in obtaining space in local and national newspapers and magazines to advertise their activities. As a result, homophile activities are reported either in those publications which are devoted to alternative life styles, in the 'house journals' of the various homophile organizations, or in *Gay News,* a fortnightly paper for homosexuals.

19. The way in which homosexual people are coming to organize their lives around their homosexual experience is fast becoming a significant part of the homosexual scene today. Such behaviour may be common to a number of emerging minority groups, but in this case, where the sub-culture is organized around the basic desire for sexual expression, human differences can be sharply exacerbated. Some homosexual Christians, as we have seen, feel drawn to join Christian homophile organizations, but it remains to be seen whether an increasing number of homosexuals will form 'Gay Churches', as has happened in the United States.

ONE SOCIOLOGICAL VIEW

20. One explanation of the nature of the stigma which is felt by homosexuals is advanced by the sociologist, Kenneth Plummer.[5] He argues that hostility towards homosexuals is due to a three-fold challenge which their existence presents to others. It is a challenge to 'classification systems', that is, to patterns of thought which we use to make sense of a bewildering world. One set of classification systems surrounds the ideas of the family and marriage; another is concerned with gender; a third is concerned with our own sexual experience. The existence of the homosexual minority disturbs and threatens all these classification systems.

21. Plummer goes on to argue that hostility towards homosexuals is greater amongst those who adopt what he would categorize as a 'conventional' stance on social matters. Their outlook depends on fixed stereotypes, so that the perceived threat of homosexuality is correspondingly greater. Thus Plummer's understanding of hostility against homosexuals takes

account of the fact that it is not homosexual behaviour alone which excites hostility; simply to be a homosexual and to declare oneself as such is a sufficient trigger.

22. We could put this more simply by saying that the sex drive is of universal importance. Each individual learns to come to terms with it through his experience of ordinary life. Social conventions, modes of address, the conversational banter of school, office, or workshop, all help in this process. However, the homosexual person does not match the expectation which the process has created. He presents a disconcerting problem in a sensitive area of social behaviour, almost as if a woman had come by misunderstanding to what had been planned as an all-male gathering, or vice versa. There may be no threat of any sexual approach. The very existence of a homosexual creates an awkwardness and a tension. All this shows itself much more strongly when the homosexual is sexually active; and this antipathy seems to be out of all proportion to the moral judgement that may accompany it.

23. Plummer goes on to explore the effect of stigma on the pattern of social behaviour of the stigmatized minority. The hostility which the majority of the community may feel towards homosexuals serves to isolate and strengthen a subculture in which a person's homosexuality becomes the central fact of his existence. In one sense the homosexual subculture produces a pull towards itself as an attractive way of solving the problems of isolation. In another sense the hostility of heterosexual people provides a push which segregates homosexuals into a subculture of their own. It is possible that the pull of such a subculture has been present for a fairly long time. The push may have been accelerated since the passing of the Sexual Offences Act, which has brought with it the freer discussion and the increased hostility mentioned above. This hostility in its turn can provide the push for many homosexual men and women away from a heterosexual society, which they believe has rejected them, and by which they believe themselves to be oppressed.

CONCLUSION

24. It is within this social context that the Working Party has pursued its task. In the features to which it has drawn attention in this chapter it has inevitably been selective and perhaps impressionistic. This is inevitable when one is describing in brief a scene which is far from homogeneous. The most one can hope for is that the selection of data has been fair and that the picture drawn conveys the basic truth.

25. It is uncertain in what way the social life of homosexual men and women is likely to develop. Until now they have experienced only ten

years of 'public' history. In these they have become more free to declare themselves and to express their sexual feelings. They have, however, brought with them a 'covert' history. This has been geared to the necessity of survival in a hostile world, and it may include some patterns of behaviour which are imperfect adaptations to life in a society in which growing toleration is afforded to a sexual minority.

26. There is thus an interim character to any description of the social context of homosexuality today. We cannot easily speculate on the way that this social context will develop as a result of changes in moral judgment or an increased toleration of homosexuals. We may be clear about the fruits of negative reactions, but we cannot but be uncertain about the possibilities which might be opened up by a positive response.

27. Readers may find something of this uncertainty reflected in the interim nature of some of the judgments expressed in this report. This chapter has attempted to describe the social background which has given rise to it.

# 2

# *Sex, Identity and Human Relationships — A Medical View*

SEXUALITY

28. From the outset the Working Party has sought to consider homosexuality in its medical dimension in the context of sexuality as a whole. In the present state of medical science the causes of homosexuality are uncertain, and although a summary of what is known follows, it cannot be overstressed that at the present time the medical evidence is inconclusive. Some readers may find the use of technical language hard to follow. However, the Working Party has used medical terms in this chapter, believing them to be necessary in the interests of accuracy.


DEFINITION OF TERMS

29. The word 'homosexuality' is commonly applied both to the practice of engaging in a sexual (genital) act in which both persons are of the same sex, and to the psychological state that motivates a person to desire such an act. It is used when the act is participated in either by two men or two women. The word 'homosexual', when used as a noun, is frequently though inaccurately employed to describe people who are able to enter into sexual relationships with partners of the opposite sex as well as with those of their own sex. The term 'bisexual' has come into common use to describe these people. This term does not entirely avoid confusion with hermaphroditism (a completely different phenomenon which will be discussed later); because of this we propose to use the term 'ambisexual' instead.

30. 'Pederasty' has been used for genital relationships between adult males and children, who may be of either sex, but in common parlance has come to be thought of chiefly in relation to boys. This is an unsatisfactory term, partly because the etymology relates to the practices of the Graeco-Roman world, in which the younger partner was at least pubescent and usually older; and partly because it is also sometimes used, misleadingly, to describe buggery.

13

31. The more comprehensive term 'paedophilia' is now increasingly used. It refers to all types of sexual relations between adults and pre-pubertal children, whether or not these are the same sex as the adult, and irrespective of whether there is genital contact. There is a general medical consensus at present that this is pathological (abnormal) and should be considered as separate from homosexuality as defined initially; indeed it was regarded differently in the Graeco-Roman civilization.

## THE CENTRAL ISSUE

32. The question 'Can they help it?' with reference to homosexual orientation was raised early on in the deliberations of the Working Party. If homosexuality was, for instance, genetically determined in the same way as red hair, then taking a moral attitude towards it might seem irrelevant. The facts, as far as they are known, indicate a much more complicated reality, and they will be reviewed briefly in what follows. However at this point it might be useful for those readers who are convinced of their own heterosexuality to ask whether this depends on any element of choice on their part.

33. The difficulty is that there is no objective test for sexual orientation; it is a subjective view about oneself. Only behaviour can be observed, and knowledge even of this may depend largely on the evidence of the individuals concerned. Enquiry into sexual fantasies might give additional information, but the accuracy of this depends entirely on the probity of the witness. The self-assessment of someone whose sexual relationships have been exclusively homosexual and who asserts that no other sort of sexual relationship is possible for him or her cannot readily be checked. A heterosexual person would not be in any stronger position if asked to prove his or her heterosexuality.

34. The position is complicated by the fact that some people's orientation appears to lie between the exclusively homosexual and the exclusively heterosexual. The preference for a partner of the same or the opposite sex is what is in question, and the ambisexual may be attracted to people of either sex. Ambisexual orientation is part of the spectrum of biological variation. When we enquire further into the relationships into which ambisexuals enter, it is clear that some at least of them are able to choose between heterosexual and homosexual relationships.

35. Homosexual behaviour also depends partly on the social setting. Some who exhibit exclusively heterosexual behaviour in their usual social setting will turn to homosexual practices in circumstances where they have the opportunity of meeting persons only of the same sex, as in single-sex institutions.

14

## HOW WIDESPREAD ARE HOMOSEXUAL PRACTICES?

36.   The controversial question of the incidence of homosexuality among various peoples, in different countries, at different times, and under a multitude of conditions, is obscured first by the general difficulty of obtaining information from those involved; second by the problem of classifying those who are completely so, mainly so or partly so (and those who may change their pattern in the course of time); and third by the difficulties that face any enquiry into the distribution of differences.

37.   The question is often asked how widespread homosexual practices are. The answer is likely to depend on the society we are considering as well as the period of history.   It also depends on which definition of homosexuality we use.   Kinsey (1948),* in his study of American men, classified individuals in seven groups, ranging from exclusively homosexual to exclusively heterosexual.   According to Kinsey, writing in terms of sexual acts, four per cent of white American males were exclusively homosexual throughout their lives after the onset of adolescence; eight per cent were exclusively homosexual for at least three years between the ages of 16 and 55; ten per cent were more or less exclusively homosexual for such a three year period; and thirteen per cent were more homosexual than heterosexual for such a period.   In the companion study of American women Kinsey (1953) did not produce exactly comparable figures.   The age range was restricted to women between the ages of 20 and 35, and the highest overall figure for homosexual behaviour in women was six per cent.

38.   While more than one in three men had been actively homosexual for a period of at least three years between the ages of 16 and 55, it must be stressed that only about one in twenty-four had been exclusively so, the remaining majority being ambisexual.

39.   Although the accuracy of Kinsey's studies has been challenged by some, it is generally conceded that Kinsey demonstrated, and all available evidence supports his conclusions, that millions of white Americans are exclusively homosexual.

40.   What people prefer may vary with time and circumstances.   Most people seek to conform to the social behaviour of those around them, whether this is heterosexual or homosexual in character, and may then come to realize their essential preference more fully.   However, Kinsey's work relates to their behaviour; preference cannot be inferred directly from his statistics.

41.   What does not emerge from the study is whether those in the intermediate categories participated in homosexual activity as a phase in the

---

* Full details of publications cited in this chapter are given in the notes at the end of the report.

maturing process of their own sexuality; whether they changed because of social or other external pressures which drove them away from such activity; or whether there is a form of sexuality which can relate to either mode.

42. Paedophilia is a predominantly male activity; it is orientated towards children of either sex. Boys make up three-quarters of the total number of children concerned. Any propensity towards homosexual orientation does not seem to be increased in the case of boys affected by this practice.

THE DEVELOPMENT OF GENDER AND SEXUAL ORIENTATION

43. In their growth from conception to adulthood people develop as sexual beings in two different though related ways. They are developing into people we speak of as 'men' or 'women', that is, beings of one sex or another. They are also developing as sexual beings, that is, people with an orientation towards physical relationships with others. Normal development, leading to the adult person with a predominant or exclusive orientation towards sexual relationships with persons of the opposite sex, involves the unfolding and interaction of several biological and psychological processes during embryonic and postnatal life.

44. Biologically, there are three components in the sex of an individual. There is the genetic or chromosomal sex, the gonadal sex (the type of sex gland), and the phenotypic sex (the type of internal and external genitalia). Psychological aspects of sexual development include hormonal 'imprinting' of the brain during embryonic life, postnatal parental influences, and adolescent influences.

45. Chromosomes bear the hereditary material and are present in every cell of the body. They are thread-like structures, and the genes, responsible for inherited characters such as hair and eye colour, occur along their length. There are 23 pairs of chromosomes in each cell, and one pair constitutes the sex chromosomes, for they carry certain factors which influence sex determination. A female has two identical sex chromosomes, referred to as X chromosomes, while the male has one of these X chromosomes and a morphologically distinct Y chromosome. A normal female is thus termed XX, and a normal male, XY. Chromosomal sex is determined from the moment of conception.

46. The gonads are present in the embryo from a very early stage. At first, however, they are 'neutral' or 'indifferent', being neither male nor female, but later they are induced to develop into either an ovary or a testis. This process is brought about by sex hormones which the primitive gonad produces. If the genetic sex is male, certain constituent cells produce male sex hormones (androgens) while if the genetic sex is female, then female

16

hormones (oestrogens) are made. Later, these sex hormones also direct the differentiation and development of the internal and external genitalia, thus creating the 'phenotypic' sex.

47. Androgens and oestrogens are chemically very similar. They are synthesized from a common precursor and both are actually produced by each sex. In both sexes the precursor is metabolized first into androgen and then by a further step into oestrogen. However, in males the formation of oestrogen can be inhibited so that an accumulation of androgen occurs, while little oestrogen is produced. The difference between male and female pattern is therefore finely quantitative.

48. The sex hormones are also important in imprinting the sex of the individual on the developing brain. There is a precise area of the brain where there are some cells which have receptors for oestrogens only and other cells which have receptors for androgens as well. Martinez-Vargas and Fox (1975) suggest that in this way the cells can detect differences in the proportion of the two hormones and that on this basis a 'male' or 'female' neuronal circuitry is established in the brain, independently of the genetic sex.

49. Post-natally, psychosexual development involves the acquisition of a 'gender role' whereby a child 'learns' to be masculine or feminine. There is disagreement as to how this occurs, but agreement that it is established within the first five years of life. In Money's research (1957) 'gender role' is defined as all those things that a person says or does to disclose him or herself as having the status of boy or man, girl or woman, respectively. Acquisition of a gender role seems well under way by the time a child begins to have a command of language, around the age of two years, and by the fourth birthday it is firmly established in most children and remains fixed. However, it is possible for an individual to establish a defective, erroneous or ambiguous gender role compared with their assigned sex.

50. It is important to note that a good deal of masculine or feminine behaviour is a cultural expression, and what is masculine in one culture may be considered feminine in another (Mead, 1959).

51. In adolescence, the final phase of psychological sexual development is triggered by the powerful action of hormonal influences occurring at that time. This brings the previously developed sexuality to full maturity. The sex drive and responsiveness in both sexes appear to be dependent on androgens. Puberty is a period of intense physical growth and maturation of the secondary sex characters. As each individual matures biologically adult relationship patterns are developing and the personality crystallizes. Inter-personal interaction is important, and good and bad experiences at this time may have a profound effect upon psychological maturity.

17

52.   Thus, normal sexual development is extremely complex.   Genetic sex is a foundation upon which gonadal, phenotypic and psychological sex is built.   At any stage, the mechanisms may so operate that the functional result can appear to contradict the structural foundation.

## ABNORMAL SEXUAL DEVELOPMENT

53.   Genetically, there may be a deficiency or an excess of sex chromosomes, producing individuals with XO, XXX, XXY or XYY sex chromosome complements.   XO and XXX individuals are female, XXY and XYY are male.

54.   Faulty gonadal and phenotypic sex development result in inter-sexes—individuals where there is a discrepancy in the sex organs and parts, giving a mixture of male and female characters.   True hermaphrodites have both ovarian and testicular tissue present, pseudohermaphrodites have gonads of one sex and external genitalia of the other sex (or sometimes ambiguous sex).   A female pseudohermaphrodite, for instance, has ovaries, but looks male.   It is here that the importance of phenotype sex becomes obvious, for sex assignment is made at birth from the appearance of external genitalia, and it is on this basis that all the parental and social rearing process is founded.   In cases of aberrant biological development, even professionals may make a mistake, and certain individuals are reared as one sex, but should on other grounds be thought of as belonging to the other sex.   It is interesting to note, however, that such individuals do not constitute all those who seek a 'sex change'; many of those requesting sex change operations do so solely on psychological grounds.

## THE DEVELOPMENT OF HOMOSEXUALITY

55.   Is homosexuality an illness?   People differ in a multitude of ways, as everbody knows.   In some ways everyone is unique or nearly so (consider the variation of fingerprints, which means that one set of prints can almost certainly relate to only one individual).   Variation in height, skin, colour and so on are not necessarily indications of a disease process.   Psychosis is.   In which class does homosexuality lie?

56.   In this section we review some studies which are based on the biological data.   It is important to remember however, that homosexuals are not concentrated amongst those who have abnormal biological development; indeed, homosexuals are usually biologically normal.   Even where homosexuality co-exists with biological abnormalities, the latter do not necessarily provide an explanation for the orientation.   This is well

demonstrated by a female who was XXX (instead of XX) and who took the male role in a lesbian relationship. One might have expected maximum femininity if the sexual role depended on the chromosomes.

57. Studies of twins suggest that there is some genetic predisposition towards homosexuality, although what genotypic form (inherited character) it takes, and how it is mediated, for example through hormones, is not understood. A review of the evidence by Heston and Shields (1966) shows that there is a greater likelihood of both male twins of an identical pair being homosexual than is the case in a pair of non-identical male twins. This suggests that the ante-natal and post-natal environments are not sufficient alone to explain the fact that if one identical twin is homosexual it is likely that the other one will be too. There is no evidence that identical twins *per se* are particularly prone to homosexuality. Kallman (1952) also showed that if one male identical twin was homosexual, there was a high chance that the other twin would be too. This study has been criticised because many of the individuals included were psychotic. (This makes it difficult to be sure about their sexual orientation, for some psychoses produce a general disturbance of sexuality which might properly be called chaotic and may involve either the same or the opposite sex as a preference. Further, one of the earlier manifestations of schizophrenia may be difficulties with sexual orientation or even overt homosexual behaviour and, possibly, vague feelings about changing sex.) Twin studies in females are less clear cut. Nevertheless the available evidence suggests that genetic factors contribute to the aetiology of homosexuality, however indirectly. Environmental factors do, of course, play a part in most genetically influenced conditions. That they play such a part in homosexuality is shown by the occurrence of identical twins with different sexual preferences. On the evidence to date, it is likely that the aetiology of homosexuality is due to a combination of genetic and environmental factors, but their relative importance as a whole and in any individual remains uncertain, according to Pare (1965).

58. A theory of homosexuality based on an imbalance between androgens and oestrogens was postulated as long ago as 1944 by Lurie. By 1954, Swyer felt able to state that there was no convincing evidence that human homosexuality was dependent on hormonal aberrations in the adult. However, with further advances, the picture has again become less clear. As previously described, it is now known the sex hormones have a part to play in 'imprinting' the sex of an individual on the developing brain. Neuronendocrinological studies have shown that minute amounts of sex hormones can also have an effect on the brain centres concerned with sexual behaviour. Dorner (1969) showed that androgen (male sex hormone) treatment of female rats in the newborn period and again in adulthood resulted in predominantly male behaviour. Donovan and Bosch (1965) also

19

emphasized that androgens loom large in importance in the behavioural development of the individual.

59. One further consideration which may be dealt with at this stage is the question of body-build (somatotype). The concept is based on the work of Sheldon, who investigated types of body-build in relation to personality. As long ago as 1926 Hirschfield attempted to define a male homosexual somatotype, but Coppen (1959) found that the somatotype described correlated better with neuroticism than sexual preference. Henry (1951) and Kenyon (1968) investigated the same possibility in regard to homosexual woman. Henry's sample included a majority of individuals whom he categorized as 'bisexual or narcissistic', so he produced no clear-cut result. Kenyon agreed with Coppen that the somatotype correlated better with neuroticism than sexual preference. Thus the appearance of the individual seems to be largely unrelated to sexual preference, a conclusion shared by many other professionals who have worked with homosexual people for various reasons.

60. With regard to the rearing process many sorts and combinations of parent-child relationships have been postulated from Freud onwards as the cause of homosexuality. Homosexual men tend to have elderly mothers and elderly or absent fathers. A number of studies including Fisher (1962) and Wolff (1971) suggest that the mother is the more important parent in the consciousness of male *and* female homosexuals, but many of the theories cannot easily be tested. Nevertheless it seems that the sexual identity and sexual orientation are established at an early age, and certainly before any conceivable 'age of discretion'.

61. Adolescence has often been considered a crucial period in determining whether a person becomes a homosexual but the evidence is inconclusive. Some homosexual men have been found to have lower levels of male sex hormone than normal, but it is uncertain whether this is cause or effect. West (1965) considers that it may be causal, and notes that male homosexuality seems often to be associated with earlier than normal puberty. He further suggests that there seems to be a drift towards heterosexuality as the male individual ages in the adolescent period. Sexual development in homosexual women, on the other hand, appears to be late.

62. People often ask whether homosexuality is caused by homosexual seduction. Kenyon (1968) considers that it appears to be a minor factor and West (1965) considers that it is usually a case of confirming the sexual preference than actually producing it. Sexual identity is often insecure in adolescence and a number of adolescent males are afraid that they may be homosexual when they are really anxious about their potency (though this anxiety *may* have a homosexual basis). Homosexual behaviour in the

adolescent may only be part of a crisis of identity, a passing phase, and should not in itself be looked upon as evidence of a fixed sexual orientation.

63. It is likely that in adolescence it is the ambisexually orientated who are most susceptible to what Bancroft describes as the push-pull factors. These may incline an individual either towards a heterosexual or homosexual preference at a time when his or her identity is crystallizing, the sexual drive is strongest, and many new relationships are likely to be formed (in the period leading to adulthood). At this period an ambiguous orientation may be swayed one way or another by the proclivities of those with whom the adolescent is associated.

GENITAL INTERCOURSE

64. Human genital intercourse is unique in the animal kingdom in certain respects. Human beings can have sexual intercourse at all times, while animals have mating seasons. Also the vagina is transposed forwards anatomically speaking, which makes face-to-face intercourse possible, and intercourse usually last much longer than in most species. This might support a case for the importance, in human terms, of the biologically secondary function of sexual relationships, namely, the relational rather than the reproductive.

65. The most obvious distinction between heterosexual and homosexual practice is that only the former can achieve reproduction, which is the primary function of sexual intercourse *in vaginam* from the biological standpoint. That apart, however, heterosexual and homosexual genital behaviour are very similar. Heterosexual couples can, and many do, enjoy mutual masturbation, intracrural intercourse, oral-genital intercourse and anal intercourse. Their use by heterosexual couples would not call for medical comment by most doctors. Virtually all human beings have tendencies to engage in these kinds of sex acts. Kinsey (1948, 1953) and his associates have pointed out that manifestations of extra-vaginal sexual activity are part of our mammalian heritage, and it would be a rare individual who had no such tendencies.

66. Transvestism consists in deriving sexual gratification from dressing in the clothes of the opposite sex. There are no entirely satisfactory data on this activity, but most workers in the field would probably agree that the substantial majority of transvestites of the fetishistic kind are basically heterosexual, using masturbation for sexual release, with a small proportion having homosexual tendencies (altogether not very different from the population as a whole). However, it may form part of a homosexual pattern when cross-dressing becomes part of seductive behaviour.

21

67. Transsexualism is a wish to change one's sex, and this, in the absence of hermaphroditism, where a 'truer' sex may be achieved by medical means, involves altering the given bodily structure and function by such radical measures as castration and hormonal treatment together with complicated plastic surgery. The aim is to adjust the body to fit with the person's sexual identity, which is a psychological phenomenon as previously described. A proportion of transsexuals may be strongly pushed in the transsexual direction because of a fear of homosexual identity, or a wish to avoid it.

## THE PSYCHOLOGICAL UNDERSTANDING OF HOMOSEXUALITY

68. We have already seen (para. 60 above) that Freud sought to explain homosexuality in terms of the relationship between parents and their children. Homosexuality has been extensively studied by psychologists. Their findings depend very much on the constitution of the sample studied, and the homosexuals studied may have little in common apart from their homosexual behaviour. Homosexuality is apparently compatible with mental health and as good a social adjustment as society will allow. On the other hand it would be naive to consider that those homosexual people who are seriously disturbed are ill merely because of a reaction to a hostile environment, although in many cases homosexual people become depressed at least partly as a response to society's attitude towards them.

69. Measurable psychological variables have been extensively studied. In a published symposium Maccoby (1967) provided an annotated bibliography of some 500 articles of relevant research. Many have pointed to this or that set of characteristics, but all the findings may best be seen in the context of Klein's (1946) review of the concept of femininity (which would seem to be applicable *mutatis mutandis* to masculinity). Her summary contains the passage:

> The impression one gains from this variety of disciplines is definite on only one point, namely, the existence of a concept of femininity as the embodiment of certain distinctive psychological traits. What, however, is considered essential to this concept depends to a large extent on personal bias and valuations and on the social-historical vantage point of the observer.

70. In psychoanalytical terms homosexuality is considered as a failure to reach full maturity in development. The liturature is large and complicated and only a brief review is possible here. Freud stated that the belief that in man sexual life only begins at puberty is incorrect. On the contrary signs of it can be detected from birth onwards, it reaches a first culminating point on or before the fifth year after which it is inhibited or interrupted until the age of puberty, which is the second climax of its development.

All experiences during the first period of childhood are of the greatest importance to the individual and, in combination with his inherited sexual constitution, form the dispositions for the subsequent development of character or disease. It is, according to Freud, a mistaken belief that 'sexuality' coincides with 'genitality'. The sexual instincts pass through a complicated course of development, and it is only at the end of it that the 'primacy of the genital zone' is attained. Before this there are a number of 'pre-genital organizations' of the libido—points at which it may become 'fixated' and to which, in the event of subsequent repression, it will return (so-called 'regression').

71. Social factors play an important part in the development of sexually appropriate behaviour, whether one adopts the social learning hypothesis or the cognitive-development one. The former emphasizes the fact that acquisition of sexual behaviour can be described by the same learning principles used to analyse any other aspects of behaviour—for example, conditioning, reward, punishment; the latter stresses the cognitive aspect in the active nature of the child's thought as he organizes his role perceptions around his basic conceptions of his body and his world.

72. There have been various attacks on the psychoanalytical theories in recent years. In the field of sexual functioning Masters and Johnson (1966) have questioned the distinction between clitoral and vaginal orgasm which is an important Freudian concept in connexion with the maturing process of female sexuality. Kenyon (1968) on the other hand studied a sample of overtly homosexual women and found that 58 per cent. had had heterosexual intercourse, and in that mode only 10 per cent. had experienced regular orgasm compared to 45 per cent. of the control group. This supports the psychoanalytic point of view.

73. The behaviourist school have attempted to test the hypothesis that homosexual orientation is the product of abnormal learning processes during the development of the individual. With patients strongly motivated towards changing their homosexual orientation into a heterosexual one, so-called 'aversion therapy' has been used by members of this school, but according to Bancroft (1974) without success.

74. It will be seen that in general, neither the psychoanalytic nor the behaviourist view of the development of sexuality is at variance with the known basic facts of that development, but the detailed steps in the development have been made the subject of several interpretations, some of which are mutually incompatible and all of which are difficult to test.

75. When we come to consider definite psychiatric disorders, a neurotic depressive reaction is common in homosexual people; this may be precipitated by conflict over being a homosexual person in contemporary

society, a broken sexual relationship, or some other stress not related to sexuality in any obvious way. It is not clear whether homosexual people are more prone to such reactions than the general population.

76. Brain-disease or damage may be associated with chaotic sexuality (as in the case of some psychoses), with homosexual orientation in some cases. This may be due to the removal of the normal control mechanisms built up by the individual during development (dis-inhibition) or to altered perceptions consequent on the changes in the brain.


THE QUESTION OF TREATMENT

77. Consideration of treatment requires us first to decide whether homosexuality is rightly understood as a pathological state, i.e. an illness. If it is not, but is, rather, a variant in sexual development (a view we hold), treatment would be appropriate only if the condition was unacceptable to or unwanted by the individual concerned.

78. The question then is whether he or she can be helped to change, or at least to learn to experience and enjoy heterosexual relationships instead of homosexual ones. This help, it should be stressed, would be an educational developmental process of adaptation, rather than a cure of a sickness.

79. There is no doubt that certain individuals do approach doctors, psychotherapists and counsellors to help them with their homosexual feelings, and that some are able with guidance and help to develop and enjoy heterosexual relationships. These people are presumably within the ambisexual range. The help given to them differs from the counselling offered to homosexual people who have no wish for, or for whom it would be difficult or impossible to develop, heterosexual relationships. Such people suffer distress from the fact that they are homosexual in a preponderantly heterosexual society. It should be stressed that it does not follow from the fact that some people can be helped to change in this way, that all could, let alone should, receive such help.

80. In saying this, we must however remember that it is possible that only 4 per cent. of people are exclusively homosexual: another 29 per cent. may have had homosexual experience but in greater or less degree be capable of heterosexual relationships. Whether it is possible to change a person's orientation by any means is uncertain. Psychoanalysis has made certain claims in this direction, and so has aversion therapy. It is difficult to validate the former objectively, and it seems the success of the latter is in doubt. All treatment or re-learning depends on the motivation to change expressed by each homosexual individual. It must be emphasized however that, medically speaking again, it is very undesirable to put

pressure on homosexual people to try to 'solve their problem' simply by marrying, as this false solution may bring misery to the spouse and children.

## SUMMARY

81. The development of homosexuality does not seem to depend on any gross genetic, gonadal or phenotypic abnormality. Its origins seem much more likely to lie in hormonal imprinting in embryogenesis and/or in the rearing process by parents or parental surrogates. This is not to say that the hormonal processes do not depend on some genetic basis, or that the rearing process does not depend on the apparent phenotype to some degree. The various inter-acting factors in adolescence appear to be confirming rather than formative processes.

82. How then can we understand the differences of sexual orientation, apparently ranging from exclusively homosexual to exclusively heterosexual?

83. There are various possibilities. First, during the phase of hormonal imprinting during embryogenesis an alteration of the proportion of oestrogen and androgen may affect the development of the neuronal circuitry to promote a homosexual orientation under the stimulus of the surge of hormone activity at puberty. This presupposes that the neuronal circuitry is 'neutral' with regard to such orientations until the balance of hormones at the critical phase selects a dominant pattern, just as the internal and external genitalia are selected from a 'neutral' basis under the influence of genetic and hormonal influences. Second, it may be that the rearing process, usually by parents, may produce an inappropriate or ambiguous gender role in the child. For instance Bene (1965) adduced some evidence to suggest a relationship between the parents' wish for a son and the homosexuality of their daughter. It would seem that the pressure on children, when their ability to perceive is rather weak, and when the influence of the parents' world is strong, may be overwhelming. It is hardly surprising if some people's gender-identity is displaced away from what would be expected from the genetic sex, even when the external genitalia are unambiguous.

84. Thirdly, it is possible that homosexuality is a psychological process equivalent to a neurosis. As there is no agreement on how the latter is caused, it is perhaps idle to speculate as to whether the developmental processes are similar or not. Certainly many homosexuals appear to have a good social adjustment, unlike many people with a neurosis, although some homosexuals develop neuroses or psychoses, just as heterosexual people do.

85. Ambisexuality may be seen as a partial shift caused by the same

processes which produce exclusive homosexual orientation. Such a shift might result from relatively weak hormonal or family rearing influences, or alternatively from a mild form of some definitely neurotic process.

86. At present medical science can give only a very incomplete account of the formation of sexual orientation. What we do know suggests that people have the responsibility for deciding whether or not to express their orientation in sexual acts, though the very strong nature of the sexual drive must be reckoned with. It can after all make people who are exclusively heterosexual in their usual social context behave in a homosexual way when confined to a society exclusively of their own sex.

87. Sexual relationships between human beings, we have seen, are rooted in biological existence. Between men and women they are the means by which the life of the species is carried on. Nevertheless in saying this we have only begun to speak of their importance.

# 3

# Homosexuality: The Biblical Evidence

THE OLD TESTAMENT BACKGROUND

88. References in the Bible to actual homosexual behaviour are comparatively infrequent. As far as the Old Testament is concerned, the Authorized Version makes mention of 'sodomites' in such passages as Deut. 23.17, I Kings 14.24, 15.12, 22.46 and II Kings 23.7. But the Hebrew word so translated really means 'male cult-prostitute' and it is unclear whether the persons so described had intercourse with men or with women. Given the fact that such cultic prostitution was concerned with the promotion of fertility, the latter seems to be more likely. Otherwise, the only directly relevant passages are the story of Sodom in Gen. 19.4-11 and the brief references in Lev. 18.22 and 20.13.

89. Behind the Sodom episode, there lies a long and complicated history of the development of the tradition but there are certain elements in it which may be noted as being of particular relevance to the present enquiry.

90. First, in recent years, some commentators have considered that the story is not concerned with homosexual behaviour at all. They interpret Gen. 19.5 not as referring to intercourse but as a request to know the credentials of the strangers who have entered the city. However, there seems to be a connection between the story of Sodom and the episode in Judges 19 which has a number of similar features; and the context of the demand in Judges 19.22, 'Bring out the man who came into your house, that we may know him', strongly suggests that sexual intercourse is there in question. It seems likely, therefore, that the Sodom story does contain a reference to homosexual behaviour.

91. Second, as the comparison with Judges 19 also indicates, the crime of the inhabitants of Sodom is viewed primarily as a failure to respect the duty of hospitality, which was regarded so much more seriously in the ancient Semitic world than it would be today. The purpose of the homosexual attack is to demonstrate the ultimate breach of the obligation of hospitality. It is noteworthy that, in the Old Testament references to Sodom outside of Genesis, homosexuality is not explicitly picked out, but the inhabitants are depicted as guilty of a wide range of religious and

27

social sins, for example in Jer. 23.14 or Ezek. 16.49. Only later in Jewish and Christian tradition does homosexuality come to be regarded as the specific sin which brought down the divine judgement on Sodom.

92. Thirdly, the narrative in Gen. 19 is a variant of a widely diffused folk-tale dealing with the inhospitable treatment accorded by the inhabitants of a particular place to divine visitants whose identity was not realized. We are dealing not, it would appear, with history but with legend.

93. Fourthly, this consideration is reinforced by the clear aetiological element in the narrative, i.e. part of its purpose is to explain the occurrence of a natural disaster in the Dead Sea region and to account for the desolate character of that area.

94. Fifthly, the story exemplifies what may be found even more obviously in other Biblical and extra-Biblical passages, namely, the Israelite judgement on Canaanite society. Sodom is depicted as a stereotype of the peculiar wickedness and corruption of Canaanite culture.

95. Two points may be made by way of summary, in view of the great weight which has commonly been given to the Sodom story as indicating, clearly and beyond all doubt, the Biblical reaction to homosexual behaviour. On the one hand, while, as we have argued, the narrative does express abhorrence of homosexuality, that is not its sole, or even its primary, concern. In assessing its relevance for the question of homosexuality in our contemporary society, we have to view the story as a whole and to take full account of its particular character and of all its concerns.

96. On the other hand, if, as we have argued, the account is not historical, it cannot be taken, as so commonly in the past, to record an instance of divine action intended expressly to condemn and punish homosexual behaviour. It is a reflection, rather than a cause, of existing attitudes and beliefs, the nature and origin of which must be sought elsewhere.

97. By contrast, the laws of Leviticus are intended to regulate the real situation of an actual community. We may perhaps pick out three characteristics of them. First, although there are some unimportant differences in the formulation of the commandments in Lev. 18 and 20 respectively, they are both embedded in legal collections dealing with the family as that was known in ancient Israel. In their existing context, they are presented as direct commands of Yahweh, and we shall see the justification of this presently, but it would be generally agreed by Old Testament scholars that this is a later setting of the material and that the laws themselves originally existed independently, probably once without any explicit divine sanction. They were not basically moral commands of universal application, although to say this is not necessarily to pre-judge the validity of the development by which they have become so. Rather

their aim was to strengthen and preserve the family group, which was really the Israelite totality, the only social organization the Israelites knew, by forbidding anything which, from the standpoint of that group, disturbed its harmony or prevented its growth and continuance. Marriage—although here we must be careful not to invest that word with all the connotations of the commonly presented Christian ideal of marriage today—was one of the most vital bonds in such a society, and homosexual behaviour was seen as a grave threat to it and its social purpose. For this reason, the death penalty was prescribed for such behaviour, not so much as punishment, but rather to root out, in the only way open to the Israelite of those days, a potentially destructive element in the social organism.

98. Second, in both passages we are discussing, homosexual acts are described by the Hebrew word *toebah*, commonly translated as 'abomination'. A good deal has often been built on this term, so it is necessary to try to look briefly at its meaning. It has commonly been defined by some such statement as 'a strong Divine aversion from the violation of certain principles'. But, in the most thorough study yet devoted to the term, P. Humbert comments that, in Leviticus, 'the offence of *toebah* is formulated without direct reference to Yahweh but with reference to Canaanism. *Toebah* is something in itself and not only with reference to Yahweh'.[1] In the Old Testament the word is frequently used of the worship of idols and the significance of this and its connection with Canaanite religion will be discussed below.

99. But it also has a much wider use, often to describe actions which would not arouse in us anything like the same intense reaction as does homosexuality. For example, in Genesis it is an 'abomination' for Hebrews to eat with Egyptians, and in Proverbs false scales are an 'abomination'. What appears to lie behind the use of the word in the Old Testament is the concept of an order of being which runs through the entire world and of which human society is a part. And basic to this concept is the idea that everything and everyone has a proper nature and a proper sphere: the clearest expression of this is found in the priestly picture of creation in Genesis 1, where God creates by making a distinction or separation between the different parts of the universe and by assigning creatures with appropriate characteristics to each part. So whatever disrupts the proper ordering of the world and society is an 'abomination' and such disruption is particularly shown whenever any creature diverges from its proper nature or proper sphere. So another dimension is added to the condemnation of homosexuality, indicated by the words in Lev. 18.22 and 20.13 'as with womankind' and by the close connection of Lev. 18.22 with the forbidding of bestiality, which is significantly described by the word 'confusion' or, in the New English Bible rendering, 'violation of nature'. Put very simply, men are created to have intercourse only with

women, not with men or beasts. Here then we have something which can be called a doctrine of natural law—although no doubt not in the Stoic meaning of that term—and what we shall want to say about it will tie up with our discussion about law in general. However, there is one point to be made about the Old Testament view in particular. It is doubtful if its conception of homosexual behaviour as unnatural—although, since Hebrew has no term corresponding to 'nature' in this sense, we must be cautious here—rests on the belief that sexual activity must only be with the deliberate object of procreation. Of course, that is of prime importance for the preservation of human-kind and society. But the Old Testament contains a number of carefully defined lists of females with whom intercourse is forbidden and it is implied that intercourse with other females outside these categories is permissible. It is not marriage which is envisaged here but simply intercourse. No doubt, in the case of women with whom intercourse was allowed, offspring would often be the result; but, since the object of the intercourse rules was to preserve and define the family structure, such children had no status in society and so their birth was not the *purpose* of sexual intercourse in this instance. It is not perhaps possible to go much further than to say that the Old Testament does not question what it sees as the divinely ordered pattern of sexual differentiation and relationship.

100.   The third consideration which must be noted concerning the Levitical prohibitions of homosexuality is that the most explicit reason given for them is that homosexuality, along with many other practices, was characteristic of the Canaanite population of Palestine. They are part of what it means to be a heathen and it was because of these practices that God's judgement fell on the Canaanites in the form of the Israelite conquest. Israel must be completely separate from Canaan and it must avoid behaving in their ways lest it too suffer dispossession of its land. So it has often been said that one reason why homosexual activity was abhorrent to the worshippers of Yahweh was that it was associated with idolatrous Canaanite worship. How far this was in fact the case and, still more, how widespread homosexual practices were among the Canaanites, is much less clear than is often supposed, but, in any event, the view we are discussing is the theological interpretation of history of the compilers of the Law of Holiness (Lev. 17-26), fashioned by the circumstances of the Exile and by their hopes for a restored Jewish community. This interpretation they grafted on to the much older legal material which they wished to preserve. The main concern is to establish the separateness and distinctiveness of the people of God. This, of course, is not to deny that homosexual practices as such are condemned in Leviticus but only to underline that they are seen as peculiarly characteristic of heathen religion and society and that in Leviticus this is the basic reason for avoiding them.

THE NEW TESTAMENT

101. When we turn to the New Testament, the key passage is Romans 1. 18-32. In considering these verses, we are led beyond the brief and infrequent references to homosexual behaviour in the Bible to a deeper understanding of the nature of man and the world which underlies them. For the context of Paul's argument in Romans 1 is the doctrine of Creation. Some reference has already been made to this in connection with the Old Testament, but it is necessary to say a little more about it at this point.

102. In the creation accounts in Genesis 1 and 2, humanity is divinely created as male and female. One purpose of this is that human beings should 'be fruitful and increase', that is, that sexuality should properly be only in the context of a man-woman relationship. There is a creation pattern for human sexuality and that pattern is heterosexual. Nor is it simply a question of the procreative function of sex here, for as D. Daube has recently pointed out,[2] the words of Genesis 1.28 indicate a blessing which human beings enjoy, parallel to the blessing of 'dominion' over other creatures, not a duty which they have to fulfil. Elsewhere in these accounts, most notably in Genesis 2.18, the emphasis falls on the complementarity and companionship of male and female; while in Genesis 2.24, the phrase 'they become one flesh' implies the coming together of two persons into a new and unique personal union.

103. Paul's argument in Romans 1 is to be seen against the background of the Old Testament doctrine of the creation of men and women. Because humanity in general has departed from the knowledge of the one true God, so it fails to recognize the divine purpose in sex and hence misuses it, and of this misuse homosexual practices are the clearest example. What Paul means by 'unnatural' is 'unnatural' to mankind in God's creation pattern. All homosexual behaviour is a divergence from God's creation scheme and, in the words of one writer, 'when set in the context of creation, all homosexual relations are unnatural relations'.[3]

104. But also, in this passage, as will be clear from what has been said already, Paul can be seen to inherit the concern of the Old Testament with the distinctiveness of the chosen community over against the world in general, a concern which had become increasingly sharpened in the later Judaism of his own time. As with the Old Testament, his basic idea is that the sins of the heathen are punishments for their basic error of being heathens, that is, their abandonment of man's proper role in the creation which involves the recognition of the one God. It is easy to claim that Paul is merely reproducing the stock Jewish reaction to the Gentile world and to point out that his description of the pagans even of his own day is exaggerated and unfair: not everyone in the Roman Empire behaved in the way his sweeping statements would suggest. It is also easy to say that

31

Paul does not treat the problem of homosexual behaviour in isolation and to make the perfectly valid point that the Church has generally been much harsher in its attitude to homosexuality than to many of the other sins listed in verses 29-31. Nevertheless, all the offences he lists are wrong and ought not to be found among the Christian community. Paul gives special prominence to homosexual practices, partly no doubt because of their widespread acceptance in the Graeco-Roman world compared with their comparative infrequency in the Jewish community which he knew, but also, more profoundly, because these represented one of the most fundamental ways in which man, though called to be the crown of creation, diverged from his proper place and function in the natural order of being as that was viewed in the Old Testament. What is legitimate to emphasize, as far as Paul is concerned, is that he is in this passage primarily concerned with the sinful state of the world outside the Church, in sharp distinction from the people of God; again, homosexual behaviour is part of what it means to be a heathen. In this, as we have noted, he is very much in line with the Old Israel.

105. The same concern seems to be reflected in the two other New Testament passages bearing directly on homosexuality, I Timothy 1.10, where the whole passage in verses 8-11 may well rest on the Ten Commandments, and I Corinthians 6. 9-11, where the picture is of the new life of the Corinthians in the kingdom of God in contrast with their sinful condition before they became members of it. Discussion of these passages, as far as homosexuality is concerned, has largely centred on the precise meaning of the Greek terms they employ, and here there is a good deal of uncertainty as can be seen from the different renderings of them in current English translations. It seems clear that certain forms of homosexual activity, along with other sins and offences, are being condemned, whatever exactly they may have been. The real nub of the discussion, however, is whether the author or authors had in view the homosexual *condition* or merely certain homosexual *practices*. However, this is an issue which is raised by the whole of the biblical material relating to homosexuality and must be considered later.

106. This review demonstrates what was said at the beginning of the chapter, that in both the Old and the New Testaments there is comparatively little about homosexuality. Furthermore, on some of what is said, particularly the episode of Sodom, when it is carefully examined, not as much weight can be placed as has been done in the past. Nevertheless, what evidence there is seems clearly to show condemnation of homosexual behaviour. For many, this will settle the matter. They will hold that the Bible so plainly indicates the divine disapproval of such behaviour that it must be wrong in all circumstances, and especially so for Christians, who recognize the Bible as an inspired collection of writings which gives authoritative guidance for the conduct of human life.

107. But this at once raises the very large and disputed problem as to the kind of authority we are to give to Bible statements, particularly in the moral and ethical spheres. The issue is not, primarily, between those who would hold to a literal interpretation and a simple acceptance of every biblical injunction and those who would not, because the former category does not exist in practice. Even those who would call themselves 'fundamentalists' recognize different levels of authority in different biblical statements: for example, the Sydney Archdiocese's Report on Homosexuality builds its discussion of the Law of Moses and Modern Society on the distinction drawn in Article VII of the Articles of Religion between ceremonial and civil precepts, on the one hand, and moral commandments on the other, a distinction which is quite foreign to the Old Testament law itself, and which can be justified, within the biblical context, only by reference to what is viewed as a higher authority such as the prophets or the New Testament. Rather, the issue is how far specific biblical statements on moral and ethical behaviour and attitudes provide, to quote the Sydney Report again, 'timeless principles and patterns of morality'.

108. Here various considerations arise. First, the biblical writings certainly reflect the social ethos, needs and structure of a particular society or a particular group at various stages of its development. We live in a society which is in many ways very different from anything to be found in the Bible and we are often able to see a degree of relativity in biblical attitudes and standards, in a way that was not possible to previous generations, in the light of historical, anthropological, sociological and psychological knowledge which was not available to them. In other words, even when we can be confident that our text of the Bible is fixed and constant, the Church's understanding and use of it, and hence the attitudes and actions which derive from this, are not.

109. It is important to bear in mind how many moral and ethical precepts which in the Bible are presented as the direct commands of God have been re-interpreted in the course of Christian history and even in some cases abandoned as guides or standards for the conduct of individual and social life. One might instance the doctrine of the 'holy war', a theme which looms very large in the earlier parts of the Old Testament, according to which the cause of the God of Israel was advanced through actual warfare and the Israelites were required by him totally to exterminate his and their enemies when they had conquered them. Today our evaluation of this custom will be determined by our seeing it against the background of the assumptions and practices of the ancient Near Eastern world in which the life of Israel was set: we may even wish to argue that it was a necessary stage in the unfolding of God's plan for his people and that Israel's distinctive faith and society could not have been preserved in

33

any other way in the actual circumstances of history. But surely most contemporary Christians would not take it as a principle or pattern for their own behaviour. Nor would they hold that their faith and their Church needed to be protected by such means. Nor, even if they did not renounce war altogether as an instrument of national policy, would they think it right for military operations to be conducted in such a manner.

110. If we apply such considerations to the question of homosexuality, we may note that, as was said in paragraph 97, one of the motives for the strong condemnation of homosexual practices in the Old Testament was that these were seen as a threat to the preservation of the family group. But this is not just a sociological or anthropological question: in the Old Testament it has a theological aspect as well. In the Old Testament, to quote DeKruijf, 'contact with God was connected with their being the people of God, because in this chosen people God dealt with man. Therefore it was important for every man and woman in Israel to receive this life and pass it on in marriage'.[4] Sexual activity was closely linked with the covenant and the handing down of the promise from generation to generation. But in the New Testament, the people of God is constituted on a different basis, through baptism and not through human descent. Marriage, however important it remains, no longer has the same imperative religious significance that it has in the Old Testament, and other options are open to members of the divine society, notably celibacy, which, it is important to remember, has often been viewed in Christian tradition as the ideal, in marked contrast to the outlook of the Old Testament.

INTERPRETING THE BIBLICAL EVIDENCE

111. It does not follow from this that the Church should necessarily sanction homosexual behaviour, even to a limited extent. Many, for instance, would wish to argue that homosexual activity always poses a threat to family life, directly or indirectly, and that for this reason it cannot be tolerated. What is being claimed is that the question cannot be settled by reference simply to biblical texts that deal directly with homosexuality. These have to be considered in the light of the underlying message of the Bible, especially the New Testament, and in assessing and interpreting this, we need to take account of knowledge not available to biblical writers, and moral intuitions formed in the Christian tradition. Thus the bearing of the biblical material on how we should think and act in our present situation has also to be evaluated in the light of those other theological, philosophical, medical and social insights which are discussed in other chapters of this Report. What follows is not intended to prejudge this question but to illustrate what has been said about the use of the Bible in answering it.

34

112. One of the important conclusions of the previous chapter is that there are a considerable number of people who are sexually attracted only to members of their own sex, so that we can properly speak of a person as being 'homosexual'. Here again is an area of human personality which has been identified only in comparatively recent times and which seems to have been largely unknown to the biblical writers. They appear to have had no conception of the 'true' homosexual or the exclusively orientated homosexual condition as such. Rather, they are speaking of homosexual behaviour undertaken by those they presume to be heterosexually inclined by nature. If this is so, it is right to ask how far it is proper to apply the biblical prohibitions of homosexuality to those people whom they could not possibly have had in view. The Church today, in its pastoral concern for the individual, has to determine what it will say to such persons, guided not so much by particular commands or statements which were not directed, and may have little relevance, to their case, but by the light of the biblical revelation taken as a whole. Again, it is to this question that other sections of our report are addressed.

113. Many Christians, however, would still take the view that there is nothing wrong or sinful in a homosexual disposition, in having strong feelings of attraction towards the same sex, but that it is wrong and sinful to translate those feelings into overt sexual behaviour. They would regard this distinction between disposition and acts as still requiring that the biblical condemnations of homosexual activity should apply unconditionally. But it is necessary to give a warning against such a possible solution, not least because many in the Church have perhaps tended to adopt it somewhat uncritically in the recent past. However much such an attitude marks an advance in Christian understanding of homosexuality and however convenient it may be for the Church in practice, it is doubtful if biblical support can be claimed for the distinction on which it is based. While we may wish to distinguish clearly between a strong desire to do something and a firm intention to do it, the Old Testament at least is much less clear in drawing a sharp line between such a strong desire to do something and the actual doing of it. In Pedersen's words: 'the action and its accomplishment are a matter of course, once the thought is there'.[5] If one is wrong, the other will be too. Presumably the same outlook is reflected in the famous saying of the Sermon on the Mount about looking on a woman to lust after her. Thus in Romans 1, when men abandon the true worship of God and embrace idolatry, they are delivered over to the unchecked operation of their own homosexual desires and passions and these are viewed as blameworthy, as much as, if not more than, the actions which result from them.

114. Against the line of argument which proceeds by questioning the absoluteness of biblical condemnations of homosexual behaviour, at least

35

two objections may be urged. It has been pointed out earlier that the New Israel has abandoned many of the things which the Old Israel saw as vital for the preservation of its distinctive religion and society and to which it ascribed the status of divine commands. We also noted that many of these, for example, circumcision, are set aside in the New Testament because of the further revelation of God's nature and purposes found in the gospel of Jesus, who claimed a higher authority than the Jewish Law. However, as we have also noted, this is not the case with homosexuality, where the attitude of the Old Testament is reinforced by Paul and the other New Testament writers. There is nothing, it would seem, in the New Testament to justify the Church in relaxing the condemnations of all homosexual behaviour which it inherits from the old covenant.

115. But the matter cannot simply be left there, for many of the considerations about the character of the Old Testament material which have been raised earlier apply also to the New Testament. Paul, too, was a child of his age and was as limited by its outlook as were the men of the Old Testament. The particular problems he had to face and answer for his own time were not always the same as ours and we cannot necessarily expect him to give complete guidance for every moral dilemma in the situation in which the Church finds itself today.

116. Further, we have to take seriously what has been called the 'discontinuous aspect of Jesus's ethics' over against the Old Testament and the claim that the new and fundamental aspect of his teaching is the demand for unconditional love in conduct. It would be consistent with this to maintain that the Church in every age should set forward specific directions for the regulation of sexual behaviour and expect its members to conform to them, even when such obedience involves great suffering on the part of the individual. But it would mean that such directions may vary at different periods, for they express, not timeless principles, but 'second-order' rules. These are binding only insofar as they derive from the principle of love, on the one hand, and from what is seen as necessary for the preservation and furtherance of the distinctive message of the gospel at any particular time, on the other.

117. The modern philosophical distinction between first-order principles and second-order rules arguably has its counterpart in the New Testament itself, as when Paul differentiates between commandments which come from him, as the one who has 'the care of all the churches', and those which derive from the Lord. If this is so, it is at least possible to ask whether, granted our greater knowledge, as compared with the New Testament, of the homosexual and his condition, homosexual relationships might not in some cases, although by no means all, be as genuine expressions of love as other human relationships. On this view, the abiding significance of

the biblical condemnation of homosexuality for the contemporary Church would be as a witness to the need always to stand fast against the misuse of sex in this as in other areas.

118.   Second, it may still be objected that the biblical doctrine of creation, which we have argued is of fundamental importance for this whole area, clearly rules out any kind of homosexual activity for those who accept its teaching.   There is only one God-given pattern for human sexuality and to depart from it is to deface the image of God which makes humanity what it ought to be.

119.   This consideration, however, is not conclusive.   First, it can be argued that there is a dynamic as well as a static element within the biblical view of creation and the material order itself.   It is proper, and indeed helpful, to speak of a concept of 'natural law' in the Bible, but this must not be misunderstood.   It does not imply a fixed pattern in nature which precludes any change or development.   In the Bible God remains sovereign over the natural world that he has made, and the fact that he intervenes in it means that it is controlled by the purposes of a personal being and not by immutable laws.   Further, for the Bible, this personal being is directly concerned with the condition and needs of every individual, a concern which the Church, as an agent of his loving care, must also exemplify.   Hence Christians have not hesitated to modify aspects of at least the Old Testament view of creation which Israel saw as of binding significance.   Thus, for example, the Old Testament concept of the order of being in creation, described in paragraph 99, finds its clearest expression for the actual situation of human life in the distinction between clean and unclean animals.   For Leviticus, the non-observance of the regulations which safeguard the distinction between clean and unclean is a serious matter, and the debate about this in the New Testament clearly shows that the early church fully realized their importance.   But finally Christianity abandoned them.

120.   In the second place, it can be argued that according to the creation accounts in Genesis, complementarity and companionship are as much a part of the divine pattern for sexual relationships as is procreation.   The Bible does not clearly separate these two aspects, and it is difficult to imagine that in Genesis the relationship between men and women does not find its true and supreme expression in marriage.

121.   But if it is the case, as again we have previously argued, that there are those who genuinely cannot achieve this ideal with members of the opposite sex, is their condition an aspect of the fallenness of creation, or is there a place for them in the divine order wherein they may fulfil the sexuality which is theirs?   It is to this central question that the following chapter of this Report is addressed.

# 4

# *Theological and Ethical Considerations*

122.  Taking account of the medical and social evidence before us we now have to make recommendations as to the view Christians should take of the phenomenon of homosexuality, remembering all the time that it is people we are dealing with.  The task is a difficult one both because of the intrinsic complexity of the subject and because opinion is divided within the Church as well as outside it.  Some, at least, of these differences have been reflected in the Working Party itself—indeed it could not have been at all representative otherwise.

123.  We shall proceed as follows.  First we shall state as clearly and as sympathetically as we can what we take to be the main approaches in our society to the moral questions posed by the phenomenon of homosexuality. Then we shall endeavour to identify the elements of truth to be found in them.  And finally we shall attempt to develop a position which will, so far as possible, do justice to all of these.  We shall do our best to make the argument at each stage clear enough for the reader to be able to decide to what extent, if at all, he is prepared to accept it.  It will be apparent from this statement of intention that we do not think that any very simple solution is available.

## (i) THE TRADITIONAL VIEW

124.  The Christian tradition is a complex one and there are today, and have always been, varying opinions within the Church as to the relation between scripture and tradition and as to the extent to which, and the means by which, the tradition of the Church may be interpreted, modified and developed.  There can be no doubt that the Church has traditionally condemned homosexual acts as sinful, and this is a fact to which any Christian must attach considerable weight.  But, as can be seen from the case of contraception, which has also been traditionally condemned, this fact cannot of itself be decisive for the Christian conscience.

125.  The traditional arguments have tended to fall into two groups. There are those based upon scriptural passages from both Old and New Testaments and those based upon Natural Law.  Here indeed is one

example of the diversity of Christian tradition, for the direct appeal to Scripture has been characteristically protestant and the appeal to nature characteristically catholic.

126.   The appeal to Scripture, as has been argued in Chapter 3, if confined to those passages which refer specifically to homosexuality, provides us with a rather narrow and somewhat ambiguous base for contemporary Christian teaching.   The Old Testament passages that prohibit homosexual practices prohibit equally behaviour of other kinds that Christians today, however traditionally minded, would regard as unexceptionable.   Paul regards homosexual vice as characteristic of the sexual licence and disorderliness of the Graeco-Roman world at its worst.   In so doing he attacks disordered sex in all its manifestations, but does not specifically address himself to the question whether homosexual relationships must always be disordered and, if so, why.   Neither does he recognize as something distinct the predicament of the individual who is homosexual but not by choice.   Hence we do not think that it would be possible on the strength of these passages alone to rule out of court the contentions of those who claim to find in the ethical teachings of Jesus, and indeed of Paul himself, the germs of a personalist understanding of sex which would require us to revise the traditional judgement of the Church upon homosexuality.

127.   Nevertheless, as we also argue in that chapter, there is in these passages an underlying assumption, which cannot be entirely dismissed, that homosexual practices represent a departure from man's proper nature or sphere as ordained by God.   How or why this should be so is not made fully explicit in them.

128.   One way of making it explicit is through the developed Natural Law approach.   The appeal to nature in relation to sexual morality has been extensively discussed and assessed in the course of the debate about the morality of contraception in the Roman Catholic Church.   If the form of the natural law argument against contraception used in *Humanae Vitae* is valid, it holds *a fortiori* against homosexual practices.   If it is not valid, discussion of it should help us to see whether the appeal to nature in some other form has force and, if so, what its bearing is upon the homosexual question.

129.   The argument in its simplest form holds that the sexual act by its very function is aimed at the transmission of life and that it is against nature, and consequently wrong, to engage in sexual activity in which this aim is frustrated.   It concludes that each act of intercourse should be open to conception, and it is this conclusion that rules out contraception.   As has frequently been noted, the argument in this form, with its emphasis upon procreation as the primary end of intercourse, proves both too much and too little for its proponents.   It rules out any intercourse, even in

marriage, which it is known will not in fact lead to conception on account of age, pregnancy or permanent or temporary infertility; and it permits artificial insemination by the husband, where procreation is secured, although by artificial means. In order to avoid these implications the argument has to be supplemented by a further criterion of what is natural. This is expressed in terms of a particular pattern of genital behaviour which must not be interfered with. However, the further difficulty is then encountered that we do not feel bound to require animals to conform to this anatomical pattern. In their case we have no hesitation in using artificial methods of contraception or insemination. There may be good reasons for differentiating in this respect between animals and human beings, but they are not to be discerned simply by examining the mechanics of human reproduction. This suggests that attention needs to be paid to the whole context in which human sexuality finds its meaning. To enlarge the context in this way is to take account of the function of sexual intercourse in expressing and confirming love between the sexes. The official Roman Catholic position recognizes and indeed emphasizes this. Before Vatican II it was customary to set the 'ends' of marriage in a hierarchical order and to insist that the expression and confirmation of love in intercourse must be subordinated to the primary 'end' of marriage, *viz*. procreation. In the Pastoral Constitution *Gaudium et Spes* the language of a hierarchy of ends was dropped. Nor was it re-introduced in the Papal Encyclical *Humanae Vitae*. The latter, however, continued to insist that each act of intercourse must be completed without direct interference in the generative process. This requirement tends to conflict not only with the demands of the personal relationship between the partners, but also with any adequate interpretation of the end of procreation itself. For this involves the rearing of children as responsible human beings, which in turn is held to require a family of manageable size and a happy and relaxed relationship between the parents.

130. If these criticisms of the standard Roman Catholic position are justified, as we believe them to be, the appeal to nature in that particular form is both invalid and incompatible with a satisfactory understanding of marriage.

131. Reference has been made, in the course of the Roman Catholic debate about contraception, to a principle of totality, by which the morality of individual acts might be assessed in terms of the morality of the total married relationship. Although rejected by *Humanae Vitae* there are the germs of this position in Aquinas, for whom the content of the Natural Law is provided by man's inclinations, among which are the inclinations to sexual intercourse and to the upbringing of children. This is the basis for the Natural Law argument for monogamy. which depends on the claim that it is the institution best adapted to the care and education of children.

132. When interpreted in this way the Natural Law approach relates more convincingly to the psychological and social realities of human life and becomes to that extent morally more persuasive; but it ceases to have the character of a single tight and definitive argument. That biologically the primary function of sex is procreation is evident enough, and that this is related to the rearing of children; but in order to arrive at a satisfactory theology of marriage this simple appeal to the biological function of sex would need to be supplemented by a wide range of other considerations.

133. However, an argument may be controversial and yet have force; it may require to be supplemented by others and yet have its own independent weight. And it remains possible that both the traditional approaches we have considered have a contribution to make to a final judgement. Thus it could be argued that, although the norm of monogamous heterosexual marriage is not straightforwardly derivable from nature, it can draw rational support from the biological relationship between sexuality and procreation. That human and animal species reproduce themselves sexually; that sexual differentiation is essentially connected with generation and with the rearing of the young; that tenderness between mates and between them and their young plays an important part in the whole process; all this is undeniable. That in human societies family relationships are of central importance both to the individual and to society is also clear. The traditional Christian doctrine of marriage, although not based solely on these facts, can claim to derive considerable support from them. If it makes sense at all to talk of 'the purpose of sex', it is hard to deny that these facts have a bearing on it. We are, however, bound to conclude that neither of the traditional approaches, in the form in which they have generally been presented, provides us with an understanding of sexuality that is adequate to the task of forming a Christian judgement about homosexuality. The appeal to Scripture, if it is to be illuminating, must look to the biblical treatment of the central themes of human love and marriage rather than to the occasional and somewhat peripheral texts that mention homosexuality itself; and the appeal to nature must be made in a broader context than the merely biological.

## (ii) THE LIBERTARIAN VIEW

134. On this view there is no need for any morality relating specifically to sexual behaviour. This is not to say that there are no moral constraints upon sexual activity. Care should be taken to prevent the birth of unwanted babies (which with effective contraception is now possible); beyond this, the moral constraints which apply to sexual behaviour are simply those that apply to human conduct in general. Thus in sexual matters, as in all others, people ought not to injure or exploit one another

but, so long as they avoid this, everything is permitted. No doubt some uses of sex are 'higher' or more profoundly satisfying than others, but that is no reason for condemning these others. In this respect the pleasures of sex resemble those of eating and drinking. No one condemns the simple satisfaction of hunger or thirst, or eating and drinking for pleasure, merely because these activities can sometimes also have the character of a spiritual or aesthetic experience. The sexual capacities of men and women can be used and enjoyed in an indefinite variety of ways and this variety, within the sort of moral constraints mentioned, is to be welcomed and encouraged. It follows that homosexual practices are in no way to be condemned as such; and it makes no difference whether they are undertaken by persons who are aroused erotically only by members of their own sex or not.

135. This approach is individualistic. It takes as its basic concern the question, 'What do I really want: what will give me the greatest satisfaction in life?'. Each individual is to ask and answer this question for himself. The answer can be discovered only by a process of growing self-awareness based upon experience and experiment. Although prudence may counsel enduring rather than fleeting relationships, this is a matter for the individual to decide and individuals may well decide it differently. As homosexual relationships are non-procreative, one of the strongest arguments for a permanent and exclusive relationship, *viz.* that of family stability for the benefit of children, is absent.

136. From this standpoint homosexual practices are 'natural' in the sense that many people feel an inclination towards them and find them satisfying. Whether in any other sense of the word such behaviour is 'natural' is considered to be morally irrelevant. It follows that what have traditionally been regarded as 'unnatural practices' such as bestiality, paedophilia and incest are either not to be condemned or to be discouraged for some other reason than their 'unnaturalness'. It is arguable that both bestiality and paedophilia lack the element of consent which ought to characterize a sexual relationship, that paedophilia may cause psychological harm and that incest threatens the security of a family and is to be avoided on that account. Libertarians may differ as to the force of such considerations, as is shown in recent discussions of paedophilia, but they agree as to the sort of case that would have to be made out in order to justify moral condemnation of these practices. It seems best to postpone an assessment of this libertarian view until we are able to compare and contrast it with the remaining position we wish to discuss.

## (iii) THE PERSONALIST VIEW

137. According to this view what matters in sexual behaviour is the quality of personal relationship that it serves to express and confirm.

A sexual relationship thus has a symbolic character which makes it inappropriate to regard it simply as a way of giving and receiving pleasure, a character which would be unlikely to survive in an entirely permissive society. Hence there is need for a specifically sexual morality, since some sexual behaviour must be ruled out as not properly personal. Bestiality and prostitution would be cases in point, and doubtless paedophilia too. Incest would be more problematical; the relationship is personal enough in itself and, if condemned, would have to be rejected on account of its effect on other family relationships.

138. The personalist approach tends to be found in a stronger and a weaker form. In the stronger form the emphasis upon the personal dimension results in a comparatively strict moral imperative. Sexual intercourse (or other sexual behaviour) is thought of as the uniquely appropriate expression of profound erotic love and as such, therefore, not to be engaged in where genuine love is absent. Some would hold that genuine love involves a life-long exclusive commitment, but a more characteristic view is that the relationship should be exclusive but need not be permanent; it should last as long as love lasts and no longer.

139. In this stronger form the personalist view is anti-permissive, since it finds unacceptable sexual relationships which fail to express the quality of love that it demands. But many personalists adopt the weaker position that, so long as a sexual relationship is minimally personal, it is at least to be accepted, even if a more completely loving relationship would be better.

140. Much of the evidence we received on behalf of homosexual equality was given from a personalist standpoint. It was argued, especially by Christian homosexuals, that the Church's teaching about the ends of marriage lays great stress upon the unitive or companionate aspect of marriage, and that a homosexual relationship may reflect this value to the same extent and in the same fashion as a heterosexual one. We received a good deal of persuasive testimony along these lines from correspondents and those who talked with us in the course of our work. Some of them, indeed, complained about what seemed to them an over-emphasis upon various genital acts, whereas, they claimed, for many homosexual people themselves these are secondary and what counts is the relationship as a whole.

141. The personalist argument was often supported by another, which is in effect a variant of the traditional natural law approach. This maintains that it is as natural for the homosexual person to be homosexual as for the heterosexual to be heterosexual. An 'equivalent' or 'alternative' ethic therefore applies. A homosexual couple would expect to treat each other, and be treated by the community, exactly as would a heterosexual couple. They are 'by nature' constituted differently and have, therefore, developed in a different sexual direction.

43

142. It is evident that the 'personalist' approach covers a fairly wide range of possible attitudes and it remains to be seen whether they are all consistent with one another. Some, but not all, personalists would accept two of the main features of the traditional outlook, *viz.* (i) the appropriateness of asking 'what sex is for' and (ii) the insistence upon permanence and exclusiveness in sexual relationships. These are features which the libertarian explicitly rejects. He regards the question whether behaviour is natural as of doubtful meaning and of no moral relevance; and he considers the question of the degree of permanence or exclusiveness of a sexual relationship to be entirely a matter for personal choice.

143. Thus, in one of its forms, the personalist approach would seem to point strongly in the direction of homosexual 'marriages' or at any rate of a bond which would be as permanent and exclusive as marriage is normally taken to be. This would be to accept to the full the givenness of the homosexual orientation in those concerned, taking them completely seriously in this condition. But other personalists would regard the traditional model as being unduly restrictive for homosexuals and, indeed, often for heterosexuals too.

## THE APPROACHES REVIEWED

144. In reviewing these different approaches it seems appropriate to start from the libertarian end. The libertarian approach has the merit of simplicity. It is tolerant and realistic and leaves as much as possible to individual choice. It calls attention to the extent to which sexual morality in the past has been influenced too much by social conventions and irrational taboos. It is, as a rule, presented in criticism of the influence of historical Christianity, but it receives support from some Christians who value its freedom from the prejudices of the past and who hear echoes of the Gospel in its refusal to judge people.

145. Nevertheless it seems to us that its excessively individualistic and atomistic approach does not do justice to what is known about the fundamental importance of sex in human life, which remains as in some sense given and involving social relationships, whether individuals choose to recognize it or not. Hence it fails to appreciate the need for disciplines and constraints in the realm of sexual behaviour, which are widely held to be required, and not only by Christians. The sexual impulse is too strong and affects too much of human life to be left entirely to be determined by purely individual and subjective judgements. The universal acceptance of the libertarian approach would prove unsatisfying to the individual and damaging to society.

146. The reluctance of many of its advocates to go all the way with it provides some evidence of this. They feel bound to condemn certain forms

of sexual activity as inappropriate but are hard put to justify this by their own essentially hedonistic criteria. That bestiality is sub-human and paedophilia objectionable because (among other reasons) one of the partners is immature are considerations which they cannot altogether discount; yet to give any weight at all to such considerations is to admit the validity of constraints upon sexual behaviour which are not freely chosen but arise out of the nature of sex itself as an inescapable part of human life. By contrast the personalist approach is able to do full justice to the conviction that sexuality is important, and provides a persuasive rationale for it, *viz.* that sexual activity is the uniquely appropriate expression of profound erotic love between the sexes (and, perhaps, between those who are erotically attracted, whatever their sex). But it can do so only in its stronger form, in which it emerges as severely restricting the limits within which sexual activity is permissible. So that on this point, it would seem, a crucial decision has to be made. Either the significance of sex is something that individuals may or may not choose to give it—they are free to accord their love-making deep personal meaning, but they need not do so—or the significance is something there to be discovered, which men ignore at their peril. If the first line is taken 'personalism' collapses into permissiveness, and the personalist is doing no more than express his own individual preference for enduring and deeply personal relationships, while providing no stronger warrant than the libertarian does for rejecting an entirely hedonistic approach to sex on the part of those who prefer it.

147. If the second line is taken, the personalist is open to a challenge that can also be directed against the traditional Christian teaching about marriage. Both employ the argument that sexual intercourse is implicitly an act of *total* self-giving and so an unspoken promise of *continuing* care and love. This is, in effect, to claim that the act has a symbolic character. But what is the force of this claim? It may indeed be the case that sexual intercourse *can* signify and symbolize such a total and continuing relationship, and also that Christians and personalists are right in wishing to restrict its practice so that it *shall* signify and symbolize this. But may it not also in practice signify and symbolize a number of other kinds of personal relationship which are neither as deep nor as lasting as this? No doubt there are psychological and emotional causal processes involved which have to be taken into account as more or less 'given' but, granted these, may not sexual intercourse to a large extent signify and symbolize what we *choose* it to signify and symbolize? This seems, for example, to be the clear implication of Father John J. McNeill's challenging book *The Church and the Homosexual,* in which the 'radical freedom of man' in relation to his sexuality is strongly emphasised.

148. If we are inclined to say 'No: we are not free to make of sex just what we will (subject only to the sort of moral and prudential constraints

45

that apply to any other activity)', we are recognizing implicitly that there is something in the nature of human sexuality which is determinative for us. Many who have no religious beliefs are intuitively convinced that this is so, but it is notoriously difficult to find a satisfactory rationale for this intuition in wholly non-religious terms.

## THE TRADITIONAL APPROACH RECONSIDERED

149. At this point, therefore, we are led to reconsider the traditional approach, for with its explicitly theistic assumptions it is in a position to raise and answer questions about 'the purpose of sex' which are not questions simply about the purposes to which men choose to put sex.

150. The traditional approach that we considered earlier was based upon scriptural passages which refer specifically to homosexuality, and upon Natural Law arguments in the form in which they have been developed in the official teaching of the Roman Catholic Church. We concluded that neither of these provides a foundation broad enough or secure enough for a sound contemporary judgement upon the problems of homosexuality. We need to draw upon the teaching of Scripture about the more fundamental themes of love and marriage; and we need to conceive of Natural Law in a broader context than the merely biological. In proposing to reconsider the traditional approach we assume that, in order to form a Christian judgement upon any contemporary problem, a distinction has at some point to be made between what is of underlying and permanent validity and relevance in the Bible and in the tradition of the Church, and what is appropriate to a particular time and place. Such a distinction may be made in the faith that the Holy Spirit continues to guide and enlighten the Church.

151. The early formation of the Christian tradition derived not only from the Scriptures, which were not afraid to celebrate the sexual love between man and wife, but also from the Fathers of the Church, whose attitudes and opinions were shaped by a very different cultural environment. There were those who praised the virtues of marriage, and there were others who praised the virtues of virginity, reckoning that marriage was at best a remedy against lust and a necessity for peopling God's kingdom. What seems to have been widely accepted among Christian theologians was the view that sexual activity was suspect. It was not that it was inherently evil; but it was, since the Fall, disordered. Passion bordered on concupiscence and concupiscence merged with sin. Consequently Christians, inside or outside marriage, must exercise a discipline of self-control. Outside marriage this meant celibacy; inside marriage this mean the subordination of sexual pleasure to the duty of procreation.

152. Within such a context, in which human sexuality was confessed to be disordered and marriage was considered first and foremost as a necessity, it was hardly to be expected that there should be any emphasis on the links between sex and love.

153. The recognition of the unitive aspect of married love has had an uneven course. Now here, now there, it has had acclaim. Today, however, it would be generally agreed among Christians that sex has been given for the purpose of expressing and confirming love between the sexes in a life-long union. This is consonant both with Christ's reaffirmation of the Genesis one-flesh doctrine and with what we have later come to learn about the deeply pervasive influence of sex in human life. It is indeed unsatisfactory (as McNeill and others have insisted) to regard human beings as wholly subject to the demands of 'mere biology', but it is equally unrealistic to treat men and women as pure spirits whose sexual identity is entirely a matter of individual or cultural choice, and thus to ignore the profound physical and psychological complementarity of the sexes. The appeal to scriptural doctrine and the appeal to nature provide converging reasons why sex should be uniquely important for personal and social relationships.

154. Because the Christian doctrine of marriage gives it a sacramental character—marriage represents for us a sacramental mirroring of the divine love—it explains how the sexual act can have a significance which does not derive simply from human choice or convention. This understanding of marriage is influenced by the use of sexual language in the Scriptures to speak of the relation of God to Israel and of Christ to his Church. God's love for us—strong, faithful, jealous—finds at least one of its most adequate expressions within our experience in the highest forms of sexual love.

155. If marriage is taken as the norm, as we believe it must be, the question that has to be faced in relation to homosexuality is whether a homosexual relationship can be regarded as an equivalent of marriage (whether or not it is given formal recognition). Many homophile writers argue that it can, and that 'homosexual equality' must be conceded as soon as the 'unitive' end of marriage is seen to be independent of the 'procreative'; and that means, so they would claim, as soon as contraception is agreed to be legitimate. For sex may have precisely the same effect in expressing and confirming a loving relationship between persons of the same sex as it does between married couples, and also the same symbolic character. It is true that Christian tradition has consistently taught otherwise, but this, it is argued, is one of those instances which must occur from time to time in the history of the Church, when later and more profound reflection upon certain central doctrines leads to the abandonment of more peripheral judgements which are seen to have been erroneous or of merely temporary validity.

156. As has already been remarked, the tendency of this line of reasoning is towards the recognition of homosexual 'marriages'. If it were possible to separate entirely the requirement of permanence from that of procreation a way would be open for the traditionalist as well as the personalist to accept the claims of homosexual equality. Whether such a reconciliation is actually possible, however, depends not only upon the willingness of the traditionalist to accept this severance but also upon the readiness of the personalist to insist upon permanence. In fact we were somewhat surprised to discover how little enthusiasm there seems to be among homosexual people for 'homosexual marriage'. Although many, if not most, of those who advance the claims of homosexual equality do so from a broadly personalist position, the dominant opinion among them seems to be that permanence and exclusiveness, while necessary in a sexual relationship that is characteristically procreative, are not in the same way necessary (though they may be desirable) in one which is not. Formal recognition and legal restraints are, they believe, equally inappropriate. If there is a heterosexual equivalent to the desired kind of homosexual relationship it is not marriage but a more or less serious 'affair'.

157. It may be urged that homosexual relationships should be considered in their own right and not forced into categories formed for heterosexual ones, so that we should not ask whether a particular homosexual relationship is tantamount to a marriage or an affair. (It is misleading to use the word 'affair' in this context because in the heterosexual case there is normally the alternative of marriage.) There is some force in this objection but, to the extent that it has force, it points to significant differences between the two which may affect the claim that they are equally 'valid'. The crucial issue is that of fidelity. Traditional Christians and many 'personalists' attach paramount importance to fidelity in sexual relationships. Even if the former could be persuaded to give up their insistence upon procreation as an 'end of marriage', many would continue to insist on its permanence. They would in that case be taking the view that the primary purpose of sexual activity is to express and confirm a personal relationship marked by permanence and mutual fidelity; and that an additional, but separable, purpose is the procreation and raising of children. Fidelity would accordingly be demanded as much in homosexual as in heterosexual relationships. In this way, and this way only, the personalist element in the traditional doctrine of marriage could be stretched to cover homosexual partnerships. If, however, homosexual partnerships are held not to be subject to the requirement of fidelity and permanence, this difference would seem to suggest that they differ in other important respects from marriages.

158. One way of dealing with the problem which is favoured by some personalists is to maintain that the fidelity requirement does indeed go with

procreation and is based solely on the needs of children. So it applies only to fertile marriages and applies to them only so long as there are dependent children. Sexual relationships not constrained by the needs of children can safely do without long-term commitments and should last as long as love lasts, but no longer.

159. The question, then, would in that case turn on the Church's understanding of marriage. Is the Church prepared to countenance a loving but impermanent attachment whether heterosexual or homosexual so long as there are no dependent children? Or should permanence (i.e. marriage) be required for heterosexuals but not for homosexuals? Or for both? The decisive question seems to be whether the institution of marriage is thought to consist in a deep sexual relationship between two individuals, to which children may be added without affecting its essential character; or in a relationship whose entire nature is decisively influenced by the fact that it characteristically results in children. On the first view a homosexual marriage is entirely intelligible; it would exhibit one of the characteristics of ordinary marriage and that, arguably, the most important one. On the second view it would be impossible to regard as equivalent to a marriage a sexual relationship in which not only procreation, but the act of coitus itself was impossible. It is difficult not to reach the conclusion that a concept of marriage in terms of which a case for homosexual equality could be made out would be a defective one. It would imply the possibility of detaching the 'unitive' end of marriage from everything else that makes marriage what it is. When two people marry they enter into a status (they 'consent together in Holy Matrimony'), in which they complement each other biologically, psychologically and spiritually, and in which they accept responsibility in the sight of God and men for one another and for any children of the marriage. The marriage represents a personal union and a social unit of an unparalleled kind, upon which the existence and character of a society uniquely depends.

160. The shape of the institution of marriage is moulded to fit the sexual and personal needs of the partners, and the needs of children for continuous love and security, in such a way that the satisfaction of each of these different needs tends to aid the satisfaction of the others. There is, therefore, in marriage, a possibility of personal fulfilment, to which the personalist approach is sensitive, but which depends to an extent that the personalist sometimes fails to appreciate, upon its character as an institution. Not every marriage need issue in children. but the partners in a childless marriage share in a pattern of life which is available to them only because most men and women have children. By contrast a sexual relationship in which the partners, however deeply and intensely it may engage them, do not undertake a permanent commitment, is bound to lack

the many dimensions of marriage, the complex interweaving of diverse strands, which give it solidity and strength. In a homosexual relationship one strand, the deep biological complementarity of the partners, is lacking altogether. Hence the ideal of sexual love as deeply personal, which many thinkers today rightly insist upon, is not readily detachable from its roots in the sexual polarity of men and women; and men and women are sexual beings through and through and not just biologically, although their sexuality cannot be adequately understood without some reference to the biological function it subserves and the social patterns which go with it. In marriage all these strands run together and it is this fact that engages the personality at all levels and makes the sacramental language of the Christian tradition appropriate. This is not to subordinate the personal to the biological or the institutional, but simply to recognize that personality has biological foundations and that persons require appropriate institutions for their full development.

161. Thus we believe that Anglicans should continue to teach that the norm for sexual relationships is one of mutual love, expressed and nurtured in life-long and exclusive marriage, based on the givenness of biological and psychological potential, and open to the future in respect both of permanence and procreation. At the same time the Church leaves to each married couple the liberty to determine responsibility for themselves whether they shall use contraception or not, and presumably also the liberty to decide the details of their sexual behaviour. We believe that this is a proper development of Christian tradition and can be supported from Scripture, tradition and experience.

162. In saying that marriage is the norm, we intend more than that it is an ideal to which men and women should, so far as possible, approximate. It represents for Christians something given which has the character of a demand upon us. It does not, of course, follow from this, as the Victorians may often have supposed it did, that the status of marriage automatically confers a spiritual superiority, no matter how loveless the marriage, over those who fail in various ways to achieve the norm. But it would also be a mistake to assess sexual relationships by grading them all alike upon a single scale of lovingness and ignoring other morally relevant distinctions which human relationships, individual and social, require.

163. If the Church seeks to maintain this norm, which is an exacting one, it has a special responsibility for those who, for whatever reason, find it difficult or impossible to satisfy it. Pastoral sensitivity and discernment will be needed and unsympathetic and undiscriminating judgements must be avoided. We must now ask what implications our discussion has for the Church's attitude to homosexuality.

## THE HOMOSEXUAL PREDICAMENT

164. Traditionally the Church has ruled out homosexual practices entirely and we are not persuaded that this was a judgement that can now be seen to be totally erroneous or of merely temporary validity, for it does follow in principle from an understanding of sexuality which we believe to be fundamentally sound and defensible. But there is one important respect in which the situation has changed. It was assumed until quite recently that every mature individual was capable of a heterosexual response. It is now clear that for a significant proportion of the population this is not the case. Whatever the cause or causes may be—and we have seen that there is no agreed view—there are many men and women who find themselves able to respond erotically only to members of their own sex. For most there is little prospect of altering their condition, which, indeed, feels to them 'natural'. They cannot, therefore, enter into a heterosexual marriage which has any chance of being complete and it would normally be very unwise to try to persuade them into it. Yet they may not be called to celibacy and may long for that tenderness in genital relationships which heterosexuals can hope to experience in marriage. It is true that many people who would like to marry cannot, and the whole tenor of our discussion makes clear that we cannot accept the view that everyone has an unqualified moral right to sexual self-expression. But the frustration to which the homosexual man or woman is exposed is of a different order. It is not only that individuals cannot, as a matter of fact, find a partner with whom to share a complete and satisfying and socially acceptable sexual relationship. That is something that is allowed, if at all, only to exceptional individuals, and even then in the face of considerable reserve and sometimes active disapproval, and this in a society which attaches enormous—and, indeed, exaggerated—importance to sex in all its manifestations and encourages people to think of themselves and value themselves pre-eminently as sexual beings.

165. It is not surprising that in this situation many homosexuals have sought to vindicate their own identity as homosexuals by claiming that a homosexual relationship is as such in every way as 'natural' and as 'valid' as any heterosexual one can be. We have not found it possible to accept this claim and we think that many homosexuals would not accept it. But we have an obligation to consider how a homosexual can best witness to that 'sacramental mirroring of the divine love' which the Christian Church sees in marriage.

166. It is of first importance that he should not condemn himself or be condemned by others because of his homosexual orientation, and this means that he should be enabled to recognize it and encouraged to believe in the possibility of coming to terms with it and putting it to good use. We have received evidence from Christian homosexuals for whom abstinence has

not been a merely negative response but who have achieved a full and active life of enhanced sympathy and sensitivity. We have also received evidence from others who have taken a careful and responsible decision to enter into or maintain a relationship in which homosexual genital acts will take place and who have found in their love for each other the source of a wider care and concern.

167. The difficult question we have to consider is how to view this latter response on the part of those who have no choice in their homosexual orientation. There are those who would urge us to condemn unreservedly any such decision as being plainly contrary to the divine will. There are others who would counsel us with equal vehemence to recognize that for some people homosexual relationships are the only deep sexual relationships possible, and to declare unequivocally that for them to enter into such a relationship is the appropriate way to 'mirror the divine love'. In effect we are being urged to declare that the Church should either totally forbid or explicitly sanction homosexual practices. Total prohibition, it is claimed by some, would be true to Christian tradition. Explicit recognition, it is equally strongly maintained by others, would be a legitimate development of tradition based upon a dynamic conception of God's creative and redemptive grace.

168. We feel the force of both these appeals, contradictory though they are. But neither, to our mind, is sufficiently sensitive to the truth which the other represents. On the one hand, the celebration of homosexual erotic love as an alternative and authentic development of the living Christian tradition which ought to be accepted as such by the Church today would involve the repudiation of too much that is characteristic, and rightly characteristic, of Christian teaching about sex. On the other hand, to declare that homosexuals may not in any circumstances give physical expression to their erotic love is unduly to circumscribe the area of responsible choice, to lay on individuals a burden too heavy for some to bear, and, by restricting the options open to them, to hinder their search for an appropriate way of life. In the light of some of the evidence we have received we do not think it possible to deny that there are circumstances in which individuals may justifiably choose to enter into a homosexual relationship with the hope of enjoying a companionship and physical expression of sexual love similar to that which is to be found in marriage. For the reasons which we have given such a relationship could not be regarded as the moral or social equivalent of marriage; it would be bound to have a private and experimental character which marriage cannot and should not have. Nevertheless, fidelity and permanence, although not institutionally required, would undoubtedly do much to sustain and enhance its genuinely personal commitment and aspirations.

169. Because of the inevitable lack of the sort of conventions and formalities which still to some extent surround courtship and marriage, a decision to seek a homosexual relationship has its evident risks. It is nevertheless notable that well established and stable homosexual unions are often recognised by society as such and afforded a certain measure of acceptance. The maintenance of a relationship in which fidelity and constancy have been experienced and demonstrated is more readily accepted by others than the initiation of a new relationship in which their presence and persistence are problematic.

170. Homosexuals, through no fault of their own, find themselves in a situation of great difficulty, in which many of the guidelines normally available do not apply, and in which there is little general understanding or sympathy. They need the assurance that solutions adopted by them in good faith—and we assume that we are here talking of mature adults capable of responsible choice—will not be condemned out of hand by people who cannot know all the circumstances of each case.

171. We would ask those who wish the Church to condemn such homosexual relationships unreservedly to have regard to the Church's pastoral concern for those who cannot conform to the norm of marriage. This concern, we believe, must show itself in a willingness to help men and women who are homosexual to decide in hope and confidence what they shall do, while recognizing that those who are members of the Church will, as such, make their own individual contribution to the exacting task which we have attempted here of interpreting the Christian tradition in relation to the problems of today. Upon this basis we believe that the Church can and should speak pastorally and positively and present the values which can be found in different choices, while recognizing also the restraint that needs to be exercised.

# 5

# *A Legal Perspective on Homosexuality*

## THE HOMOSEXUAL MINORITY

172. This chapter is concerned primarily with the legal expression of the relationship between the homosexual minority and the wider society of which it forms a part. We are very conscious of the land-mines which await anyone venturing into this area. For example, the phrase 'the homosexual minority' suggests a readily identifiable group; it obscures the difficulties of defining that minority and the problem of ambisexuality. Again, as soon as we think of a minority, a special class, we find ourselves wondering what 'we', the majority, should do to 'them', assuming that something should and can be done, and this may be the outsider's version of the ghetto mentality. For all that, it remains proper to ask how the wider society should react in terms of social convention and possibly of legal regulation to the existence of the homosexual condition and of homosexual acts and relationships, and also how the needs and interests of the majority should affect the attitudes and actions of the homosexual.

173. Some homosexual men and women who have 'come out' and who wish to take part in homosexual social activities or enter into homosexual relationships complain of discrimination against them by the institutions of society and by the agents of those institutions. So, for example, there is dissatisfaction with the present state of the criminal law, and there are complaints of harassment by the police. We consider these criminal law matters later. But complaints are made in many other contexts: of discrimination in employment, in education, in the attitudes of courts and social work agencies, in adoption and in child custody cases, and, in the case of established homosexual couples, in relation to mortgages and taxation.

## DISCRIMINATION

174. It is important in considering these matters to be clear about the use of the word 'discrimination'. It means to distinguish between, to observe and in appropriate cases to act upon a distinction. In some contexts discrimination is proper and praiseworthy; we honour a discriminating judge of art, for example. In other cases, as in racial discrimination, we

54

refer to *improper* distinction in treatment: the prior judgement that the races are to be treated equally is implied but unspoken.

175. If we were able to accept the view that homosexuality, despite being the sexuality of a minority, is entitled to full equality in social, educational and theological terms, it would of course follow that we would regard the differential treatment of homosexuals as in all cases improper. Insofar as we cannot accept such a claim to full equality, we cannot accept a rule of general application. Instead it becomes necessary to look at particular situations and individual cases, seeking always to avoid the use of shallow stereotypes and generalized labels.

176. As an illustration it is possible to consider cases of unfair dismissals. One possible approach would be to urge employers to react to the known homosexual activities of an employee as they would react to the corresponding heterosexual activities: if this man is not put at a disadvantage if he is known to have a disorderly heterosexual private life, his homosexual colleague should be in no worse state. Some in the homophile organizations might object that this approach could retain an element of unfair discrimination because of the absence of a socially-approved homosexual equivalent to marriage. Others might argue that homosexuality has special features which are often relevant in those employment situations in which an employee's private life is likely to be taken into account.

## PARENTHOOD AND CHILDREN

177. Decisions concerning children raise acute difficulties. The reader may care to consider the following cases:

(1) A marriage founders when the wife declares that she prefers a lesbian relationship. She proposes to live with another woman who she has known for some time; the prospects for that relationship being stable and secure are good. The husband will make his home with his sister, a young childless widow. There is a child of the marriage, a boy of seven. Each parent claims custody of the boy. What weight is to be given to the lesbian nature of the wife's new relationship?

(2) A lesbian couple wish to adopt an orphaned child. The child's parents both died in an air disaster, while the child was staying with the couple. Under present law two persons not being spouses cannot adopt. Should the law be changed? Should the nature of the relationship prevent adoption in this case by one of the couple?

(3) Before a child can be adopted, its natural parents must either agree to the adoption, or have their agreement dispensed with by the court on the ground that it is being unreasonably withheld. Should a court be more willing to dispense with the consent of a parent if he is of homosexual disposition? (cf the reported case of *Re D (an infant)*, 1977).

178. These cases raise a number of issues. In what sense is it harmful for a child to grow up in a homosexual environment, or aware that one of his parents is a homosexual? (The difficulties are perhaps increased by

the duty laid upon the courts and the social work agencies by the Children Act 1975 to have regard to the child's own wishes.) What weight is to be given to the fact that an adult party to a case has entered into a relationship which is non-procreative? And how far is the reaction to these questions coloured by fears, often quite groundless on the facts, that a child will be the victim of a sexual assault?

179. The belief that adult male homosexuals are always a threat to children is an important element in public attitudes to homosexuality generally. It is the most prevalent of the misconceptions which exist and it is understandably resented. It is clear that there is a class of child-molester, who is typically attracted by young children (often of either sex) whom he wishes to fondle or whom he invites to touch or inspect his genitals. Such behaviour, more pathetic than immediately dangerous, is understandably greatly shocking to the parents of the child, and in some cases the child himself will be frightened and disturbed, though there may be no long-term ill effects.

## YOUNG PEOPLE

180. Of much greater relevance is sexual activity between adults and children at the age of puberty or in the immediate post-pubertal period. Some men are particularly attracted by boys at this stage of development. Other homosexuals occasionally find a partner aged 14 or 15. One American study, using a large sample of men convicted of homosexual offences involving adults, put the proportion who had had sexual experience with boys of that age since they themselves attained the age of 18 at one-third.[1] Some pornographic material directed at the male homosexual market includes photographs of boys of this age as well as mature men. For some of the men involved the preference for boys seems to be part of a general emphasis on youth; in other cases, it is merely a question of availability.

181. One comment on the practical working of the law in relation to homosexuality is to be found in a conference paper of the Campaign for Homosexual Equality published in 1975:

> The law is designed to afford protection to young people. In practice it does not. On the contrary it often causes suffering. A number of researchers have demonstrated that homosexual contacts between boys under 16 and adults do no harm, do not have subsequent adverse effects, are not traumatic and are not a factor in bringing about a homosexual orientation. It is clear that much more harm is caused by police investigations, court appearances and the emotional reaction of the adults who become involved, including parents and teachers, than by the individuals themselves.

182. That passage calls for a number of comments, all of which need to be considered against the background of Kinsey's evidence of a 'spectrum'

in sexual orientation: here, as elsewhere, it must be remembered that sexual preferences are not necessarily wholly heterosexual or wholly homosexual in any one individual.

183. The passage quoted attacks the view that one homosexual experience by an under-16 year old leads to a permanent corruption. As our chapter on the physical aspects of homosexuality indicates, we agree that such a simplistic 'seduction' argument is false. But a continuing homosexual relationship over a period of time might have a different effect, and a habitual pattern of behaviour at variance with the individual's predominant sexual orientation on the Kinsey spectrum could be established. It is significant that the Netherlands Speijer report,[2] so often cited in this context, reached a carefully qualified conclusion: 'The Committee is of the opinion that *generally speaking* a minor of 16 years and older will not be made a homosexual by a homosexual contact' (para. 7.4(10); italics added). It will be noted that the Speijer Committee restrict their conclusion to minors of 16 years and older. This was dictated in part by their terms of reference, which were similarly restricted; but it is clear from the text of the report that they were influenced by evidence that post-pubertal development is still continuing up to the age of 16, and in some cases is not completed by that age. In England, the Wolfenden Committee[3] reached a similar conclusion on this aspect of the question, although their ultimate recommendation was to fix the age of 21 as the age of consent (see para. 68 of their report).

184. We cannot accept the view that it is established by research that homosexual contacts between boys and older men (especially if by contact is meant intercourse or a near equivalent) 'do no harm, do not have subsequent adverse effects, are not traumatic'. Clearly the reactions of others to the discovery of the conduct are very important, and this applies to those of friends and siblings as well as to those of the parents; but this is part of the social context in which the seducer acts. He really cannot argue that the act is 'harmless' when the predictable consequences are so painful and distressing for those properly concerned; this remains true, even if the reactions of the parents and others may in particular cases be exaggerated or irrational.

185. We do not, of course, overlook the fact that what may be termed a 'seduction' is often much less one-sided than the term suggests. That is a proper matter for investigation in cases where it applies, but it does not constitute any argument for a general change in the law which would make lawful homosexual contacts between adults and minors under 16.

186. Finally, we must assert that the law *does* afford protection to young people. The dangers of exploitation are real, and in our view, it is imperative that minors should be protected from those dangers. This applies to adolescents and *a fortiori* to young children.

CHANGES IN THE LAW

187.  Any discussion of the law's function in the protection of the young inevitably raises the controversial question of the age of consent and wider issues as to the role of the criminal law in areas often seen as being the concern of 'private morality.' The period during which our Working Party met saw the launching of a major campaign aimed at securing further changes in the law as to homosexual conduct, and the reference of the law of sexual offences in general to the Criminal Law Revision Committee.

188.  The present law can be summarized as follows.  Subject to the very important changes made by the Sexual Offences Act 1967, the law prohibits intercourse *per anum* (the offence of buggery), acts of gross indecency (described by the Wolfenden Committee as usually taking one of three forms: mutual masturbation, some form of intercrural contact, or oral-genital contacts, and the procuration of another to commit buggery or gross indecency with a third person.  Other offences include indecent exposure, solicitation for immoral purposes, offences of brothel-keeping, and other offences of indecency contained in local by-laws.

189.  The 1967 Act affected only some of the items in this list.  Buggery and acts of gross indecency ceased to be offences provided the parties had attained the age of 21 and were consenting and the act took place in private. Members of the armed forces and the crews of merchant ships were excluded.  The Act applies only to England and Wales, though a number of proposals to bring the law of Scotland and of Northern Ireland into line with that of England have been made in recent sessions of Parliament, most recently in 1977.

190.  It is strongly argued by the homophile organizations that the law as it stands is in many respects anomalous, and that it does not reflect the principle enumerated in the Wolfenden Report, and widely accepted, that the function of the criminal law in this field 'is to preserve public order and decency, to protect the citizen from what is offensive or injurious, and to provide sufficient safeguards against exploitation and corruption of others, particularly those who are specially vulnerable because they are young, weak in body or mind, inexperienced, or in a state of special physical, official or economic dependence'.[4]  We accept the tenor of these arguments and believe that law reform is needed.

191.  The present law is unsatisfactory in a number of respects.  The first is its reliance on the distinction between conduct 'in private' and other conduct.  The Law Commission in its review of the law of conspiracy touched upon a related area and proposed a new offence of 'offensive sexual behaviour in public view':

'A person who (a) has sexual intercourse, or
                 (b) whether alone or with anyone else engages in any other sexual behaviour

is guilty of an offence if he does so in such circumstances that he knows or ought to know that his conduct is likely to be seen by other persons to whom it is likely to cause serious offence' (clause 21, draft Bill in Law Com. No. 76). Although not drafted with homosexual practices principally in mind, this seems to most of the Working Party to express a satisfactory principle.

192. A second and more serious defect in the law concerns offences of conspiracy and of counselling and procuring homosexual acts. The view was expressed after the passing of the 1967 Act that homosexual acts remained unlawful though not directly punishable by the criminal law, so that for two men to conspire to provide homosexual acts, or for one man to procure a second to engage in homosexual acts with a third, remained criminal under the common law. As Lord Reid expressed it in *Knuller v DPP* (the *International Times* case, 1973),

> I find nothing . . . to indicate that Parliament thought or intended to lay down that indulgence in [homosexual] practices is not corrupting. I read the Act as saying that, even though they may be corrupting, if people choose to corrupt themselves in this way that is their own affair and the law will not interfere. But no licence is given to others to encourage the practice.[5]

193. The Law Commission has now recommended the abolition of common law conspiracy and of any common law offences the substance of which consists in the fact that the conduct constituting the offence tends to corrupt, undermine or otherwise injure public morals or affronts or outrages public decency (clause 6(1) and 22(1) of the draft Bill). We welcome this proposal, which does not of course involve any abdication by the State of its role as a guardian of public morals; specific and clearly-defined offences would remain, and new offences be created, but the common law offences, uncertain in scope and unpredictably and erratically applied, would disappear. In the Criminal Law Act 1977 reforms were made in the law of conspiracy, but offences involving the corruption of public morals or the outraging of public decency were not affected (see Section 5(3) of the Act). Reform in this area awaits the report of the Criminal Law Reform Committee on sexual offences generally.

194. Until the law is fully clarified in these respects, there are difficulties for *bona fide* counselling and supportive organizations for homosexual people. It is unfortunate that those acting as counsellors to homosexuals or as organizers of social clubs and groups should have to fear criminal prosecution by the use of one of the common law offences. The organizers can find themselves in a situation in which they appear to condone (and this can easily be presented as encouraging) illegality, which brings them within the possible scope of the common law offences. Although a homosexual club can promote a ghetto mentality, and can be an undesirable stimulus to promiscuous sexual activity, these dangers must be

put alongside the very real benefits such organizations may confer. Similar arguments can be applied to groups arranged by or for those attracted by young children or by any sort of sexual perversion.

195. The exclusion of members of the armed forces and some others raises different issues. In relatively 'closed' institutions there is a lack of privacy, especially where the institution is a single-sex one. When this is found together with a hierarchical system of command, which puts some in a position of power over others, there are dangers of exploitation and the possibility, in the military context, of a threat to security. Fears are also voiced of male prostitution occurring in some units. Some of us would maintain the present exclusions on account of these considerations. Others would maintain the present position but would wish to see the matter treated more clearly as one of discipline rather than of criminal law. Others, conscious of the unfairness of the present law, feel that the above arguments do not justify the full extent of the present exclusions, which apply where the parties are off duty and where none of the special institutional factors applies, but recognize that it is difficult to draft a flexible code which could give full expression to all the variables in the situation. Others would insist on the removal of all rules applicable to military personnel from the criminal law.

THE AGE OF CONSENT

196. The most controversial matter remaining is that of 'the age of consent'. The phrase is not altogether satisfactory but is well-established. Heterosexual intercourse is prohibited by law up to the sixteenth birthday; the corresponding age for homosexual conduct is 21. The Sexual Law Reform Society in a report published in 1974 urged the lowering of the age limit for all types of sexual behaviour to 14, but the homophile organizations' draft Bill of 1975 advocates rather the age of 16, that is, the application of the present heterosexual limit to the homosexual categories. The latter proposal would be in line with the Dutch reforms following the publication of the Speijer report in 1969, a report which was however limited to purely medical and scientific aspects, the committee being instructed that 'ethical, sociological and pedagogical considerations can be ignored'.[6]

197. Discussion of age-limits is sometimes confused as a result of a failure to appreciate the precise significance of the age-limit in this context. Although any proscribed conduct one party to which is below the chosen age will be a criminal offence, this is not to say that there will be a prosecution (even where the offence is known). For example, sexual intercourse between a 16-year old boy and a 15-year old girl is criminal, but a prosecution is at present extremely improbable.

198. Discretion on the part of prosecuting authorities is an essential feature of our criminal justice system. Where age-limits are used it is particularly important: it scarcely needs to be said that children develop at very different speeds, both physically and emotionally. One 17-year old may be the equivalent on one or more relevant criteria of another 13-year old.

199. It would be a mistake to fix an age-limit in such a way that a large and identifiable class of acts would be technically criminal but seldom in practice made the subject of prosecution. In the present context, the aim should be to fix an age-limit high enough to protect a late developer within the normal range.

200. Some members of the Wolfenden Committee, whose careful review of this question repays close study,[7] favoured an age-limit of 18; a majority settled for 21, then the legal age of majority for most purposes, including marriage without parental consent. The age of majority is now 18, and on the reasoning of the Wolfenden Committee itself there is a very strong case for a corresponding change in the age for our present purposes. The Wolfenden Committee were influenced by the existence of National Service, now abolished, and by the numbers of young people leaving home for educational reasons at age 18; but a student is now a voting adult, not subject to the quasi-parental control of his college authorities as he was twenty years ago.

201. One member of the Wolfenden Committee, the Marquess of Lothian, has recently expressed his opposition to the lowering of the age from 21 to 18. He was speaking in the debate in the House of Lords on 14th June 1977 which ended in the rejection by 146 votes (including the three bishops present) to 25 of a Bill designed to make that change in the law. Lord Lothian's view was that the 18-21 age group was still at risk of exploitation, and he referred to a medical view that many young men do not establish a definite gender role until they are between those ages. Lord Stamp expressed a similar fear, pointing to the vulnerability of those at university or at the start of certain careers.

202. The Working Party remains in favour of a reduction in the age to 18. We believe that that age is high enough to protect the normal late developer, and that there are no strong reasons for fixing the age of maturity (as it was referred to in the Lords' debate) higher than the present age of majority. We should, however, refer to the different view expressed by the then Bishop of Birmingham. He did not regard the lowering of the age of consent as warranted by the present state of public opinion or as likely to be supported by those whose standards of personal conduct were derived from Christian sympathies; he stressed the protective function of the law.

203. The crucial point in the argument is whether or not there is a significant number of young men aged between 18 and 21 who are at risk in the sense of Lord Lothian's, Lord Stamp's and the Bishop's speeches. The Working Party does not believe that there is.

204. Many in the homophile organizations would press for a further reduction to age 16, which is of course the relevant age in the heterosexual context. The arguments for and against such a change are similar in character to those advanced in the Lords' debate just referred to. The case for a further reduction to 16 rests upon the argument that if the criminal law regards the heterosexual as mature enough to make responsible decisions at age 16, and if orientation is established in almost all cases by that age, there can be no justification for withholding an equivalent liberty from the homosexual. To maintain a higher age-limit is to apply the moral judgements of the heterosexual majority, and to enforce those judgements (however prejudiced) via the criminal law, contrary to the libertarian view that law and morals must not be confounded.

205. The case against a further reduction (leaving aside any appeal to public opinion as inappropriate at this level) must be paternalistic in the sense of the Wolfenden Committee's own concern for the inexperienced and vulnerable. A young person of 16 or 17, whose primary heterosexual orientation might be established, may be led into homosexual experiments with very unhappy social consequences. The law should protect him and other groups from this temptation.

206. One possible approach would be to lower the age of consent to 16, but to create specific criminal offences concerned with the exploitation of those between 16 and 18 (or between 16 and 21) who are especially vulnerable. For example, the Swedish Penal Code as amended in 1969 has an offence of 'carnal abuse of youth' which covers sexual relations with someone who is in the offender's charge at school, an institution or some other establishment or is otherwise subject to his supervision, care or authority, or if the act occurs by taking advantage of the young person's dependent situation. A similar offence, 'seduction of youth', is committed by one who, by promising or giving compensation, obtains or tries to obtain a temporary sexual relationship with a young person (Code, Chapter 6, ss 4,8). The Dutch Penal Code (Article 249) is amongst those with similar provisions. (It is notable that these provisions apply to girls as well as boys; it is well known that the English criminal law carries no express provisions dealing with lesbian acts.) The Working Party had no information as to the practical operation of these provisions. They have the merit of identifying cases in which the need for protection is greatest, but this would be at the cost of uncertainty in the law, for the definitions leave many questions unanswered.

207. Our conclusion is that the age of consent should not be reduced below 18; we bear in mind the operation of prosecutorial discretion in respect of those below this, or any other age-limit, where the exploitative element is judged to be absent.

## EQUALITY UNDER THE LAW

208. The point which has been made several times in this chapter about the implications of the deviant minority status of homosexuality is relevant to one further matter raised in the 1977 House of Lords' debate on the law of Scotland. The same point also features in a draft Bill prepared by the homophile organizations in 1975. Clause 2 of that Bill reads:

> It shall not be alleged in any proceedings that any conduct or thing is unlawful, *contra bonos mores,* obscene, lewd, indecent, likely to cause offence or likely to lead to a breach of the peace by reasons only of its being or relating to sexual conduct between persons of the same sex; and in deciding whether any conduct or thing amounts to conduct or thing described as aforesaid . . ., such conduct or thing shall be deemed to have taken place or relate to conduct taking place between members of opposite sexes.[8]

209. This proposal assumes that homosexuality is a valid alternative, parallel to heterosexuality, and that the two should be equated as far as possible, an assumption that underlies the homophile organizations' proposals in the legal and educational fields. In fact the proposal may operate to give a specially protected status, not merely equality, to the homosexual. Because homosexuality has a deviant minority status, there are situations in which public displays of affection, or enthusiastic commendations of sexual practices, are more likely to create public offence in a homosexual than in a heterosexual context. The Bill proposes to ignore this fact by deeming it not to exist, a procedure which seems unacceptably artificial.

## THE POLICE

210. Whatever limits are set to the criminal law, there is always an element of discretion in its enforcement. By far the greater part of this discretion is exercised by the police, both at policy and at actual operational levels. At the policy level, a Chief Constable has to set priorities in the use of police resources. His men cannot be everywhere, and not every aspect of the criminal law can be enforced with equal vigour. At one and the same time, a Chief Constable may face demands for increased police activity to check the spread of drugs amongst the young, to cope with a growing problem of vandalism in an industrial area, to increase patrols in a residential area in which burglaries are becoming more frequent, and to

deal with crowd problems created by the success of one of the football clubs in his territory. The choices are delicate, and fickle public opinion is an important element in the range of considerations.

211. At a more particular level, similar problems arise. An area becomes known as a meeting-place for homosexual men and women. There may be complaints about noise from particular clubs or pubs. There may be complaints of soliciting or of indecency in public. There comes a time when the officer in charge of the local police division feels that something must be done to demonstrate a willingness to respond to the public complaints, and for a time at least the law will be more strictly and zealously enforced.

212. From the point of view of homosexual men and women the position is very unsatisfactory. Police behaviour seems unpredictable and arbitrary. There are sudden 'drives' against homosexuals in particular cities. Because of the vagueness of some of the legal concepts, such as 'soliciting', even the law-abiding feel at risk. A local police commander may seek to solve a difficult problem by 'moving on' the homosexual groups to some other officer's territory, and an element of harassment directed at clubs and individuals may creep in (and the police exercise indirect control over the licensing of clubs through the evidence they present to licensing justices).

213. A number of features of police work cause special difficulties. The police tend to rely on stereotypes in much of their work; a constable has to develop the knack of identifying a stranger whose behaviour is out of the normal pattern. But the difficulties this technique can cause for minority groups within society are well-known. Studies of the work of specialist 'vice squads' have highlighted other problems. Members of these squads face special temptations, reflecting a very human ambivalence on sexual matters.[9] In the enforcement of some areas of the criminal law, where there is no 'victim', or where fear of embarrassment discourages specific complaints from the public and offers of actual evidence, only police testimony is available, and this is sometimes obtained by devices such as the use of *agents provocateurs*.

214. There is ample evidence of a serious lack of communication between the police on the one hand and organized homophile groups on the other. The homophile organizations make no secret of their distrust of the police. In clause 14(4) of their draft Bill they seek to prevent reliance on the evidence of police officers alone in certain prosecutions. The police argue that reliance on police evidence is essential if the criminal law in this area is to be enforced, since most private citizens will not get involved in giving evidence for fear of undesirable publicity. Homophile groups on the other hand say that the police manufacture or at least 'improve' their evidence in order to justify intervention.

215.  Distrust works the other way too.  The police are sometimes very inflexible in dealing with homosexual offences, and elements of prejudice, or mere embarrassment, no doubt help to explain this in some cases. Perhaps more significant is the reluctance of some senior police officers to meet representatives of homophile organizations, apparently from fear of the consequences of the publicity which would inevitably attend such a meeting.

216.  There are no easy solutions to these difficulties.  At one level, there is a need for a more consistent policy as to the enforcement of the law in this area, and we are aware of research in progress within the Home Office which may provide more adequate data as to regional variations in practice. Individual Chief Constables may well seek to retain considerable discretion; homosexual people do tend to congregate in particular areas and a policy designed for the Earls Court district of London might be wholly inappropriate in, say, Canterbury or York.

217.  It is perhaps more important for chief officers of police to recognize that members of established and reputable homophile organizations are a good deal less likely than isolated secret homosexual individuals to be involved in the sort of activities which give offence and involve breaches of the criminal law.  It is true that a pub or club much used by homosexuals may be unpopular with local residents, and there may be complaints; but these are often influenced by prejudice rather than the interests which the criminal law seeks to protect.  In short the homophile organizations and the police could be allies.  That would involve considerable adjustment of attitudes; but we would encourage both sides to a greater readiness to meet and to discuss the difficulties they face.  The resultant clarification of aims and practices could be very beneficial.

# 6

# *Social Implications and Pastoral Care*

218.   It will be evident to those who have read the preceding chapters that the subject of homosexuality raises many issues which require further study and research.   There is much in the social setting which remains confused and confusing.   The medical evidence is tantalisingly inconclusive.   Scholars disagree about the nature and weight of biblical references to homosexuality.   Our examination of various moral approaches leads us to conclusions expressed in carefully qualified terms.   The legal position, even after further reforms, will still include anomalies and uncertainties.

THE PASTORAL NEED
219.   Nevertheless, we must now go on to consider what might be said which is consistent with our conclusions in these various fields, and which may help those with educational and pastoral responsibilities in Church and society.   Never far from the thoughts of members of the Working Party were those for whom decisions about homosexuality are not theoretical or academic, but immediate, pressing and personal.   An individual man or woman may come quite suddenly to a realization of his or her homosexual condition.   Homosexuality may present a crisis in a marriage, or within a family.   It may become a factor to be weighed by those who have to make decisions as part of their responsibility in educational institutions, or in the Church, or elsewhere in society.   In all these areas, the matter cannot be deferred indefinitely pending further scientific evidence or the emergence of a scholarly consensus.   In this final chapter of our report, we hope to provide some help for those who face such decisions.   We believe that the suggestions which we shall make are consistent with the moral position marked out earlier in this report, and we hope that they express a spirit and an approach which can be recognized to be both sensitive and constructive.

220.   Within society itself, the primary need is for greater understanding of the complex issues involved.   We have drawn attention in the first chapter of this report to the polarization of attitudes on a number of issues connected with homosexuality, and also to the increasing self-confidence and even aggressiveness of some of the groups campaigning in this field.   However, this picture needs to be balanced by noting that the great majority

of people are perplexed and uncertain. Moreover, most homosexual people themselves share in this general perplexity. They too hope for a period of more open discussion and greater understanding. The impression can sometimes be given by those who write or comment on homosexuality that homosexual people are either totally 'permissive' or totally 'traditionalist' in their own attitudes. This is certainly a mistake. Greater understanding in society as a whole will be of special benefit to those homosexual people who are genuinely troubled by the personal and practical decisions with which their homosexuality confronts them.

221. We have made it clear that we do not accept the claim to full homosexual equality—the claim that homosexual relationships and practices should be treated in all respects as equivalent to heterosexual ones. But we believe that men and women who are homosexual should be freed from the excessive pressure which they now experience either to pass for heterosexual or to commit themselves entirely to a specifically homosexual culture whose values they may or may not wholly share. They need the opportunity to work out their own individual solutions without having to conform to stereotypes created for them, either by society at large or by the homophile groups.

222. But even given greater understanding and good will among all concerned, it has to be admitted that the process of adjustment is not likely to be easy. For example, our present conventions in society make friendship particularly elusive and difficult for homosexual people. A homosexual woman, for example, may find an incipient friendship with a man she has met in the normal course of affairs frustrated, since he invests the relationship with a sexual dimension which is abhorrent or irrelevant to her. On the other hand, she could conceivably find that, as she develops a friendship with another woman, she comes to feel an element of sexual attraction which leads to painful misunderstandings. Such experiences, or even the fear of them, may make it sometimes difficult for homosexual people to enjoy the great blessing of friendship, and emphasize the painful web of alienation in which they can become enmeshed. To understand such experiences can help the rest of the community to respond more sympathetically to homosexual people. It must also help to explain why homosexual people (of both sexes) often congregate together, more or less exclusively, in certain clubs and public houses: in these places the possibility of these misunderstandings and frustrations is largely removed and people feel free to be themselves.

223. In this and in other ways, homosexual people are subject to real handicaps and deprivations, and one may sympathize with the claim that this has amounted to oppression. At the same time, we need to recognize and take the measure of the antipathy and revulsion which so many in

67

the community feel towards homosexual practices, and even towards the homosexual condition itself. Sometimes the antipathy is thoughtless and bigoted, or attributable to cruelty or fear. But not always. Even when allowances have been made for conditioning factors of various kinds, it remains remarkable how, in the comparatively tolerant and non-judgmental climate of current opinion, so many people feel conscientiously compelled to condemn homosexual practices. Although the cruder reactions against homosexuality largely evaporate when people take the trouble to gain more knowledge and understanding of the matter, it would be naive to suppose that enlightenment of itself will remove all antipathy.

224. Exaggerated as these prevailing attitudes all too often are, they derive from a basic conviction about the proper use of sex which is, in general, well-founded. Attempts, therefore, to dismiss this conviction as unreasoning prejudice are misplaced and unlikely to succeed. We have argued that the situation of those who have no choice but to be homosexual is such that they could not, even if they wished to, conform to a norm which is rightly felt to hold for others. We plead for a wider recognition of this fact and greater understanding of the homosexual condition. This plea has a better chance of being heeded if those to whom it is addressed, both within and outside the Church, realize that they are not being asked to repudiate their deeply-felt convictions about the nature and purpose of human sexuality. They are rather being asked to acknowledge a difficult, but limited, human problem with honesty and compassion. One consequence of the increased polarization of attitudes has been that many people have been led to fear that homosexuality as such represents a serious threat to the conception of the family and its place in society which they are determined to uphold—a view that is lent some colour by the more extreme homophile groups.

225. We believe that this fear is largely unjustified. It presupposes a wide extension of homosexual practices among the great majority of people whose predominant disposition is not homosexual. Even if temporary fashions in a particular milieu may occasionally involve numbers of people who are not basically homosexual, creating a local problem which causes genuine concern, there is, so far as we can tell, no reason to believe that homosexuality, if better understood and more widely tolerated, would spread through the community like a contagious disease.

226. Among the obstacles to a better understanding and a greater toleration of homosexuality are certain common misunderstandings. In the course of its enquiries, the Working Party encountered ignorance and inaccuracies in the minds of a surprising number of people. Although several of these misunderstandings are referred to elsewhere in the report, it is relevant to mention them again.

227. Chief among them is the mistaken belief that homosexual men are always attracted to boys under the age of puberty—in other words that homosexuality is a form of paedophilia. This misunderstanding seems so widespread that it is scarcely possible to call attention to it too frequently. (The concern felt for adolescents who may be exposed to homosexual advances is, of course, a separate issue: this is also referred to earlier in our report.) Hence attempts which have occasionally been made to link propaganda on behalf of paedophilia with the campaign for a more sympathetic understanding of homosexuality seem to us to be altogether regrettable and misleading.

228. Many people also believe that all homosexual men are physically effeminate and that all homosexual women are 'masculine'. This is not so.

229. Perhaps because only male homosexuality is subject to legal restriction, it is still sometimes believed that the homosexual condition is largely, if not entirely, confined to the male sex. This belief may be connected with the notion (also inaccurate) that physical homosexual lovemaking appeals only to male couples.

230. A more open recognition of the existence and needs of homosexual people in the community is bound to pose problems, both for them and for society at large. It may be painful for a homosexual person to recognize and accept his or her own homosexuality, and the process may call for the ministry of a friend, counsellor, or pastor. Then the homosexual needs to decide whether to allow his or her homosexuality to be generally known. The consequences of this decision—at work, in the family, or among friends —can be considerable. Some, especially in the homophile groups, would argue that a positive duty is laid on every homosexual to 'come out'. But circumstances differ so much that the Working Party cannot endorse this view; the unequal burdens which would result, and the possible damage to the individual's right to privacy, lead us to conclude that no general rule is possible, but that individuals can be justified in reaching differing solutions.

THE PUBLIC EXPRESSION OF AFFECTION

231. We have already indicated that 'there are situations in which public displays of affection . . . are more likely to create public offence in a homosexual than in a heterosexual context' (see para. 209 above), and that this cannot be entirely ignored in relation to the law. Social milieux vary so greatly that it is impossible to generalize about the sorts of behaviour which ought to be regarded as socially acceptable on the part of homosexual people. It clearly follows from our recommendations that there should be places where homosexuals are able to express themselves with the freedom

normally permitted to heterosexuals; it also seems to us that homosexual people should be expected to exercise greater restraint than others in ordinary public places and situations.

## FRIENDSHIP

232. A more open recognition of the existence and needs of homosexual people in the community is bound to pose some problems also in the realm of ordinary human friendship. We may accept that there is often a relationship, subtle and intricate, between sexual attraction and friendship. Nevertheless, the possibility of deep and close friendship between people, devoid for all practical purposes of any sexual connotation, is an extremely valuable aspect of the life of any society. If society comes to accept homosexual unions more freely than at present, conventions may need to be devised to distinguish the one from the other. The conventions surrounding the institution of marriage and the family perform this function for heterosexual people, generally speaking, and we are at a loss to know how corresponding conventions could grow up to define or protect homosexual unions which society might find acceptable, especially since we find ourselves unable to validate the concept of 'homosexual marriage'. But it would be unfortunate if the 'liberalization' òf society in regard to homosexuality resulted in close friendships being automatically interpreted as involving genital expression. If, in other words, it ever came to be assumed that every Sherlock Holmes and Dr Watson, or even Starsky and Hutch were homosexually related, the value of friendship would be greatly threatened. This is one of the ways in which the phenomenon of homosexuality may threaten, for better or for worse, our 'classification systems' in the manner described by Plummer (see para. 20 above). A problem is also created in this context for homosexual couples who, while recognizing that their affections have a sexual dimension, have chosen to live together as friends.

## ABSTINENCE AND CELIBACY

233. To say, as we have said, that there are circumstances in which individuals may justifiably choose to enter into a homosexual relationship involving the physical expression of sexual love, is not to imply, of course, that this is or ought to be the choice normally made. Abstinence from sexual activity, whether accepted by homosexual or by heterosexual people, is not a merely negative response or a failure to choose. It may be actively embraced in the interests of true friendship, or for some wider purpose. But abstinence is not the same thing as celibacy, and it is necessary to distinguish between the two. Failure to do so may lead pastors and counsellors to recommend 'celibacy' as the proper response of homosexual people to their condition when what is meant is abstinence.

234. Celibacy is essentially a vocation, and cannot with integrity be interpreted as an expedient, let alone a remedy. Part of the Christian tradition about sexuality is that some men and women are called to renounce the possibility of marriage for the sake of the Kingdom of Heaven. Indeed one part of the tradition affirmed that the life of consecrated celibacy was higher than the married state. Not many educated Christians today would accept this theoretical grading of states of life. If we think of higher and lower at all, it is more realistic to think of it in relation to particular individuals. People vary enormously. Temperament, personal history and circumstances all have a bearing on what is possible or what is best for an individual. What is highest for one person might not be the highest for another, indeed it might be totally impossible. But the Christian tradition, which gives an honoured place to the vocation of celibacy, witnesses to a truth of permanent importance: that some, not because they are incapable of becoming partners in a good and stable marriage but in pursuit of some spiritual goal—whether a more intensely realized relationship with God or for the sake of some ministry which marriage would effectually rule out— are called to give up marriage and the genital expression of their sexuality. This renunciation need not necessarily mean forgoing the possibility of deep and intimate relationships with others, whether of their own or the opposite sex. Rather those who make this choice renounce the particular love for one person, and its genital expression, which marriage consecrates, for the sake of a more wide-reaching love for God and their neighbour.

235. This is the understanding to which those called to celibacy would adhere. The fact that most celibates fall short of it does not invalidate the ideal any more than the fact that most marriages fall short of the ideal invalidates matrimony. The fact that some are able to find fulfilment in this life does not imply that this is a satisfactory way for all for whom marriage is ruled out. For genuine vocation imparts to the person called a strength which makes possible a way of life that without that strength would be beyond his capacity. It is a road which only a minority is called to walk. But one of the means by which God discloses his will for a person is the circumstances of his life including his personal make-up. For this reason the homosexual person who is also a Christian should consider whether the fact of his sexual orientation may perhaps be one of the signs that God is calling him to consecrate himself as a celibate, perhaps with other people, for the service of God and his fellows.

## THE MEDIA AND EDUCATION

236. We have referred more than once to the misunderstandings about homosexuality which are widely prevalent. We hope that those who may

have the means and the skill to remove these misunderstandings through the media, or teaching, will do all they can to this end.

237. There is at least one way in which the mass media can help. Recognizing that homosexuality is a subject which immediately arouses anxieties and emotional reactions in so many people, broadcasters and journalists might reasonably agree to treat it with special sensitivity, and exercise great care in preparing their material. In particular, we ask them to accept that public figures and members of certain professions, well-known nationally or locally, stand to suffer cruelly and unjustly if the media publish, without permission, suggestions that they are, or might be, homosexual.

238. Sex education in schools usually forms part of a course on Health Education or Personal Relationships. It is concerned with physical, social, emotional and moral development, and frequently the teaching on the course is shared between different professional disciplines. Pupils gain factual information and are encouraged in their search for personal identity, maturity and satisfactory relationships with others.

239. There is more than one responsible opinion on the question of the desirability of including teaching about homosexuality in such a course. We believe that if teaching is given it should be done with sensitivity and concern for the needs and feelings of the pupils. It is reasonable to assume that most secondary school pupils have at least heard something about homosexuality. To ignore the subject, and to confine all sex education to a consideration of heterosexual relationships, does not help to prevent misunderstandings about homosexuality and runs the risk of aggravating the anxieties of pupils who believe they may be homosexual. Resource material such as that supplied by the Nuffield Education Foundation is available to teachers, and they are also able to receive training in the skills needed to undertake group discussion.

240. In addition to class work and discussion pupils who are worried about their sexual development may need more specialized help. In some schools this can be provided by the school counsellors, the school medical service, school chaplain, and other responsible counselling agencies. Parents too may ask for help and guidance in talking to their children.

COUNSELLING

241. The Working Party is aware of a need for counselling services to be available and recognizes that a number are already in existence. There are services such as 'Friend' which are provided by the homophile organizations themselves for homosexual men and women, and those such as the

Albany Trust, Marriage Guidance Councils or the Samaritans, which are prepared to offer help in a wide variety of psychosexual problems or where the individual is unsure of his or her sexual identity.

242.   In this field there is, perhaps, a need to distinguish between counselling properly so called and the giving of pastoral or moral advice. In our view, there is a place for both.   Both are, or should be, non-directive in the sense that the eventual decision is left in the hands of the individual, but the latter admits of the giving of positive advice in a way that the former does not.   Counselling services should meet professional standards, and the client must be satisfied in advance that the agency is neutral in its attitude.   Only so can the client be sure of being free to 'sort himself out' without undue pressure being brought upon him.

243.   Often, however, the individual may be perplexed more by the moral or spiritual aspects of his homosexuality than by the practical ones, and may reasonably seek advice and help from those who have given thought specifically to these aspects of the matter and whose judgement he respects and whose values he largely shares.

244.   This distinction between counselling and advice is not, of course, a sharp one.   There are likely to be some broadly expressed values which even professional counselling agencies would feel bound to represent to a client in certain circumstances; and pastors or other advisers will take care to respect the individual's freedom of conscience.   Nevertheless, we think it useful to mark the distinction and recommend that it be more widely and explicitly recognized.   There might then be less danger of confusion between the two sorts of agency and a better chance of fruitful co-operation between them.

PRINCIPLES OF PASTORAL CARE

245.   At this point we wish to draw attention to two fundamental pastoral principles which, we believe, should govern the counsel and care offered by the Church to its own members, clerical and lay, and to others who may seek its advice and help.   The first concerns the integrity of the individual, the second the integrity of the community to which the individual belongs. For the Christian the latter will involve his loyalty to the Church and his witness to the Gospel which it proclaims.

246.   First, the individual.   If we are right in allowing to the homosexual man or woman a liberty of conscience in deciding whether or not to enter into a homosexual union, then that person's conscientious decision, once made, should be respected.   The primary task of the Christian pastor is to enable him or her to reach such a decision based on an informed understanding of Christian insights and values, and on a responsible

judgement what in his or her specific circumstances is the right course to pursue. The values to be taken into account should include that expressed by the traditional virtue of 'chastity', where chastity is understood to signify, not necessarily total abstinence from sexual activity, but certainly its subordination to the deeper and more inclusive demands of personal relationships. The questions to be asked and answered are particular questions. In a situation in which there is no possibility of finding fulfilment in the kind of relationship which the Church believes to be the norm for all sexual relationships, what is God calling him or her here and now to be and to do? What are the individual's existing obligations? What are his own needs and potentialities? What are the needs and claims of others whom his decision will directly affect? Where every option has its dangers and drawbacks, which affords the greatest opportunity, not only for the individual's own growth in Christ, but also for his Christian witness and service?

247. Closely linked with our concern for the integrity of the individual's own conscience, in an area where moral judgements are honestly disputed, is a concern for the individual's right to privacy. Admittedly, such a right cannot be absolute. Nor is it the case that there is an area of human behaviour in which it does not matter what a person thinks or does. There is no hiding place from God and conscience. Nevertheless, we believe that every individual has a right to a 'private space' which should not be invaded except for the most compelling of reasons. Privacy is one of the constituents of personal existence. Reserve is as important as openness. Certainly the pressures which exist to make everything a matter of public inquisition, not least in matters of sex, are to be resisted. The fact that it is not possible to draw a clear-cut line between a person's private life and his public life is no reason for denying he has a right to any privacy at all.

248. Our concern for the right to privacy leads us to affirm that, before any suggestion is made that someone is a homosexual, or has entered into a homosexual relationship, or has performed homosexual acts, great attention should be paid to the consequences of making such a suggestion. The man or woman in question may well be put in the almost impossible position of having to prove a negative, so that if the allegation is in fact untrue, it yet remains on the record and in people's minds. Even if it happens to be true, given current attitudes and prejudices, very great damage may be done, to no one's benefit. We are not, of course, suggesting an absolute right to privacy; rather we urge a responsible restraint. The need for such restraint is well understood by many working in the media; but it is equally needed in ordinary conversation. The suffering which can be caused by what we thoughtlessly call 'innocent' gossip is all too often underestimated or simply ignored.

249. Second, the community to which the individual belongs. The well-being of the whole Body of Christ should be of concern to each of its members. Hence no individual should deliberately cause another to stumble: he should be wary of causing 'scandal'. In the New Testament, the word 'scandal' meant a stumbling-block and was used in two distinct ways. First, there was the sin of causing others to stumble. Jesus spoke with the utmost severity concerning those who caused his little ones to stumble, while Paul counselled those who were clear that a certain action was right, *viz.* eating meat offered to idols, to refrain from making their own liberty of conscience an occasion of damaging the conscience of their weaker brethren. Second, there was the way in which Jesus considered that he himself was a stumbling block to the world, and so, by extension, that his followers too would be. There was a sense in which the Gospel was to challenge the world's preconceived ideas and to incur hatred towards those who proclaimed it.

250. In our own day these two meanings have tended to become debased and confused. The concept of a stumbling block has changed into a concept of giving offence to the respectable, while the politics of conflict has produced those who seek to further their cause by confrontation and clash with the established order. Neither of these attitudes appears to reflect the depth of biblical insight, according to which membership of a community calls for both honesty and charity. We are members one of another, and each of us has a duty to bear in mind not only his own convictions and the actions to which naturally they give rise but also the convictions of his fellows and the well-being of the community as a whole.

HOMOSEXUALITY AND CHURCH LIFE

251. It is with these principles in mind that we must look at the place of homosexuals within the life of the Church. Here Christians meet each other on the basis of their common life in Jesus Christ. It follows that the mere fact of being homosexual should not be regarded as any hindrance to Church membership and communion. We are therefore dismayed by the evidence submitted to us by homosexual men and women who have experienced nothing but suspicion, or even outright rejection, on the part of their fellow Christians. Furthermore, it seems clear to us that, if the substance of our ethical and theological argument is correct, there is no good reason, considerations of scandal apart, for excluding from Church membership and communion those who in good conscience have entered into a responsible homosexual union. Christians whose advice and counsel have been sought need not feel bound to condemn out of hand and without further reflection every homosexual relationship. At the pastoral level there is room for careful and sensitive discrimination according to individual circumstances and needs.

252.   At the same time Christian homosexuals have to realize the stresses and strains which the Church fellowship may be called to accept on their behalf, especially if they have made no secret of their homosexual union with another person.   We understand the feelings of Christian homosexuals who desire to reform what seems to them to be a mistaken tradition in the Church, but the Working Party believe that the aggressive policy of confrontation which is sometimes urged on that account is likely to disrupt the life of the local church.   The Church, like any other social institution, is a body which contains strong conservative strains, including people who, without manifest prejudice, hold sincere convictions that homosexual relationships are morally wrong.   The more prominent the person is in the life of the church, the more necessary it is for him or her to realize that the right to privacy is thereby limited, and that the possibility of becoming a stumbling block to others within the Christian fellowship has correspondingly increased.

## THE CLERGY AND ORDINANDS

253.   Our enquiries left us in no doubt that there exists at present some variety in the ways in which bishops respond to the existence of homosexuality in clergy and ordinands in their dioceses.   This is only to be expected; as the Church is divided, so we must expect the bench of bishops to reflect the divisions.   Nevertheless, we should be failing in our task were we not to point out that this variety of attitude and practice can have uncomfortable and undesirable consequences for some ordinands and clergy.

254.   The clergy should be able to expect reasonable privacy in their private and domestic lives, and a 'presumption of innocence' in all matters concerning their personal behaviour.   Thus, for example, the simple fact that two priests live together in the same house should not, in our opinion, entail a presumption that they are living in a homosexual union.   Nor would any enquiry into the nature of their relationship be justified, unless a strong case were made out to the bishop or archdeacon that such enquiry was necessary for the good of the Church.

255.   Nevertheless, the clergy must accept the fact that their domestic affairs, insofar as they are common knowledge, inevitably affect their standing as leaders of the congregation and examples to the flock of Christ. This is especially true of the parish priest, living amongst the people of the parish.   We have already come to the conclusion that the only sexual union to which the Church can give public recognition in the lives of her members is marriage.   A homosexual priest who has 'come out' and openly acknowledges that he is living in a sexual union with another man should not expect the Church to accept him on the same conditions as if he were married.

256. What then should a priest in this situation do? We recognize that he might be absolutely clear in his own conscience about the relationship, and that he and others might think it a matter of regret that the Church has no way of accepting or validating it. Could he be justified therefore in insisting on continuing in his position as a parish priest, regarding any consequent trouble in the parish or diocese as a proper challenge placed before a pusillanimous Church? In the end we came to the conclusion that a priest in this position ought to offer his resignation to the bishop of the diocese, so that he as the minister bearing responsibility for the Church in the locality could with the pastoral care appropriate to his office decide whether it should be accepted or not.

257. We realize that the obligation to offer his resignation would be a moral one. It would not be enforceable. Furthermore, it is not likely that, if the homosexual union involved were within the law, a legal action against the priest aimed at depriving him of the living would be desirable.

258. Delicate and difficult problems are bound to arise from time to time in connexion with homosexual ordinands, some of whom are likely to believe conscientiously that homosexual relationships are sometimes justified. As we have already noted, bishops themselves will differ in their personal responses to a homosexual ordinand presenting himself for ordination, and they are likely to be more keenly aware than the ordinand of the formidable difficulties involved in finding parochial employment for an ordinand who is a practising homosexual.

259. Honesty and charity are required from both bishop and ordinand if these situations are to be dealt with successfully and the bishop may need all his pastoral skill and experience if confidence and frankness are to be preserved. It is extremely difficult to suggest adequate guide-lines but we offer the following suggestions.

260. We do not think that a bishop is justified in refusing to ordain an otherwise acceptable ordinand merely on the ground that he is (or is believed to be) homosexually orientated. But an ordinand would be wrong to conceal deliberately from his ordaining bishop an intention existing in his own mind to live openly in a homosexual union after ordination or to campaign on behalf of a homophile organization.

261. We would hope that the atmosphere of pastoral confidence between an ordinand and his bishop, or diocesan director of ordinands, would normally allow questions about sexuality to be broached freely. But we do not think it desirable that every ordinand should be required to declare whether he believes himself to be homosexual or heterosexual. This would be an unjustifiable intrusion on an individual's rightful privacy.

AMBISEXUALITY

262. In considering the pastoral care of individual men and women we have so far had in mind those who have no choice in their homosexual orientation. Indeed, it was the fact that they had no choice which weighed so heavily with us in our judgement that in certain circumstances a genital relationship might for such persons be justifiable. We are however, aware that there is not always a clear-cut distinction between a heterosexual and a homosexual orientation. There are some, it seems, who are ambisexual, at least to the extent that they are susceptible, in varying degrees, to erotic attraction by people of either sex. What shall we say to such as these?

263. In so far as they have what may be called a 'real' choice, our whole argument suggests a straightforward answer. They should seek to restrain their homosexual inclinations and develop a heterosexual orientation. We do not believe that ambisexual relationships somehow make an individual more complete than a heterosexual relationship, as is sometimes argued. Nor do we believe that in this matter we should allow personal preferences to prevail. We have, on the contrary, argued for marriage as the norm.

264. The pastoral problem becomes potentially more acute, the more homosexual the individual discovers himself or herself to be. There may be a point at which, although it would be untrue to say that there is no choice, the alternatives are barely comparable: they do not offer a like fulfilment.

265. Fulfilment is by no means the sole relevant consideration. There are commitments to others—for the married, to spouses and children—whose needs claim priority. It has been the reported experience of some married lesbians that they have achieved a greater depth of loving in a homosexual relationship than in their marriage. This may be so, but even if it is, this does not of itself justify marital infidelity, any more than a wife's falling deeply in love with another man justifies her in being unfaithful to her husband. Fidelity, too, has its claims.

266. There are others, however, who are unmarried, who are to some extent ambisexual, but in whose development a homosexual orientation has seemingly come to predominate. We believe that it would be irresponsible to advise them, on the grounds of their potential ambisexuality, to enter into a marriage and in this way to attempt to re-direct their sexual orientation. Even were this outcome possible, prudence would tell against the attempt to achieve it. Such a course would expose them to psychological stresses which they might not be able to bear and so bring tragedy upon their spouses and themselves. If they are unable to restrain their homosexual inclination and to develop a heterosexual orientation, they might be better advised, depite their potential ambisexuality, to regard themselves as

homosexual and to act on the assumption that they no longer have a 'real' choice in the matter.

267. If it is said that pastoral advice of this kind might in some cases encourage homosexual behaviour among those who are in fact capable of heterosexual relationships, we should have to admit this risk. Nevertheless, its significance should not be exaggerated. We have consistently argued that marriage continues to be the norm of sexual relationships, and that the truly ambisexual, no less than the truly heterosexual, should be bound by this norm. On the other hand, in so far as Kinsey is correct in suggesting that there is a spectrum of sexual orientation, there are bound to be some uncertain cases. In such cases a person's own honest self-assessment must be respected. Furthermore, in counselling those who have problems of ambisexuality, one needs considerable sensitivity to discern whether a person is truly ambisexual or whether in fact a homosexual orientation underlies that person's history and self-awareness. Such discernment cannot easily be achieved outside a context of mutual trust and confidence.

CONCLUSION
268. There is much we do not yet know or understand. Indeed, perhaps the one thing of which we can be sure is that those who claim to know the whole truth about homosexuality are misleading us. We are still emerging, half-dazzled, from a long period of darkness in which the whole subject was regarded as shameful and unmentionable. It is too soon to expect clear and final answers, not least in matters of pastoral practice. We need, and may hope for, a period of responsible and increasingly informed study and discussion, during which the differing convictions and opinions of concerned groups and individuals will be taken seriously and regarded sympathetically by all concerned. During such a time, Christians have a responsibility in society to soften and reconcile, wherever they can, those who may be tempted to aggressiveness, provocation, scornfulness, bigotry, or malice. So more of the truth, spoken and heard in love, may emerge, and clearer light be thrown upon the many moral and pastoral problems which still face us.

# Notes

## CHAPTER 1

[1]Kinsey, A. C., *et al., Sexual Behaviour in the Human Male* (W. B. Saunders, 1948), pp. 636 ff.
It is not the intention of this chapter to trace the history of homosexuality, as to which see
Montgomery Hyde, H., *The Other Love* and
Sherwin Bailey, D., *Homosexuality and the Western Christian Tradition* (Longmans, 1955).

[2]Wolff, C., *Love between Women* (Duckworth, 1971).

[3]For example, see
Pittenger, N., *Time for Consent* (SCM Press, 1971).
Kimball-Jones, H., *Towards a Christian Understanding of the Homosexual* (SCM Press, 1967).
Oberholzer, W. D. (Ed.), *Is Gay Good?* (Westminster Press, 1971).
Blamires, D., *Homosexuality from the Inside* (Religious Society of Friends, 1973).
Beaumont, T. (Ed.), *A* New Christian *Reader* (SCM Press, 1974).
McNeil, J. J., *The Church and the Homosexual* (Darton, Longman and Todd, 1977).
Macourt, M. (Ed.), *Towards a Theology of Gay Liberation* (SCM Press, 1977).

[4]*The Truth in Love* (Nationwide Festival of Light, London, 1975).
For an Evangelical approach, see for example
Davidson, A., *The Returns of Love* (IVF Press, 1973).
Field, D., *The Homosexual Way—A Christian Option?* (Grove Booklets on Ethics, 1976).
Moss, R., *Christians and Homosexuality* (Paternoster Press, 1977).

[5]Plummer, K., *Sexual Stigma* (Routledge and Kegan Paul, 1974).

[6]Weinberg, M. S. and Williams, C. J., *Male Homosexuals—their problems and adaptation* (OUP, 1974).
*Sexual Offenders and Social Punishment* (CIO, 1956), p. 84, also hints at this.


## CHAPTER 2

Bancroft, J., *Deviant Sexual Behaviour: Modification and Assessment* (Clarendon Press, 1974).
Bene, E., *Brit. J. Psychiat.* 111, 815 (1965).
Coppen, A.J., *Brit. Med. J.* ii, 1443 (1959).

Donovan, B. T., *et al.*, *Physiology of Puberty* (Arnold, 1965).

Dorner, G. J., *Endocr.* 42, 163 (1968).

Ehrhardt, A. A., *Endrocrinology and Human Behaviour* (Ed. Michael, R. P.) (OUP, 1968).

Fisher, S. H., in *Sexual Inversion* (Ed. Marmor, T.) (Basic Books, New York, 1965).

Fox, T., *Proceedings of the U.S. Academy of Science* 72, 4303 (1975).

Henry, G. W., *Sex Variants, a Study of Homosexual Patterns* (Cassell, 1951).

Heston, L. L. and Shields, J., *Arch. gen. psychiatric* 18, 149 (1968).

Hirschfield, M., *Sexual Anomalies and Perversions* (revd. ed. Haire, N.) (Encyclopaedic Press, London, 1952).

Kallman, F. J., *J. Nerv. and Mental Dis.* (1952).

Kenyon, F. E., *J. Neurol. Neurosurg. Psychiat.* 31, 487 (1968).

Kenyon, F. E., *Brit. J. Psychiat.* 114, 1337 (1968).

Kinsey, A. C., *et al.*, *Sexual Behaviour in the Human Male* (W. B. Saunders, 1948).

Kinsey, A. C., *et al.*, *Sexual Behaviour in the Human Female* (W. B. Saunders, 1953).

Klein, V., *The Feminine Character: History of an Ideology* (Kegan Paul, 1946).

Lurie, L. A., *Amer. J. Med. Sci.* 208, 176 (1944).

Maccoby, E. E. (Ed.), *The Development of Sex Differences* (Tavistock Publ., 1967).

Martinez-Vargas, C., *Science* 190, 1307 (1975).

Masters, W. H. and Johnson, V. E., *Human Sexual Response* (Churchill, 1966).

Mead, M., *Male and Female* (William Morrow, 1949).

Money, J., *et al.*, *Arch. Neurol. Psychiat.* 77 (1957).

Pare, C. M. B., in *Sexual Inversion* (Ed. Marmor, J.) (Basic Books, New York, 1965).

Slater, E., *Lancet,* i, 69 (1962).

Swyer, G. I. M., *Practitioner* 172, 374 (1954).

West, D. J., *Homosexuality* (Pelican, 1965).

Wolff, C., *Love between Women* (Duckworth, 1971).

CHAPTER 3

[1]Humbert, P., 'Le substantif *to 'eba* et le verbe *t'b* dans l'Ancien Testament', in *Zeitschrift für die Alttestamentische Wissenschaft,* vol. 72, 1960, p. 232.

[2]Daube, D., 'The Duty of Procreation', in *Proceedings of the Classical Association,* vol. LXXIV, 1977, pp. 10-11.

[3]Field, D., *The Homosexual Way—A Christian Option?* (Grove Booklets on Ethics, 1976), p. 16.

[4]DeKruijf, T. C., *The Bible on Sexuality* (De Pere, Wisc.: St. Norbert's Abbey Press, 1966), p. 53; quoted in J. J. McNeill, *The Church and the Homosexual,* p. 63.

[5]Pedersen, *Israel,* I-II, p. 128.


CHAPTER 5

[1]Gebhard, *et al., Sex Offenders* (Heinemann, 1965).

[2]States General of the Netherlands, Session 1969-70—10-347: Withdrawal of Article 248*bis* of the Penal Code.

[3]Report of the Committee on Homosexuality and Prostitution (HMSO, 1957).

[4]*Op. cit.,* para. 13.

[5][1973] AC 435 at 457; see also Edwards, Q., *What is Unlawful?* (Church Information Office, 1959).

[6]*Op. cit.,* para. 1.2(6).

[7]*Op. cit.,* paras. 65-71.

[8]Draft Homosexual Law Reform Bill 1975; see also Clause 14(3).

[9]See e.g. Skolnick, *Justice without Trial* (Wiley, 1966).

# Acknowledgements

The setting up of the Working Party attracted some notice both in the press and from the general public, and a considerable amount of correspondence was generated. The Chairman and Secretary received letters from well over one hundred and thirty correspondents as well as reports from the Archdiocese of Sydney, the Church of Scotland and the Church of Ireland. The Working Party also received a number of papers from the Nationwide Festival of Light.

In addition, the Secretary met 18 individuals including representatives from the following organizations:

'Centre' Charitable Trust
The Campaign for Homosexual Equality
Sappho
Parents' Enquiry
Reach
Integroup
The Open Church Group
The Albany Trust
The Gay Christian Movement
SIGMA (An organization for the spouses of homosexuals)

In the course of gathering evidence, the Working Party met:

Dr John Bancroft
The Hon. Mrs Lil Butler ⎰
Mr Antony Grey            ⎱ from the Albany Trust
Mr Wallace Gravatt  ⎰
The Rev. Denis Nadin ⎱ from the Campaign for Homosexual
Ms Angela Needham   ⎰ Equality
Dr Charles Rycroft
The Rt Rev. and Rt Hon. the Bishop of London

They were also joined at their first residential session by the Rev. Dr Oliver O'Donovan, at that time tutor at Wycliffe Hall.

The Working Party would like to express their gratitude to those people who took the time to write or appear personally, and who in some cases commended others whose evidence also proved valuable. They would also like to thank those diocesan bishops and principals of theological colleges who responded so readily to their enquiries.

# Acknowledgements

The authors, ay of the Working Party solicited some mode trok in the press and from the several publicand a considerable amount of correspondence, not generated, of the Churches and Secretary received letters from well over one hundred and thirty correspondents, as well as reports from the Archdiocese of Southwark, the Church of Scotland and the Church of Ireland, the Working Party also received a number of reports from the Mennonwele Fellowship.

In addition, the Secretary met or individuals, including representatives from the following organisations:

Courage Christian Trust
The Campaign for Homosexual Equality
Baptist
Parents Enquiry
Reach
Quest
The Open Church Group
The Albany Trust
The Gay Christian Movement
SIGMA (An organisation for the spouses of homosexuals)

In the course of gathering evidence, the Working Party met:
Dr John Bancroft
The Hon. Mrs J.H. Butler
Mr Anton Gray
Mr Wallace Craven
The Rev. Denis Nadin
Mr Angus Stedman
Dr Charles Knevitt
The Rt Rev. and Rt Hon. the Bishop of London

There were also joined at their residential session by the Rev Dr Oliver O'Donovan at that time tutor at Wycliffe Hall.

The Working Party would like to express their gratitude to these people who took the time to write or appear personally and who in some cases commended places whose help was also proved valuable. They would also like to thank those diocesan bishops and principals of theological colleges who responded so readily to their enquiries.

# PART II

# Critical Observations of the Board for Social Responsibility on the Report

# Members of the Board

The Rt Rev. G. D. Leonard, Bishop of Truro (*Chairman*)

Rev. Dr J. Atherton, Joint Director, The William Temple Foundation

Professor R. J. Berry, Professor of Genetics at The Royal Free Hospital School of Medicine

Mr M. Chandler, public relations consultant

Mrs Margaret Cornell, Meetings Organiser, Overseas Development Institute

Rev. Canon E. N. Devenport, Canon Missioner in the Diocese of Leicester

Mr Gervase E. Duffield, publisher

Rev. Professor G. R. Dunstan, F.D. Maurice Professor of Moral and Social Theology in the University of London

Rev. D. R. J. Holloway, Vicar of Jesmond, Diocese of Newcastle

Canon L. Lloyd Rees, Chaplain General of Prisons

Professor J. D. McClean, Professor of Law at the University of Sheffield

The Rt Rev. H. W. Montefiore, Bishop of Birmingham.

The Rt Rev. Simon Phipps, Bishop of Lincoln (from 1.9.79)

Dr Mary Seller, experimental biologist, Guy's Hospital Medical School

Mr L. C. Smith, company director

Canon I. Smith-Cameron, Diocesan Missioner in the Diocese of Southwark

Rev. Dr Norman Todd, Training Adviser, Southwell Diocesan Education Committee

Rev. Keith Ward, Dean and Chaplain, Trinity Hall, Cambridge

Dr J. R. Winter, retired consultant anaesthetist (abroad when decision taken to publish report)

The Rt Rev. R. W. Woods, Bishop of Worcester (until 31.8.79)

Mr G. S. Ecclestone (*Secretary*)

# Critical Observations of the Board

A1.   The working party's report was the subject of prolonged and detailed discussion within the Board over a period of ten months.   This went on both at meetings of the Board and in correspondence.   Members of the Board have obviously not been able to give the same amount of time to the report as was available to the working party in preparing it.   Nor do they have the particular expertise possessed by a working party convened for this purpose.   Nevertheless it is their responsibility to assess the material and arguments in the report, and the composition of the Board is such that it is competent to undertake this task.   Members differed among themselves in their attitude to the subject-matter of the report, and their judgments on the report have been equally varied.   These observations summarise the most important criticisms of the report advanced within the Board.   In reading them it should be borne in mind that some members did support the main conclusions of the report, while dissociating themselves from some of its arguments.

A2.   The following criticisms are published not as evidence of lack of appreciation for the diligence with which the report has been prepared, or for the many valuable passages which it contains.   Still less do they evidence any posture of the Board 'against' homosexuals.   On the contrary some members of the Board felt that the report did not entirely do justice to the pressures of society which make life difficult for homosexuals.   The critique is however necessary in order to ensure that criticisms of the report, made by members of the Board and carrying weight, in varying degrees, with all the Board's members, are published as widely as the report itself. This is not the first opportunity the Board has had to consider the results of the working party's thinking, and to offer criticisms.   Some criticisms, made when an interim version of the report was presented to the Board, were accepted by the working party and the draft was amended accordingly. Others were not accepted, and the working party holds its present draft to be final.   It is for a wider public now to judge their cogency.

A3.   In its criticisms of the report the Board recognises that the heart of the report is to be found in its biblical and theological chapters (chapters 3 and 4).

A4.   In Chapter 3 the working party examine the biblical evidence which has traditionally been regarded as settling the matter conclusively for Christians reflecting on homosexual behaviour.   The view of the working party is that that evidence cannot now be regarded as conclusive.   In considering the chapter the Board has tried to be just.   It recognises that

87

among its own members there are diverse attitudes to the Bible and to its authority in moral questions. The exegesis of particular books, and passages in them, gives rise to differences among biblical scholars; in consequence questions to do with the moral authority or relevance of particular passages are bound to be disputed. The Board was careful not to criticise the chapter merely because to some members its methods and conclusion were unfamiliar or even disturbing. Some members of the Board would regard the biblical testimony on homosexual behaviour as by itself settling the matter once and for all: others do not. Nonetheless the treatment in this chapter of the biblical material read to most members of the Board, including some who support its conclusions, as an 'explaining away' of the evidence; it was seen as minimising the fact, noted by the working party themselves, that 'what evidence there is seems clearly to show condemnation of homosexual behaviour' (para. 106). An interpretation is often put upon the biblical text which gives the impression that the conclusion came first and influenced the way in which the evidence was interpreted. Passages in the chapter where this appears to have occurred are noted in the following paragraphs.

A5.  In its treatment of the Sodom story (paras. 89-96) the report relates a number of interpretations familiar to Old Testament scholars. It concludes that the Genesis narrative 'does express abhorrence of homosexuality' but says that 'that is not its sole, or even its primary concern'. It goes on to say that because 'we are dealing not . . . with history but with legend', the account 'cannot be taken . . . to record an instance of divine action intended expressly to condemn and punish homosexual behaviour'. But historical narrative is not the only literary form which the biblical writers used to record Israel's moral judgments: they used legend—as they used parable—with the same intent and with equal effect; and such narratives are received as canonical scripture as much as the histories. Abhorrence of homosexual behaviour is entrenched in the text of Genesis, whether or not the ensuing disaster is regarded as punitive.

A6.  Reflecting upon the condemnation of homosexual behaviour in Leviticus and in Paul's Epistle to the Romans, the report notes that in both books such behaviour is 'part of what it means to be a heathen' (paras. 100, 104). But this crucial point is not followed up. If there is one moral theme constant in the Old Testament and in the New, it is that the people of God are not to conform to the sexual immoralities of the world around them, because God has shown them, and called them to, a better way. Neither in the biblical chapter nor elsewhere in the report is there sufficient awareness that the tension between the old and the new nature is of primary importance for every generation of Christians. As chapter 4 demonstrates, homosexual behaviour was not among those aspects of the Jewish law which Paul felt free to set aside. At the very least therefore, members of the Board considered, the report should have faced the question whether homosexual behaviour is to be regarded as compatible with new life in Christ.

A7. Chapter 3 says in para. 112 that the biblical writers appear to 'have had no conception of . . . the exclusively oriented homosexual condition as such [and are] speaking of homosexual behaviour undertaken by those they presume to be heterosexually inclined by nature'. It goes on to ask 'how far it is proper to apply the biblical prohibitions of homosexuality (*sic*) to those people whom they could not possibly have had in mind'. Such an important statement should have been backed up by some evidence, but none is given. Para. 164 in Chapter 4 makes the point again: 'it was assumed until quite recently that every mature individual was capable of a heterosexual response'. Any student of the canon law of marriage and of its interpretation in consistory courts of the medieval Church will recognise that this statement is false: the tests for impotence were, in the modern journalistic sense, explicit.[1] Moreover, Jesus spoke of 'eunuchs' who were so from their birth,[2] and Clement of Alexandria, writing in the third century, recorded a current interpretation of this to the effect that 'some men, from their birth, have a natural sense of repulsion from a woman; and those who are naturally so constituted do well not to marry'.[3] Whether or not Paul could distinguish a condition from practices, he undoubtedly condemned practices, while accepting those who had given them up (I. Cor. 6.11). The hypothesis that in this respect 'the situation has changed' (para. 164) and that 'our new knowledge gives us a pastoral obligation not recognised before' is therefore not made out. Whether or not the pastoral obligation has been properly fulfilled in the past is another matter.

A8. Related to this is the assertion in para. 113 that biblical support cannot be adduced for our moral distinction between dispositions and feelings on the one hand and practices on the other. In support of this Pedersen's *Israel* is quoted. The thrust of the paragraph appears to be to establish the conclusion that one cannot cite biblical authority for regarding homosexual practices as sinful without also holding that the homosexual condition is intrinsically sinful. This cannot however be deduced from an unbiased reading of the biblical material. In the first place Pedersen's quotation relates to a period early in the history of Israel, not to sophisticated Jews or Christians of the New Testament era. Secondly, and most importantly, the paragraph, by speaking indifferently of 'a homosexual disposition', 'having strong feelings of attraction', and 'a strong desire to do

[1] e.g. R. H. Helmholz, *Marriage Litigation in Medieval England* (CUP, 1974), p. 89.
[2] Matth. 19.12.
[3] Miscellanies III 1.1 in J. E. L. Oulton and H. Chadwick (eds.), *Alexandrian Christianity*, (SCM Press, 1954), p. 40.

something', actually blurs distinctions which ought to be borne in mind throughout the Report, besides misrepresenting the thrust of both the Old and the New Testaments. If we consider the moral distinction between disposition, desires, intentions and actions, it is clear that the Old and New Testaments recognise that temptations may occur to anyone and are not necessarily sinful; what *is* sinful is to succumb to temptation by action. The distinctive feature of Jesus' moral teaching in the Sermon on the Mount is not, as para. 113 suggests, that temptation comes under the same condemnation as the sinful action, but that internal *intentions* are as sinful as external *acts*.

A9. Para. 114 ends with the apparently uncompromising statement: 'there is nothing, it would seem, in the New Testament to justify the Church in relaxing the condemnations of all homosexual behaviour which it inherits from the old covenant'. 'But', the report immediately continues, 'the matter cannot simply be left there'. The reasons why not which are given seem to many members of the Board inadequate and unconvincing. The first is that Paul 'was a child of his age and was as limited by its outlook as were the men of the Old Testament'. This is at best part of the truth about Paul. An adequate judgment on what he had to say about homosexual behaviour would also have to take into account the striking *transformation* of Jewish thought which is a feature of his teachings. The fact that in this area—and not in some others—Paul reiterated the Old Testament prohibition surely itself requires further examination. As it is, it is merely ignored.

A10. The second reason concerns 'the discontinuous aspect of Jesus' ethics' and the view that he demanded 'unconditional love in conduct'. But the words of Jesus on love which were experienced as most demanding, so far from being discontinuous, were in fact direct quotations from the Old Testament; and his real demand was not for unconditional love but for unconditional obedience to the Kingdom, or rule, of God.

A11. In any case it is an error to reduce ethics to an undefined emotively elastic principle of 'love'—and then to treat all other rules, as the report does, as binding only insofar as they derive from that principle (para. 116). This 'elasticity' is evident in the following paragraph, where it is asked 'whether, granted our greater knowledge, as compared to the New Testament, of the homosexual and his condition, homosexual relationships might not in some cases, although by no means all, be as genuine expressions of love as other relationships'. If by 'relationships' is meant ties of brotherly love, the observation is true but commonplace; if, as members of the Board assume, it refers to a relationship involving genital contact, the question in effect invites us to bring under the 'love' principle actions expressly forbidden in the authorities from which the principle derives. We are free to scrutinise the authority of those prohibitions for our own day, but there should be a greater awareness of what is here involved than is shown in the report at this point.

A12.  The distinction between first-order principles of Christian ethics, which are of permanent validity, and second-order rules, which may vary from one period to another, is a valuable one but seems to be used at this point in the argument about homosexual practices in order to arrive at a particular conclusion.  The use of the 'first-order principles/second-order rules' analysis must be questioned when it leads to the implied conclusion that there are no moral standards unrelated to culture.  Here again there is an expression of the relativism which is simply asserted, and not argued for, in this chapter.

A13.  In paras. 118-9 the biblical doctrines of creation and the natural order are cited in support of the view that to depart from the 'God-given pattern for human sexuality' (i.e. heterosexual union) 'is to deface the image of God which makes humanity what it ought to be'.  The report argues against this that in the Bible 'God remains sovereign over the natural world'; he 'intervenes in it', and this fact 'means that it is controlled by the purposes of a personal being and not by immutable laws'.  But the implications of belief in God's ordering of the world, and his concern with the needs of every individual, need more careful consideration than they are given here.  God's sovereign interventions must be consistent with his own nature.  In consequence we cannot conceive of him arbitrarily altering the created natural order, including men and women.  While it is possible and relatively easy, to point to examples of where the Church has superseded elements of the Jewish law, more is needed to apply this approach to homosexual practices than a brief reference to 'the condition and needs of every individual'; yet this is all that the report offers at this point.  At the very least it is necessary to develop a criterion for determining what is inherent in the divine order of creation and what is not; and that the report does not give us.

A14.  Members of the Board commented in some detail on Chapter 3 not only because of unease about its method of argument but also because the conclusions are accepted as a premise for further enquiry in Chapter 4.  'Hence we do not think that it would be possible on the strength of these passages alone (i.e. in the Old Testament and in Paul) to rule out of court the contentions of those who claim to find in the ethical teachings of Jesus, and indeed of Paul himself, the germs of a personalist understanding of sex which would require us to revise the traditional judgment of the Church upon homosexuality' (*sic*) (para. 126; cf. para. 112, where the appeal is to 'Biblical revelation taken as a whole', and 150).  The burden of proof must be heavy on anyone who would counter the specific and unqualified condemnation of practices with an appeal to unspecified 'ethical teachings'. As has already been noted, the task *must* include an examination of the biblical meaning of 'love'. Such an examination is essential at a time when the term frequently conceals a basic selfishness which is fundamentally opposed to the generous self-giving comprehended in the New Testament term *agape*. The teaching of Jesus about love has been understood as more demanding precisely because it was related to the inward intention of the Law and not merely with external obedience; it was not regarded as entitling one to supersede the moral obligation enshrined in the Law by a private decision that another course was 'more loving'.

A15. In spite of all the excellent things said in paras. 160-2 about marriage, some members of the Board are unconvinced by the application of the words 'norm' and 'demand' to marriage without further elucidation. Jesus, followed by Paul, used the term 'gift'. Thus marriage *normally* is the gift to be received; but it is not specifically 'normative' when compared with another gift such as the celibate state. For the New Testament there are no norms among the gifts: 'Each has his own special gift from God' (I Cor. 7.7).

A16. If sexual relationships are to be analysed in terms of a 'demand' which must be met, and the possibility of its being frustrated, the relevant demand would be that of *chastity* (in its Christian rather than its popular sense) which is laid upon all Christians, married and unmarried, rather than that created by elevating marriage as a state to which all should aspire.

A17. The report recognises that some people with a homosexual orientation may not have a vocation to celibacy as the Church understands that term (para. 164; cf. paras. 234-5). It acknowledges that the homosexual in that situation faces a problem similar to that faced by the heterosexual person who would like to marry but cannot, but points out that the homosexual has to bear additional burdens of frustration. When however the conclusion of the discussion is reached in para. 168, the reason given for rejecting the Church's prohibition of homosexual practices is that the effect of it is 'unduly to circumscribe the area of responsible choice, to lay on individuals a burden too heavy for some to bear, and, by restricting the options open to them, to hinder their search for an appropriate way of life'. All of which could with equal truth be said of heterosexual people in a comparable dilemma. There is a second view of homosexual behaviour which is held by many members of the Board. They believe that people with a homosexual condition do have, as the report accepts, a moral choice, but consider that the right choice is abstinence rather than the genital expression of love in a homosexual relationship. They regard the attempt to justify the latter, as the report does, as a denial of the teaching of both Scripture and tradition, and observe that the central conclusion of the report, in para. 168, is unsupported by ethical argument. A third view is held by other members. They would hold that homosexual relationships, although objectively speaking disordered, should be viewed with differing degrees of culpability in relation to the subjective situations in which people find themselves.

A18. Chapter 5 was read by the Board as a useful and well-argued analysis of the legal perspective on homosexuality. The Board takes no view on the judgments in favour of or against reform of particular points of law advanced by the Working Party; it was not the function of the Board at this stage to do so. Individual members of the Board registered their personal dissent from the proposal to lower the age of consent to homosexual practices to 18.

A19. Chapter 6 of the report deals with counselling and the pastoral care offered by the Church, pointing out quite properly that the two are not identical. The treatment of the latter however neglects, in the judgment of several members of the Board, those distinctive features which Christian theology impresses upon Christian pastoral care. In particular there is no consideration of sin and forgiveness in an area of life in which it is likely to be a real issue. While insisting, in para. 246, that 'a conscientious decision, once made, should be respected', the report does not raise the possibility, recognised in moral theology, that that decision, objectively viewed, may be erroneous. The problem of the relationship between a conscientious decision, honestly made but erroneous, and the Divine will, is therefore not dealt with. But without some recognition of the possibility of a divergence between the human will and the Divine will, that is, of sin, there can be no ministry of forgiveness, and no application of the Gospel of which the Christian pastor is *ex officio* a minister.

A20. Many members of the Board would recognise the outstanding pastoral work done by priests of homosexual orientation who, perhaps because of their orientation, consecrated in Christ, demonstrate singular qualities of sensitive pastoral care. They would therefore acknowledge the problems involved in spelling out adequate guidelines for those responsible for the pastoral care of the clergy and ordinands, a point also taken by the working party (para. 259). Nonetheless they believe there is a particular problem facing bishops and clergy in the present climate of opinion, of which readers of the report should be aware. A man may be quite unsuitable as an ordination candidate or may, if ordained, be failing in his pastoral ministry because of serious defects which have nothing to do with his homosexual disposition and which are to be found in heterosexuals and homosexuals alike. Yet if a homosexual is not accepted as an ordinand or is taken to task for his behaviour once ordained, it will most likely be attributed to the fact that he is a homosexual.

A21. A separate problem would be created if the recommendation in para. 256 were to be adopted. The report concludes that in certain circumstances a genital relationship may be for some persons justifiable. This implies that it is a decision which could be made in good conscience. The report then says that a priest who had made such a decision ought to offer his resignation to the bishop, though his resignation would not be enforceable. This seems to some members of the Board to put a quite unacceptable onus on a person to act contrary to his conscience. If the Church believes that a practising homosexual priest should not continue in office it must take the responsibility for removing him and for doing so in a way which is legally and morally defensible, and must be prepared to spell out its reasons. A priest may decide in good conscience to live in a sexual union with another man; yet clearly he must realise that he is not thereby exempt from the pastoral discipline of the Church.